TWO GOSPELS
FROM ONE

TWO GOSPELS
FROM ONE

*A Comprehensive Text-Critical Analysis
of the Synoptic Gospels*

Matthew C. Williams

Kregel
Academic & Professional

To Willa

Two Gospels from One: A Comprehensive Text-Critical Analysis of the Synoptic Gospels

© 2006 by Matthew C. Williams

Published by Kregel Publications, a division of Kregel, Inc., P.O. Box 2607, Grand Rapids, MI 49501.

Cover photo © Bill Wittman
Cover design by Frank Gutbrod

Library of Congress Cataloging-in-Publication Data
Williams, Matthew C.
  Two Gospels from one: a comprehensive text-critical analysis of the synoptic Gospels / by Matthew C. Williams.
      p. cm.
  Includes bibliographical references and index.
  1. Bible. N.T. Mark—Criticism, Textual. 2. Bible. N.T. Matthew—Criticism, Textual. 3. Bible. N.T. Mark—Relation to Matthew. 4. Bible. N.T. Matthew—Relation to Mark. 5. Synoptic problem. I. Title.
BS2585.52.W55   2006   226'.066—dc22   2005035947

ISBN 0-8254-3940-X

Printed in the United States of America

06 07 08 09 10 / 5 4 3 2 1

CONTENTS IN BRIEF

CONTENTS

PREFACE

FOR MANY PEOPLE, DISCUSSIONS ABOUT the Synoptic Problem, Marcan priority, Q, and so forth are irrelevant and another example of the impractical nature of academic studies. But the relationship of the Gospels to one another is not a trivial matter. Rather, it is relevant for matters of apologetics, exegesis, counseling, and for finding the theology of the individual gospels.[1] It makes a difference whether Mark used Matthew, or vice versa, or whether these two gospels were written independently of one another.

This book examines the so-called text-critical (or linguistic) argument for the Synoptic Problem, which says that Matthew improved the language and style of Mark's gospel and is, therefore, the later gospel. The classic statement of this argument was articulated by B. H. Streeter nearly one hundred years ago in his five heads of evidence for Marcan priority (see pp. 28–33). While many in the early twentieth century thought that Marcan priority was "an assured result" of the scientific examination of the Synoptic Problem, recent criticisms have shown that such assurance is not quite so clear. Many scholars today tentatively hold that the Synoptic Problem is, in fact, probably insoluble.

The goal of this book is to examine the linguistic argument in hopes of finding objective criteria for determining which gospel was written first. Chapter 1 briefly surveys the history of the Synoptic Problem, giving possible solutions, as well as giving a proposed methodology for solving the Synoptic Problem, namely, the use of text-critical criteria for determining which gospel was written first. Chapter 2 analyzes the text-critical criteria that are used in all literary disciplines to determine original texts. Chapter 3 examines significant portions of Mark's textual apparatus in order to establish scribal tendencies while "copying" gospel texts. With this information, the text-critical criteria that were examined in

---

1. See Kloppenborg, "The Theological Stakes in the Synoptic Problem," 93–120; and Farmer, *The Gospel of Jesus.*

chapter 2 are reevaluated. Eight criteria then will be used to explore the textual differences between Matthew and Mark.

In chapter 4's exploration of Matthew and Mark, the text-critical criteria are used to compare pericope after pericope of texts in order to determine which Evangelist's reading was primary and which was secondary. Finally, chapter 5 compares the types of scribal changes to Mark's gospel with the types of differences found between the gospels of Matthew and Mark. Three conclusions will be drawn in this book:

1. The kinds of readings found in Matthew in comparison to Mark are the kinds of readings found in Mark's textual apparatus in comparison to Mark's text.[2] In other words, Matthew made the same types of changes to Mark's gospel that Marcan scribes made.
2. Text-critical criteria clearly and consistently support Marcan priority and Matthean posteriority.
3. Using the Nestle-Aland Greek New Testament and not agreeing with Marcan priority demonstrates inconsistency since the *same* text-critical arguments that were used to establish the present Nestle-Aland text also establish that Matthew has secondary readings and Mark has original readings.

The Greek text and textual apparatus of the New Testament used herein is that of Nestle-Aland[27].[3] Discussions of the Greek text use my own translations. The translations that are found in parentheses immediately after the Greek words come from Robert K. Brown and Philip W. Comfort, *The New Greek-English Interlinear New Testament*.

I owe thanks to a number of people: Scot McKnight, my mentor and friend—I'm not sure where I'd be in my scholarship without your continual guidance and encouragement; and to Jim Weaver, who accepted this title for publication and who, along with the editors, Jarl Waggoner and Paulette Zubel, worked hard to make it a better book.

Special thanks go to my community at Biola University. Biola University's Vice Provost Faculty Research and Development office granted some of the funds needed to complete the research on this book. Thanks to Deans Michael Wilkins and Dennis Dirks and my department chair, David Talley, for allowing

---

2. Mark's "textual apparatus" is a list of purported changes that scribes made to Mark's gospel.
3. The "27" refers to the 27th edition of Nestle-Aland's Greek New Testament.

me a research leave in spring 2005, which allowed me to complete my research and writing without sacrificing my family at the altar of "scholarship"—my wife, Willa; Joshua (age 5); and Jordan (age 4) will forever thank you! Finally, thanks to two students—Melissa Phillips, who helped in the bibliographical research, and Max Sternjacob, who helped in the insertion of the English translations.

How to Read This Book

THIS BOOK IS DESIGNED TO BE useful to many different types of readers. On the one hand, because of the extensive examinations of Greek texts, the scholar will be guided into discussions of textual variants found in Mark's textual apparatus and will find as well detailed analyses of the textual differences between Matthew's and Mark's gospels. On the other hand, for those who are interested in the Synoptic Problem and in these textual differences but are unable to read Greek fluently, Greek words and phrases have been translated throughout the body of the book. Literal translations have been given so that the non-Greek reader can see word order changes in the texts. As a result, these textual examinations will be helpful to almost everyone.

Below is a guide to various ways of reading this book. In order to be persuaded by the full weight of the argument it will, of course, be necessary to wade through the lengthy and detailed textual examinations. An understanding of the argument, however, can be attained—without reading all of the intricate textual discussions—by reading the summaries at the beginning of each chapter, along with the concluding summaries at the end of each chapter. Chapter 5 gives an overall summary of the book, along with the suggested conclusion—which is reached as a result of this current study—to the Synoptic Problem that seems to best fit with text-critical criteria.

- *Quick Reader:* Read the summaries at the beginning of each chapter, along with chapter 5 in its entirety, which explains the argument of the book and gives overall conclusions.
- *Interested Reader:* Read the summaries at the beginning of each chapter, along with the "Concluding Summaries" sections at the end of each chapter, and read chapter 5 in its entirety, which explains the argument of the book and gives overall conclusions.

- *Detailed Reader:* Read and investigate in detail the textual examinations. This can be done using the translations of the Greek texts but is preferably done by reading the Greek. The reader will need a synopsis, either in Greek or in English, at hand and open.

Abbreviations

AB	Anchor Bible
AJP	*American Journal of Philology*
ANRW	*Aufsteig und Niedergang der römischen Welt: Geschichte und Kultur Roms im Spiegel der neueren Forschung.* Edited by H. Temporini and W. Haase. Berlin, 1972–.
ANTC	Abingdon New Testament Commentaries
BAGD	Bauer, Walter, William Arndt, F. Wilbur Gingrich, and Frederick Danker. *A Greek-English Lexicon of the New Testament and Other Early Christian Literature.* 2d ed. University of Chicago Press, 1979.
BDF	Blass, F., A. Debrunner, and R. W. Funk. *A Grammar of the New Testament and Other Early Christian Literature.* Chicago: University of Chicago Press, 1961.
BETL	Bibliotheca Ephemeridum Theologicarum Lovaniensium
Bib	*Biblica*
BNTC	Black's New Testament Commentaries
BR	*Biblical Research*
BSac	*Bibliotheca sacra*
BT	*The Bible Translator*
CBQ	*Catholic Biblical Quarterly*
CBQMS	Catholic Biblical Quarterly Monograph Series
ConNT	*Coniectanea neotestamentica*
CTM	*Concordia Theological Monthly*
DRev	*Downside Review*
EBC	*Expositor's Bible Commentary*
EFN	Estudios de filología neotestamentaria. Cordova, Spain, 1988–.
EKKNT	Evangelisch-katholischer Kommentar zum Neuen Testament

ETL	*Ephemerides theologicae lovanienses*
ExpTim	*Expository Times*
FN	*Filología Neotestamentaria*
HTKNT	Herders theologischer Kommentar zum Neuen Testament
HTR	*Harvard Theological Review*
ICC	International Critical Commentary
ISBE	*International Standard Bible Encyclopedia.* Edited by G. W. Bromiley. 4 vols. Grand Rapids: Eerdmans, 1979–1988.
JAAR	*Journal of the American Academy of Religion*
JBL	*Journal of Biblical Literature*
JBLMS	Journal of Biblical Literature Monograph Series
JHC	*Journal of Higher Criticism*
JSNT	*Journal for the Study of the New Testament*
JSNTSup	Journal for the Study of the New Testament: Supplement Series
JSOTSup	Journal for the Study of the Old Testament: Supplement Series
JTS	*Journal of Theological Studies*
LCL	Loeb Classical Library
LXX	Septuagint
NAC	New American Commentary
NCB	New Century Bible
Neot	*Neotestamentica*
NIBCNT	New International Biblical Commentary on the New Testament
NICNT	New International Commentary on the New Testament
NIDNTT	*New International Dictionary of New Testament Theology.* Edited by Colin Brown. 4 vols. Grand Rapids: Zondervan, 1975–1986.
NIGTC	New International Greek Testament Commentary
NovT	*Novum Testamentum*
NovTSup	Novum Testamentum Supplements
NRTh	*La nouvelle revue théologique*
NTL	New Testament Library
NTS	*New Testament Studies*
NTTS	New Testament Tools and Studies
OCBC	Oxford Church Biblical Commentary
PSB	*Princeton Seminary Bulletin*
PSTJ	*Perkins (School of Theology) Journal*
ResQ	*Restoration Quarterly*
RevBib	*Révue Biblique*
RevExp	*Review and Expositor*

RNT	Regensburger Neues Testament
RTR	*Reformed Theological Review*
SBLDS	Society of Biblical Literature Dissertation Series
SBLMS	Society of Biblical Literature Monograph Series
SBLSCS	Society of Biblical Literature Septuagint and Cognate Studies
SBLSP	*Society of Biblical Literature Seminar Papers*
ScrB	*Scripture Bulletin*
SecCent	*Second Century*
SJT	*Scottish Journal of Theology*
SNTSMS	Society for New Testament Studies Monograph Series
SP	Sacra Pagina
SR	*Studies in Religion*
TDNT	*Theological Dictionary of the New Testament.* Edited by G. Kittel and G. Friedrich. Translated by G. W. Bromiley. 10 vols. Grand Rapids: Eerdmans, 1964–1976.
THKNT	Theologischer Handkommentar zum Neuen Testament
ThS	*Theological Studies*
TNTC	Tyndale New Testament Commentary
TrinJ	*Trinity Journal*
TynBul	*Tyndale Bulletin*
TZ	*Theologische Zeitschrift*
WBC	Word Biblical Commentary
WTJ	*Westminster Theological Journal*
WUNT	Wissenschaftliche Untersuchungen zum Neuen Testament
ZNW	*Zeitshcrift für die neutestamentliche Wissenschaft und die Kunde der älteren Kirche*

A Proposed Method for Solving the Synoptic Problem

....

CHAPTER SUMMARY

After defining the Synoptic Problem, this chapter gives a brief history of the problem, along with solutions that have been proposed through the centuries. B. H. Streeter's arguments for Marcan priority are examined, especially his linguistic argument that Mark's more primitive wording points to Marcan priority. After an examination of scholarship on the linguistic argument since Streeter, it is suggested that text-critical criteria, which are used to determine original and secondary texts, might be used to determine whether evidence exists that either Matthew or Mark used the other gospel as a literary source when composing his own gospel.

....

Albert Einstein wrote:

> In our endeavor to understand reality we are somewhat like a man trying to understand the mechanism of a closed watch. He sees the face and the moving hands, even hears its ticking, but he has no way of opening the case. If he is ingenious he may form some picture of a mechanism which could be responsible for all the things he observes, but he may never be quite sure his picture is the only one which could explain his observations. He will never be able to compare his picture with the real mechanism.[1]

---

1. Cited in Allison, "Plea for Thoroughgoing Eschatology," 667.

The Einstein quote above offers a parallel to the Synoptic Problem. Numerous other parallels have been offered as well. In brief, though, the Synoptic Problem consists of having the finished product—three Synoptic Gospels—but only clues as to the exact history of how these three gospels were produced.

Because of this lack of clarity regarding history, scholars have struggled to reach a consensus for the solution to the Synoptic Problem. A recurring critique of proposed solutions is the lack of objective criteria: "Not tens but hundreds of thousands of pages have been wasted by authors on the Synoptic Problem not paying attention to errors of method."[2] The purpose of this book, then, is to find the elusive "objective" criteria by which to solve the Synoptic Problem. Criteria already exist, though, that have been used successfully for centuries in textual criticism to determine the original of various literary texts. Can't these same criteria be applied to the Synoptic Problem?

An Introduction to the Synoptic Problem

The "Synoptic Problem" is the term that has been used to describe the task of determining the precise relationships between the first three gospels. Scholars note the alternating array of agreements and disagreements among the three gospels and wonder why and how the disparities came to be. Why, on the one hand, do the Synoptic Gospels have so much material in common? About 90 percent of Mark's material is found in Matthew, while about 50 percent of Mark is found in Luke.[3] In addition, nearly 235 verses in Matthew and Luke are similar to one another. In those places where agreement appears, incredible similarities can extend even to identical tense and mood for every word in an entire verse (or more). Given that Jesus probably spoke in Aramaic, these similarities are even more astounding. In some places, the Evangelists have identical parenthetical material (for example, "let the reader understand" in Mark 13:14 and Matt. 24:15).

On the other hand, why do the Gospels not have more material in common? Even pericopae in which vast similarities are found still have tremendous differences in vocabulary, grammar, and syntax. Each Evangelist has his favorite vocabulary, themes, and emphases.

Also disturbing among the three gospels is the alternating agreement and disagreement of the order in which material is presented. Sometimes Matthew

---

2. Goulder, "Some Observations," 99.

3. Tyson and Longstaff, *Synoptic Abstract*, provide exhaustive statistics. Cf. Honoré, "A Statistical Study," 95–147.

and Luke have many pericopae in a row in the same order as Mark.[4] At other times, there is very little agreement in order.

The Synoptic Problem, briefly stated, is the attempt to explain how Matthew, Mark, and Luke agree, yet disagree, in these three areas: content, wording, and order. Did one Evangelist use another as a source for writing his own gospel? And, if so, who wrote first? Answering these questions is the goal of this present study.

This current study offers a method for analyzing the similarities and differences between the Synoptic Gospels, the purpose of which is to determine their literary relationship. First, though, a brief history of the Synoptic Problem will be offered. Various solutions that scholars now hold will be presented, and B. H. Streeter's linguistic argument for Marcan priority will be examined.

A BRIEF HISTORY OF THE SYNOPTIC PROBLEM

Because the history of the Synoptic Problem has been examined fully in many other places, including a recent and massive summary by David Dungan,[5] only a brief history will be offered here before examining the primary solutions.[6]

Some of the early Fathers made comments about the relationships among the Synoptic Gospels. Clement (150–215) said that "those Gospels were first written which include the genealogies."[7] Origen (185–253) is said to be the first Christian thinker to examine these differences systematically. Augustine (354–430), who was most interested in a harmonization of the Gospels, suggested an order of Matthew, then Mark, then Luke.

---

4. Examine, for example, the nearly identical parallel order of Matthew and Luke to Mark 1:21–3:19; 8:27–9:50; and 10:1–52.

5. The main surveys include Reicke, "History of the Synoptic Discussion," 291–316; Stoldt, *Geschichte und Kritik der Markushypothese;* Farmer, *Synoptic Problem,* 1–198; Meijboom, *Origin of the Marcan Hypothesis, 1835–1866,* 9–96; Dungan, *History of the Synoptic Problem;* Peabody and Reicke, "Synoptic Problem," 2:517–24; Goodacre, *Synoptic Problem;* and Dungan and Kloppenborg, "Synoptic Problem," 1231–40.

6. This study does not examine all of the proposed solutions to the Synoptic Problem. It does not, for example, include Lukan priority solutions, such as Lindsey, "New Approach," 87–106, who suggests that Luke was the first written Gospel, followed by Mark and then Matthew. For a more technologically advanced survey of the various options, see http://www.mindspring.com/~scarlson/synopt/. This Web site "surveys proposed solutions and provides a clearing-house for materials related to its resolution." It is also helpful in giving color-coded diagrams that depict the literary relationships of the various sources. Also see Farmer, "Present State of the Synoptic Problem," 11–36, along with the updated version at http://www.bham.ac.uk/theology/synoptic-1-farmer.htm.

7. Eusebius *Hist. Eccl.* 6.14.5. Stein, *Synoptic Problem,* 16, though, mentions Tatian (c. 110–172) as the first serious attempt to resolve the problems of unity and diversity in the Gospels.

Thereafter, a long gap in time ensued before a concentrated emphasis upon the synoptic relationships was renewed. The impetus to this renewed study came from the publication, within a few years of each other, of works by Henry Owen (1764) and J. J. Griesbach (1783 and 1789). These two works closely examined the precise wording of the first three gospels.[8] These works also questioned the Augustinian consensus for the order of the Gospels, suggesting the order of Matthew, then Luke, then Mark, who was thought to have conflated the first two gospels. This new theory, now called the two-gospel (or Owen-Griesbach) hypothesis, inspired a plethora of works on the literary relationships of the Gospels and was for nearly a century held by the majority of scholars, including the Tübingen school.

During the latter half of the nineteenth century, however, a new hypothesis took center stage. Renewed textual examinations in Germany (by Christian Gottlob Wilke, Christian Hermann Weisse, Heinrich Julius Holtzmann, Paul Wernle, and Bernhard Weiss)[9] and in England (mostly by the Oxford school—William Sanday, Sir John C. Hawkins, B. H. Streeter, and W. C. Allen)[10] reached the conclusion of Marcan priority.

Those who held to Marcan priority, now called the two-source or four-source or Oxford hypothesis, were so certain of this solution that this view soon became an "assured result." The majority of scholars in the twentieth century were, in fact, so certain of the correctness of the two-source hypothesis that it was presupposed as the solution to the Synoptic Problem when they began their own studies of the Gospels. In 1909, V. H. Stanton said that the priority of Mark "was one of the most widely accepted results of modern criticism of the Gospels."[11] In Albert Schweitzer's summary of gospel criticism, he stated, concerning the certainty of the two-source hypothesis, "Indeed, it has been established on the basis of evidence to a degree that it can no longer even be called a hypothesis."[12] Vincent Taylor wrote in the introduction to his commentary on Mark, "Significant of the stability of critical opinion is the fact that, in a modern commentary, it is no longer necessary to prove the priority of Mark."[13]

---

8. See M. C. Williams, "OWEN Hypothesis," 126–58. Owen, *Observations on the Four Gospels*. Griesbach, "Commentatio qua Marci Evangeluim totum e Matthaei et Lucae Commentariis Decerptum esse monstratur," 74–102; English translation may be found in Orchard, "Mark Was Written After Matthew and Luke," 103–35.

9. See bibliography in Stoldt, *Geschichte und Kritik der Markushypothese*, 265–67.

10. Sanday, *Studies in the Synoptic Problem*; Hawkins, *Horae Synopticae*; Allen, *Matthew*; idem, *Mark*; and Streeter, *Four Gospels*.

11. V. H. Stanton, *Gospels as Historical Documents*, 30–31.

12. Schweitzer, *Von Reimarus zu Wrede*, 201, "ja sie ist durch Holtzmann auf einen solchen Grad der Evidenz gebracht, daß sie nicht mehr eine hypothese genannt werden kann."

13. Taylor, *Mark*, 11.

Even as late as 1970 in a gathering of scholars at the Pittsburgh Festival on the Gospels, it was stated that "perhaps the only major agreement among a wide circle of scholars is the priority of Mark." At the end of the conference, attendees merely posed the question, "Is the priority of Mark a conclusion too solid to be challenged, or is it a question open to reexamination?"[14] In 1976, O. Lamar Cope wrote, "All of the recent studies of Matthew known to me have presupposed the two-document hypothesis."[15]

The Marcan priority consensus has, though, faced an onslaught of challenges. In 1951, B. C. Butler published the first major critique of Marcan priority, *The Originality of St. Matthew: A Critique of the Two-Document Hypothesis.*[16] Among other things, Butler examined the main heads of evidence for Marcan priority. He showed, for example, that the argument from order merely places Mark in a middle position rather than in a prior position (the Lachmann Fallacy). He also made a comparative examination of the actual wording of parallel passages of the Gospels to see if this detailed comparison might show that one gospel was prior to another. Butler concluded this comparison by postulating Matthean priority. His analysis of the linguistic data, however, was performed without any objective criteria by which to determine priority. As a result, most of his exegetical study presents subjective analyses for literary priority. Butler's study did succeed, though, in redirecting later scholars' efforts, it being followed by many others, including those of Bernard Orchard and Thomas R. W. Longstaff, who examined the "scientific" evidence for conflation.[17]

Perhaps, though, the greatest challenge to the two-source hypothesis came from William Farmer. He began by examining the historical circumstances that contributed to the predominance of the two-source theory.[18] He then continued

---

14. Buttrick, *Jesus and Man's Hope,* 1:7–8.
15. Cope, *Matthew,* 5 n. 25.
16. Butler, *Originality of St. Matthew.*
17. Orchard, *Matthew, Luke and Mark;* Longstaff, *Evidence of Conflation in Mark?*
18. Farmer's "'Skeleton in the Closet,'" 18–42, was his foundational work prior to *The Synoptic Problem.* While Farmer has provided a useful historical summary in *The Synoptic Problem,* overstatements abound. He says, for example, concerning the influence of the Ur-gospel theory and Schleiermacher's interpretation of Papias's Logia on the two-source hypothesis, "Without these two ideological presuppositions, pure products of the creative imagination of Lessing and Schleiermacher, the Marcan hypothesis . . . would probably never have been accepted by New Testament scholars acquainted with the realities of the Synoptic Problem." Such statements by Farmer falsely suggest that there are no precise linguistic data upon which the two-source theory was founded.
     The most important critiques of Farmer's monograph are by Tuckett, "Griesbach Hypothesis in the 19th Century," 29–60; idem, *Revival of the Griesbach Hypothesis,* esp. 9–11; and Fitzmyer, "Priority of Mark," 131–70. Fitzmyer says that "though [Farmer] sets out to 'investigate the history of the Synoptic problem,' the number of American, English, French, and German writers who have dealt with some

by both writing extensively in the area of the Synoptic Problem,[19] and, perhaps more importantly, supervising a host of doctoral students who carried on his revival of the Griesbach hypothesis.[20]

As a result of these challenges to the two-source hypothesis, Synoptic Gospel scholarship today stands on uncertain ground. "The critical consensus regarding gospel relationships now appears to have been shaken, if not shattered."[21] Although scholars as late as 1970 could claim Marcan priority as a majority belief (see above), by 1979 this was no longer the case. At the close of the Cambridge Gospel Conference, on August 18, 1979, B. Ward Powers wrote that general agreement existed among the participating scholars: "To speak now of the Two-Source Hypothesis as an 'assured result' of scholarship is no longer possible; the consensus of the past century or so concerning this hypothesis has gone."[22]

POSSIBLE SOLUTIONS TO THE SYNOPTIC PROBLEM

We now live in a pluralistic age with regard to almost everything, including possible solutions to the Synoptic Problem. Five main solutions are held by scholars today: two-gospel hypothesis, two-source hypothesis, multiple-source hypotheses, oral or independent solutions, or insoluble.[23]

The first two solutions were examined earlier in the brief history of the Synoptic Problem.[24] Multiple-source hypotheses are held in general by French scholars,[25]

---

phase of the Synoptic question and who are passed over in silence is surprising. Farmer proposed to write a 'critical review of the history of the Synoptic problem,' but it has turned out to be a sketch interlaced with value judgments and remarks of a 'non-scientific' or 'extra-scientific' character" (160).

19. A full bibliography of Farmer's works before 1988 may be found in Longstaff and Thomas, *Synoptic Problem,* 42–47.

20. The latest work to be done by Farmer's friends is Peabody, Cope, and McNicol, *One Gospel from Two.*

21. W. O. Walker, *Relationships Among the Gospels,* 3.

22. Farmer, *New Synoptic Studies,* xx. Some, though, still believe that Marcan priority is assured. G. N. Stanton, *Gospel for a New People,* 51, says, "After a century of discussion of the synoptic problem, Matthew's dependence on Mark is the single most assured result."

23. Regardless of rhetoric to the contrary, none of the proposed solutions is more or less conservative or liberal. The important matter is to examine the evidence to determine what the Evangelists did, under the inspiration of the Spirit, when they wrote their gospels. See M. C. Williams, "Case for the Markan Priority View," 74–75.

24. There are many alternate forms of the two-document hypothesis, including the "three-document hypothesis" (Luke knew Mark, Q, and Matthew—held by Gundry and Ron Price) and the hypothesis that dispenses with Q altogether (held by A. M. Farrer, Michael Goulder, and Mark Goodacre), etc.

25. Although Stoldt, *Geschichte und Kritik der Markushypothese,* 248, includes B. H. Streeter in the multiple-source camp, I do not. A new multisource theory has recently been proposed by Burkett, *Rethinking Gospel Sources.*

with L. Vaganay being the main proponent.[26] A more recent defense of the multiple-source (or stage) hypotheses is by Marie-Émile Boismard, who wrote,

> The diverse theories of the Multiple-Source Hypotheses have in common a fundamental principle . . . the relationship between these Gospels is due not to direct dependence, but rather upon older, hypothetical resources upon which they depend.[27]

One problem with multiple-source hypotheses is that postulated sources are always speculative; the more sources one postulates, the higher the possibility that the theory is no longer acceptable. As a result, few scholars are persuaded by multiple-source hypotheses.

Some scholars, to show that the Synoptics are independent of one another, have held to an oral influence in the composition of the Gospels.[28] This theory has recently been revived, however, by Eta Linnemann, John Wenham, and Robert Thomas.[29] Linnemann's theory is based on detailed statistical evidence that, in theory, demonstrates that the Gospels are independent creations.[30] Wenham, though, while "denying literary dependence as the primary explanation of the likenesses of the gospels," remains open to the possibility of the Evangelists writing "with knowledge of the early gospels . . . but they are not seen as systematically altering their predecessors' work."[31]

---

26. Vaganay, *Le Probleme Synoptique*. German multiple-source scholars are found in Stoldt, *Geschichte und Kritik der Markushypothese*, 248. Further bibliography is found in Bellinzoni, *Two-Source Hypothesis*, 11 nn. 17–20.

27. Boismard, "Théorie des Niveaux Multiples," 231, "Les diverses théories des Niveaux Multiples ont en commun le principe fondamental . . . les rapports entre ces évangiles non par dépendance directe, mais en faisant appel à des sources hypothétiques plus anciennes dont ils dépendent." His solution is very complex: our Matthew is independent of our Mark, and is instead dependent on an earlier version of our Matthew and Mark. See also, idem, "Two-Source Theory at an Impasse," 1–17; and Rolland, "La Question Synoptique Demande-t-elle une Réponse Compliquée?" 217–23.

28. Dyer, "Do the Synoptics Depend on Each Other?" 242–43, concluded that the Gospels were independent and that the similarity in wording resulted from the "supernatural work of the Holy Spirit which would enable the disciples to recall all of Christ's words" (243).

29. Linnemann, *Is There a Synoptic Problem?* J. W. Wenham, *Redating Matthew, Mark and Luke*. R. L. Thomas and Farnell, *Jesus Crisis*; Farnell, "Case for the Independence View," 226–309. Cf. Reicke, *Roots of the Synoptic Gospels*, 180, who holds that the "relative parallelism between the Synoptic Gospels is fundamentally due to common traditions of the early church"; Riesner, *Jesus als Lehrer*, 2–6, 512–14.

30. Although her statistical data are impressive, they nonetheless remain unconvincing. See a critique by M. C. Williams, "Review of *Is There a Synoptic Problem?* 97–101.

31. J. W. Wenham, *Redating Matthew, Mark and Luke*, xxiii. Wenham seems to want his cake and to eat it too! See a critique of Wenham's earlier article by Moo, "Gospel Origins," 24–36.

The last option of the five primary theories suggests that the Synoptic Problem is insoluble.[32] It is true, as Dungan said, "As time goes on, matters are getting more confusing, not less."[33] Walker, at the close of the "Colloquy on the Relationships among the Gospels," concluded, "The possibility that the problem of Synoptic sources is finally insoluble may turn out to be the most significant and far-reaching suggestion made at the Colloquy."[34]

B. H. Streeter and the Linguistic Argument for Marcan Priority

In the midst of these pluralistic options, should it be concluded that the Synoptic Problem is, indeed, insoluble? Should hope for a solution be abandoned? Should further analyses of the texts be foregone? No—further study on the Synoptics is required. But, given that detailed studies have been performed for at least the past two centuries, how should such a study be continued? Research should continue in that area in which most scholars think the solution may be found, namely, textual criticism.[35]

Before explaining textual criticism, however, it will be helpful to examine B. H. Streeter's five heads of evidence for Marcan priority,[36] the "classic statement" of the evidence.[37]

Streeter's five heads of evidence for Marcan priority are as follows:

1. Matthew and Luke reproduce 91 percent and 55 percent, respectively, of Mark's material, much of which is identical wording.
2. Matthew and Luke rarely agree with each other in wording, yet alternatively reproduce the wording of Mark, using the exact wording 30 to 60 percent of the time.
3. Matthew and Luke generally agree with the order of Mark: wherever Mat-

---

32. See, e.g., Fitzmyer, "Priority of Mark," 132, followed by Moo, "Gospel Origins," 34.
33. Dungan, *Interrelations of the Gospels*, xi. See also Wright, "Doing Justice to Jesus," 364, who concludes that "it is fairly likely that Matthew used Mark. . . . But, after twenty-five years of study and teaching, I am, as a historian, nowhere near as convinced about these points . . . as I am that Jesus of Nazareth was a Jewish eschatological prophet."
34. W. O. Walker, *Relationships Among the Gospels*, 11. See Hengel's hypothesis in *Four Gospels and the One Gospel*, 184–85.
35. Streeter's evidence is only presented here for Marcan priority. Further arguments for Marcan priority may be found in M. C. Williams, "Case for the Markan Priority View," 35–42.
36. Streeter, *Four Gospels*, 157–69.
37. So, Rist, *Independence of Matthew and Mark*, 1.

thew departs from Mark's order, Luke supports Mark; and wherever Luke departs from Mark's order, Matthew agrees with Mark.

4. Matthew and Luke improve Mark's more primitive wording [i.e., linguistic analysis].

5. The distribution of Marcan and non-Marcan material throughout Matthew and Luke seems to be explicable only on the theory of Marcan priority.

Streeter concluded as follows:

> The net result of the facts and considerations briefly summarised under the foregoing five heads is to set it beyond dispute that Matthew and Luke made use of a source which in content, in order, and in actual wording must have been *practically identical* with Mark.[38]

Analysis of Streeter's Evidence

Streeter's first line of evidence is that Matthew and Luke reproduce 91 percent and 55 percent, respectively, of Mark's gospel, much of which is identical in wording.[39] As has been shown over and over again in the literature, though, this statistic only proves that a literary relationship exists between the three gospels, and that Mark is somehow the common element but not necessarily the prior element.[40] The two-gospel hypothesis can, in fact, use this same data as evidence: in composing his gospel, Mark reproduced much of the wording of his sources, namely Matthew and Luke. Streeter's first line of evidence does not prove Marcan priority.

Streeter's second line of evidence—that Matthew's and Luke's wording rarely agrees with one another when compared to the wording in Mark—has faced serious difficulties because similarities can, indeed, be cited between Matthew and Luke. Although Streeter went into great detail to explain away these similarities,[41] most scholars disagreed with him. The two-gospel hypothesis, in fact, uses the agreements between Matthew and Luke as one of the main arguments for their

---

38. Streeter, *Four Gospels*, 168. Notice that Streeter did not say *identical* with Mark. He saw two problems in such a statement: (1) large omissions of Mark by Matthew and Luke; (2) minute agreements of Matthew and Luke in passages that clearly show overall dependence on Mark.

39. The most important critiques of Streeter's evidence include Dungan, "Mark," 54–71; Butler, *Originality of St. Matthew*, 62–71; 161–64; and Farmer, *Synoptic Problem*, 118–77.

40. See Butler, *Originality of St. Matthew*, 62–67; and Dungan, "Mark," 55.

41. Streeter, *Four Gospels*, 168–81.

theory.[42] Two-gospel scholars suggest that the postulation of a "Q" document is unnecessary because the similarities between Matthew and Luke are explained by their direct literary dependence upon one another.

Streeter's third line of evidence is that Matthew and Luke generally agree with the order of Mark: wherever Matthew departs from Mark's order, Luke's order supports Mark; wherever Luke departs from Mark's order, Matthew's order agrees with Mark. This argument has been conclusively rejected as proving Marcan priority. Butler said that these data prove only that "Mark is necessarily the connecting-link between Matthew and Luke in these passages, but not necessarily the source of more than one of them."[43] In other words, Mark is merely the common element between Matthew and Luke, not necessarily the prior element. This logical error is known as the "Lachmann Fallacy."[44] Neville's recent study of the phenomenon of order concludes, "All formal arguments based on the phenomenon of order are inconclusive."[45]

Streeter's fifth head—that the distribution of Marcan and non-Marcan material throughout Matthew and Luke seems to be explicable only on the theory of Marcan priority—is not a new argument but merely a summary of the previous four arguments. Thus, no critique is needed.

The fourth head of evidence—Matthew and Luke improve Mark's more primitive wording—is saved here until last because of its importance. What exactly did Streeter mean by improving "more primitive wording"? He listed numerous examples in two categories: (1) elimination or toning down of phrases that might cause offense or suggest difficulties (such as Mark 6:5: "he could do there no mighty work"); (2) stylistic (elimination of repetitions, redundancies, and digressions such as Mark 1:32, "evening coming on, when the sun set") or grammatical improvements.[46] Streeter comments that these improvements are cumulative in character: "Its full force can only be realised by one who will take the trouble to go carefully through the immense mass of details."[47]

Streeter was not, of course, the first scholar to notice the primitive nature of Mark's text. As early as 1838, C. H. Weisse noted the "clumsy and accidental" nature of Mark.[48] In 1863, Heinrich Julius Holtzmann mentions the "accidental

---

42. So, Farmer, "Two-gospel hypothesis," 138, 143.
43. Butler, Originality of St. Matthew, 65.
44. Lachmann himself, though, did not formally make this error. See full discussions in Butler, Originality of St. Matthew, 64–67; and Farmer, Synoptic Problem, 65–67.
45. Neville, Mark's Gospel—Prior or Posterior? 335.
46. Streeter, Four Gospels, 162–64.
47. Ibid., 164.
48. C. H. Weisse, Die evangelische Geschichte, 1:67: "Man kann diesen Charakterzug nach der einen Zeite hin als Unbeholfenheit und Schwerfälligkeit bezeichnen."

and clumsy" nature of Mark, which hints of its originality in comparison to the other Evangelists.[49] English scholars also were aware of Mark's awkwardness. E. A. Abbott wrote,

> Our present Mark . . . contains, as might be expected, many roughnesses, obscurities, and vernacular expressions—some of them specially condemned by Greek grammarians—likely to be removed by the earliest Evangelists using this Gospel.[50]

Scholarly Agreement with Streeter's Linguistic Argument

Scholars after Streeter usually agree on the importance of the fourth argument. G. D. Kilpatrick said, "The [Matthean] stylistic changes from Mark increase lucidity. Unnecessary and distracting details are omitted"; and "the crudities and irregularities of Mark's Greek are removed, while often a more unexceptionable vocabulary replaces the undignified words of the earlier Gospel [i.e., Mark]."[51] Butler, although disagreeing with Streeter's overall conclusion, did agree that "only the fourth head of evidence contains any argument tending to support the theory of Marcan priority to the exclusion of all other solutions. Not five converging sets of evidence, but one only."[52] Ned B. Stonehouse also agreed that Streeter's fourth argument "confronts us with weighty issues which need to be evaluated with due care."[53] O. Lamar Cope, another defender of the two-gospel hypothesis, comments that "most critics would probably agree that the crux of current belief that Mark is the earliest Gospel is the evidence that Matthew has altered Mark in several instances in unmistakable ways."[54] Davies and Allison's massive commentary on Matthew admits that "Matthew's style is superior to Mark's."[55] They comment that as they began work on their commentary, they were, in fact, open to the recent criticisms of Marcan priority. They found, however, as they analyzed the texts of Matthew and Mark, that "the theory of Matthean antecedence has

---

49. Holtzmann, *Die synoptischen Evangelien*, 289: "Auf diesen Hebraismen in Styl und Sprachgebrauch beruht zum grossen Theil jener Eindruck der Schwerfälligkeit und Unbeholfenheit, den die Lectüre des Marcus im Gegensatz zu Matthäus und Lucas macht, der aber eben damit auch für die Ursprünglichkeit des zweiten Evangelisten zeugt."
50. Abbott, *Diatessarica—Part II*, 52.
51. Kilpatrick, *Origins*, 72, 76. See also Johnson, *Griesbach Hypothesis*, 137; and O. E. Evans, "Synoptic Criticism Since Streeter," 296.
52. Butler, *Originality of St. Matthew*, 68.
53. Stonehouse, *Origins of the Synoptic Gospels*, 78.
54. Cope, "Argument Revolves," 144.
55. Davies and Allison, *Matthew*, 1:103.

failed to commend itself while the postulation of Marcan priority has consistently brought illumination."[56] John Wenham comments that "all that is left of Streeter's evidence is his head number 4."[57] Finally, Graham Stanton notes that Matthew "abbreviates Mark's verbosity and improves his clumsy Greek style; he clarifies many of the Marcan theological enigmas."[58]

Disagreement with Streeter's Linguistic Argument

Although the majority of scholars—defenders of both the two-source hypothesis and supporters of the two-gospel hypothesis—agree with Streeter concerning the importance of this fourth head of evidence, a few scholars have disagreed. These dissenters, while they might agree that Mark's gospel is more awkward and redundant than Matthew and Luke, do not agree that this is evidence for the priority of Mark.

Farmer commented, "In literary criticism there is no canon by which questions of literary dependence can be settled on the basis of good or bad grammar"; and "If it is true that one Evangelist wrote better Greek than another it probably indicates more about his private education or that of his intended readers than it does about the date of composition of his Gospel, or its relationship to the other Gospels."[59] Farmer was seconded by H. P. Hamann: "[Mark] is capable of marring beyond recognition the best bit of Greek. It is just as easy to imagine clumsy Mark botching up competent Matthew as to imagine competent Matthew tidying up some of Mark's inelegancies."[60] Dungan agrees:

> We may argue back and forth about aspects of Streeter's literary criteria, what they mean, and so forth, "till the cows come home," and fail to come to a much more fundamental problem at the root of this entire tree of arguments. When has a single one of these four arguments ever been itself scientifically tested to see whether and to what extent it is a reliable criterion for deciding between early or late traditions?[61]

David Alan Black, in a recent presentation at the Society of Biblical Literature, said, "Thus, from the perspective of Greek discourse analysis, there appears to

---

56. Ibid., 1:98.
57. J. W. Wenham, *Redating Matthew, Mark and Luke*, 90.
58. G. N. Stanton, *Gospel for a New People*, 326.
59. Farmer, *Synoptic Problem*, 122; cf. 121. Cf. Butler, *Originality of St. Matthew*, 164–67.
60. Hamann, "Sic et Non," 463.
61. Dungan, "Mark," 68.

be no *linguistic* basis for assuming that Marcan grammar is inferior to that of Matthew and Luke."[62]

Although these critics have accused Streeter and his followers of failing to provide "scientific evidence" for their claims that Mark's inferior grammar is evidence of Marcan priority, they also have failed to prove their case that Streeter's fourth head of evidence is invalid. E. Earle Ellis said, "[These] advocates have been more successful in their critique than in the establishment of their alternative."[63] They have placed the burden of proof on Streeterians without taking up the challenge themselves. In other words, it remains to be shown that an author who is using a source writes in the same style as he or she would if composing a work without using an existing source.

Farmer and others have a valid point in that different authors write in better or worse Greek depending on their educational background. What happens, though, if an author who normally writes in a poor Greek style uses a written source that employs good Greek style? Does the former become a better, or more grammatically refined, author? In terms of the Synoptic Problem, it may be true to say that Mark composed his gospel in a grammatically unrefined Greek, but it is an altogether different proposition to say that Mark wrote his gospel in a grammatically unrefined Greek while using grammatically sophisticated sources, that is, Matthew's and Luke's gospels. Herein lies the crux of the argument: Could Mark have written a grammatically "worse" gospel given that he had two grammatically "refined" gospels before him as he wrote? Thus, the question is not simply one of linguistic style but of source criticism, namely, the influence upon one's style from another, more refined, source.[64]

Major Studies on the Linguistic Argument

A few scholars have furthered Streeter's fourth head of evidence by examining in detail either the gospel texts or the ideas behind Streeter's argument.[65]

---

62. D. A. Black, "Discourse Analysis, Synoptic Criticism," 2. See also, idem, "R. Stein's *Synoptic Problem* and Markan 'Errors,'" 95–101.

63. Ellis, "Historical Jesus and the Gospels," 96.

64. See the comments on the unlikelihood of such changes by Kilpatrick, "Matthew on Matthew," 179; idem, *Principles and Practice of New Testament Textual Criticism*, 252. Shin, *Textual Criticism and the Synoptic Problem*, 40, concluded, "One may prefer less polished readings . . . especially when the author's style is itself unpolished."

65. Concerning the amount of work that has been performed on the Synoptic Problem, Stoldt, *Geschichte und Kritik der Markushypothese*, 1, makes the exaggerated suggestion that "an entire army of scholars has employed its acumen and developed a high degree of philological precision and an almost detective-like sagacity; one can truly say that no other enterprise in the history of ideas has been subjected to anywhere near the same degree of scholarly scrutiny."

B. C. Butler

The first important exegetical study that examined texts linguistically was published by B. C. Butler in 1951.[66] Butler, who wrote his monograph as a critique of the two-source hypothesis, sought to "undertake an investigation (never, so far as I am aware, attempted in modern publications of the two-document school) of the actual point-to-point relations revealed by a comparative study of the texts of . . . Matthew and Mark."[67] Butler examined nearly all of the Matthew-Mark parallels for signs of priority. Most of his analysis, however, is short and lacks details. The analysis of Matthew 23:1–8 (Mark 12:37b–40), for example, covers a mere three pages, hardly enough to make detailed comments on the Greek text of these two gospels. In addition, because of his lack of objective criteria by which to judge priority, many of Butler's conclusions are too subjective to be of any ultimate value. He compares, for example, Matthew 23:5b (πλατύνουσιν γὰρ τὰ φυλακτήρια αὐτῶν καὶ μεγαλύνουσιν τὰ κράσπεδα) ("For ~ they enlarge the phylacteries of them and make large the tassels.")[68] to Mark 12:38 (τῶν θελόντων ἐν στολαῖς περιπατεῖν) ("the ones desiring in long robes to walk about") and concludes,

> Clearly Mark, unwilling to explain what Jewish phylacteries and fringes were, and why specially large ones were signs of religious ostentation, has substituted his own bizarre phrase, which suggests at most mere childish vanity. Matthew cannot possibly be supposed to have invented his version from Mark's jejune phrase.[69]

By what criteria did Butler make such a conclusion? It is unclear. Further, he fails to see that Matthew invented this saying, whether he used Mark as a source or not. Which is easier to say?—that Matthew invented the saying, or that Matthew was triggered by Mark's "bizarre phrase" and then invented the saying. Butler's argumentation does not merit the confident conclusions that he draws: "The conclusion must be accepted that Mark is here excerpting from Matthew."[70] Butler fails to provide the necessary objective criteria by which to decide prior texts.

---

66. Butler, *Originality of St. Matthew.*
67. Ibid., 69–70.
68. The "~" symbol indicates that the word order of the English translation differs from the Greek word order.
69. Butler, *Originality of St. Matthew,* 74.
70. Ibid., 75.

W. R. Farmer

The next author to examine texts linguistically was W. R. Farmer in 1963.[71] Farmer devised a sixteen-step plan for proving that Mark was written after and dependent on Matthew and Luke.[72] The sixteenth-step lists four canons of criticism (actually, three, because he deletes one in the revised edition) by which to judge secondary texts. These canon are as follows:

1. That form that reflects an extra-Palestinian, or non-Jewish, provenance is to be adjudged secondary to a form of the same tradition that reflects a Palestinian or Jewish provenance;
2. [The second canon was retracted after E. P. Sanders's study showed that there is not a tendency to become more specific];
3. That form of a tradition that exhibits explanatory redactional glosses and expansions aimed to make the tradition more applicable to the needs of the church is to be adjudged secondary;
4. That form of a tradition that exhibits words or phrases characteristic of a redactor whose hand is clearly traceable elsewhere in the same gospel is to be adjudged secondary.[73]

Farmer's first canon is inconclusive since the Jewishness of a saying may be more related to the particular author and his audience rather than to chronological development.[74]

The third canon is useful, but it must be used with caution because explanatory glosses may be due more to the author's audience than to chronological development. In Mark 2:7, for example, is found an explanatory phrase after βλασφημεῖ ("he blasphemes"), namely, τίς δύναται ᾿αφιέναι ἁμαρτίας εἰ μὴ εἷς ὁ

---

71. Farmer, *Synoptic Problem*.
72. Ibid., 199–232. Cope, *Matthew*, 5 n. 26, himself a defender of the two-gospel hypothesis, said that Farmer's sixteen-step plan is "too simplistically stated to be compelling." W. O. Walker, *Relationships Among the Gospels*, 283, said, "I have always seen them [Farmer's canons of criticism] as an unnecessary weakness."
73. Farmer, *Synoptic Problem*, 227–32. One example of Farmer's own analysis of texts can be found in "The Passion Prediction Passages and the Synoptic Problem," 558–70. It can be quickly seen, though, that Farmer's argumentation lacks objectivity, for he makes assertion after assertion regarding priority with no real objective criteria by which to make these decisions. Burton, *Some Principles of Literary Criticism*, 198, listed six criteria by which to judge secondary texts, although this current work does not offer a critique of them (see Farmer, *Synoptic Problem*, 229, for a critique).
74. So, for example, Tuckett, *Revival of the Griesbach Hypothesis*, 10; idem, "Response to the Two-gospel hypothesis," 57–58, and Sanders, *Tendencies of the Synoptic Tradition*, 190–255.

θεός; ("Who is able to forgive sins except [the] one—God?"). Matthew 9:3, however, does not contain this explanation. It cannot be concluded, however, that Mark's text is secondary, as Farmer proposes. Mark may have added the phrase to Matthew, but it is just as plausible that Matthew deleted this phrase from Mark's gospel because his Jewish audience would not need this explanation.

Farmer's fourth criterion is helpful, and it will be used in the analysis in this current study of Matthew and Mark. Although Farmer followed his sixteen-step plan with specific examinations of the Gospels, because of his brief discussions (Mark 1:1–20, for example, receives a mere page and a half of analysis), his work remains inadequate.

E. P. Sanders

In 1969 E. P. Sanders initiated a study on the Synoptic Gospels, using the known criteria for determining secondary texts. He soon halted his study, however, realizing that these criteria were not as objective as he had previously thought. As a result, his study became an examination of the *criteria* for determining secondary texts.[75] Which criteria are useful? He concluded, "There are no hard and fast laws [criteria by which to determine] of the development of the Synoptic tradition. On all counts the tradition developed in opposite directions."[76]

Although this statement is oft quoted, it should not be understood as applying to *all* criteria used to judge priority; it must be understood in light of the actual study that Sanders did and be taken in context. Sanders examined only *three* general criteria: length, amount of detail, and amount of Semitism. Thus, his conclusion of inconclusiveness cannot be applied to all criteria for determining chronological development but should be applied only to those three mentioned.

Many scholars also fail to notice that Sanders did not conclude a lack of probability in using these three general criteria. Sanders himself devised the "relative strength of each of the *useful* criteria" for determining lateness: not very strong, fairly strong (including addition of subjects), strong, and very strong.[77] Sanders's study has thus taken us a long way toward the development of "scientific" criteria for determining priority.

---

75. Sanders, *Tendencies of the Synoptic Tradition*, xi.
76. Ibid., 272.
77. Ibid., 275 (italics mine).

C. M. Tuckett

Another example of a linguistic study that furthers Streeter's line of evidence was done by C. M. Tuckett in 1983.[78] His study minutely examines numerous gospel texts to determine which synoptic relationship hypothesis best explains these texts.[79] He concludes, "In the detailed examination of the wording of the individual pericopae, the results frequently suggested some form of 2DH [two-document hypothesis]"; and "insofar as the 2DH can often apparently give a more coherent and consistent set of explanations of why the later changes were made (i.e., by Matthew and Luke on the 2DH), that hypothesis is to be preferred."[80] Tuckett's conclusion challenged the two-gospel hypothesis to "give a more detailed explanation for Luke's and Mark's behaviour."[81]

Eighteen years after Tuckett penned this challenge, Blomberg reiterates that "the major weakness in the Griesbach theory to date is that its proponents have not demonstrated how Marcan style and theology emerge more consistently and coherently from their hypothesis than from the alternatives. Until I see such a demonstration, I will remain unconvinced."[82] Scot McKnight concurred: "[T]he Griesbach proponents have yet to come up with a counter argument to the cumulative force of the linguistic arguments."[83]

When examining Tuckett's analysis, though, the reader is again struck by the lack of objective controls on his redactional analysis. Certainly defenders of the two-gospel hypothesis could answer many of Tuckett's explanations of the data.[84]

International Institute for Gospel Studies

After nearly twenty years of challenges, the research team of the International Institute for Gospel Studies, a group of two-gospel scholars including Lamar

---

78. Tuckett, *Revival of the Griesbach Hypothesis.* For a critique of Tuckett, see McNicol, "Two Gospel Hypothesis Under Scrutiny," 5–13; and W. O. Walker, "State of the Synoptic Question," 14–21. Tuckett himself responds to these critiques in "Two Gospel Hypothesis Under Scrutiny: A Response," 25–31.

79. Tuckett, *Revival of the Griesbach Hypothesis,* 95–185. Tuckett not only examines numerous pericopae but also makes detailed comments on the Greek text and the theological overtures of each gospel.

80. Ibid., 186–87.

81. Ibid., 187.

82. Blomberg, "Synoptic Problem," 32.

83. McKnight, "Generation That Knows Not Streeter," 83.

84. A good example of the differing explanations for the differences among the same pericope can be found in Dungan, *Interrelations of the Gospels,* 63–76, 157–200, 265–88. In Dungan's volume, two-source, two-Gospel, and multiple-source hypotheses defenders give a textual explanation of the eschatological discourse. Such alternative explanations for the source history of the same pericope show the need for objective criteria.

Cope, David Dungan, William Farmer, Allan McNicol, David Peabody, Philip Shuler, and Thomas Longstaff, took pen in hand and tried to provide "considered and detailed responses to these long-standing requests" to show how "Mark, writing third, made use of both Matthew and Luke."[85] This response was "founded on more than twenty years of detailed, critical re-examination of scholarship on the synoptic problem."[86] While Peabody and friends list six categories of evidence for Mark's posteriority, only some of these relate to the linguistic argument.[87] While the book claims to present new evidence for Marcan posteriority, it is highly dependent on previous work done by two-gospel scholars. Peabody's earlier works are referred to on 127 pages; many times two or three references appear on a single page.[88] Very little interaction is undertaken with two-source scholars. Tuckett, for example, is referred to just ten times, but Peabody et al never interact with his scholarship (in contrast, Zeller's writings from 1843 are referred to more often than Tuckett's). This lack of interaction is especially surprising given that other scholars had previously responded to similar arguments that are made in the Peabody et al book.[89]

The writers had a wonderful opportunity to show how their explanations of the Synoptic differences are *better* than those of the two-source hypothesis. Instead, over and over again are found general comments that presuppose Matthean priority instead of a "critical defense" of Marcan conflation. In-depth explanations of texts are rarely given. Mark 4:14–19, for example, is skipped entirely; 12:19–23 gets three sentences of discussion; 13:15–22 gets a mere half page.

On those occasions where Peabody et al present evidence for conflation, it is often done with no objective criterion by which to judge priority. Depending on the argument needed to explain why Matthew is prior, their understanding of the ability of Mark as a conflator changes. In some places Mark is seen as "clever," "creative," "skillful," even "careful,"[90] while in other places he is seen as inept at understanding Matthew's argument and even as introducing errors into the text.[91]

---

85. Peabody, Cope, and McNicol, *One Gospel from Two*, xii.

86. Ibid., xiv.

87. Ibid., 20.

88. Peabody, Cope, and McNicol, appendix 3 to *One Gospel from Two*, 383–88, for example, refers to Peabody's *Mark as Composer* sixty times in just six pages.

89. Peabody, Cope, and McNicol, acknowledgment to *One Gospel from Two*, xv.

90. Ibid., 61, 127, 162, 186, 190, 192, 251, 263, 344, etc.

91. Ibid. See the most important examples on pages 72 ("discrepancy in the text"), 109 (Mark "contradicts the biblical record"), 126 ("evidence of fatigue"), 129 ("awkwardness"), 163, 168 (geographical problem), and 250 (Mark 12:8).

Contradictory arguments are given, too, for Mark's either retaining or rejecting the content of his sources. While Mark "uses material that would contribute to his theological vision of Jesus' life," a different argument is used to explain why Mark does not retain Luke's sermon in Nazareth, which clearly emphasizes Jesus' death through foreshadowing, two Marcan characteristics.[92] Another example can be found in the reasons given for not retaining Matthew's Sermon on the Mount: "Because the content of Matthew's version of Jesus' inaugural Sermon on the Mount differed so much from Luke's version of Jesus' Inaugural Sermon in Nazareth, he simply could not harmonize them."[93] On other occasions, however, Mark is capable of conflating "great" differences in his sources, such as in the eschatological discourse.[94]

The result leaves the reader with a continued desire for a set of objective criteria by which to judge priority in synoptic texts. Peabody said it best: "Unfortunately much of the discussion of conflation relies too heavily on speculation and often on rhetorical questions, about what an author may or may not be expected to do."[95] Psychological hypotheses as to why Mark either used or rejected his sources will simply not convince readers to conclude that Mark is the "last of the synoptics to be composed," a claim that is made in the conclusion of their book.[96]

A significant issue in all this, of course, is their late dating of the gospel of Mark. This late date is in contrast to the most recent studies on the dating of Mark, which place it in the "mid to late thirties and mid-forties."[97]

Other Studies on the Linguistic Argument

Other studies have analyzed Streeter's linguistic argument on a smaller scale, namely those of T. R. W. Longstaff, J. A. Fitzmyer, G. M. Styler, and S. McKnight.[98] Although Longstaff's main goal was to see whether evidence of conflation could

---

92. Foreshadowing is seen as a key Marcan characteristic (ibid., 384f.), as is an emphasis on Jesus' death (ibid., 41f., 86).

93. Ibid., 85.

94. Ibid., 268.

95. Ibid., 93.

96. Ibid., 346.

97. Crossley, *Date of Mark*, 208. Casey, *Aramaic Sources of Mark's Gospel*, 260, gives a "purely critical argument for an earlier date than is conventional" for Mark's gospel: "a date c. 40 CE must be regarded as highly probable."

98. Longstaff, *Evidence of Conflation in Mark?* Fitzmyer, "Priority of Mark"; Styler, "Priority of Mark," 285–316; and McKnight, "Source Criticism," 136–72.

be found in Mark's gospel, he did a partial linguistic examination of twenty-nine verses of Mark's text.[99]

Fitzmyer wrote an essay that was mostly an examination of Q, but he did touch on the evidence for Marcan priority based on awkwardness in Mark's grammar.[100]

Perhaps due to the broad influence of C. F. D. Moule's *Birth of the New Testament*, G. M. Styler's appendix on the priority of Mark has been similarly influential.[101] Styler concluded, "When challenged to state my criteria for assessing priority, I could only make the feeble-sounding reply 'We must use our judgment in every case.'"[102] The problem with this methodology is that Orchard and Riley—Griesbach-hypothesis defendants—cite opposite arguments to Styler's on every case.[103]

One of the more recent studies that uses Streeter's fourth head of evidence is Scot McKnight's analysis of Luke's redactions of Mark in Luke 9:18–27.[104] Much of his argument is based on "grammatical or stylistic improvements" to Mark's text by Luke. McKnight concludes,

> So far as I can see, the Griesbach proponents have not dealt with the most decisive argument favoring the Oxford Hypothesis, namely, the argument from primitive language. The most telling argument against the Griesbach Hypothesis is the accumulated answers to this question: which reading most likely gave rise to the other readings.[105]

Although they contribute valuable insights, a recurring failure of these linguistic studies is the lack of objective criteria by which to judge secondary texts.[106]

---

99. Longstaff, *Evidence of Conflation in Mark?* Given Longstaff's small data sample (only 29 verses), it is worth wondering whether his assurance in his introduction is actually true: "In my opinion, the inclusion of further examples in either category would not materially affect the structure of the argument or the conclusions" (6). See Downing's critique, "Compositional Conventions and the Synoptic Problem," 69–85: "It makes as much sense to suggest such a procedure [i.e., conflation] at the time as it would to presuppose the use of electronic word-processors" (85). Cf. the critiques by Joanna Dewey and William Walker, with a response by Longstaff in Tyson, "Order in the Synoptic Gospels," 65–109.

100. Fitzmyer, "Priority of Mark." See the reply to Fitzmyer in Farmer, "Response to Joseph Fitzmyer's Defense."

101. Styler, "Priority of Mark," 285–316.

102. Ibid., 292 n. 3.

103. Orchard and Riley, *Order of the Synoptics*, 100–104. See also Hamann, "*Sic et Non*," 462–69.

104. McKnight, "Source Criticism," 136–72.

105. Ibid., 148.

106. See, for example, the comments by Stoldt, *Geschichte und Kritik der Markushypothese*, 202.

"Not tens but hundreds of thousands of pages have been wasted by authors on the Synoptic Problem not paying attention to errors of method, which are extremely common."[107] What is needed is a set of scientifically based criteria by which to determine chronological priority in the Synoptic Gospels.[108] Are such criteria available?

Criteria for Analyzing the Data of the Synoptic Problem

It is as obvious today as when Sanders first penned these words: "It is obvious, then, that criteria for determining the relative age of two or more parallel passages, based on knowledge of the tendency of the tradition, are needed."[109]

Although Farmer has concluded that there are "no convincing arguments for the priority of Mark" because "all arguments are either circular or inconclusive,"[110] such criteria are, nonetheless, available. Such criteria, however, must move beyond reversible arguments and seek a solution to the Synoptic Problem that is more objective.

Because of the similarities between textual criticism and source criticism (both disciplines seek the prior text), text-critical criteria may be applied in an analysis of the gospel texts in order to determine priority. Gordon Fee said,

> Textual criticism may yet have a contribution to make to the historical task. If we allow, as the majority of scholars on both sides do, that there is a *direct* literary relationship between any two of the Synoptists, then the kinds of questions textual criticism brings to such literary relationships are a pertinent part of the analytical task.[111]

---

107. Goulder, "Some Observations," 99.
108. *Contra* Rist, *Independence of Matthew and Mark*, 13, who concluded, "Discussion of primitivity must go hand in hand with a necessary exercise of the imagination."
109. Sanders, *Tendencies of the Synoptic Tradition*, 8. Such "objective" criteria would eliminate the need to rely merely on "the individual reader's judgment" as Goodacre proposes, *Synoptic Problem*, 65–66.
110. Farmer, "Case for the Two-gospel hypothesis," 134. Farmer seems to be echoing Dungan, *History of the Synoptic Problem*, 390: "At present, no formal arguments [are] left that will justify [Marcan priority] and the compositional arguments are just as questionable. It has rightly earned the sobriquet 'the Teflon hypothesis.'"
111. Fee, "Modern Text Criticism," 168. See the similar conclusion in Kilpatrick, "Some Thoughts on Modern Textual Criticism," 283; and Burton, *Some Principles of Literary Criticism*, 3: "Indeed, the work done in formulating the task of textual criticism may well furnish the starting-point for the effort to formulate corresponding principles applicable to the problem of the relation of the gospels to one another."

Streeter's fourth head of evidence is, in fact, similar to many of the text-critical criteria. It has even been said that "one would expect that the same general principles which apply to scribes copying texts would also apply to Matthew and Luke copying Mark."[112] In other words, "that Gospel is to be preferred as having priority which best explains how the others came into existence."[113] "Even though the specific goal may be different for each area, the types of questions utilized are comparable enough to allow for the application of textual questions to problems of synoptic relationships."[114]

Thus, the following examination applies text-critical principles to the gospel texts to determine priority.

The Similarities Between Textual Criticism and Source Criticism

First, the precise relationship must be shown between textual criticism and the Synoptic Problem, that is, between textual criticism and source criticism.[115] Matthew did not, after all, treat the text of Mark in the same manner as would a scribe, did he? Scribes were merely transcribers, weren't they?

Whereas scribes were merely supposed to duplicate the manuscript before them, many scribes were more than just copyists. Not only did scribes make unintentional errors,[116] they also often made intentional changes to the text they were copying.[117] Origen commented that the diversity of copies of the New Testament was immense, "be it from the negligence of certain scribes, or from the evil daring of some who correct what is written, or from those who in correcting add or take away what they think fit."[118] Aland agrees:

---

112. Royse, "Scribal Habits," 149.

113. Fee, "Text-Critical Look at the Synoptic Problem," 13.

114. Wheeler, *Textual Criticism and the Synoptic Problem*, 397.

115. See D. C. Parker, *Living Text of the Gospels*, 34–35, for an example of how textual and source criticism are similar as Parker lines up three manuscripts of Luke 6:1–10 and notes their differences.

116. Metzger, *Text of the New Testament*, 186–95.

117. Metzger (ibid., 195–203) lists seven types of intentional scribal changes: changes involving spelling and grammar, harmonistic corruptions, additions of natural complements, clearing up historical and geographical difficulties, conflation, doctrinal alterations, and additions of miscellaneous details. See Hurtado, *Text-Critical Methodology*, 68, 77–80, for some examples of significant changes to the gospel of Mark made by the scribe of codex W. D. C. Parker, *Codex Bezae*, 121–79, indicates specific textual corrections that scribes made to Codex Bezae (D). Many of the corrections impose significantly different meanings on the text. Cf. C. S. C. Williams, *Alterations to the Text*, 3; and G. N. Stanton, *Gospel Truth?* 35–36.

118. Origen, *Comm. on Matt.* 3:671, cited in Sturz, *Byzantine Text-Type*, 118.

They [scribes] also felt themselves free to make corrections in the text, improving it by their own standards of correctness, whether grammatically, stylistically, or more substantively. This was all the more true of the early period, when the text had not yet attained canonical status, especially in the earliest period when Christians considered themselves filled with the Spirit.[119]

Larry Hurtado, in his study of W, shows that scribes made significant changes to the text: *"Codex W shows conscious care to 'improve' the sense of the text of Mark."*[120] "There was considerable scribal freedom exercised in the text represented by W, but that freedom was exercised with responsibility and with purpose. It is the freedom exercised by translators today who wish to free the text from outmoded or unfamiliar expressions."[121]

Because of these scribal changes, no two New Testament manuscripts are identical. As scholars saw that different texts had different readings, they began to draw up criteria by which they could determine the earliest or original reading. The attempt to determine which textual variant in any given variation-unit is original is known as the art and science of textual criticism.

These text-critical criteria are now in use by the majority of scholars and were used to determine the main New Testament texts used today. These criteria are widely used and widely held to be valuable guides for determining the original reading from among multiple readings. Thus, these "scientifically" developed criteria also will be valuable for determining priority between the Synoptic Gospels.

To date, no one has analyzed these criteria to see whether they might be useful in solving the Synoptic Problem. Fee agrees:

That there is an interrelationship between textual criticism and the Synoptic Problem is the presupposition of most Synoptic studies.

---

119. Aland and Aland, *Text of the New Testament*, 69. See also Epp and Fee, *Studies in the Theory and Method of New Testament Textual Criticism*, 9, which says that the scribes were "more interested in making the message of the sacred text clear than in transmitting errorless manuscripts." Head, "Christology and Textual Transmission," 128, agrees when he states, "The scribes were interested in 'transmission' of texts, rather than in the creation of new texts. Nevertheless the transmission of gospel texts should not be seen as a neutral activity. The scribe of the New Testament was a participant in the life and faith of the church, and this life and faith clearly influenced the process of transmission." Further examples of changes may be found in Ehrman, *Orthodox Corruption of Scripture*.

120. Hurtado, *Text-Critical Methodology*, 68 (italics his). His category of "significant sense changes" also shows that scribes affected "the content of the passage and not merely the style" (77).

121. Ibid., 81.

Nonetheless, the specific nature of that relationship, especially as it affects the finding of solutions, is seldom spelled out, and, it would seem, is frequently neglected.[122]

Although it is true that the methods of scribes and those of the Evangelists differed, it is here proposed that many of the types of changes made by scribes also might have been made by Matthew, if he were using the text of Mark as a source when he composed his gospel, or by Mark, if he were using the text of Matthew as a source.[123]

Can text-critical criteria be applied to the Gospels in determining priority?[124] The remainder of this book will analyze these criteria to see if my proposal is correct.

THE NEED FOR PERICOPE-BY-PERICOPE ANALYSIS

Given that text-critical criteria may be useful for analyzing the Synoptic Gospels, how should they be applied? The best application would be a direct comparison of parallel portions of the gospel texts, pericope after pericope, word by word.[125]

The legitimacy of such detailed comparison is all but unanimously agreed upon in literature related to the Synoptic Problem: "It is now generally agreed that the only legitimate approach to the question of the relation of Matthew to Mark is the detailed comparison of their material."[126] "Ultimately the problem can be solved only by minute study of the actual texts."[127] "We believe that the most formally relevant evidence is . . . that which consists of the results of a direct comparison of parallel passages in their respective contexts."[128] "It is right

---

122. Fee, "Corrections of Papyrus Bodmer II," 257, shows that the scribe who copied 𝔓⁶⁶ "displays a marked tendency to smooth over certain harshnesses in the original text." This is, in essence, the so-called "text-critical" argument for the Synoptic Problem made by Streeter's fourth argument, namely, that Matthew smoothed Mark's rough areas.

123. Fee, "Modern Text Criticism," 154.

124. Shin, *Textual Criticism and the Synoptic Problem*, 317–18, has recently concluded that "the criteria used in textual criticism, in Synoptic Studies, and in historical Jesus research all share one basic similarity: they were all designed to distinguish prior or initial tradition from its later developments." On account of their similarities, we can adapt their methods, especially their criteria, from one of these areas of research for use in the other two areas.

125. Holtzmann, *Die synoptischen Evangelien*, 274: "über das synoptische Verhältniss nur Stand halten, wenn sie sich, als durch eine genaue philologiesche Untersuchung begründet, ausweisen."

126. Rist, *Independence of Matthew and Mark*, 12. Cf. Orchard, "Solution of the Synoptic Problem," 11.

127. Marshall, "How to Solve the Synoptic Problem," 2:315.

128. Butler, *Originality of St. Matthew*, 163; cf. 70.

that one should examine various individual pericopes within the gospels to see which hypothesis can best explain the texts."[129] Finally, Reginald H. Fuller wrote, "Farmer has compelled those who accept the two-document hypothesis to demonstrate its tenability pericope by pericope."[130]

One important scholar, though, disagrees with this methodology. In a reply to Fuller, Farmer said, "Such a demonstration is not likely ever to be completed; the time and energy required would be virtually prohibitive. For another, there is no consensus among scholars that demonstrating the tenability of any particular hypothesis 'pericope by pericope' will ever solve the Synoptic Problem."[131]

Tuckett replied to Farmer, "If a source hypothesis is to be accepted as a viable solution to the Synoptic Problem, then it must be capable of explaining the detailed wording of the gospel texts of each pericope. A hypothesis which fails to account for the detailed wording within each pericope can hardly be said to be satisfactory."[132]

The goal herein is to show that such a textual comparison *is* helpful for determining priority. Further, it really cannot be known whether or not the comparison is tenable until the study has been completed. As Walker states,

> I, myself, am inclined to agree with Farmer that, if the Synoptic Problem is ever to be solved, it will not be done exclusively (or perhaps even primarily) upon the basis of an "atomistic" or "pericope by pericope" approach such as that advocated by Fuller. Nevertheless, it is my judgment that this type of approach should not be abandoned, since the cumulative weight of its results might well eventually "tip the scales" toward one or another of the possible solutions.[133]

Thus, such an examination is, indeed, worthwhile.

Given that a pericope-after-pericope examination of the Synoptic Gospels should be performed, does such as examination need to be performed on all three gospels together? Gordon D. Fee said it best:

> Since both Marcan and Matthean priorists allow (1) that Luke is secondary, and (2) that Mark and Matthew have a *direct* literary relationship,

---

129. Tuckett, *Revival of the Griesbach Hypothesis*, 95.
130. Fuller, "Synoptic Problem," 67.
131. Farmer, "Basic Affirmation with Some Demurrals," 310.
132. Tuckett, *Revival of the Griesbach Hypothesis*, 207 n. 1.
133. W. O. Walker, "Son of Man Question," 263.

then a crucial part of a Synoptic solution must be the careful pericope-by-pericope, word-by-word analysis of Matthew and Mark (preferably where Luke is absent) to determine the most likely direction of literary dependence.[134]

Concluding Summary

Despite the minority opinion to the contrary, it is a worthwhile goal to analyze and compare pericope after pericope from the gospels of Matthew and Mark, using the criteria from textual criticism to determine evidence for priority. Such an analysis and comparison is, in essence, an analysis of Streeter's fourth head of evidence: Is the text-critical argument for the priority of Mark a valid argument?

An analysis is best begun, however, by examining the textual apparatus of Mark.[135] Thus, using text-critical criteria, it will be necessary first to categorize the "types of changes" made by scribes when "copying" a gospel. This set of "types of scribal changes" will yield categories by which to compare the gospels of Matthew and Mark. The ultimate goal will be to determine whether the kinds of changes found between the two gospels show similarity in any way to the kinds of scribal changes.

In other words, in order to approach the question of priority between the gospels of Matthew and Mark with as much objectivity as possible, an examination will be necessary of later changes made to Mark's gospel, thereby determining the types of changes that were actually made by scribes. These "types of changes" can then be used as a control to analyze the differences between Matthew and Mark, thereby finding which gospel makes the same types of changes to the other gospel that are found in Mark's textual apparatus. That is, if Mark displays the same types of text-critical changes to Matthew's gospel that later scribes made to Mark's text, it constitutes evidence, based upon text-critical principles, that Mark is the later gospel. If, on the other hand, Matthew displays the same types of text-critical changes to Mark's gospel that later scribes made to Mark's text, it constitutes evidence, based upon text-critical principles, that Matthew is the later gospel.

---

134. Fee, "Modern Text Criticism," 169; *contra* Farmer, "Two-gospel hypothesis," 134. See Fee's reply to Farmer in "Modern Text Criticism," 169.

135. In analyzing the textual apparatus of Matthew, the same types of changes would be found that are also found in Mark's apparatus.

A few limitations must, of necessity, be placed upon this study. First, not all of the Matthew-Mark parallels will be examined. Rather, to be examined is a total of 173 verses of Mark's gospel with the corresponding Matthean parallel. This amounts to 27 percent of Mark's total gospel, and, of course, a higher percentage of Marcan verses that are parallel with Matthew.[136] A complete study of all texts of Mark would, however, lead to the same conclusions.[137]

Second, the goal herein is not to perform a complete analysis of the Synoptic Problem. Rather, the goal is more modest—that of examining one argument, albeit the most important argument, for determining priority. Thus it will not be necessary to comment on, for example, the argument from order, or the document Q.

Third, because problems and inaccuracies tend to occur in every major textual apparatus, the well-prepared and relatively accurate apparatus from the Nestle-Aland *Novum Testamentum Graece,* 27th edition, will be used.[138] In addition, the text of Matthew given in Nestle-Aland's *Synopsis* will be accepted, with only occasional forays into the apparatus of Matthew.[139]

Finally, the synopsis of Nestle-Aland, *Synopsis Quattuor Evangeliorum,*[140] will be used for an analysis of the parallels between the gospels of Matthew and Mark.[141]

---

136. The 173 verses were not chosen for any *a priori* reason but were chosen based upon two criteria: (1) the pericopae chosen were portions of longer parallels between Matthew and Mark; (2) portions were chosen from the entire gospel of Mark (except the Passion narrative) in order get an overall impression.

137. See, for example, the comments of Marshall in "How to Solve the Synoptic Problem," 2:315–16.

138. See Kilpatrick, "Western Text and Original Text," 30–34. The Nestle-Aland textual apparatus is accurate per Elliott, "Examination of the 26th edition of Nestle-Aland *Novum Testamentum Graece,*" 26–27: "All the information there [in the textual apparatus] has been checked against photocopies of the original manuscripts, and . . . therefore we can use the information with confidence."

139. See J. W. Wenham, "Why Do You Ask Me About the Good?" 116–25; and Holmes, "Text of the Matthean Divorce Passages," 651–64, for examples of the influences that textual variations in Matthew's gospel have on an examination of the Synoptic Problem.

140. Nestle-Aland, *Synopsis Quattuor Evangeliorum,* 13th ed. (Stuttgart: Deutsche Bibelgesellschaft, 1993).

141. There has been some discussion that all synopses are biased based upon the editors' conclusions to the Synoptic Problem. Dungan, *Interrelations of the Gospels,* 317–42, concludes that the text, arrangement of text, and division into pericopae in synopses cannot be neutral. Elliott, "L'importance de la Critique Textuelle pour le Problème Synoptique," 57, replied to Dungan, "le texte lui-même ne révèle pas une préférence quelconque de la part de l'éditeur et dans ce sens il peut être appelé 'neutre'" [the text itself does not reveal any preference from the editor, and in this sense it can be called "neutral."]. Cf. Elliott, "Relevance of Textual Criticism," 348–59; idem, "Examination of the Text and Apparatus, 557–82; idem, "Printed Editions of Greek Synopses," 1:337–57; Neirynck, "Order of the Gospels," 357–62; idem, "Once More," 363–76; and Orchard, "Are All Gospel Synopses Biased?" 149–62.

— 2 —

HISTORY AND CRITERIA
OF TEXTUAL CRITICISM

CHAPTER SUMMARY

Since the goal of this book is to compare Matthew's and Mark's gospels using text-critical criteria, an understanding of the basics of the discipline will be needed. Thus, this chapter examines the current state of scholarship on textual criticism. A brief history of the discipline is given along with a critique of the various criteria presently being used. The chapter concludes with a list of text-critical criteria that may be used in chapter 3 for examining Mark's textual apparatus.

SCHOLARS AGREE THAT THE STRONGEST argument for Marcan priority is based on the so-called text-critical argument. Before applying this argument to gospel texts, however, an understanding is needed in regard to the discipline of textual criticism. This chapter, then, presents a brief history of textual criticism, along with a summary of and critique of the criteria that are used in textual criticism for determining original texts.

A BRIEF HISTORY OF TEXTUAL CRITICISM

Although textual criticism has become more "scientific" in the last two hundred years, even the early church Fathers made textual comments.[1] Some Fathers,

---

1. A thorough history of textual criticism is beyond the scope of this chapter. For more information, the reader should examine Vincent, *History of the Textual Criticism;* Kenyon, *Handbook to the Textual Criticism,* 265–313; Vaganay and Amphoux, *Introduction to New Testament Textual Criticism,* 129–71; Metzger and Ehrman, *Text of the New Testament,* 95–118 (Pre-Critical Period), 119–46 (Modern Critical Period: Griesbach to the Present); Epp, "Eclectic Method," 211–57; and Aland and Aland, *Text of the New Testament,* 3–47.

in fact, made text-critical decisions as to which reading was original when faced with variant readings in multiple manuscripts based on somewhat critical procedures.[2] Irenaeus (d. ca. 202) made reference to four distinct criteria: the critic should prefer as being more original (1) the reading that is older, (2) the reading that is found in better manuscripts, (3) the reading that best appeals to internal probability, and (4) the reading that accounts for the origin of the corrupted reading.[3] Metzger states that Origen (d. 253 or 254) was "an acute observer of textual phenomena but was quite uncritical in his evaluation of their significance."[4] He noted when other readings were found, usually without stating his preference for the more original reading. Jerome, in the late 380s, employed canons such as "an older MS carries more weight than a recent one, and a reading is preferable [more original] that fits the grammar or context of its passage."[5]

While important text-critical comments such as these were made by some church Fathers, those commentators were in the minority. Most early scholars and students of the Bible were not very interested in textual criticism. Only recently has textual criticism grown as a discipline, as the result of mainly two factors: the invention of the printing press and the availability of increasing numbers of manuscripts resulting from numerous new discoveries.[6]

The first printed version of the Greek New Testament was completed by Cardinal Ximenes of Toledo, Spain, in 1514. This work was withheld from the public, however, until 1522, leaving Erasmus's 1516 edition as the first available edited Greek New Testament. Various Greek New Testaments were subsequently printed, with the apparent climax in the 1633 edition published by Bonaventure and Abraham Elzevir in Holland. The preface to the second edition, claimed that this was the "Text received by all" *(Textum ergo habes, nunc ab omnibus receptum).* Scholars soon, though, began to question the principles and manuscripts upon which the "Textus Receptus" had been published. Thus began the modern era of textual criticism.

---

2. Metzger, "Practice of Textual Criticism," 189–90. See also idem, "St. Jerome's Explicit References," 179–90; and idem, "Explicit References in the Works of Origen," 78–95.

3. Irenaeus, *Adv. Haer.,* 5.30.1. See also, Metzger, "Practice of Textual Criticism," 190.

4. Metzger, "Explicit References in the Works of Origen," 93. In this essay, Metzger examines twenty-two references of Origen's text-critical observations on variant readings. For example, in *Matt. frag.* 74, Origen noted that some manuscript witnesses to Matthew 4:17b, μετανοεῖτε· ἤγγικεν γὰρ ἡ βασιλεία τῶν οὐρανῶν, did not contain the word μετανοεῖτε in their texts. Origen accepts the shorter reading based on the reasoning that the people had already repented at John the Baptist's preaching and did not need to repent again at Jesus' preaching.

5. Epp and Fee, *Studies in the Theory and Method of New Testament Textual Criticism,* 18.

6. See, for example, the interesting story by Tischendorf concerning his finding of Codex Sinaiticus at the monastery of St. Catharine at Mount Sinai in Tischendorf, *Codex Sinaiticus,* 15–32.

In 1711 Gerard von Mästricht drew up forty-three rules for finding the [more original] variant.[7] With Johann Albrecht Bengel (1687–1752), however, "we reach a new stage in the history of New Testament textual criticism. While a student in theology at Tübingen, his pietistic faith in the plenary inspiration of the Bible was disturbed by the 30,000 variants, . . . and he resolved to devote himself to the study of the transmission of the text."[8] In 1734 he published his *Novum Testamentum Graecum* (basically the Textus Receptus) with variants in the margins, graded according to five different classifications: original readings, readings better [more original] than the printed text, readings equally good, less good, and no good at all.[9] Bengel, besides devising new criteria dealing with external evidence,[10] was the first to state that "the difficult reading is to be preferred [as more original] to the easy reading" *(proclivi scriptioni praestat ardua,* normally shortened today to *difficilior lectio potior).*[11] This criterion was based on scribes' attempting to explain passages that seemed obscure.

Less than twenty years later Johann Jakob Wettstein (1693–1754), in his *Novum Testamentum Graecum,* 1751–1752, followed the principles that "a reading with a more pleasing sound is not to be preferred [as being more original] above a harsher one, so long as the context is not disregarded"; and "a shorter and more concise reading is more likely to be correct than a longer one, although omissions must be considered possible"; and "a reading is usually to be preferred if it agrees with the style of the writer."[12] All three of these rules are important today in textual criticism.

Johann Jakob Griesbach (1745–1812), who is well known for his Synoptic studies, formulated no new text-critical criteria himself. He listed fifteen criteria for textual criticism that were based on other scholars' conclusions. Griesbach did, however, go beyond earlier writings in listing six instances in which the criteria

---

7. In Bengel, *Gnomon of the New Testament,* 1:20–39.

8. Metzger and Ehrman, *Text of the New Testament,* 112. Bengel, *Gnomon of the New Testament,* 1:20–39, analyzed Mästricht's 43 criteria and reduced them to 27; Griesbach later reduced these to 13.

9. Bengel, *Gnomon of the New Testament,* 1:19–20; cited as α, β, γ, δ, and ε readings. See also Vaganay and Amphoux, *Introduction to New Testament Textual Criticism,* 140.

10. Bengel, *Gnomon of the New Testament,* 1:12–16, 25–26. Besides being the first to distinguish between two great manuscript groups, he noted that manuscripts must be weighed and not counted (as opposed to, for example, John Mill and most scholars before Bengel, who counted manuscripts).

11. Bengel first formulated these criteria in 1725 in an essay titled "Prodromus Novi Testamenti recte cauteque ordinandi," which was included as an appendix to his edition of *Chrysostomi libri VI de sacerdotio* (Denkendorf, 1725), cited in Metzger and Ehrman, *Text of the New Testament,* 112 n. 2. See also, Vincent, *History of the Textual Criticism,* 88. Epp, "Eclectic Method," 217–18, sees the seed for this criterion in John Mill, who said that smooth and easy readings are not necessarily genuine (1707).

12. Wettstein, Η ΚΑΙΝΗ ΔΙΑΘΗΚΗ, 2:851–74. The English translation of the criteria are found in Bristol, "New Testament Textual Criticism in the Eighteenth Century," 107. See also Epp, "Eclectic Method," 223–25.

of the shortest reading would not hold true as being the more original, including instances of homoeoteleuton (accidental shortening) and "if the shorter reading is less in accord with the character, style, or scope of the author."[13]

Constantine Tischendorf (1815–74) agreed with most of the existing criteria. His most important accomplishment is that he explained in detail, for the first time, a criterion that originated with Bengel, namely "that reading is to be preferred which could have given occasion to the others, or which appears to comprise the elements of the others."[14] It will be seen that this is probably the most important criterion used today in textual criticism.

The final scholars to be discussed are B. F. Westcott and F. J. A. Hort, who published their *Introduction to the New Testament in the Original Greek, with Notes on Selected Readings* in 1881–82. Metzger says that they "refined the critical methodology developed by Griesbach, Lachmann, and others, and applied it rigorously."[15] While Westcott and Hort, by classifying groups of manuscripts more precisely, moved beyond previous scholarship in terms of external evidence, they made little headway in terms of devising new internal criteria. They did, however, formulate the helpful distinction between transcriptional probability and intrinsic probability. The former deals with criteria that relate to what copyists do, the latter with criteria that relate to what authors do.[16]

A Discussion of the Text-Critical Criteria

The above brief survey of the history of textual criticism reveals that most of today's criteria were devised many years ago, sometimes two hundred years or more. Thus, a critique of the criteria used in textual criticism is not without cause. One of the best outlines of the criteria is found in Metzger's *A Textual Commentary on the Greek New Testament*:

I. External Evidence
   A. The date and character of the witnesses.
   B. The geographical distribution of the witnesses.
   C. The genealogical relationship of texts and families of witnesses.

---

13. Metzger and Ehrman, *Text of the New Testament*, 120.
14. Finegan, *Encountering New Testament Manuscripts*, 63. See also Tregelles, *Account of the Printed Text*, 119–21. Fee, "Text-Critical Look at the Synoptic Problem," 13, thinks that Griesbach was the first to spell out this principle clearly (though he does not cite where Griesbach did this). Although Bengel originated this criterion, he did not explain it in detail, as Tischendorf did.
15. Metzger and Ehrman, *The Text of the New Testament*, 129.
16. Westcott and Hort, *Introduction to the New Testament*, 19–30. A summary of Westcott and Hort's criteria may be found in table-form in Epp, "Eclectic Method," 243.

    D. Witnesses are to be weighed rather than counted.

II. Internal Evidence
    A. Transcriptional Probabilities depend on considerations of the habits of scribes.
        1. In general the more difficult reading is to be preferred as the more original reading.
        2. In general the shorter reading is to be preferred.
        3. That reading which is not a harmonization with another gospel's text is to be preferred as the more original.
        4. Scribes would sometimes
            a. Replace an unfamiliar word with a more familiar synonym;
            b. Alter a less refined grammatical form or less elegant lexical expression in accord with contemporary Atticizing preferences;
            c. Add pronouns, conjunctions, and expletives to make a smoother text.
    B. Intrinsic Probabilities depend on considerations of what the author was more likely to have written.
        1. In general this is determined by
            a. The style and vocabulary of the author throughout the book;
            b. The immediate context;
            c. Harmony with the usage of the author elsewhere.
        2. In the Gospels this is determined by
            a. The Aramaic background of the teaching of Jesus;
            b. The priority of the gospel according to Mark;
            c. The influence of the Christian community upon the formulation and transmission of the passage in question.[17]

External Evidence

Because the emphasis herein is placed on the text-critical argument's role in solving the Synoptic Problem, with its focus on internal criteria, the criteria for external evidence will not be critiqued.[18]

---

17. Metzger, *Textual Commentary*, 11*–14*. See also his *Text of the New Testament*, 209–19. Similar lists may be found in most introductions to textual criticism: e.g., Aland, *Text of the New Testament*, 280–82; Greenlee, *Introduction to New Testament Textual Criticism*, 114–15.
18. This limitation of discussion of the criteria in no way implies agreement with thoroughgoing or rigorous eclecticism; rather, the focus of this current study is on those elements—that is, the internal criteria—that are most helpful for analyzing the Synoptic Problem.

Internal Evidence

Following Metzger's outline, each of the internal criteria will be discussed in order to see if all of these criteria are equally valid for examining Matthew and Mark for priority.[19]

A. Transcriptional Probabilities

Transcriptional probabilities depend on considerations of the habits of scribes. It is no longer possible, of course, to interview the scribes who transmitted the New Testament in order to determine the motives behind their changes. As Ehrman says, however, "It is possible to evaluate the fruit of their labors by determining, that is, how the text appeared before they copied it and seeing how it had been altered once it left their hands."[20] Different scribes had different habits. In order to do a complete study of transcriptional probabilities, it would be necessary to examine each and every manuscript in order to see how each and every scribe treated the text before him. This, too, is, of course, impossible. In the end, however, this type of study is not necessary since this current study is interested in the average scribe and the general types or kinds of changes made to texts by copyists. Such studies have been done on enough manuscripts to convey a good idea of what an average scribe did when copying a text.[21]

Throughout the critique of these criteria, but especially of the transcriptional criteria, caution must be exercised in the use of these criteria. While their use is not completely objective, it is not, however, as subjective as some would claim.[22] As Vincent says, we have extensive knowledge of the habits of scribes, and thus transcriptional criteria are somewhat objective.[23] With these introductory comments, the transcriptional criteria are as follows:

1. *In general the more difficult reading is to be preferred as the more original.* As

---

19. Shin, *Textual Criticism and the Synoptic Problem*, 35–59, contains an examination of Metzger's transcriptional probabilities. It is unfortunate that Shin, given that he finished his dissertation in 2003, did not read a copy of my original doctoral dissertation (1996), which overlaps significantly with his overall thesis that there is much in common between textual criticism and the Synoptic Problem.

20. Ehrman, *Orthodox Corruption of Scripture*, 275.

21. Colwell, "Scribal Habits in Early Papyri," 370–89. See also Royse, "Scribal Habits," 139–61; idem, "Scribal Tendencies," 239–52; Hurtado, *Text-Critical Methodology*; Head, "Observations on Early Papyri," 240–47; and D. C. Parker, *Codex Bezae*.

22. Petzer, "Eclecticism and the Text of the New Testament," 57, claims that the use of transcriptional criteria "is very subjective and arbitrary. It rests mainly on hypothesis and speculation."

23. Vincent, *History of the Textual Criticism*, 79.

mentioned above, this criterion was initially devised by J. A. Bengel (1687–1752), who said, *proclivi scriptioni praestat ardua* ("the difficult reading is to be preferred to the easy reading"). This criterion is usually stated in the shorter form: *lectio difficilior placet*. The logic behind this criterion is that scribes often "corrected" texts they did not quite understand, thus making them "easier."[24] "The cleverer a scribe thinks he is, the more he is inclined to modify his text."[25] The more difficult reading, it is concluded, is therefore the more original reading.[26]

Nearly all scholars since Griesbach have agreed with Bengel on the importance of this criterion.[27] The majority of scholars, in fact—and not just New Testament scholars—are in agreement that this is the most important criterion for determining priority "One must not imagine that this principle of the priority of the 'harder reading' is restricted to the analysis of New Testament texts. This same principle of textual analysis has proven to be sound in the case of all kinds of textual reconstruction."[28]

This criterion, however, is not without its problems. The scribe may have misunderstood the passage and, in an attempt to "correct" the passage, actually made it more difficult. In such cases, the more difficult variant is actually not the original reading. It is because of such problems, says Tov, that Bengel's criterion is "problematic and impractical," and "the application of the rule is so subjective that it can hardly be called a textual rule or canon."[29]

The majority of scholars, however, disagree with these overly negative statements. They think that the criterion does play a role in textual criticism but must be used with caution. "One must not see this principle as a hard-and-fast rule. It must be used flexibly and in light of the total text-critical situation."[30] It is obvious, though, that none of these criteria are hard-and-fast. They must all be used with care. Even then, a subjective element remains. Still, the criterion stands as a valid general principle: all things being equal, the more difficult reading will normally be the more original reading (this is the intention of the

---

24. Westcott and Hort said such readings had "the appearance of improvement with the absence of its reality" (*Introduction to the New Testament*, 27).
25. Vaganay and Amphoux, *Introduction to New Testament Textual Criticism*, 81.
26. Note that this principle examines the most difficult reading from the perspective of the scribe, not from our perspective.
27. For example, see the more recent surveys by Fee, "Textual Criticism," 828–29; and Holmes, "Textual Criticism," 929.
28. Nida, "'Harder Reading' in Textual Criticism," 106.
29. Tov, "Criteria for Evaluating Textual Readings," 439–40. Sturz, *Byzantine Text-Type*, 114, adds that because of Atticizing, the simpler reading is often original, since scribes often changed to more difficult, Atticistic readings.
30. Edwards, "Using the Textual Apparatus," 129.

"in general" in Metzger's formulation).[31] Scholars have reached this conclusion from numerous studies on scribal habits.

2. *In general the shorter reading is to be preferred as more original.* Of all the criteria that will be examined, this one has recently come under the strongest attack. Griesbach's initial logic for this criterion is based upon the assertion that "scribes were much more prone to add than to omit."[32] Even Griesbach, though, understood that this was not always the case. He himself listed six cases in which the longer reading would be preferred as more original—including omissions of obscure or harsh words and omissions due to harmonizations.[33] Thus, even from the beginning, the dangers of this criterion were realized.

Nevertheless, scholars have shown that there is simply too much subjectivity in this criterion for it to be of value. Colwell, in his study of scribal habits, found that the more common tendency of the three scribes he studied was not addition to the text but omission. Traits of the scribe of $\mathfrak{P}^{45}$, for example, include the following: "The dispensable word is dispensed with. He omits adverbs, adjectives, nouns, participles, verbs, and personal pronouns—without any compensating habit of addition. He frequently omits phrases and clauses."[34] Colwell thus concluded that the longer reading is actually the original. Sturz has shown that some Byzantine longer readings are demonstrably early. He concludes that "the length of a reading has nothing to do with its age: long readings are old and short readings are old."[35] E. P. Sanders, in *The Tendencies of the Synoptic Tradition,* concludes that "on all counts the tradition developed in opposite directions. It became both longer and shorter. . . ."[36] Peter Head concluded just the opposite of Metzger: "Scribes were more likely to omit words and phrases from their texts (for whatever reasons),"

---

31. Just because the criterion cannot be used with mathematical certainty does not mean that it should be thrown out. Tov, "Criteria for Evaluating Textual Readings," 446–47, says, "This procedure is as subjective as subjective can be. Common sense is his main guide, and not abstract rules. This is not to say that the rules must be abandoned. They will always be of use, but one must recognize their limitations."

32. Cited in Metzger and Ehrman, *Text of the New Testament,* 120.

33. Ibid.

34. Colwell, "Scribal Habits in Early Papyri," 118–19. Colwell's conclusions were supported by Head, "Observations on Early Papyri," 240–47, who says, "Most fundamental is the support given to the conclusion that omission is more common than addition." Cf. Royse, "Scribal Habits," 154; Tov, "Criteria for Evaluating Textual Readings," 441; Hurtado, *Text-Critical Methodology,* 74–76; A. B. Lord, "Gospels as Oral Traditional Literature," 43; and Frye, "Synoptic Problems and Analogies in Other Literatures," 285.

35. Sturz, *Byzantine Text-Type,* 89.

36. Sanders, *Tendencies of the Synoptic Tradition,* 272. It should be noted that Sanders was not doing text-critical research, but his conclusions are nonetheless appropriate to this criterion of textual criticism.

and "it follows that we should not prefer the shorter reading, but rather prefer the longer reading (other factors being equal)."[37]

As a result, this criterion—as it is worded—will not be used in this current study. Instead, this criterion shall be subsumed under the previous criterion, namely, *Which is the most difficult reading?* Thus, this study will ask, *Why did the scribe add to or omit part of the text?*[38] The following questions will be much more productive than merely looking for the shorter reading: Is the omission due to stylistic, grammatical, or theological objections? Is it due to harmonization tendencies? Such questions that probe the logic of scribal motives help to make this criterion usable to some degree.

3. *That reading which is not a harmonization is to be preferred as more original.* Little needs to be said about this criterion since there is general agreement in its application. The basic logic here is that scribes, either intentionally or unintentionally, conformed parallel passages. Whether the motive was because of a belief that inspired Scripture would always be written in the same words,[39] or whether it was done unconsciously due to the scribes's familiarity with the wording of one or another of the gospels (recall that Matthew was the most used and thus most familiar gospel in the early church), we know that scribes harmonized readings. Thus, that reading which is not a harmonization is, in general, the more original reading.[40]

4. *Scribes would sometimes*
   a. *Replace an unfamiliar word with a more familiar synonym.* This aspect shall be discussed below, under the style of the author.
   b. *Alter a less refined grammatical form or less elegant lexical expression in accord with contemporary Atticizing preferences.* F. G. Downing, G. D. Kilpatrick, and J. K. Elliott are the main scholars to assert that Atticizing principles were at work in textual transmission.[41] Again,

---

37. Head, "Observations on Early Papyri," 247.
38. See the discussion by Royse in "Scribal Habits," in which he addresses the sometimes haphazard and contradictory arguments used by Metzger regarding arguments on the basis of text length in his *Textual Commentary*.
39. Aland and Aland, *Text of the New Testament*, 290, " . . . because it was impossible that sacred texts should not be in agreement."
40. See the discussion of the Matthean divorce passages in Holmes, "Text of the Matthean Divorce Passages," 651–64, for an example of the impact of harmonizations.
41. Downing, "Redaction Criticism," 49, shows that Josephus often made Atticizing improvements to his sources in both vocabulary and syntax. Kilpatrick, "Atticism," 125–37; Elliott, "Atticist Grammarians," 65–77.

however, there are opposing views. Carlo M. Martini, after discussing Kilpatrick's claims, says that "the claim of atticistic influence on Egyptian manuscripts should be carefully examined case by case before we could arrive at a general conclusion" since the Atticist reviser only partially corrects texts.[42] Gordon Fee goes further in saying that "Atticism may indeed be a cause of some corruption in the second century, but it is hypothetically equally probable (to this writer, *far* more probable historically) that a Christian scribe in the second century altered a less common form (= the alleged Atticism) to a more common, if less literary, form."[43] It should be concluded, then, that this criterion is of little value for determining the more original reading, and it shall be used in this study only with the greatest caution.

   c.   *Add pronouns, conjunctions, and expletives to make a smoother text.* Since much of the logic of this criterion is based upon the criteria of the more difficult reading and the shorter reading, this criterion shall be subsumed under those headings. Thus, this criterion *per se* shall not be used in this study.[44]

B. Intrinsic Probabilities

The second set of internal criteria are intrinsic probabilities, which depend on considerations of what the author was more likely to have written. As said above concerning transcriptional probabilities, intrinsic probabilities are also somewhat subjective. Petzer says that they are "even more subjective and speculative in nature" than transcriptional probabilities.[45] Westcott and Hort said, "There is much literature, ancient no less than modern, in which it is needful to remember that authors are not always grammatical, or clear, or consistent, or felicitous."[46] Again, it will be well to remember these cautions in the course of discussing these criteria.

   1. *In general, Intrinsic Probabilities depend on*
      a. *The style and vocabulary of the author throughout the book;*

---

42. Martini, "Eclecticism and Atticism," 155. See Kilpatrick's reply to Martini in "Eclecticism and Atticism," 107–12.
43. Fee, "Rigorous or Reasoned Eclecticism—Which?" 131.
44. This criterion runs into trouble for many of the same reasons that the "shorter reading" criterion does. See, for example, Sanders's conclusions in *Tendencies of the Synoptic Tradition*, 272–75.
45. Petzer, "Eclecticism and the Text of the New Testament," 57.
46. Westcott and Hort, *Introduction to the New Testament*, 21.

b. *The immediate context;*
c. *Harmony with the usage of the author elsewhere.*

Since all three of these criteria ultimately relate to an author's style, they will be discussed simultaneously.

As early as Origen, the criterion of style was used by biblical scholars to determine the preferred reading in variation-units.[47] That authors had a consistent style[48] and that scribes often made stylistic changes to the texts they were copying[49] has been shown many times. It is clear that different authors have different vocabulary and stylistic preferences. One need only dip into the conclusions of redaction criticism to see that each gospel writer had his own theological preferences.

A few questions concerning this criterion about stylistic considerations must, of course, be asked: Are authors completely consistent in style, or do they vary? Must it be concluded that the variant more in conformity with an author's style must be the more original? As Gordon D. Fee says, "The fact is that a variant may be regarded as original *because it conforms* to the author's style, or it may be regarded as secondary *because a scribe may have made it conform* to the author's prevailing style."[50] Petzer goes even farther in concluding that it is "clear that

---

47. See Epp, "Eclectic Method," 216. Style was used even before Origen by classical scholars attempting to determine the original texts of Homer's *Iliad* and *Odyssey*. See Peabody, "Chapters in the History of the Linguistic Argument," 47; cf. idem, *Mark as Composer*, 167, 173–75.

48. Engelbrecht, "Language of the Gospel of Matthew," 199, says, "It is an undeniable fact that there are definite differences between the style and language usage of the various writers of the synoptic Gospels"; and "Matthew, for instance, has his own composition, characteristic narrative style, as well as a predilection for certain words and constructions." Elliott, "Can We Recover the Original New Testament?" 353: "The individual style of the separate authors is recognizable." See also, for example, the vocabulary preferences of Matthew in Luz, *Das Evangelium nach Matthäus (Mt 1–7)*, 49–73; Hawkins, *Horae Synopticae*; Gundry, *Matthew*, 674–82; and Davies and Allison, *Matthew*, 1:72–96.

49. According to Colwell, *Methodology in Textual Criticism*, 118, "These three papyri ($\mathfrak{P}^{45}$, $\mathfrak{P}^{66}$, $\mathfrak{P}^{75}$) are enough to show that scribes made changes in style, in clarity, in fitness of ideas, in smoothness, in vocabulary. They created readings which can properly be called 'editorial.'" Colwell shows how the scribe of $\mathfrak{P}^{45}$ "does not actually copy words. He sees through the language to its idea-content, and copies that—often in words of his own choosing, or words rearranged as to order," and "writes with great freedom—harmonizing, smoothing out, substituting almost whimsically" (117). It is ironic that Colwell writes this about $\mathfrak{P}^{45}$, a manuscript that Aland rates in Category I. Kilpatrick, "Atticism," 125, adds that "Anyone who has studied the readings of $\mathfrak{P}^{66}$ will agree with this: apart from mere mistakes the largest single class of variants is stylistic." Finally, Metzger and Ehrman, *Text of the New Testament*, 192–93, note that scribes often substituted synonyms due to the nature of copying a text, namely that a scribe often forgot exactly what he had read "while a copyist was holding a clause or a sequence of letters in his (somewhat treacherous) memory between the glance at the manuscript and the writing down of what he saw there."

50. Fee, "Modern Text Criticism," 174–82. A similar conclusion was made by Metzger and Ehrman, *Text of the New Testament*, 178. See also Sturz, *Byzantine Text-Type*, 17.

consistency in style cannot easily serve as a basis for the analysis of language and style, or as a norm for determining originality in text-critically disputed passages in the New Testament."[51]

It is obvious that an author's overall style and vocabulary preferences may be determined from passages that are not text-critically disputed.[52] Each debated variation-unit that depends on an author's style, therefore, must be examined through the lens of this knowledge. It must then be asked, *Which is more probable—that a scribe changed the wording into an author's preferred style or away from an author's preferred style?* Often, reasons for the change can be determined. In a comparison of Matthew and Mark, this stylistic criteria will be valuable because each of these authors had a fairly consistent style and vocabulary.

2. *In the Gospels, Intrinsic Probabilities depend on*

   a. *The Aramaic background of the teaching of Jesus.* E. P. Sanders concluded that the presence or absence of Semitisms is inconclusive for determining original readings since different writers had different inclinations.[53] Thus, this criterion shall not be used in this study.

   b. *The priority of the Gospel According to Mark.* Since this criterion is exactly what is being examined, this criterion will not be used at all.

   c. *The influence of the Christian community upon the formulation and transmission of the passage in question.* Words and phrases that were theologically problematic for the Christian scribe might have been altered in the transmission process. A thorough and recent work on this topic is Bart Ehrman's *The Orthodox Corruption of Scripture: The Effect of Early Christological Controversies on the Text of the New Testament*, which concludes that "scribes occasionally altered the words of their sacred texts to make them more patently orthodox and to prevent their misuse by Christians who espoused aberrant views."[54] This criterion, too, has its uncertainties. Ehrman admits that it's not always clear which direction scribes have altered the words since texts were altered in seemingly arbitrary directions because "some textual changes work to *emphasize* aspects of Christ's human nature whereas others work

---

51. Petzer, "Author's Style," 195.

52. An examination of Neirynck and van Segbroeck's *New Testament Vocabulary* shows that each gospel writer had vocabulary preferences.

53. Sanders, *Tendencies of the Synoptic Tradition*, 272–75, who is followed by Engelbrecht, "Language of the Gospel of Matthew," 199–213.

54. Ehrman, *Orthodox Corruption of Scripture*, xi. See also, Head, "Christology and Textual Transmission," 105–29; and idem, *Christology and the Synoptic Problem*.

to *de-emphasize* it; some work to *heighten* his divinity, whereas others work to *diminish* it."[55] This criterion may be used but, as with all of them, with caution.[56]

Conclusion on Internal Criteria

It will now be helpful to summarize which of Metzger's criteria are useful. The most important criteria are as follows:

1. In general, the more difficult reading is to be preferred as the more original reading.
2. Stylistic criteria which help one to determine the original reading based upon the author's normal writing style:
   a. the style and vocabulary of the author throughout the book;
   b. the immediate context;
   c. harmony with the usage of the author elsewhere;
   d. replacement of an unfamiliar word with a more familiar synonym.

The next best criteria are the following:

3. That reading which is not a harmonization with another gospel's text is to be preferred as the more original.
4. The influence of the Christian community upon the formulation and transmission of the passage in question.

Criteria that are of limited value include the following:

5. In general, the shorter reading is to be preferred as the more original.
6. Alteration of a less refined grammatical form or less elegant lexical expression in accord with contemporary Atticizing preferences are less preferred as the more original reading.
7. Addition of pronouns, conjunctions, and expletives to make a smoother text are less preferred as the more original reading.

---

55. Ehrman, *Orthodox Corruption of Scripture*, 278. These alternating motives are the result of orthodox Christians' having to defend their view from two opposing forces: those working against Christ's deity (e.g., adoptionists) and those working against his humanity (e.g., docetists).
56. Head, "Christology and Textual Transmission," 126–27, concludes, "There are also enough exceptions to the rule to provoke caution in the use of a tendency to increasing reverence of Christ as a major text-critical principle. Nevertheless, that it is *one* important text-principle should not be denied."

Criteria that have no value include the following:

8. The Aramaic background of the teaching of Jesus.
9. The priority of the Gospel According to Mark.

For purposes of the current study, however, two of Metzger's criteria will be altered, namely "alteration of a less refined grammatical form or less elegant lexical expression in accord with contemporary Atticizing preferences," and "addition of pronouns, conjunctions, and expletives to make a smoother text."

Modifying the former criterion by eliminating any reference to Atticizing tendencies results in, "Alteration of a less refined grammatical form or less elegant lexical expression." This criterion is now of value, especially for a comparison of the differences in the Synoptic Gospels. Under Metzger's scheme, the wording of this criterion would fall under his "more difficult" criterion. Thus, the more difficult reading would be that one that is grammatically less refined. For the purposes of this study, however, it is better to make "grammatically less refined" a separate criterion.

Modifying the latter criterion by eliminating the types of changes made in order to bring about a smoother text (pronouns, conjunctions, and expletives), results in, "Modification of the text to make it smoother." This allows a greater degree of freedom in determining which text is smoother, rather than being limited by Metzger's formulation, which stipulates that only additions to the text help to make it smoother. Sometimes scribes deleted items in order to make it smoother. These changes result in four criteria of great value and two of slightly less value.

In perusing Metzger's *Textual Commentary*, however, it seems that he is operating with another criterion that he does not mention in his introductory list. Aland, along with many other text critics, places the highest importance, in making text-critical judgments, upon the determination of that variant that best explains the others.[57] Vaganay, who shows that this criterion has been in existence since Griesbach's day, calls this criterion the "source-variant," for it accepts as more original that variant that best explains the existence of all the others and cannot itself be explained by the others.[58] It is agreed that this crite-

---

57. A sample listing of modern text critics who think this is the premier criterion include Epp and Fee, *Studies in the Theory and Method of New Testament Textual Criticism*, 14; Sturz, *Byzantine Text-Type*, 17; Holmes, "Textual Criticism," 113; D. A. Black, *New Testament Textual Criticism*, 35; Ehrman, *Orthodox Corruption of Scripture*, 63; Edwards, "Using the Textual Apparatus," 129; and G. N. Stanton, *Gospel Truth?* 40–42.

58. Vaganay and Amphoux, *Introduction to New Testament Textual Criticism*, 82. He quotes Tischendorf, who called this criterion the *"omnium regularum principium"* ("the chief of all rules").

rion is the most important. To use this criterion, "each [variant] in its own turn must be assumed as a hypothetical original, and an endeavour made to deduce from it all the others."[59]

CONCLUDING SUMMARY

Seven criteria have now been established for use in an examination of gospel texts:

1. Source variant: that variant which best explains the existence of all the others and cannot itself be explained by the others is more original;
2. In general, the more difficult reading is more original;
3. That variant which is most in conformity with the author's style and usage elsewhere is more original;
4. The less refined grammatical form or less elegant lexical expression is more original;
5. The text that is less smooth is more original;
6. That reading which is not a harmonization with another gospel's text is more original;
7. That reading which is less orthodox is more original because of the influence of the Christian community upon the formulation and transmission of passages, since that influence generally produced more orthodox readings.

THE ART AND SCIENCE OF TEXTUAL CRITICISM

One final matter must be discussed before turning to an analysis of Mark's textual apparatus. Although the criteria give the appearance that textual criticism is a straightforward, scientific endeavor, such is not quite the case:

> Textual criticism is not a branch of mathematics, nor indeed an exact science at all. It deals with a matter not rigid and constant, like lines and numbers, but fluid and variable; namely the frailties and aberrations of the human mind, and of its insubordinate servants, the human fingers. It is therefore not susceptible of hard-and-fast rules.[60]

---

59. Westcott and Hort, *Introduction to the New Testament*, 23.
60. A. E. Housman (1921), cited in Metzger and Ehrman, *Text of the New Testament*, 219.

Textual criticism uses the preceding criteria, but these principles are a bit slippery. Thus results the basic problem of textual criticism: it is not mathematically conclusive. It is an art as well as a science.[61] The critic must, then, proceed cautiously and weigh the evidence carefully.

Such an admission does not, however, imply that textual criticism is totally subjective. The methodology can be improved, but it must be remembered that the criteria for determining the original text have been worked out over many centuries by many scholars. The principles of textual criticism consist of criteria used not only by New Testament scholars for determining the original New Testament but by all scholars who seek to determine the original text of any written document.[62] When the text-critical criteria are used properly, they "appeal to objective reasons which are strong enough to give backing to serious judgment."[63]

---

61. One example may be cited: Royse, "Scribal Habits," 145, says, "one reading will be judged superior on one criterion, but another reading is judged superior on another criterion. In the face of such a conflict, and in the absence of a clear understanding of the foundations for such criteria, the critic is free to choose that reading which 'seems' best, and thus to introduce what often appear to be simply arbitrary choices of one reading instead of another."

62. Westcott and Hort, *Introduction to the New Testament*, 19. Luck, "Textual Criticism Today," 164–94, a nonbiblical scholar, lists the criteria used by textual critics of all traditions. His criteria are almost exactly those listed by Metzger.

63. Vaganay and Amphoux, *Introduction to New Testament Textual Criticism*, 84.

— 3 —

EXAMINING MARK'S
TEXTUAL APPARATUS

CHAPTER SUMMARY

The text-critical criteria that were established in the preceding chapter
as valid criteria will now be applied to Mark's textual apparatus in order to determine the typical changes that scribes made to gospel texts.
The textual variants of approximately 27 percent of Mark's gospel will
be examined in order to see what scribes did to Mark's text.

SCRIBAL ACTIVITY IN MARK

BEFORE EXAMINING THE TEXTUAL DIFFERENCES between Matthew and Mark
to determine whether there is text-critical evidence that one of these Evangelists
used the other as a literary source, it is necessary to know the types of changes
that scribes made to gospel texts. Thus, starting below, this chapter examines
significant portions of Mark's textual apparatus to establish these scribal tendencies.[1] The seven text-critical criteria from the preceding chapter will be used
as a guide for distinguishing the types of changes.[2] Based on the results of this
investigation, these text-critical criteria will be reevaluated before exploring the
textual differences between Matthew and Mark.

---

1. Granted, wading through the following evidence may be tedious. Solid, detailed evidence must be
   presented, however, to demonstrate that the current study is not offering merely subjective preferences
   but is trying to encounter the elusive "objective" solution to the Synoptic Problem. A summarizing
   conclusion can be found at the end of this chapter for those who do not wish to wade through the
   following discussions.
2. Any variant that agrees with either Matthew or Luke has been labeled a harmonization, usually
   with no attempt to examine whether Marcan scribes did or could have independently made this

The Marcan texts that parallel Matthew will be examined with little or no regard for whether or not a parallel is found with Luke, since the goal of this study is to determine the more original source—Matthew or Mark. A total of 173 verses from Mark (27 percent of Mark) will be examined.[3] As each of the following pericopae is examined, the type of change that scribes made to the Marcan text will be italicized.

Mark 1:40–45: The Cleansing of the Leper

Mark 1:40. There are four different substitutions for [καί γονυπετῶν] καί ("and kneeling down and"). (1) ℵ* drops the second καί ("and"). (2) B 2427 sa^mss drop the entire phrase, perhaps due to a *harmonization* with Matthew 8:1. (3) D W Γ *pc* it omit the words in brackets, perhaps also due to an attempt to *harmonize* with Matthew 8:1. Alternatively, it is important to note that the phrase καί γονυπετῶν ("and having knelt") occupies one complete line in Greek manuscripts ℵ and Θ.[4] It would have been very easy for a scribe to *omit a line accidentally* by skipping over the phrase to the second καί ("and"), thus eliminating the bracketed phrase (homoeoteleuton).[5] (4) A final option, found in manuscripts A C 0130 *f*^13 33 𝔐 (q), inserts αὐτόν ("him") after γονυπετῶν ("kneeling"), presumably to *make the text clearer* by making explicit who is being worshiped and also to make this phrase parallel with the previous phrase, which contains the personal pronoun, παρακαλῶν αὐτόν ("begging him"). Metzger concludes that the bracketed phrase was included in the original reading due to the similar ideas of "falling on the knees" (Luke 5:12) or "worshiping" (Matt. 8:1) in the parallel accounts.[6]

Mark 1:41. Many of the same manuscripts that inserted αὐτόν (him) in 1:40

---

change. There are, admittedly, difficulties with this procedure. A similar method and reasoning was used by Hurtado, *Text-Critical Methodology*, 25, 69–71: "Some of the readings under this heading [harmonizations] might not have been conscious harmonizations; they may have been created simply because the scribe felt that alterations were needed. But whenever in this study there seemed any chance that a reading might have been introduced into the Marcan text of W from the other Gospels, the reading has been listed [under harmonizations]."

3. Because of the nature of the text-critical argument for the Synoptic Problem, the discussion will, in the following variation-units, concentrate on internal evidence rather than external evidence. While reasoned eclecticism requires that the text critic must balance the probabilities reached by both external and internal criteria, the text-critical argument for the Synoptic Problem is based solely on internal evidence.

4. C. H. Turner, "Marcan Usage," 28:157.

5. So, Gundry, *Mark*, 102.

6. Metzger, *Textual Commentary*, 76.

insert ὁ Ἰησοῦς here ("Jesus," A C L W Θ 0130 $f^{1.13}$ 𝔐 [q]). Again, it must be assumed that this is done to *make the subject clearer* since in verse 40 the leper is the subject of the main verb.

A few manuscripts replace σπλαγχνισθείς ("being filled with compassion," 5x in Matthew, 4x in Mark) with ὀργισθείς ("being angry," used only 1x each in Matthew and Luke, 0x in Mark).[7] The words ὀργίζω ("to be angry") and ὀργή ("anger") are used only a few times in the Gospels and only once directly of Jesus (Mark 3:5); where Jesus is angry and he extends his hand. Here in 1:41 there is also an extension of a hand. Is it possible that a scribe recalled the context of 3:5 and made a *mistake* here in 1:41 by inserting the idea of anger? The majority of commentators think that ὀργισθείς ("being angry") was the original reading due to the more probable direction of change from "being angry" to "having compassion," in essence, an *orthodox improvement*.[8] Elliott says that it is not "likely that human emotions such as anger would have been added by scribes to a text which would have seemed to them to be perfectly appropriate and innocuous had it originally read σπλαγχνισθείς ("being filled with compassion")."[9]

---

7. Metzger notes that a possible confusion between similar words in Aramaic may have led to the change from σπλαγχνισθείς to ὀργισθείς (*Textual Commentary*, 76–77). See also the discussion of this hypothesis in J. R. Harris, "Artificial Variants," 259–61. Metzger also guesses that ὀργισθείς may have been "suggested by ἐμβριμησάμενος of ver. 43."

8. So, Taylor, *Mark*, 178; C. H. Turner, "Marcan Usage," 28:157; and Idem, *Mark*, 17, says the Lord's anger was due to the doubt the leper exhibited in Jesus' willingness to cleanse him (ἐὰν θέλης δύνασαί με καθαρίσαι). Doubt, however, is not expressed in the text (ἐὰν θέλης). Rather, it seems to be hesitation based on respect. Cranfield, *Mark*, 91, says, "This is more an expression of confidence in Jesus' ability than of doubt about his willingness." Lane, *Mark*, 84 n. 141; Pesch, *Das Markusevangelium*, 1:141, notes that ὀργισθείς is the *lectio difficilior*; Guelich, *Mark 1–8:26*, 1:74, thinks the "anger" "is a 'righteous anger' that recognizes the work of the Evil One in the sick as well as the possessed"; Cave, "The Leper," 246; cf. Hooker, *Mark*, 78 n. 1; Mann, *Mark*, 218; Cranfield, *Mark*, 92; Davies and Allison, *Matthew*, 2:13. Grundmann, *Das Evangelium nach Markus*, 66, includes "anger" in the original text; he quotes the verse as "und er ward zornig (er erbarmte sich) streckte seine Hand aus . . . ," as does Gnilka, *Das Evangelium nach Markus (Mark 1–8,26)*, 1:89, "und voll Zorn streckte er seine Hand aus."

   Lake, "[ἘΜΒΡΙΜΗΣΑΜΕΝΟΣ and ὈΡΓΙΣΘΕΙΣ], MARK 1, 40–43," 197, thinks that ὀργισθείς was original. He makes a possible, though doubtful, suggestion that a punctuation change can help: "And there came to him a leper beseeching him and kneeling and saying to him, If thou wilt, thou canst make me clean; and he [the leper] put out his hand in a passion of rage and touched him. And he [Jesus] said, I will, be thou clean. And he rebuked him and immediately drove him out." Thus, ἐμβριμησάμενος (v. 43) is now understood as a "natural rebuke of Jesus for the leper's unwarrantable act in a moment of passion," i.e., a leper touching someone when instructed not to do so in the Law. Cf. Head, "Christology and Textual Transmission," 126.

9. Elliott, "Eclectic Textual Commentary," 53. He also notes that if Matthew did use Mark as a source, and if σπλαγχνισθείς were original, Matthew certainly would have retained it since he was fond of the theme of Jesus' compassion (4x).

Another substitution, ἥψατο αὐτοῦ ("he touched him") or αὐτοῦ ἥψατο αὐτοῦ ("of him he touched him") for αὐτοῦ ἥψατο ("of him he touched"), seems to be due to a *harmonization* with Matthew 8:3 and Luke 5:13. Some manuscripts *omit the personal pronoun,* αὐτῷ ("him") following λέγει ("[he] says"). Such omissions are very common.[10]

Mark 1:42–43. Many of the same manuscripts (A C Θ 0130 f^1 𝔐 lat sy^h) that inserted αὐτόν ("him") in verse 40 and ὁ Ἰησοῦς ("Jesus") in verse 41 insert εἰπόντος αὐτοῦ ("when he said this") here, presumably again to *make the object clearer.*

Two omissions in this verse attempt to *make the text easier/smoother.* The first omits the first finite verb phrase ἀπῆλθεν ἀπ᾽ αὐτοῦ ἡ λέπρα, καὶ ("departed from him the leprosy, and," sy^s). The second omission eliminates the second finite verb phrase beginning with καί ἐκαθαρίσθη ("and was cleansed") in verse 42 and extending through verse 43, καὶ ἐμβριμησάμενος αὐτῷ εὐθὺς ἐξέβαλεν αὐτόν ("and having sternly warned him, immediately he sent out him"). These omissions *eliminate the redundancy* in these verses.[11] It is noteworthy that Matthew 8:3 has Mark's second finite verb, ἐκαθαρίσθη ("was cleansed"), while Luke 5:13 has the first, ἀπῆλθεν ("departed"). The second omission may also be an *orthodox improvement* that attempts to lighten the strong—possibly negative—wording describing Jesus: ἐμβριμησάμενος ("having sternly warned"), which is "an expression of anger and displeasure."[12]

Mark 1:44. The omission of μηδέν ("nothing") is due to *harmonization* with Matthew 8:4 and Luke 5:14 or is an independent scribal improvement that attempts to *eliminate the double negative,* which is characteristically Marcan (pleonasm).[13]

---

10. C. H. Turner, "Marcan Usage," 28:157, says that there are numerous examples of deletion of the personal pronoun, even by "good authorities, up and down the Gospel."
11. Marcan style is fond of redundancy. See, for example, Taylor, *Mark,* 50–52; and Allen, *Mark,* 12–15, for a discussion of different types of redundant expressions. For a discussion of the difficulties of determining "Marcan style," see Pryke, *Redactional Style in the Marcan Gospel,* 25–31, who tries to delineate the style of Mark as a redactor and Mark as an author (or composer).
12. BAGD, 254. Swete, *Mark,* 30, disagrees; he says that the "idea of anger is not inherent in the word." He notes that the word is used in John 11:33, 38 and Matthew 9:30 without the idea of anger or of "correction" by scribes. Swete paraphrases the phrase as, "he gave him a stern injunction." Gundry, *Mark,* 96, agrees: the word is not used "to express displeasure but to emphasize the forcefulness of the thrusting out and of the instructions which accompany it (v. 44)." Whether or not the word was expressing anger in this particular context, the basic meaning of the word connotes anger, and that alone might have been enough for some scribes to eliminate it.
13. Taylor, *Mark,* 46, 189; cf. C. H. Turner, "Marcan Usage," 28:158.

Mark 2:1–12: The Healing of the Paralytic

Mark 2:1. The substitution of the pronoun εἰς οἶκον ("into a house") for ἐν οἴκῳ ("in/at home") may be an *assimilation* to the immediate context (εἰς Καφαρναούμ, "to Capernaum") or may be due to a preference in Hellenistic Greek for the accusative case with the preposition.[14] The change to εἰς ("to/into") also may have been made to avoid the idiomatic meaning of ἐν οἴκῳ ("at home").[15] Thus, scribes may have changed the preposition to insure that the meaning "in a house" would be understood. In other words, this change *eliminates the possible misunderstanding* that Jesus was in a house that he himself owned. Such a change would eliminate a potential discrepancy with Matthew 8:20 and Luke 9:58, where Jesus says that he has nowhere to place his head.

Mark 2:2. Many manuscripts insert εὐθέως ("immediately") after καί ("and"). While Mark often used the phrase καί εὐθύς ("and immediately," 25x), he uses καί εὐθέως ("and immediately") only once, in 7:35, where it is bracketed in Nestle-Aland[27]. It appears that this insertion is an *assimilation to Matthean style.*

Mark 2:3. Perhaps due to the *difficulty* of not following the finite verb with the prepositional object πρὸς αὐτόν ("to him"), some scribes altered the word order so that this adverbial prepositional phrase indicating direction followed immediately after the verb. Although the wording as found in Nestle-Aland[27], ἔρχονται φέροντες πρὸς αὐτὸν παραλυτικὸν αἰρόμενον ὑπὸ τεσσάρων ("they come carrying to him a paralytic being carried along by four [men]"), is acceptable, the *difficulty* of having two participles next to one another (φέροντες αἰρόμενον, "carrying being carried") may have caused some scribes to seek a little *smoother reading.* The first substitution, ἔρχονται πρὸς αὐτὸν παραλυτικὸν φέροντες αἰρόμενον ὑπὸ τεσσάρων ("they come to him a paralytic carrying being carried by four [men]"), is not as smooth as the second, ἔρχονται πρὸς αὐτὸν φέροντες παραλυτικὸν αἰρόμενον ὑπὸ τεσσάρων ("they come to him carrying a paralytic being carried by four [men]"). A third substitution, made only by W, is a complete rewrite, ἰδού ἄνδρες ἔρχονται πρὸς αὐτὸν βασταζόντες ἐν κρεβαττω παραλυτικὸν ("behold men coming to

---

14. M. J. Harris, "Prepositions and Theology," 3:1173; cf. N. Turner, *Syntax,* 3:236, 261: "The increasing vagueness of its [ἐν] meaning contributed to its ultimate disappearance; in MGr [modern Greek] it no longer survives in the spoken language." See also the discussion in C. H. Turner, "Marcan Usage," 26:14–20, who claims that εἰς οἶκον is original here because of the more likely change from εἰς to ἐν, rather than vice versa.

15. See, for example, Swete, *Mark,* 32.

him carrying on a mat a paralytic"). This variant uses a *synonym* for "carrying," though with little, if any, change in meaning, βασταζόντες.[16] It also changes the idea of "four men" carrying the paralytic, to the paralytic lying on a "mat," which is not found in either Matthew or Luke.

Mark 2:4. We find προσεγγίσαι ("to draw near," A C D $f^{1.13}$ 𝔐 it?) or προσελθείν ("to come to," W sa^ms it?) substituted for προσενέγκαι ("to bring"). These changes might be due to one of the following: (1) the emphasis in the context is drawing near; thus, both "to draw near" and "to come to" are *more refined lexical expressions* than "to carry to"; (2) Mark has no object for προσενέγκαι ("to bring"), which is odd.[17] Thus, either of these substitutions improves the reading by making the wording *clearer and more precise.*

ὁ Ἰησοῦς ("Jesus") is inserted after ἦν ("was") to *make the subject clear.* Without this subject, there is some confusion whether the subject is Jesus or the paralytic since the paralytic is directly mentioned in the preceding verse but Jesus has not yet been mentioned by name in this pericope.

A final variant is the substitution of ἐφ᾽ ᾧ ("upon which," 𝔓^45 A C f^1 𝔐), ἐφ᾽ οὗ ("upon which," Θ f^{13} 33. 565. *pc*) or εἰς ὃν ("in/on which," W) for the second ὅπου ("where"). These prepositions are *more refined expressions* for indicating the location of the paralytic's body: "the mat upon which the paralytic lay" rather than "the mat where the paralytic lay." Ὅπου is obviously the *most difficult reading* since one lies "upon" rather than "where."

Mark 2:5. The perfect passive verb, ἀφέωνται ("has been forgiven"), is substituted for the present passive, ἀφίενταί ("are forgiven"), which is probably a *harmonization* to the Lucan text.[18] On the other hand, this change may have been made independently by Marcan scribes in an attempt to emphasize the perfective or "stative" nature of Jesus' forgiveness, that is, the forgiveness was complete with continuing effects, or "reflected a given state of affairs."[19] This latter explanation is a *more elegant expression* since it indicates the proper perfective nature.

---

16. While Mark uses φέρω 16x to Matthew's 4x (2x in parallel to Mark), he uses βαστάζω only 1x to Matthew's 3x. It seems that in this variant this scribe is using more Matthean language than Marcan.

17. Cf. Swete, *Mark,* 33, who says that "προσεγγίσαι [is] possibly a correction due to the absence of αὐτόν." Without αὐτον as the object, there is also the possibility of confusion since the indirect object, αὐτῷ, follows directly after προσενέγκαι. The change to a different verb *eliminates this potential misunderstanding.*

18. BDF, §320, calls ἀφίενται an aorist present, denoting "your sins are forgiven at this moment." Reicke, "Synoptic Reports on the Healing of the Paralytic," 324, thinks the change from ἀφέωνται to ἀφίενται was made to replace the "Doric-Ionic archaism" with a "simpler form."

19. Porter, *Idioms of the Greek New Testament,* 22.

Mark 2:7. A few manuscripts change the interrogative pronoun, τί ("why"), to ὅτι ("why/that/because"). This may be significant in that Matthew also contains a question rather than a statement. Since there was no punctuation in the first manuscripts, there would not have been a question mark in the text. Thus, later scribes may have seen verse 7a as the continuation—that is, the cause—of the scribes' thoughts in 2:6 rather than as a completely new sentence. Therefore, this change would improve the reading by *making the text clearer.* Alternatively, the change may be a *change to Marcan style* because both τί and ὅτι can be used to indicate a question, *Why?* which is a characteristically Marcan usage of ὅτι.[20]

Numerous manuscripts change the verb βλασφημεῖ ("he blasphemes") to a direct object noun, βλασφημίας ("blasphemy"). This could be either a stylistic improvement or a misreading due to the lack of punctuation in the original texts. It would have been easy to misread βλασφημεῖ ("he blasphemes") and think that it was not a second statement against Jesus (i.e., "Why is he speaking in this manner? *He is blaspheming.*") but a direct object of the first statement ("Why is he speaking *blasphemies* in this manner?") This change is either an intentional change to *eliminate possible misunderstandings* or a scribal error.

Mark 2:8. Some manuscripts *omit the unnecessary* adverb, οὕτως ("in this manner"). However, then is seen the *insertion of the personal pronoun* αὐτοι ("they") as the subject of the verb, διαλογίζονται ("they are dialoguing"), another unnecessary addition. Later in the verse, is the *omission of a personal pronoun,* αὐτοῖς ("to them"). There seems to be no rationality in these various changes.[21]

Mark 2:9. The form ἀφέωνταί ("has been forgiven") is again substituted for ᾿αφίενταί ("are forgiven"), as in verse 5—and in many of the same manuscripts. Again, this is either a *harmonization* with Luke 5:23 or an independent improvement to create a *more elegant expression.*

Also is found the middle imperative ἐγείρου ("raise yourself up") substituted for the active ἔγειρε ("rise"). Due to the parallelism in Mark 2:9c, which contains three active imperative verbs (ἔγειρε ["stand"], ἆρον ["pick up"], and περιπά-τει ["walk"]), ἔγειρε ("stand") must be the original reading. Nonetheless, the

---

20. See Taylor, *Mark,* 195, where he notes ὅτι used with the meaning "Why?" in Mark 2:16; 8:12; 9:11, 28. He says that since "the tendency of scribes was to replace ὅτι by τί or διὰ τί," ὅτι was probably the original reading.

21. Scribal changes are not always rational. Examining only one manuscript reveals, for example, that an individual scribe sometimes eliminated personal pronouns from the text and sometimes inserted them into the text. Thus, not every scribal change can be explained by some particular motive. See Colwell, "Scribal Habits in Early Papyri," 106–24; Royse, "Scribal Habits," 139–61; and Head, "Observations on Early Papyri," 240–47, for examples of scribal changes in individual manuscripts.

substitution to the middle voice is a subtle *refinement in lexical expression* since it would imply "raising oneself up," which is what the context demands.[22]

The phrase καί ἆρον τὸν κράβαττόν σου ("and pick up the mattress of you") is either placed in a different order by some manuscripts (none of which is significant) or deleted altogether (only a few MSS do this, probably as a *harmonization* with Matt. 9:5 and Luke 5:23).

One final variant is the change from περιπάτει ("walk") to ὕπαγε ("go") or ὕπαγε εἰς τὸν οἶκόν σου ("go to the home of you"). This is an *assimilation* to similar wording in Mark 2:11.

Mark 2:10. Many manuscripts alter the order of ἀφιέναι ἁμαρτίας ἐπὶ τῆς γῆς ("to forgive sins upon the earth") in order to conform to Matthew's order. There are two variations in this variation-unit, both of which are *harmonizations* to either the Matthean text or a Matthean variant reading. Some manuscripts, W *pc* b q, eliminate the geographical restriction, ἐπὶ τῆς γῆς ("upon the earth"). This elimination is probably due to theological reasons since it may imply that Jesus' authority to forgive sins is geographically limited to the earthly region,[23] thus possibly being a change to a *more orthodox reading*. It is interesting that neither Matthew nor Luke eliminate this phrase. It should be noted that the Nestle-Aland[27] reading is contained in only a few manuscripts, B Θ 2427 *pc*.

Mark 2:12. The preposition ἔμπροσθεν ("in front of") is changed to either ἐναντίον ("before") or ἐνώπιον ("before"). Neither of these two prepositions are used by Mark or Matthew; Luke uses the latter 22x and the former 3x. This may simply be an *insignificant synonym substitution*.

The omission of λέγοντας ("saying") may be due to an interpretation of ὅτι as causal ("because") rather than introducing an indirect statement ("that"). This change may have been because λέγοντας ("saying") is four words removed from πάντας ("everyone"), the noun that it modifies. If such is the case, this change would *make the text clearer*.

Mark 2:13–17: The Call of Levi

Mark 2:14. Two names are substituted for Λευίν ("Levi"): Ἰάκωβον ("James"), which is probably a mistake due to an *assimilation* with 3:18, where

---

22. Taylor, *Mark*, 197, calls this change a "grammatical correction for the intransitive ἔγειρε."

23. Gundry, *Mark*, 120, thinks that the uncertainty of placement resulted in some manuscripts appearing with the phrase omitted altogether. This conclusion, though, seems unlikely. Scribes seldom omitted due to uncertainty; they simply placed the words where they thought they went, or placed the alternate reading in the manuscript's margin.

James is said to be τὸν τοῦ Ἀλφαίου ("the [son] of Aphaeus");[24] and Λευί ("Levi"), which is the same name but in the nominative case rather than the accusative. The same alternate spelling is found in a variant of Luke 5:27. Since the accusative case is grammatically "correct," one can only assume that scribes used the name "Levi" as indeclinable and thus substituted Λευί.

Mark 2:15. The omission of καί ("and") is probably due to its being grammatically unnecessary since verse 15a is an introductory adverbial infinitival clause. Mark 2:16b is then the main clause of the sentence. Since 2:15a is introductory, it would not need to be connected to the main clause by a conjunction. Thus, scribes have *improved the grammar.*

Mark 2:15–16. Some manuscripts *harmonize* οἱ γραμματεῖς τῶν Φαρισαίων ("the scribes of the Pharisees") with the more typical wording, which is also found in the parallel account in Luke 5:30, οἱ γραμματεῖς καί οἱ Φαρισαῖοι ("the scribes and the Pharisees"). Other manuscripts change the punctuation and insert a καί ("and") before ἰδόντες ("seeing") so that the text reads πολλοί. καὶ ἠκολούθουν αὐτῷ καὶ γραμματεῖς τῶν Φαρισαίων. καὶ ἰδόντες . . . ("many. And they were following him and scribes of the Pharisees. And seeing . . ."). This change is attempting to *make the subject* of ἠκολούθουν ("they were following") and ἰδόντες ("seeing") *clearer.* The problem with this change is that in Mark the scribes and Pharisees are never said "to follow" Jesus.[25] Thus, the scribes have inserted a "correction" that is actually an error; one can understand, though, the difficulty of deciphering the meaning of these verses with their abundance of clauses and repeated use of καί ("and") with no punctuation in the original manuscripts.[26] Again, it should be noted that the Nestle-Aland[27] reading is found in only a few manuscripts (B W 28 *pc*).

Mark 2:16. The omission of ἰδόντες ὅτι ἐσθίει μετὰ τῶν ἁμαρτωλῶν καὶ τελωνῶν ("seeing that he eats with sinners and tax collectors") is due to *harmonization* with Matthew 9:11.

The phrase ὅτι ἐσθίει ("that he eats") is replaced by ὅτι ἠσθίεν ("that he ate," 𝔓[88] ℵ D 892 c bo[pt]), ὅτι ἐσθίον ("that eating," Θ), or αὐτὸν ἐσθίοντα

---

24. For a discussion of this variant, see Burkitt, "Levi Son of Alphaeus," 273–74.

25. Lane, *Mark,* 102 n. 35, says that "'follow' is here used untechnically" (cf. 97–98). While it is true that "follow" occurs in Mark in a nontechnical sense (i.e., not in a discipleship connotation; cf. 3:7–8; 5:24; 10:32; 11:9; 14:13, 54), it is never used in reference to those who are hostile to Jesus. Thus, Lane's argumentation remains unpersuasive.

26. C. H. Turner, "Marcan Usage," 26:145, says that "Mark has made use of this expedient [i.e., the parenthetical clause ἦσαν γὰρ πολλοὶ καὶ ἠκολούθουν αὐτῷ] in a way which has misled scribes or commentators or both." See also the prolonged discussion of Marcan parenthetical clauses in Pryke, *Redactional Style in the Marcan Gospel,* 32–61.

("that eating," [ʃA] C 0130^vid *f*^1.13 𝕸 a f q). The first substitution is a change of the verb tense from the historical present to an aorist. While the aorist tense would be the *more acceptable tense,* Marcan style uses the historical present 151x.[27] The second and third substitutions are changes to participles. This change serves to subordinate the phrase about eating with sinners and tax collectors in order to emphasize ἔλεγον ("were saying") as the main verb of the sentence. While this change is not necessary, it serves to emphasize a different part of the sentence, which may be viewed as a scribal improvement in order to *make the text clearer.* This *change is toward Marcan style,* as he often has two or more participles functioning together (e.g., 1:41; 3:1; 5:15, 27, 36; 6:35, 48; 8:6, 13; 10:50; 11:13; 12:28; 14:22–23, 45, etc.).

The reversal of word order of ἁμαρτωλῶν καὶ τελωνῶν ("sinners and tax collectors") is due to *harmonization* with Matthew 9:11 and Luke 5:30.

The substitution of διὰ τί ("why") for ὅτι ("that/why") is due to *harmonization* with Matthew 9:11 and Luke 5:30. Some manuscripts substitute τί ὅτι ("why"). This change is a *grammatical refinement* that *makes clearer* that this last clause is a question. Recall from above that ὅτι may be used by itself to indicate a question.

There are numerous substitutions for ἐσθίει ("he eats") that are *grammatical improvements.* They are changes to the plural from the *more difficult* singular, thus indicating that the disciples and others were also present with Jesus.[28] They also might be due to *harmonization* with Matthew 9:11 or Luke 5:30.

Mark 2:17. The *deletion of the personal pronoun,* αὐτοῖς ("to them"), may be stylistic, since it is an unnecessary word, or it may be a *harmonization* with Matthew 9:12. On the other hand, it may have been independently eliminated due to the improbability that the Pharisees were actually eating with Jesus.[29] Note that the Pharisees spoke to τοῖς μαθηταῖς ("to the disciples," Mark 2:16), and not to Jesus himself. Thus, it is doubtful that Jesus would have replied directly to the Pharisees. Instead, he would have responded to those who were eating with him. The deletion of αὐτοῖς ("to them") *eliminates a possible misunderstanding* by eliminating the immediate reference to the Pharisees.[30]

---

27. N. Turner, *Style,* 4:20.

28. C. H. Turner, "Marcan Usage," 26:225, though, cites "21 instances in which the plural is used by Mark, denoting the coming and going of Jesus and his disciples followed at once by the singular in reference to Jesus alone."

29. Taylor, *Mark,* 207, agrees with this understanding and sees the deletion of αὐτοῖς as support for this interpretation.

30. Unless, of course, αὐτοῖς is understood as referring to the disciples and the sinners who were at table with Jesus. While this understanding is possible, it does not seem as plausible, given the need for Jesus' response to be heard by the Pharisees themselves. Gundry, *Mark,* 126, disagrees with this

The deletion of ὅτι ("that") is due to the same factors. Was the statement an indirect statement or a direct quote? Nonetheless, the ὅτι ("that") is *superfluous* and may be omitted with no loss in the sense.[31]

Mark 2:18–22: The Question About Fasting

Mark 2:18. The substitution of either τῶν Φαρισαίων ("of the Pharisees") or μαθηταὶ τῶν Φαρισαίων ("disciples of the Pharisees") for Φαρισαῖοι ("Pharisees") *assimilates* the wording to parallel οἱ μαθηταὶ Ἰωάννου ("the disciples of John") in verse 18a and with the identical wording in verse 18c. The replacement of σοὶ μαθηταί ("your disciples") by σοί ("your/to you") or μαθηταὶ σου ("disciples of you") is due to *harmonization* with Matthew 9:14.

Mark 2:19. The deletion of ὁ Ἰησοῦς ("Jesus," D W 28. 1424 *pc* b i q bo^ms) is complex. On the one hand, if it were not originally in the text, scribes may have inserted it in order to *make the text clear* by indicating the subject of the verb, as above in 1:41. On the other hand, if it were original, it may have been deleted because the subject is obvious. It should be noted that the parallels in both Matthew and Luke contain it.

The second deletion, of the long phrase at the end of the verse, ὅσον χρόνον ἔχουσιν τὸν νυμφίον μετ᾽ αὐτῶν οὐ δύνανται νηστεύειν (as long as they have the groom with them they are not able to fast), is due to either *harmonization* with Matthew 9:15 and Luke 5:34 or homoioteleuton (νηστεύειν . . . νηστεύειν,) ("to fast"), a scribal error.

Mark 2:22. Many manuscripts substitute ῥήσσει ὁ οἶνος ὁ νέος τοὺς ἀσκούς ("breaks the wine the new the wineskins") for ῥήξει ὁ οἶνος τοὺς ἀσκούς ("will break the wine the wineskins"). The addition of ὁ νέος (new) is due to *assimilation* with the earlier occurrence of οἶνον νέον ("wine new") in 2:22a. The change of the tense of ῥήγνυμι (or ῥήσσω, a by-form)[32] from the future, ῥήξει ("will break"), to the present, ῥήσσει ("breaks"), is similarly

---

latter understanding and says that Jesus "directs his statement to the scribes, not to the crowd." While Gundry's understanding is possible since all the facts are certainly not given in this condensed report, it seems more likely, given the emphasis in ἔλεγον τοῖς μαθηταῖς, that the scribes of the Pharisees were not physically present with Jesus. Perhaps he was still ἐν τῇ οἰκίᾳ (v. 15) while his disciples had gone outside of the house, interacted with the Pharisees, and then returned to the house to report the conversation to Jesus.

31. See C. H. Turner, "Marcan Usage," 28:9–15, for a discussion of over forty instances of ὅτι recitative in Mark. Many of these superfluous uses of ὅτι are deleted by later scribes. Doudna, *Greek of the Gospel of Mark*, 61–64, thinks that the presence of ὅτι recitativum points to the nonliterary character of Mark. He notes that twenty-one of the twenty-three Marcan uses are deleted by Matthew.

32. BAGD, 735

motivated since the present tense is used throughout this verse, except in ῥήξει ("will break"). A second substitution for ῥήξει ὁ οἶνος τοὺς ἀσκοὺς ("will break the wine the wineskins") is found in only a few manuscripts (W a bo^{ms}), διαρήσσονται οἱ ἀσκοί ("are burst the wineskins"). This is probably a partial *harmonization* to the Matthean text, which reads ῥήγνυνται οἱ ἀσκοί ("are burst the wineskins"), with the by-form of the verb used with a preposition for heightened effect.

A second *harmonization* with the identical wording in Matthew 9:17 is the substitution of ἐκχεῖται (-D it) καὶ οἱ ἀσκοὶ ἀπόλλυνται ("is poured out and the wineskins are ruined") for ἀπόλλυται καὶ οἱ ἀσκοί ("are ruined and the wineskins").

The final clause of the verse, ἀλλὰ οἶνον νέον εἰς ἀσκοὺς καινούς ("instead new ~ wine into new ~ wineskins"), is deleted by a few manuscripts (D 2427 it bo^{ms}) Metzger says that scribes may have omitted these words due to apparent ellipsis of the verb because they failed to see that these words went with βάλλει ("puts"). Since the omitted words did not seem to make sense in the context, this deletion would be a *grammatical improvement*. Metzger also says that a more probable explanation is that scribes may have *omitted them by accident* due to the repetition of the words οἶνος ("wine") and ἀσκός ("wineskins") in close succession.[33]

Some manuscripts, at the end of the verse after καινούς ("new"), insert either βάλλουσιν ("puts"), which is a *harmonization* with Matthew 9:17, or βλητέον ("must be put"), which is a harmonization with Luke 5:38.

Mark 2:23–28: Plucking Grain on the Sabbath[34]

Mark 2:23. A few manuscripts substitute διαπορεύεσθαι ("to travel through") for παραπορεύεσθαι ("to travel through"), which is a *harmonization* with Luke 6:1 and is an improvement in that it is a *more refined grammatical form* since the preposition διά ("through") follows.[35] Some manuscripts eliminate the preposition from the compound verb, πορεύεσθαι ("to travel"). This *more refined grammatical form* is possibly due to the disparity between the preposition

---

33. Metzger, *Textual Commentary*, 79. Gundry, *Mark*, 139, says the omission is a result of "scribal offense at the ellipsis of the verb." C. H. Turner, "Marcan Usage," 26:147, says that the variants are the result of a misunderstanding of Mark's parenthetical statement, εἰ δὲ μή, ῥήξει ὁ οἶνος τοὺς ἀσκοὺς καὶ ὁ οἶνος ἀπόλλυται καὶ οἱ ἀσκοί.

34. See Shin, *Textual Criticism and the Synoptic Problem*, 221–40, for a discussion of the original text of this pericope.

35. See Porter and O'Donnell, "Implications of Textual Variants," 126.

in the compound verb, παρά ("from"), and that of the preposition following the verb, διά ("through"). One manuscript, 565, substitutes an adverbial participle, παραπορευόμενον ("traveling through") for the infinitive. This change to *more typical Marcan style* may have been due to the rarity of using an adverbial infinitive in such a manner. Only here and in Romans 15:27 and Hebrews 9:23 is such an expression found in the New Testament. It is much more common to use an adverbial participle.

Three substitutions are found for the phrase ὁδὸν ποιεῖν τίλλοντες ("to make ~ a way picking"): (1) ὁδοποιεῖν τίλλοντες ("to make a path as they picked *or* to travel as they picked," the verb ὁδοποιέω is not used in the New Testament, except in this variant reading); (2) ὁδοιπορούντες τίλλοντες ("picking as they traveled," this verb is used only in Acts 10:9); and (3) τίλλειν ("to pick"), a possible *harmonization* with Matthew 12:1. Both of these latter two options *eliminate the awkward expression,* ὁδὸν ποιεῖν ("way/path to make"). What exactly does it mean to "make a path as one picks the ears of grain"? Does this mean that they were actually "making a road through the cornfield as they went along," or does it only signify, "as they were traveling along."[36] The substitutions imply the latter connotation is correct. The second substitution changes the verb so that it definitely means "to travel," thus *eliminating any misunderstanding.* The third substitution *eliminates the difficulty* altogether.

Mark 2:25. (1) Manuscripts A *f*¹ and 𝔐 substitute αὐτὸς ἔλεγεν ("he was saying") for λέγει ("he says"); (2) 28. 1241. 1424 *pc* substitute αὐτὸς λέγει ("he says"); (3) D (Θ) a substitute ἀποκριθεὶς εἶπεν ("having answering said"); and (4) 𝔓⁸⁸ B 565. 2427. (*l* 2211) bo^pt substitute ἔλεγεν ("[he] was saying"). The first and fourth substitutions are most likely *assimilations* to the presence of ἔλεγεν in 2:24a and 2:27.[37] The addition of αὐτός ("he") in the first and second substitutions is an addition to *make the subject clearer.* The third substitution seems to be

---

36. Both connotations are grammatically and lexically possible. Swete, *Mark,* 47, lists parallel uses for both meanings in Classical and Hellenistic Greek. Zerwick, *Biblical Greek,* 73 n. 1 (§228), though, concludes that the only possible meaning is "to make their way, to go forward." The majority of commentators conclude that the phrase refers to "traveling" (e.g., Lagrange, *Évangile selon Saint Marc,* 222; Grundmann, *Das Evangelium nach Markus,* 91; and Guelich, *Mark 1–8:26,* 1:119). Hooker, *Mark,* 102, though, thinks the phrase refers to "the disciples as 'making a way' by tramping down the standing corn." She cites Duncan Derrett's suggestion that the wording reflects the right of "the king to break through private property and build himself a road (*m. Sanh.* 2.4)." If this were the case, would not Jesus have made explicit that the reason that he could make a path was because he was the king? Instead of doing this, he argues about the right that he had to *eat* the grain rather than the right to *build a road!*

37. This variant reading may also be an assimilation to typical Marcan style since καὶ ἔλεγεν αὐτοῖς is a "typical introductory formula" in Mark (2:27; 4:2, 11, 21, 24; 6:4, 10; 7:9; 8:21; 9:1, 31; 11:17); Guelich, *Mark 1–8:26,* 1:119, 123–4.

a conflation and *harmonization* with both Matthew 12:3 and Luke 6:3—possibly only with Luke 6:3 since it contains both of these verbs, καὶ ἀποκριθεὶς πρὸς αὐτοὺς εἶπεν ("and having answered to them said").

Mark 2:26. The omission of πῶς ("how," B D 2427 r¹ t) seems to be an attempt to *eliminate the slightly obtuse wording.* The τί ("why") in verse 25 would carry over into verse 26 so that πῶς ("how") is not necessary; thus, αὐτός ("he") would simply be the subject of ἐπείνασεν ("he was hungry") in verse 25 and εἰσῆλθεν ("he entered") in verse 26.

The omission of ἐπὶ Ἀβιαθὰρ ἀρχιερέως ("during Abiathar high priest") might be a *harmonization* with Matthew 12:4 and Luke 6:4 but more likely is an independent improvement by Marcan scribes. First Samuel 21:1–6 says that it was Ahimelech, Abiathar's father, who was high priest when David and his men ate the bread of the presence. Thus, D W pc it sys may have independently "corrected" this difficulty.[38]

The replacement of τοὺς ἱερεῖς ("the priests") by τοῖς ἱερεῦσιν ("for the priests," A C D [L, Θ] W f¹ 𝔐) or τοῖς ἱερεῦσιν μόνοις ("for the priests only," Δ 33 pc sa^mss bo [∫ f¹³ it vg^mss]) is either for *harmonization* with Luke 6:4 or Matthew 12:4, or for independent *grammatical improvements* and *changes to more typical Marcan style,* since one would expect a dative case to be used in this context rather

---

38. BDF, §234 (8), followed by Gundry, *Mark,* 140, solves the apparent textual difficulty by saying that ἐπὶ plus the genitive signifies a "temporal relationship," i.e., "in the time of Abiathar the high priest." Swete, *Mark,* 48, notes that the confusion between Ahimelech and Abiathar began in the Old Testament, where "we read of Ahimelech the son of Abiathar as high-priest in the time of David (2 Sam. viii. 17, 1 Chron. xviii. 16, xxiv. 6)." Taylor, *Mark,* 217, calls the reading about Abiathar either a "primitive error or a copyist's gloss occasioned by the fact that, in association with David, Abiathar was better known than his father." Mann, *Mark,* 240, cites an Arabic custom by which a father would be known by the name of a more famous son. Thus, Ahimelech would be known as "the father of Abiathar." Mann says the original Greek text would thus read "Ab(ba)-Abiathar," "the father of Abiathar." Scribes then simply made a dittographical error, eliminating the first "Ab" in order to produce a text that read only "Abiathar." So Shin, *Textual Criticism and the Synoptic Problem,* 259. While this hypothesis is possible, the use of the term "Ab" or "Abba" (ἀββα) is found only three times in the entire New Testament, all in the context of God the Father (ἀββα ὁ πατήρ). It is never used to refer to any other father in the New Testament; πατήρ was used for this designation. This fact makes Mann's suggestion unlikely. J. W. Wenham, "Mark 2.26," 156, says the phrase ἐπὶ Ἀβιαθὰρ ἀρχιερέως refers to a passage of Scripture. Wenham says, "The problem is how to account for the retention of the phrase for so long in the oral tradition when the error was so readily recognized. Might not Mark 12:26 supply the answer? ἐπὶ τοῦ βάτου means 'at the passage of Scripture concerning (or titled) the Bush.' May not ἐπὶ Ἀβιαθὰρ ἀρχιερέως mean 'at the passage of Scripture concerning (or titled) Abiathar the High Priest'?" Rogers, "Mark 2:26," 44–45, correctly refutes Wenham; ἐπὶ Ἀβιαθὰρ ἀρχιερέως does not refer to a passage of Scripture. This construction refers to a passage of Scripture only if "immediately followed by ἀνέγνωτε (so Lagrange). Even so, Abiathar is still not mentioned close to the passage about shewbread."

than the accusative case.[39] A third replacement option, τοῖς ἀρχιερεῦσιν ("to the chief priests"; [Φ] 28. 579. 1241 *pc*), is difficult to understand because Leviticus 24:5–10 makes it clear that the bread of the presence is for all of the priests, not just the high priest. It seems this is a *scribal error*, perhaps due to assimilation to the use of ἀρχιερέως ("high priest") earlier in the verse.

Mark 2:27–28. A few manuscripts replace all of verse 27 and the first word of verse 28, καὶ ἔλεγεν αὐτοῖς· τὸ σάββατον διὰ τὸν ἄνθρωπον ἐγένετο καὶ οὐχ ὁ ἄνθρωπος διὰ τὸ σάββατον· ὥστε ("and he said to them, the Sabbath on account of man came into being and not man on account of the Sabbath. So that"), with either λέγω δὲ ὑμῖν ὅτι τὸ σάββατον διὰ τὸν ἀνθρώπου ἐκτίσθη ὥστε ("but ~ I say to you that the Sabbath on account of man was created so that," W [syˢ]) or just λέγω δὲ ὑμῖν ("but ~ I say to you," D it). The phrase λέγω δὲ ὑμῖν is a *harmonization* with Matthew 12:6. The remainder of the change attempts to improve the wording by substituting a *more refined expression*. After all, the Sabbath did not just "come into being," ἐγένετο, but was created by God. Possible misunderstandings of this phrase may have led to its *elimination by more orthodox scribes*.

Mark 4:1–9: The Parable of the Sower

Mark 4:1. The variant readings for εἰς πλοῖον ἐμβάντα ("into a boat having gotten") make little difference. The addition of the article by many manuscripts may be an attempt to *make the text clearer* by showing that it is a definite boat that was in mind. Compare to 6:32, where the definite article is used.[40] Some scholars think that perhaps Jesus and the disciples used the same boat every time. Another variant reverses the word order so that the participle is before the prepositional phrase, which *makes it a little smoother*.

Some manuscripts substitute πέραν τῆς θαλάσσης ("on the other side of the sea") for πρὸς τὴν θάλασσαν ἐπὶ τῆς γῆς ("near the sea on the land"). Since πέραν is an adverb of place, "on the other side," it is a near synonym with πρός (with the accusative case), "by, at, near."[41] This change is probably an *assimilation* to the similar wording and context of Mark 5:21. Mark (14x) seems to use πέραν only for movement to the other side of a river or sea; while πρός

---

39. Taylor, *Mark*, 217, says the accusative case was used rarely after ἔξεστιν + an infinitive. Mark follows this construction with the dative case 4x (2:26; 3:4; 6:18; 10:2) and the accusative case 1x (12:14).
40. The article was often dropped following a preposition, so the presence or absence of the article makes little difference.
41. BAGD, 643; 711.7.

is used by Mark for being alongside something (cf. 5:11). W improves the idea by substituting ἐν τῷ αἰγιαλὸς ("on the shore"), which is partially in *harmonization* to Matthew 13:2.

Mark 4:3. Many manuscripts add the definite article τοῦ ("the") before the purpose infinitive, σπεῖραι ("to sow"), in *harmonization* with Matthew 13:3 and Luke 8:5. Mark, however, never places the genitive article τοῦ before the purpose infinitive (Matthew does this 6x; Luke 20x).[42] A few manuscripts drop the infinitive, perhaps to *eliminate the redundancy* since σπείρω ("to sow") is used three times in Luke 4:3–4.

Mark 4:4. W *omits the pleonastic* phrase ἐγένετο ἐν τῷ σπείρειν ("it came about while [he went] to sow"); D omits ἐγένετο ("it came about"). The phrase καὶ ἐγένετο ("and it came about") is Semitic and characteristically Marcan (7x). The omission of the entire phrase is *stylistically smoother* since it is not needed for the meaning of the sentence.

Mark 4:5. B and 2427 add καί ("and") before ὅπου ("where"). This is probably due to *stylistic assimilation* to the immediate context, given that this pericope is loaded with καί . . . καί . . . καί (3x). A scribe added an extra καί which does not belong in the context.[43] D W it substitute καὶ ὅτι ("and because") for ὅπου ("where") in order to indicate the cause for the withering. This smoothes out the idea since ὅπου is *more difficult* conceptually.

A few manuscripts substitute ἐξελάστησεν ("to sprout up," not used in New Testament) for ἐξανέτειλεν ("to grow or spring up," used 2x in New Testament: here and in Matthew's parallel account). W substitutes ἀνέτειλεν ("to rise or spring up," 9x in the New Testament), which is a probable *harmonization* with Mark 4:6, where the sun is said to ἀνέτειλεν ("to rise or spring up"). Both of these changes are synonyms.[44]

Mark 4:6. B D a e substitute a plural verb for the singular ἐκαυματίσθη ("it was scorched"), probably to indicate that there was more than one plant that sprang up *(constructio ad sensum).* Given the use of singular verbs throughout this context, this change is clearly not needed but could be seen as a *grammatical improvement.*

---

42. Burton, *Syntax,* §§366, 397, shows that purpose infinitives may be used with or without the definite article; cf. Luke 2:22–24 where both uses occur together: παραστῆσαι τῷ κυρίῳ, τοῦ δοῦναι θυσίαν.

43. It could be said, with Swete, *Mark,* 73, that the καὶ, if original, is epexegetic.

44. These synonym changes may have been made because ἐξανατέλλω is normally transitive; so, Taylor, *Mark,* 252. Since it is intransitive in this verse, some scribes introduced synonyms that are normally used intransitively, a change to more *typical style.*

Mark 4:8. καὶ ἄλλο ("and other") is substituted for καὶ ἄλλα ("and others"), which is an *assimilation* with verses 5, 7 where the singular is used.[45] Clearly καὶ ἄλλα is the *more difficult* reading since it would be hard to understand why a scribe would change the parallel singular phraseology in order to use the plural here. Also ἄλλα ("others") could be a *harmonization* with Matthew 13, where it is used throughout the pericope instead of ἄλλο ("other"), but that would not explain its being used just once here in Mark.

The form αὐξανόμενον ("growing") is substituted for αὐξανόμενα ("growing"). Because of the awkwardness of this verse, it is difficult to know which nouns the participles modify. Does ἀναβαίνοντα καὶ αὐξανόμενα ("rising up and growing") modify ἄλλα ("others") or καρπόν ("fruit")? In order to *eliminate this confusion,* and perhaps due to the assimilation to the singular verb, ἔφερεν ("it was bearing"), some scribes changed the plural participle to the singular, αὐξανόμενον. Other manuscripts substituted the active voice αὐξάνοντα for αὐξανόμενα. This is due to *harmonization* with the immediate context, where -οντα verbs are found three times in Mark 4:8. Thus, αὐξανόμενα is best seen as the *source variant,* from which the others can be explained.[46]

Five variant readings are found for the Nestle-Aland[27] reading, ἓν τριάκοντα καὶ ἓν ἑξήκοντα καὶ ἓν ἑκατόν ("one thirty and one sixty and one one-hundred," *f*[13] *pc* lat sy[p] [A C² D Θ *sine acc.*]). Part of the difficulty in understanding this variation-unit is the possibility of understanding εις and εν as either prepositions or numerals.[47] Of the variants (1) εἰς . . . ἐν . . . ἐν (B²), which was the reading in Nestle-Aland[25];[48] and (2) εἰς . . . ἔν . . . ἔν (L) may be the *most difficult* because they either shift the gender (if they are numerals) or the preposition. Either shift is difficult to explain in the context.[49] Some of the reasons for the introduction

---

45. Notice that even though the plural καὶ ἄλλα is used in Mark 4:8, the singular verb ἔπεσεν is used, just as it was used after the singular καὶ ἄλλο in Mark 4:5, 7.

46. Metzger, *Textual Commentary,* 83.

47. Ibid., says the Aramaic חד, which is both the numeral one and the sign of multiplication ("-times," "-fold"), lies behind ἕν. He does not, though, provide reasons why εἷς or εἰς would have been introduced into the text. Guelich, *Mark 1–8:26,* 1:188, says this Aramaic idiom is normally expressed in Greek "by adding -πλασιως to the cardinal (e.g., Luke 8:8; Mark 10:30)" (cf. Zerwick, *Biblical Greek,* §158). Notice that Mark himself uses this Greek idiom, ἑκατονταπλασίονα (10:30), showing he was familiar with it.

48. McNeile, *Matthew,* 188, says the reading "εις . . . εν . . . εν is impossible."

49. Swete, *Mark,* 74, says "the change of preposition is meaningless and intolerably harsh." C. H. Turner, "Marcan Usage," 28:17, concludes that since Mark uses εἰς and ἐν interchangeably in his gospel, such interchange in this verse, then, is not as impossible as it might be for other authors. If such an interchange were, in fact, original, it might best explain the reason for sometimes having all εἰς and sometimes all ἐν; i.e., scribes were not comfortable with the interchange, so they changed the wording so that the prepositions or numerals would all be the same.

of εἰς, if ἐν were the original reading, include (a) a prepositional *assimilation* due to the phrase εἰς τὴν γῆν ("on the land") earlier in the verse, or (b) a *grammatical improvement* by using the masculine gender εἷς ("one") to agree with the masculine καρπὸν ("fruit").[50] It would be incorrect, though, to have agreement between εἷς and καρπὸν ("fruit"), since it is the seed (neuter gender) and not the fruit (masculine gender) that produces the yield of 30, 60, or 100. Another reason for using εἷς may be that it is (c) used with numbers in a manner that "is distributive, '-fold.'"[51] In other words, the verse would be translated, "and some bore thirtyfold, some sixtyfold and some one hundredfold." (3) A third variant reading is εἰς . . . εἰς . . . εἰς [אC Δ 28.700.(2427) *pc*]: again, it must be assumed that the change of preposition is due either to *assimilation* to the earlier use or that ε-ι-ς are used as numerals, εἷς, rather than as prepositions (*contra* Nestle-Aland[27]). (4) Another variant is ἐν . . . ἐν . . . ἐν (*f*[1] 33[vid] 𝔐 sy[h]): Greek sometimes uses the preposition ἐν to indicate amount—for example, Acts 7:14[52]—but it is usually followed by a unit of amount when it is used in this manner—for example, drachmas. (5) τὸ ἕν . . . τὸ ἕν . . . τὸ ἕν (W). It is herein concluded that εἰς, ἐν, εἷς, or ἕν could all have been used correctly in this context. It also seems more likely that numerals were used than prepositions. The mix-up may be due to lack of accents in early manuscripts.

Mark 4:9. The insertion of καὶ ὁ συνίων συνιέτω ("and the one understanding, let him understand") after ὃς ἔχει ὦτα ἀκούειν ἀκουέτω ("who has ears to hear let him hear") *harmonizes* it with the Isaiah 6:9 quote in Mark 4:12, where both hearing and perceiving are mentioned.

Mark 4:10–12: The Reason for Speaking in Parables

Mark 4:10. The substitution of μαθηταὶ αὐτοῦ ("disciples of him") for περὶ αὐτὸν σὺν τοῖς δώδεκα ("around him with the twelve") is probably a *harmonization* to the wording of Matthew 13:10 and Luke 8:9. Or, a scribe could have been upset that the mysteries of the kingdom of God (Mark 4:11) were given only to the Twelve and those around them, so he changed the wording to include all disciples. We should remember that there were many "around Jesus" who were not disciples. The awkwardness of Mark's περὶ αὐτὸν σὺν τοῖς δώδεκα

---

50. The numeral εἷς for the preposition εἰς is introduced here (even though the textual apparatus gives the reading as εἰς). This is a possible variant reading due to the absence of accents in many older manuscripts. Thus, there may have been confusion between the preposition and the numeral.

51. BAGD, 230.6.c; BDF, §§207 (2) and 248 (3).

52. BAGD, 261.4.2, "amounting to."

("around him with the twelve") led to a scribal improvement to *eliminate possible misunderstandings.* The improvement to μαθηταὶ αὐτοῦ ("disciples of him") would *make it clearer* that only those "around Jesus" who were disciples would receive the mysteries.

Some manuscripts (A f^1 𝔐 vg^{cl} sy$^{p.h}$ bo^{ms}) substitute the singular τὴν παραβολήν ("the parable") for the plural παραβολάς ("parables"). This change *removes a difficulty* since the text of Mark records only one parable in this context.[53] This could also be the reason that the definite article is added to this singular παραβολήν. Note that Matthew has the plural; Luke has the singular. Of course, Mark 4:10 seems to be more of a summary statement of Jesus' policy than just a comment on the parable of the sower, but this may not have been clear to some scribes. A second substitution, τὶς ἡ παραβολή αὕτη ("what [is] the parable this"), is an improvement for the same reason. This change brings the emphasis only upon this one parable in Mark's context. It is also a partial *harmonization* to Luke 8:9.

Mark 4:11. The substitution of ἔξωθεν ("outside") for ἔξω ("outside") is an *insignificant synonym change* since these adverbs are nearly identical. Mark uses the former twice and the latter ten times. The substitution of λέγεται ("called") for γίνεται ("becomes") seems to be a scribal improvement to a *more elegant expression* since parables are "spoken" and do not just "happen" or "become."

Mark 4:13–20: Interpretation of the Parable of the Sower

Mark 4:15. The substitution of ἐν ταῖς καρδίαις αὐτῶν ("in the hearts of them") or ἀπὸ τῆς καρδίας αὐτῶν ("from the heart of them") for εἰς αὐτούς ("in them") is due to *harmonization;* the former is the plural form of Matthew 13:19, the latter is the identical form of Luke 8:12.

Mark 4:16. Many manuscripts add ὁμοίως ("in the same way") before (A B 2427 𝔐 lat sy^h) or after (ℵ C L Δ 33. 892. 1241 *pc*) εἰσιν ("are") to *make the text smoother* by showing the relationship of this verse to the earlier parable (v. 5).[54] A few texts (Θ $f^{1.13}$ 28. 565. 700 *pc;* Or) delete αὐτόν ("it") at the end of the verse. This object may have been deleted if scribes thought that the definite article οἱ ("the/those who") modified both participles, ἀκούσωσιν ("hear") and λαμβάνουσιν ("receive"). The object of these two participles would then be τὸν λόγον ("the word"). If this were the case, the personal pronoun αὐτόν (it)

---

53. N. Turner, *Grammatical Insights,* 47; and Zerwick, *Biblical Greek,* 7 n. 7, call the plural παραβολαῖς a generalizing plural or plural of category.

54. Metzger, *Textual Commentary,* 83.

would no longer be needed as the object of the second participle, λαμβάνουσιν ("receive"). The text would now be translated as "those who hear and immediately receive *the word* with joy," rather than "those who hear the word immediately receive *it* with joy." Thus, the deletion may have been due to a misunderstanding of the verse, or to an alternate understanding, and serve to *make the text clearer*, based, that is, on their [mis]understanding of the text.

Mark 4:18. Some MSS omit ἄλλοι εἰσίν ("others are" [W Θ $f^{1.13}$ 28. 565. 700. 892. 1424. 2542 *pc* sy^p sa^{mss}]), while others substitute οὗτοί εἰσίν ("these are," A 33 𝔐 f q sy^h). The latter change would be an *assimilation* with the immediate context, since Mark uses the pattern οὗτοί εἰσίν ("these are") throughout this pericope to indicate a new group of individuals. The omission of the phrase is probably because a scribe saw that this instance did not follow the parallel pattern and thus omitted it altogether. Both of these are *stylistic improvements*—attempts to bring *a unified style* to the text.

The substitution of ἐπί ("upon") for εἰς ("into") is possibly an attempt to bring this phrase into agreement with the falling of the seed "upon" the πετρώδη ("rocky places," Mark 4:5, 16) since it is more "correct" for seed to fall "upon" a thorn bush than to fall "into" a thorn bush. This change, however, is probably due to an *overly simplistic* (or *Atticistic*) view of prepositions. Since the meaning of prepositions is very flexible in the Hellenistic period, εἰς ("into") can carry many of the same connotations as ἐπί ("upon"). Thus, such a change would not have been necessary but could be seen as a *grammatical improvement*. That both Matthew and Luke have εἰς ("into"), and that the same phraseology in Mark 4:7 is not changed, indicates that such a prepositional change is unnecessary.

Mark 4:19. The substitution of βίου ("of life") for αἰῶνος ("age") could be a *harmonization* with Luke 8:14. Mark uses αἰών ("age") four times (the other three times it refers to this age or the age to come) and βίος ("life") only once. While βίος ("life") can refer to an "age," it can also refer to the physical resources by which one lives.[55] Thus, βίου ("of life") should be seen as a *more refined word choice* in this context, which is emphasizing riches.

There are three different substitutions for ἡ ἀπάτη τοῦ πλούτου ("the allurement of wealth"). (1) The change to the plural, ἀπάται τοῦ πλούτου ("allurements of wealth," W [1424] f), is a *grammatical improvement* since the "allurements" of this age would be more than one. (2) If ἀπάται τοῦ κόσμου ("allurements of the world," D [Θ 565] it) were the original text, it would be hard

---

55. See the contexts in Mark and Luke that emphasize monetary existence in this age: Mark 12:44; Luke 8:14, 43; 15:12, 30; 21:4.

to explain the three textual variants that involve πλούτου ("wealth"). Thus, ἡ ἀπάτη τοῦ πλούτου ("the allurement of wealth") is the *source variant*. This is probably a substitution of a broader *synonym*, κόσμου ("of world"), since it is more than just "riches" that produce allurements. (3) The third substitution, ἡ ἀγάπη τοῦ πλούτου ("the love of wealth," Δ), is probably a *scribal mistake*—inserting ἀγάπη ("love"), a more familiar term, for the less familiar ἀπάτη ("allurement," used only 7x in the New Testament, 1x in Mark). The omission of the phrase καὶ αἱ περὶ τὰ λοιπὰ ἐπιθυμίαι ("and the desires ~ for remaining things ") is a *harmonization* with Matthew 13:22.

Mark 6:17–29: The Death of John the Baptist

Mark 6:20. The substitution of ἐποίει ("brought about") for ἠπόρει ("was disturbed," A C D *f¹* 33 𝔐 lat sy) might be an attempt at a stylistic improvement by substituting a *more refined word* because of the *difficulty of the reading*, especially with πολλά ("many/much," 21x in Mark).[56] It would have been easy for scribes to become confused as to the grammatical function of πολλά ("many/much"): subject, object, or adverb?[57] Scribes may have used ἐποίει in order to show that πολλά is the object (see 7:13). This improvement is even more obvious in the second alternative substitution (*f¹³* 28 *pc*), which inserts a relative pronoun before ἐποίει, ἃ ἐποίει, ("and when he heard him, the many things which he did"). A third attempt by scribes to deal with this difficult reading was simply to delete ἠπόρει ("was disturbed," Δ bo^ms). It also should be noted that πολλά may be acting as the subject of ἠπόρει, with the verb's being singular due to *schema atticum*; thus, "and as he listened, many things puzzled [him]" (cf. Luke 9:7).

Mark 6:22. A few alternative readings attempt to *harmonize* verse 22, "his daughter Herodias," with verse 24, where the girl is called Herodias's daughter (although the queen's name is not explicitly given in the text).[58] The Nestle-Aland[27]

---

56. BDF, §414(5), says that the clause ἀκούσας αὐτοῦ πολλὰ ἐποίει is a "translation Semitism," which has the same meaning as πολλάκις ἤκουεν, i.e., "he was hearing John often." Lane, *Mark,* 214 n. 57, thinks the change from ἠπόρει to ἐποίει was due to "an error of hearing which originated in the dictation of the text to scribes who copied what they heard." The problem with this explanation is that it does not explain the two other readings in this variation-unit.

57. Metzger, *Textual Commentary,* 89, says that the use of πολλά here as an adverb is "more in keeping with Marcan style." D. A. Black, "The Text of Mark 6.20," *NTS* 34 (1988): 143, though, says the adverbial use of πολλά always follows the verb (like we find in Mark 6:23). Gundry, *Mark,* 319, says that πολλά follows the verb (1:45; 4:2; 5:10, 23, 38, 43; 6:23, 34; 15:3) almost twice as often as it precedes its verb (3:12; 5:26; 8:31; 9:12, 26). In this verse, πολλά comes before the verb.

58. See Taylor, *Mark,* 314–15, for a listing of the alternative harmonizations, and scholars who hold to each, and Guelich, *Mark 1–8:26,* 1:320, for a discussion of some of the issues involved in making a decision.

reading of verse 22, αὐτοῦ ("of him"), says that the girl is Herod's daughter and is named Herodias.[59] Perhaps due to the moral difficulty of the king's own daughter pleasing him by dancing, other readings are found.[60] Αὐτῆς τῆς, "the daughter herself, [daughter] of Herodias" (A C Θ f^{13} 33. 2427 𝔐 sy^h), is not only awkward, but a similar grammatical construction is not found anywhere else in Mark.[61] The reading with just αὐτῆς (W) gives the name Herodias to the girl, but now she is not said to be Herod's daughter. The final alternative substitutes only τῆς [f^1 pc (aur b c f) sy^{s.p}], which would be read, "the daughter of Herodias," perfectly harmonizing with verse 24.

Καὶ ἀρεσάσης (aorist participle from ἀρέσκω, "to please") has been substituted by a number of manuscripts for ἤρεσεν ("she pleased," aorist indicative). Perhaps due to an absence of a conjunction at the beginning of the next clause in verse 22, scribes altered the aorist infinitive to an aorist participle so that εἶπεν ὁ βασιλεὺς ("said the king") would be the only main verb in the sentence. Certainly it is *more in conformity with Marcan style* to have καὶ ("and") at the beginning of the next clause. Note that many of the readings that substitute the participle are also those that insert δὲ ("and") in the next variation-unit, ὁ δὲ βασιλεὺς εἶπεν ("and the king said"). The Nestle-Aland[27] text is probably incorrect in one or the other of these two readings, since these choices go against Marcan style. Their text uses one reading from a series of manuscripts but not a reading from the same manuscripts just a few words later. The choice for these two readings must be taken in tandem: either aorist indicative with the addition of δὲ ("and"), or the aorist participle with the absence of δὲ.

Mark 6:23. The substitution of ὅτι ὃ ("because what") for ὅ τι ("what[ever]") seems to be a *misreading* of ὅ τι as ὅτι ("because"), which then calls for the addition of a relative pronoun ὃ in order to *make the text smoother*. It is more difficult to account for a switch from ὅτι to ὅ τι, rather than vice versa. D's reading, εἴ τι ("if anything"), may be due to a switch from ὅ τι, which is found

---

59. Swete, *Mark,* 125, says this reading "can scarcely be anything but an error, even if a primitive one; her name was Salome and she was the grand-niece, not the daughter of Antipas" (cf. Justin *Dial.* 49).

60. Donahue and Harrington, *Mark,* 2:198–99, say that since the narrative speaks of a young woman, perhaps a twelve-year-old girl, "the narrative could conceivably depict a child's performance rather than the sensuous and seductive dance of later art and literature." They conclude that no "sexual overtones" are present.

61. Metzger, *Textual Commentary,* 90, translates this phrase as "the daughter of Herodias herself, unless αὐτῆς be taken as the redundant pronoun anticipating a noun (an Aramaism)." Metzger notes that the Committee concluded αὐτοῦ was original due to its external strength. N. Turner, *Syntax,* 3:41, calls this a "proleptic pronoun followed by resumptive noun, an Aramaic peculiarity"; "her daughter, i.e., Herodias's." This reading is also the most difficult reading by internal evidence, as witnessed to by Elliott, "An Eclectic Textual Commentary," 55–56.

only here in Mark, to the more *characteristically Marcan style* εἴ τι, which occurs 4x in Mark.

Mark 6:24. The addition of αὐτῇ ("to her") *makes the indirect object* of the mother's speaking *clearer*. The addition of αἰτῆσαι ("to ask") in a few manuscripts *makes the reading smoother* by eliminating the need for direct address.

Mark 6:27. Some manuscripts substituted ἐνεχθῆναι ("be brought," aorist passive infinitive) for ἐνέγκαι ("to bring," an alternate form of the aorist active infinitive). It appears that the differences in voice are *grammatical improvements* due to the various functions of σπεκουλάτωρ ("an executioner"). The scribes may have thought that a courier was a literal "carrier" who would "bring the head" to the king (active voice), but if a scribe thought that a "courier" was merely one who would "have the head brought" to the king, he would have changed the voice to the passive, a *grammatical improvement.*[62]

Mark 6:29. The substitution of αὐτόν for αὐτό ("it") would be a use of a *more refined grammatical form* since the body was not a "thing" but a "person."[63] The neuter was originally used to agree with πτῶμα ("corpse").

Mark 6:32–44: Five Thousand Are Fed

Mark 6:32. Mark's somewhat *difficult wording* (ἀπῆλθον ἐν τῷ πλοίῳ εἰς ἔρημον τόπον, "they departed in the boat to a desolate place") caused some scribes to improve it. Some (A W *f*[1] 𝔐 sy) merely change the word order so that the εἰς ("to") immediately follows ἀπῆλθον ("they departed"), as it should in proper word order. The place to which one departs should immediately follow the verb, per *Mark's normal style* (of 23x; only 3x does Mark use a finite ἀπέρχομαι ["to depart"] without immediately following it with the location; 5x Mark uses a participle without noting the location). Other manuscripts (D lat sa) substitute ἀναβάντες ("going aboard") for ἀπῆλθον in order to deal with the difficulty.

Mark 6:33. A few manuscripts substitute the less intensive ἔγνωσαν ("knew") for ἐπέγνωσαν ("knew"). While the latter may be used as a near synonym for the former, the former would be the *more refined word* in this context since the people certainly did not "perceive through and through" (using the intensive meaning).[64] A second variant adds an accusative pronoun (either plural, αὐτούς

---

62. BAGD, 761, says the word literally means "spy, scout"; then it came to mean "courier, but also executioner." Thus, the various connotations of the word led to this variant reading.

63. Though, as Blomberg, *Matthew*, 374, said, "there is no great difference" in the meaning.

64. BAGD, 291.1.

["to them"], or singular, αὐτόν ["to him"]) in order to *make clear* who the people recognized (either the group or Jesus, respectively). This change makes the sentence a little smoother by inserting a *direct object*.

Perhaps it was the *difficulty* of the idea that the crowd arrived before Jesus and the disciples (καὶ προῆλθον αὐτούς, "and they arrived ahead of them") that led to a myriad of alternative readings.[65] The first is the alteration of προῆλθον ("they arrived") to προσῆλθον ("they came to," [L 579] Δ Θ [1241]. 1424 *pc*), which then led to the substitution of αὐτοῖς ("to them") for αὐτούς ("them"). This perceived *improvement* allows Jesus to arrive first with the people "coming to them" after they had arrived. A second alternative (D [28. 700. 33 *pc*] b) is the substitution of συνῆλθον ("came together with") for προῆλθον ("they arrived"), which then led to another switch of the pronoun, to αὐτοῦ ("him"). The Byzantine readings (𝔓[84vid] [A *f*[13]] 𝔐 f [q] sy[h]) have merely *conflated* these two options.

Mark 6:34. While ἐπί ("on") can be followed by either an accusative, αὐτούς ("them"), or a dative object, αὐτοῖς ("them"), it seems that the variant here is due to a *harmonization* with Matthew 14:14, where αὐτοῖς is found.

Mark 6:35. Γινομένης ("becoming") is substituted for γενομένης ("was coming") by ℵ and D. It appears that this is a *scribal mistake* (perhaps due to a misunderstood oral vowel). Γινομένης is used only once in the whole New Testament (Acts 23:10) versus thirty-three times for γενομένης.

Mark 6:37. Some manuscripts *eliminate the personal pronoun,* αὐτοῖς ("to them"). Two alternate forms of the aorist active subjunctive are substituted for the future indicative δώσομεν ("will we give"): δῶμεν ("may we give," W Θ *f*[1] 𝔐) and δώσωμεν; ("may we give," ℵ D N *f*[13] 28. 33. 565. 892. 1424 *pc*). The subjunctives are *assimilations* to the previous subjunctive before the καὶ, ἀγοράσωμεν ("and, may we buy"). It is *more difficult* to explain a change from a subjunctive, which fits the context better, to an indicative.[66] It is also possible to understand this change as due to the similarity of the sound of the letters "o" and "ω," which would be a *scribal error* (faulty hearing).[67]

Mark 6:39. The substitution of ἀνακλιθῆναι πάντας ("to recline everyone") is probably a *harmonization* with Matthew 14:19. The change to the passive voice

---

65. Westcott and Hort, *Introduction to the New Testament*, 95–97, discuss the alternatives. Swete, *Mark*, 130, does not think it difficult that the crowd arrived before Jesus. He notes that the distance across the lake is four miles, while the distance by land is ten miles. "If there was little wind, it would be easy to get to the place before a sailing boat."

66. Cranfield, *Mark*, 217, says that δώσωμεν is a "natural improvement" over the harsh future indicative reading.

67. See Metzger and Ehrman, *Text of the New Testament*, 190–92.

could also be a *grammatical correction,* since verbs of commanding use the passive infinitive instead of the active.[68] One manuscript, 700, has only ἀνακλιθῆναι ("to recline"), apparently because πάντας ("everyone") would no longer be needed: "he commanded them to be reclined."

Συμπόσια ("group") is found only here in the New Testament. Apparently scribes were uncomfortable with the repetition, so some (L W Θ *f*[13] 565. 579 *pc*) eliminated the second occurrence.[69] D changed the phrase to κατὰ τὴν συμπόσιαν ("in groups"). Zerwick states that the repetition was "characteristic of popular speech in Greek."[70] Thus, the absence of repetition would be a *more elegant expression.* Notice also that the repetition of πρασιαὶ ("group") in the following verse is eliminated by some manuscripts (although the textual apparatus of Nestle-Aland[27] does not note this variant).

Mark 6:40. 𝔓[45] may have eliminated the phrase κατὰ ἑκατὸν καὶ κατὰ πεντήκοντα ("in hundreds and in fifties") due to the *apparent disagreement* with Luke 9:14, which states that they reclined in groups of fifty. Perhaps the scribe (since only a single manuscript has this reading) made a *mistake* (it should be noted that the scribe of 𝔓[45] had just eliminated a word from the text, namely πρασιαί ["group"]; he may have found the next phrase unnecessary due to this excision).

Some manuscripts substituted ἀνά for κατά ("by, according to"). These are synonymous forms since both words can be used distributively. It is likely that this is a *harmonization* with Luke 9:14.

Mark 6:41. 𝔓[45] again has a unique reading here. It eliminates the number of loaves and fish that the disciple placed before Jesus. One can only assume that this scribe thought that this repetition from verse 38 was *too redundant.* In the opposite direction, D W insert a third occurrence of πέντε ("five") just before ἄρτους ("loaves").

Many important manuscripts eliminate αὐτοῦ ("them") after τοῖς μαθηταῖς ("to the disciples"). Marcan style includes αὐτοῦ after the inflected form, τοῖς μαθηταῖς, in every instance (2:15, 16; 3:9; 8:6, 34; 10:23; 14:32; 16:7) except one (4:34, where τοῖς ἰδίοις μαθηταῖς ["his own disciples"] is used).[71] Apparently scribes either *harmonized* to the Matthean and Lucan parallels or eliminated the pronoun since the disciples eventually became known as "the disciples" rather

---

68. BDF, §392 (4).

69. BDF, §493 (2), says such "distributive doubling is not rhetorical, but vulgar."

70. Zerwick, *Biblical Greek,* §157. Taylor, *Mark,* 323, says the repetition was used "in a distributive sense," i.e., the equivalent of κατὰ συμπόσια.

71. Mark does at times, however, refer to "the disciples" without the personal pronoun present (Mark 8:1; 9:14; 10:10, 13, 24; 14:16). Here in Mark 6, is the personal pronoun after "the disciples" in verses 1, 35, and 45.

than "his disciples."[72] Later scribes might easily have made this change if the definite article was no longer needed or used with the word *disciples*.

Many manuscripts substitute παραθῶσιν ("they might set before"), which is an aorist subjunctive—for παρατιθῶσιν ("they might set before"), a present subjunctive. Mark 8:6, a parallel text, has the παρατιθῶσιν reading. Ἵνα ("in order that") followed by an aorist subjunctive is found 59x in Mark; it is followed by a present subjunctive only 14x. It seems more likely that the aorist subjunctive παραθῶσιν was the original reading (disagreeing with Nestle-Aland[27]) and was altered to *harmonize* with verse 6; though it is difficult to make conclusive decisions on this variant.

Mark 6:43. The switch of the genitive case in the phrase κλάσματα δώδεκα κοφίνων πληρώματα ("fragments twelve baskets full") to κλασμάτων δώδεκα κοφίνους πλήρεις ("of fragments twelve baskets full") is apparently a *harmonization* with Matthew 14:20 and Luke 9:17 (which have similar wording to Mark 8:19 [cf. John 6:13]).

Mark 6:44. The omission of τοὺς ἄρτους ("the loaves") is also a *harmonization* with Matthew 14:21. It is also a bit awkward that only the loaves are mentioned and not the fish. It is more likely that these words were later omitted than the reverse (the *more difficult reading*).

Mark 6:45–52: Walking on the Water

Mark 6:45. The phrase εἰς τὸ πέραν ("to the other side") is the *more difficult reading geographically* because Bethsaida was on the northeast side of the lake. According to Luke 9:10, however, the feeding of the five thousand took place in Bethsaida. How, then, is this going "to the other side" of the lake? One may say that Mark does not use εἰς τὸ πέραν to mean crossing the width of the lake but uses it in a more general manner of an unspecified geographical goal.[73] Others surmise that there were actually two towns called Bethsaida, one on the west side of the Jordan and the other on the east.[74] John says that the disciples started

---

72. C. H. Turner, "Marcan Usage," 26:235–37, concludes that the personal pronoun was necessary early on in the history of Christian society since there were various groups of disciples from whom Jesus' disciples would have to be differentiated (John the Baptist's, Pharisees). Thus, it was only later that Jesus' disciples began to be called οἱ μαθηταί rather than οἱ μαθηταὶ αὐτοῦ.

73. So, for example, Lane, *Mark*, 233 n. 111, who lists 4:35; 5:21; 8:13; with 6:32, 53; 8:10. C. H. Turner, *Mark*, 33, says the phrase "does not necessarily mean more than 'across' by water from the northeastern to the northern shore."

74. *ISBE*, 1:475.

across the sea on the way to Capernaum, which is on the west side of the lake (John 6:16–25). Mark 6:53 says that they landed in Genneserat, which is on the west side. 𝔓⁴⁵ W f¹ 28. 2542 pc lat eliminate εἰς τὸ πέραν, so that the destination is merely Bethsaida, which still presents difficulties since it appears from Luke 9:10 that they were already in that location.

Some manuscripts (𝔓⁴⁵ A N W 33. 1424. l. 2211 pm) substitute the aorist subjunctive ἀπολύσῃ ("dismisses") for the present indicative ἀπολύει ("dismisses"). Mark follows ἕως ("until") with the indicative mood three times (Mark 9:19 [2x]; 14:54) and the subjunctive six times (4x with ἄν, 1x with οὐ μή, 1x with just the subjunctive verb following). It is possible that this is a *grammatical improvement* due to the indefiniteness of the sentence,[75] or that the variant reading is a *harmonization* with Matthew 14:22, where the subjunctive ἀπολύσῃ is used. A few manuscripts (Θ 565 syˢ) substitute a future indicative, ἀπολύσει, which is a change to *typical Matthean and New Testament style*.[76]

Mark 6:47. The insertion of πάλαι ("long ago") by some manuscripts (𝔓⁴⁵ D f¹ 28. 2542 pc it vgᵐˢˢ) is an addition to *make the text clearer* by explicitly stating that it had been a "long time" since the boat had gone out to sea. It is already clear from 6:45–46 that a long time had passed, so this is redundant. Why would it be excised from the text if it were there already, given that Marcan style is often redundant and scribes do not always eliminate his redundancy?[77]

Mark 6:48. Some manuscripts (𝔓⁴⁵ A f¹·¹³ 33 𝔐 [i] syʰ) substituted εἶδεν ("he saw") for ἰδών ("seeing"). It is clearly Marcan style to use the participle ἰδών together with καί or δέ ("and," 12x).[78] Perhaps, though, the use of two participles, ἰδών ("seeing") and βασανιζομένους ("straining"), led some scribes to change one to a finite verb, εἶδεν ("he saw"). It is doubtful, however, that εἶδεν is more original, and for two reasons: (1) Mark never has the καὶ εἶδεν construct (only 2x in Synoptics); (2) Mark regularly has the καὶ ἰδών construct (sometimes with another participle soon following, cf. Mark 11:13). It is easier to see why a later scribe would alter the participle to a finite verb because of the difficulty of having two participles so near to one another than the other way around (the *source variant* criterion).

---

75. Hurtado, *Text-Critical Methodology*, 73.
76. Mark 9:19 (2x) uses the future indicative after ἕως. Both Matthew and Luke use the future tense more regularly after ἕως, (Matt. 11:23; 13:30; 17:17; Luke 9:41; 10:15; 13:35), while John (5:17; 21:22, 23) normally uses the present tense.
77. A problem in saying that πάλαι was not originally in Mark is Matthew's having ἤδη in his text (14:24). As Metzger, *Textual Commentary*, 92, notes, it is possible that Matthew may have known a copy of Mark that included πάλαι. Other commentators agree, including Taylor, *Mark*, 328.
78. Mark 2:5; 5:6, 22; 6:48; 8:33; 9:20, 25; 10:14; 11:13; 12:28, 34; 15:39.

A few manuscripts replace the temporal infinitive clause ἐν τῷ ἐλαύνειν ("while (they) rowed"), with an adverbial participle καὶ ἐλαύνοντας, which can be translated identically.[79] Mark uses the ἐν τῷ ("while") construction only two times (here and in 4:4), whereas the adverbial participle is very common. It can be surmised that a scribe changed the less frequent infinitive construction to the participial construction in a *contextual assimilation* to the other two participles.

Different manuscripts insert either σφόδρα καί ("greatly and") or just καὶ ("and") at the end of Mark 6:48b. It is easy to see why a scribe would add σφόδρα in order to *make the text clearer* as to why the disciples were unable to row very far. It is difficult, though, to see why this word would be eliminated from the text if it were original. The addition of καὶ is understood in a similar manner; it is easy to see why it would be added (because *Marcan style* nearly always has a καὶ before each new clause).

The deletion of πρὸς αὐτούς ("to them," D W Θ 565 it) is an attempt to *correct a possible problem*, perhaps an *orthodox improvement*. The problem is found at the end of the verse, where it clearly says that Jesus intended to walk past them, apparently without going directly to the boat, which was initially his intention (ἔρχεται πρὸς αὐτούς, "he comes to them"). The inclusion of πρὸς αὐτούς, however, seems to say otherwise, causing an apparent discrepancy. A deletion of the former would solve the difficulty.

Mark 6:49. Many manuscripts (A D Θ f¹³ 2427 𝔐 [ʃ W f¹ 28. 2542 pc]) replace ἔδοξαν ὅτι φάντασμά ἐστιν ("they thought that is was a ghost"), with ἔδοξαν φάντασμά εἶναι ("they thought [him] to be a ghost"). Mark uses εἶναι ("to be") only 7x, all but one (14:64) after verbs of "saying" or "wishing." On the other hand, the construction of ὅτι ("that") followed by some form of εἰμι ("to be") is used 30x. It is difficult to surmise why scribes would have changed the wording. One possible guess is that *orthodox scribes* were uncomfortable with the indicative statement that Jesus' disciples thought that Jesus *was* a ghost. Such a statement could be taken the wrong way in terms of who Jesus was (especially in the docetic controversies) or could be taken as another negative statement by Mark about the disciples' lack of faith. Thus, scribes changed the wording into an infinitive clause to lessen the possible misunderstanding.

Mark 6:50. A variant at the beginning of verse 50 replaces the phrase πάντες γὰρ αὐτὸν εἶδον ("for everyone him saw") with just πάντες ("everyone").

---

79. Taylor, *Mark*, 329, says that the infinitival clause can be translated as a verbal noun, "in the rowing" or "in rowing." While this is possible (cf. BDF, §404 [3]), it is rare. Because of the rarity of this construction, some scribes may have been confused.

Because most of the manuscripts that eliminate these words (D Θ 565. 700 it) also *eliminated* other *"redundant" expressions* in this pericope (v. 44: τοὺς ἄρτους, "the loaves"; v. 48: πρὸς αὐτούς "to them," etc.) and obviously have taken liberties in changing the wording in other phrases (most of the variants in vv. 48–50 are found in these manuscripts), it is reasonable to conclude that these scribes (or a scribe upon which the others were dependent) have deemed these words redundant and eliminated them. It is, after all, clear from verse 49 that the disciples have seen Jesus, οἱ δὲ ἰδόντες αὐτόν ("but having seen him"), so it is not necessary to repeat it here in verse 50. Such repetition, though, is Mark's style throughout (as we have repeatedly seen and commented upon, to the readers' fatigue!).

The various substitutions for ὁ δὲ εὐθύς ("and immediately") include the change from εὐθύς to εὐθέως ("immediately"). Mark uses εὐθύς forty-one times and εὐθέως only once (although it is disputed as original, 7:35). Matthew, on the other hand, uses εὐθύς five times and εὐθέως thirteen times. Thus, it appears that a later scribe *imposed Matthean style* onto Mark's text.

Mark 6:51. While Nestle-Aland[27] reads λίαν [ἐκ περισσοῦ] ἐν ἑαυτοῖς ("very much exceedingly in themselves," A *f*[13] 33. 2427 𝔐 lat sy[h]), three alternative readings are found: (1) λίαν ἐν ἑαυτοῖς ("very much in themselves," ℵ B [L] Δ 892 [sy[s.p] co); (2) περισσῶς ἐν ἑαυτοῖς ("exceedingly in themselves," D [W *f*[1] 28. 2542] 565. 700 *pc* b); (3) περιέσωσεν αὐτοὺς καί ("he saved from death them and," Θ). First, it is impossible to make a decision based upon either Marcan or New Testament style since the New Testament shows no parallels to this phrase (περισσῶς "exceedingly" is used only 4x in the whole New Testament; λίαν "very much," only 12x). The only possible parallel is Mark 5:42b, καὶ ἐξέστησαν [εὐθὺς] ἐκστάσει μεγάλῃ ("and they were amazed immediately with amazement great"), where the astonishment seems to be "very great." Since the meaning of λίαν here in 6:51 already gives a heightened sense, the phrase in brackets is not needed. Thus the inclination is to think that the first alternate option is the original reading. If this is true, though, how does one explain the second option, where περισσῶς is used? It is, in fact, difficult to explain the different variants unless one postulates that the original expression contained both elements, which was then paired down by later scribes because of redundancy. Louw and Nida say concerning the entire phrase, λίαν [ἐκ περισσοῦ], that it is "an extremely high point on a scale of extent and implying excess," both expressions "reinforcing one another."[80] Finally, the third option,

---

80. Louw and Nida, *Greek-English Lexicon*, 78.20.

the substitution of περιέσωσεν αὐτούς καί, makes little or no sense unless περισσῶς were originally in the document. One can only speculate that a scribe was uncomfortable with the redundancy and tried to "correct" the reading by *eliminating the redundancy.*

The addition of καὶ ἐθαύμαζον ("and they were marveling") by many manuscripts (A D W Θ *f*¹³ 33. [565] 𝔐 it syᵖ·ʰ) at the end of the verse is probably the result of a *harmonization* with Acts 2:7, where the two verbs are found together, ἐξίσταντο δὲ καὶ ἐθαύμαζον ("and they were amazed and were marveling").

Mark 6:52. The replacement of ἀλλ᾽ ἦν ("but had been") by ἦν γὰρ ("had been for") may be due to an *assimilation* to the immediate context, since γὰρ ("for") is found at the beginning of verse 52. More likely, though, is that scribes were trying to bring out the causal relationship that exists between verse 52a and verse 52b: the disciples did not understand what was taking place (verse 52a), "because . . . (verse 52b)." Thus, γὰρ ("for") is a *grammatical improvement* over ἀλλ᾽ ("but") because it makes this relationship clear.

Mark 6:53–56: Healings at Gennesaret

Mark 6:53. Two alternative spellings of Γεννησαρέτ ("Gennesaret") are given: Γενησαρ and Γεν(ν)ησαρέθ. Neither of the alternate readings is found in the New Testament except in variant readings. The former reading is found in 1 Maccabees 11:67, in Josephus *Bellum judaicum* 3.10.7f.; *Antiquities of the Jews* 13.5.7; 18.2.1; and in the Targum Numbers 34:11.[81] Thus, this reading may have been an *imposition of a more familiar word.* The latter reading is an alternate spelling, similar to Ναζαρέτ ("Nazareth") and Ναζαρέθ (Matt. 2:23). The omission of καὶ προσωρμίσθησαν ("and anchored") is probably a *harmonization* with Matthew 14:34, where the phrase is not included.

Mark 6:55. Two manuscripts, D and the old Latin majority text, have major variants in this verse. They insert φέρειν πάντας ("to carry all") after κραβά ττοις ("mattress") and then substitute περιεφέρον γὰρ αὐτοὺς ὅπου ἂν ἤκουσαν ("to carry for them wherever they heard") for περιφέρειν ὅπου ἤκουον ("to carry where they heard"). The problem with the wording as it is found in Nestle-Aland²⁷ is that the infinitive, περιφέρειν ("to carry"), is located seven words after ἤρξαντο ("they began"). Ἄρχω ("to begin") is used 27 times

---

81. BAGD, 156; *ISBE*, 2:443; Lane, *Mark*, 239 n. 127.

in Mark and 26 times it is followed by an infinitive (only Mark 10:42 does not have an infinitive). Of these 26, 25 are followed *immediately* by the infinitive (either immediately or separated by one word, except 12:1, where there are three words of separation). Thus, Mark 6:55 is not the *typical Marcan style*, so scribes inserted an infinitive, φέρειν ("to carry"), closer to ἤρξαντο ("they began"). As a result of this change, the second infinitive, περιφέρειν ("to carry"), is no longer needed, so it was changed to the indicative mood. Two other minor changes appear within this variation-unit: the addition of ἂν, which may simply be an *assimilation* to Mark 6:56, where ἂν is included; the change from the imperfect tense of ἤκουον ("they were hearing") to an aorist, ἤκουσαν ("they heard"). Finally, D and the old Latin manuscripts also *make it clearer* who is coming into the region, namely, Jesus, by the insertion of his name, τὸν Ἰησοῦν εἶναι ("Jesus to be"). Many other manuscripts, mostly Byzantine (A *f*¹³ 33 𝔐 sy^h [∫ W 0278 *f*¹ 28. 565. 700. 2542]), add ἐκεῖ ("there") to ὅτι ἐστίν ("that he is") to *make it smoother*.

Mark 6:56. Some manuscripts omit the repetition of the preposition, εἰς ("to"). While it is difficult to determine typical style since this construction does not appear often, it appears that Matthew and Luke do not repeat the preposition with geographical locations (Matt. 10:11; Luke 8:1; 13:22), but Mark does in his one parallel construction (Mark 5:14). Regardless of Marcan style, scribes often *eliminated redundant expressions.*

The word ὅσος ("as much as") is used thirteen times in Mark. It is followed by ἂν only once, and there the following verb is subjunctive. Thus, Mark never follows ὅσος with ἂν with an indicative verb. In fact, the New Testament never uses this combination. It does, however, often follow ὅσος with the indicative mood. Zerwick says the ἂν plus indicative takes the place of the optative mood in the New Testament.[82] Perhaps the rarity of this construction led later scribes to *alter ὅσοι ἂν ἤψαντο ("as many as touched") to more typical New Testament style* by either deleting or changing the verb tense.

Mark 8:14–21: The Leaven of the Pharisees

Mark 8:14. D (it) replace καὶ εἰ μὴ ἕνα ἄρτον οὐκ εἶχον ("and except one loaf they did not have") with εἰ μὴ ἕνα ἄρτον εἶχον ("except one loaf they had"). This change was motivated by the differences between this text and Mark 8:16, where the disciples claim to have no bread, ἄρτους οὐκ ἔχουσιν ("they

---

82. Zerwick, *Biblical Greek*, § 358; N. Turner, *Syntax*, 3:93; cf. Mark 3:11; 6:56a; 11:19; and 15:6 in Codex Bezae.

do not have ~ loaves"). Thus, this could be an *orthodox correction*.[83] A second substitution for this phrase, which is found in numerous manuscripts ($\mathfrak{P}^{45\text{vid}}$ [W] Θ $f^{1.[13]}$ 205. 565. 700. [2542] k sa), is ἕνα μόνον ἄρτον ἔχοντες ("one only loaf having"). This change *improves* Mark's *awkward expression*, καὶ εἰ μὴ . . . οὐκ ("and except . . . not").[84] Is the Nestle-Aland[27] text saying they had no bread, "they did not even have one loaf"; or does it say they had one loaf, "except one they did not have a loaf"? Due to this uncertainty, later scribes changed the wording to make it clear that the disciples had one loaf, with ἔχοντες ("having") serving as an adverbial concessive participial phrase to modify 8:14a; thus, "and they forgot to take bread, although they did have just one loaf."

Mark 8:15. It seems that the presence of two imperatival synonyms immediately in succession, anacoluthon, ὁρᾶτε ("take care") and βλέπετε ("beware"), motivated some scribes to make changes in order to *make the text smoother*. Some manuscripts eliminated the redundancy by deleting the first verb, leaving only βλέπετε ("beware," D Θ f^1 565. 2542). Others deleted the second and left only ὁρᾶτε ("take care," Δ 700). Others provided a conjunction (maybe in imitation of Matthew 16:6) and retained both verbs, ὁρᾶτε καὶ βλέπετε ("take care and beware," $\mathfrak{P}^{45}$ C 0131 $f^{1.13}$ 28. 1424 *pc* aur c f l vg^{cl}).

Many manuscripts changed Ἡρῴδου ("of Herod") to τῶν Ἡρωδιανων ("the Herodians") due to the *difficulty in understanding the meaning* of the "leaven of Herod." Thus, scribes "corrected" Mark by assuming that he meant the Ἡρωδιανων ("Herodians"), who are mentioned in Mark 3:6 and 12:13 (and Matt. 22:16).[85]

Mark 8:16. The change to the first plural ἔχομεν ("we have") from the third plural ἔχουσιν ("they have") seems to be due to a *harmonization* to the person and number of Matthew 16:7, while the change to ἐλάβομεν ("we take") is definitely a *harmonization*. The change in number also may be due to the various interpretations of ὅτι ("why/because"). By changing the verb, the scribe is able to *make clear* exactly which meaning is intended. As it stands, there are various

---

83. Guelich, *Mark 1–8:26*, 1:421, says that these two references to bread in 8:14 and 8:16 may not be contradictory in that there is a difference between the plural ἄρτους in 8:16 and the singular ἄρτον here in 8:14. In other words, they may not have had plural "breads," but they did have a "bread."

84. Taylor, *Mark*, 365, followed by Cranfield, *Mark*, 260, calls the improvement a "smooth reading [that] appears to be a simplification of a more difficult original."

85. Lane, *Mark*, 279 n. 31, uses the term *correction*. Cf. Taylor, *Mark*, 366. Riley, *Making of Mark*, 94, thinks that Mark was influenced by Matthew 12:14 to add "with the Herodians" at 3:6 (because of his presupposition that Mark uses Matthew and Luke as his sources). This then led to the same insertion here at 8:15. Riley says further, though, that "to Mark's readers the Sadducees would be of no special interest, and he inserts the name of Herod as representing a more obvious danger." There is confusion in Riley's thought. Did Mark originally write Ἡρῴδου or τῶν Ἡρωδιανων?

interpretations: is it recitative, in which case the first person plural would be better, "They said to one another, 'It is because we have no bread'" (NRSV); or is it causal, in which case the third person plural would be better, "They discussed with one another because they did not have any bread"?[86]

Mark 8:17. The insertion of ὁ Ἰησοῦς ("Jesus") after γνούς ("having known") is a *harmonization* with Matthew 16:8, as is the insertion of ἐν ἑαυτοῖς ὀλιγό πιστοι ("among yourselves ones of little faith") after διαλογίζεσθε ("you are discussing").[87] An alternative reading for the latter insertion is ἐν ταῖς καρδίαις αὐτῶν, ὀλιγόπιστοι ("in the hearts of them, ones of little faith"), which seems to be a *harmonization* with Matthew 16:8 because of the presence of ὀλιγόπιστοι ("ones of little faith," 4x in Matt., but 0x in Mark). It appears that scribes have inserted this phrase into Mark but changed the ἐν ἑαυτοῖς ("among themselves") to ἐν ταῖς καρδίαις ("in the hearts"). It is known, of course, that the meaning of the latter change is not exactly correct because the disciples were complaining verbally, as we see from διελογίζοντο πρὸς ἀλλή λους ("they were arguing among themselves") in 8:16.

Some manuscripts insert ἔτι ("still"), and some also add ὅτι, ("because," 047. 1424 *pc*), after συνίετε ("comprehend") in order to produce οὐδὲ συνίετε ἔτι [ὅτι] πεπωρωμένην ἔχετε τὴν καρδίαν ὑμῶν ("nor comprehend still [because] having become hardened in the heart of you"), apparently to *make the text clearer.* Metzger says that this change "appears to have come from the last syllables of συνίετε ['comprehend'], the sense seeming also to justify it."[88]

Mark 8:19. The insertion of καί ("and") after πεντακισχιλίους ("five thousand") is a *harmonization* with Matthew 16:9. It could as well be an independent scribal improvement to *eliminate asyndeton.*[89] The insertion of ἀνθρώπους καί

---

86. C. H. Turner, "Marcan Usage," 27:59, translates the ὅτι as interrogative, "they discussed with another why they had no loaves." Guelich, *Mark 1–8:26,* 1:418, says that it is a "noun clause. It could also be causal, since it is uncertain and moot whether this clause tells what they were discussing or why they were discussing it. The variant reading λέγοντες . . . ἔχομεν would change its thrust to *recitativum.*" Mann, *Mark,* 334, sums up the variation-units in this verse by saying, "Unfortunately the textual state of the Greek in this verse is confused and confusing."

87. Taylor, *Mark,* 367, thinks that this insertion "deserves serious consideration" for originality because "the adjective is so much in harmony with Mark's narrative." He does not, though, explain what he means by this statement. Lane, *Mark,* 279 n. 33, follows Taylor in both his conclusion and lack of argumentation. Lane says that this phrase "is thoroughly in harmony with Mark 8:17–21 and deserves consideration." Precisely because of such harmony, though, it seems more likely that a later scribe would have inserted it.

88. Metzger, *Textual Commentary,* 98.

89. C. H. Turner, "Marcan Usage," 15–19, notes thirty-eight instances of asyndetons in Mark that are improved by either later scribes, Matthew, or Luke.

("men and") is an improvement in that it is *more explicit* in stating that there were five thousand "men."

Mark 8:20. The various alternative insertions after ὅτε ("when") seem to be due to a combination of *harmonization* with Matthew's οὐδέ and independent scribal attempts at improvement to more *typical Marcan style*, which normally includes a conjunction at the beginning of a new sentence. Therefore, scribes insert a conjunction after ὅτε ("when"), either καί ("and," ℵ Δ [ʃ 892. 2427] lat sa), or δέ ("and," A D W Θ *f*[1.13] 33 𝔐 it sy[h]), or a conflated δὲ καί (C N f). Some manuscripts *drop the personal pronoun* αὐτῷ ("to him," 𝔐 *pc*) in καὶ λέγουσιν [αὐτῷ] ("and they say [to him]"), while others replace the phrase with a different verb tense, οἱ δὲ εἶπον ("but they said," 𝔓[45] A D W Θ *f*[1.13] 33 𝔐 it sy[h]). Notice that with the exception of 𝔓[45], these are the same manuscripts that inserted δέ after ὅτε ("when") in the previous clause. Obviously these scribes are taking liberty. The change from the historical present to the aorist tense would be a *grammatical improvement* since the aorist tense is technically correct since this action took place before the action of the next clause, which contains an imperfect tense. Mark, though, was fond of the historical present.[90]

Mark 8:27–30: Peter's Confession

Mark 8:27. D it replaced εἰς τὰς κώμας Καισαρείας ("to the villages of Caesarea") with εἰς Καισαρείαν ("to Caesarea"). The scribes may have been confused by this unique (to the New Testament) expression. Does it refer to the city or to "villages near the city"?[91] Scribes inserted the *more typical New Testament* expression (8x in the New Testament) εἰς Κασαρείαν ("to Caesarea") in order to *make the text clearer*.

Mark 8:28. Either ἀπεκρίθησαν ("they answered," A f[1] sy[h]) or ἀπεκρίθησαν αὐτῷ λέγοντες ("they answered to him saying," D [W] Θ 0143 f[13] 28. [33]. 565 *pc* lat) is substituted for εἶπαν αὐτῷ λέγοντες ("they spoke to him saying"). Due to the *difficulty* of two forms of λέγω ("to say") in the space of three words (which never occurs elsewhere in Mark), some scribes altered the wording. The combination of ἀποκρίνομαι ("to answer") and λέγω ("to say") is used 16x in Mark, so this is a *change to a more typical Marcan style*. A possible *assimilation* to the wording of verse 29, ἀποκριθεὶς ὁ Πέτρος λέγει ("having answered Peter says"), is also a possible explanation for the change.

Mark 8:29. The insertion at the end of the verse of ὁ υἱος τοῦ Θεοῦ ("the

---

90. N. Turner, *Style*, 4:20, says that Mark uses the historical present 151x.
91. BAGD, 396.1.

son of God") or ὁ υἱὸς τοῦ Θεοῦ τοῦ ζῶντος ("the son of God of the living")
are due to *assimilation* with Matthew 16:16.

Mark 8:34–9:1: "If Any Man Would Come After Me . . ."

Mark 8:34. Some manuscripts replace εἴ τις ("if someone," 2x in Matthew, 6x
in Mark) with the near synonym ὅστις ("whoever," 19x in Matt., 0x in Mark).
It is difficult to know why the change was made. A guess might be that scribes
imported the more familiar *Matthean style* into this verse. It also may be because
of *harmonization* with the similar wording in the parallel idea of Luke 14:27,
ὅστις οὐ βαστάζει τὸν σταυρὸν ἑαυτοῦ καὶ ἔρχεται ὀπίσω μου, οὐ
δύναται εἶναί μου μαθητής ("whoever does not carry the cross of himself
and comes after me is not able to be my disciple").[92]

The replacement of ἀκολουθεῖν ("to follow") by ἐλθεῖν ("to come") is a
harmonization with Matthew 16:24, while ἐλθεῖν καὶ ἀκολουθεῖν ("to come
and to follow," Δ sa^mss) is both a *harmonization* and a conflation with Mark's
original reading.

Mark 8:35. Two manuscripts replace ψυχὴν αὐτοῦ ("life of him") with
ἑαυτοῦ ψυχὴν ("of himself life"). It is possible that this is a *scribal error* as
a result of *assimilation* with ἑαυτὸν ("of himself") in verse 34. Nigel Turner
calls this use of the reflexive pronoun an "indirect reflexive." He says that there
are few New Testament examples of the reflexive pronoun where it has little or
no dependence on the verb because of the intervention of a noun or a phrase.[93]
Another use of the reflexive pronoun is possessive.[94] While Matthew and Luke
sometimes used ἑαυτοῦ ("his") in this way, Mark never does (Matt. 8:22; 21:8;
25:1; Luke 2:39; 9:60; 11:21; 12:36).

The change from ἀπολέσει ("will lose") to ἀπολέσῃ ("loses," A L W 33.
2427 𝔐 *et*) may be due either to *assimilation* to the mood of the parallel form in
8:35a or to *harmonization* with Matthew 16:25 and Luke 9:24. It also could be a
grammatical improvement[95] or merely an *aural error.*

Two alternatives are found in place of ἐμοῦ καὶ τοῦ εὐαγγελίου ("of me
and the good news"): (1) τοῦ εὐαγγελίου ("the good news," 𝔓^45 D 28. 700 it
[sy^s]);(2) ἐμοῦ ("of me," 33. 579 *pc* ff²). The second is probably a *harmonization*

---

92. Cf. Taylor, *Mark*, 381. BDF, §293, says that the εἴ τις reading is "more correct." Yet, it may be more
    correct grammatically, but not more correct according to normal Marcan style.

93. N. Turner, *Syntax,* 3:43.

94. BAGD, 212.4.

95. Taylor, *Mark*, 382, calls this change a "grammatical correction" since it follows ἄν. The indicative
    mood is, though, used with ἄν in the New Testament (Mark himself uses this form 2x).

with Matthew 16:25 and Luke 9:24, which both read ἕνεκεν ἐμοῦ ("on account of me"). If the first option were original, it is *more difficult* to understand why scribes would have added ἐμοῦ καί ("of me and").[96] Besides this, the Nestle-Aland[27] reading is much more in keeping with *Mark's pleonastic style*. A similar construction to the Nestle-Aland[27] reading appears in Mark 10:29, οὐδείς ἐστιν ὃς ἀφῆκεν οἰκίαν ἢ ἀδελφοὺς ἢ ἀδελφὰς ἢ μητέρα ἢ πατέρα ἢ τέκνα ἢ ἀγροὺς ἕνεκεν ἐμοῦ καὶ ἕνεκεν τοῦ εὐαγγελίου ("there is ~ no one who left house or brothers or sisters or mother or father or children or fields for the sake of me and for the sake of the good news"). Both objects are found here, with a repetition of the preposition and the article (the parallel in Matt. 19:29 contains ὀνόματός μου, "name of me"). Thus, Mark lists both "gospel" and "me," but the other gospels never do. In fact, Luke never uses the word εὐαγγελίον ("good news"), while Matthew uses it 4x (to Mark's 8x). Upon examining Mark's purpose in 1:1 for writing his gospel, the following construction is found: τοῦ εὐαγγελίου Ἰησοῦ Χριστοῦ ("of the good news of Jesus Christ"). By taking the latter two nouns as epexegetic genitives, the same idea is found in 8:35 and 10:29. Thus, it was Marcan style to repeat these two concepts (i.e., "me" and "gospel") together. Later scribes, though, eliminated one or the other. One possible reason for the omission is a *scribal error* due to the "skipping of the eye" because of the similar endings of the three words ἐμοῦ, τοῦ, and εὐαγγελίου. It might also simply be the result of *harmonization*.

Mark 8:36. The replacement of ὠφελεῖ ("does it benefit") by ὠφελήσει ("will it benefit") may have been to effect a *harmonization* to the future tense in Matthew 16:26, ὠφεληθήσεται ("will be benefited"). More likely, though, it was done independently by Marcan scribes for *assimilation* to the future tenses and the overall futuristic implications throughout this context. Certainly the substitution of ὠφεληθήσεται ("will be benefited") by some manuscripts was a *harmonization*,[97] as was the change to ἄνθρωπος ("man") from ἄνθρωπον ("man").

The substitution of ἐὰν κερδήσῃ τὸν κόσμον ὅλον καὶ ζημιωθῇ ("if he gains the whole ~ world and forfeits") for κερδῆσαι τὸν κόσμον ὅλον καὶ ζημιωθῆναι ("to gain the whole ~ world and to forfeit") is to effect a *harmonization* with the wording of Matthew 16:26.

Mark 8:38. The deletion of λόγους ("words") changes the sense of the sentence from "whoever is ashamed of me and my words" to, "whoever is ashamed of me and that which is mine [his followers?]." C. H. Turner accepts this deletion as

---

96. Lane, *Mark,* 305 n. 97; Hooker, *Mark,* 209; Mann, *Mark,* 349; and Metzger, *Textual Commentary,* 99, think the omission of ἐμοῦ καὶ was accidental.

97. Taylor, *Mark,* 382, calls the change to the passive voice of ὠφελέω an improvement of the Greek.

the original reading (against Nestle-Aland[27]).[98] There is no doubt that the reading without λόγους ("words") is the *most difficult reading*. Scribes would have inserted λόγους due to the parallelism with ἐμοῦ καὶ τοῦ εὐαγγελίου ("of me and of the gospel") in verse 35. On the other hand, it can be understood why a scribe might make an *error* by accidentally skipping λόγους ("words") due to the similar endings on the two previous words, τοὺς ἐμούς ("my"), which is the explanation given by those who edited Nestle-Aland[27] (homoioteleuton).[99]

The phrase ταύτῃ τῇ μοιχαλίδι ("this adulterous") is replaced by either τῇ μοιχαλίδι ("adulterous," 𝔓[45] W a i k n) or by ταύτῃ τῇ πονηρὰ καὶ μοιχαλίδι ("this evil and adulterous," Θ). The latter seems to be the result of assimilation with the phrase γενεὰ πονηρὰ καὶ μοιχαλὶς ("a generation evil and adulterous") in Matthew 12:39 and 16:4. The former change may have been an attempt to extend this saying to include all generations that—because of the delay of the Parousia (a later Christian community change?)—are adulterous and not just Jesus' generation (ταύτῃ, "this").

The replacement of μετά ("with") with καί ("and") is an interesting variant. While this change may be the simple result of *harmonization* with Luke 9:26, if so, why does Luke have a different reading here than Matthew and Mark.[100] Could Luke (and possibly Marcan scribes) have made this change for theological reasons? Fitzmyer says it makes the angels both partakers in Jesus' glory and witnesses of Jesus' glory.[101]

Mark 9:1. It is difficult to determine whether or not the insertion of μετ' ἐμοῦ ("with me," D 565 it) after ἑστηκότων ("having stood") is a harmonization to

---

98. C. H. Turner, "Marcan Usage," 29:2. See also his *Mark,* 41, where he says that this reading "corresponds so closely to the emphasis in Mark's Gospel on the unity of our Lord and His followers (see e.g., 9:38; 10:39) that it may well be right."

99. This is the reason stated by Metzger, *Textual Commentary,* 99–100, followed by Gundry, *Mark,* 456. Metzger further says that it is harder "to account for the insertion of the word in a wide variety of different types of texts" if it were not original. This is, though, faulty logic. It can easily be argued that it was inserted in only one manuscript, an early one, which was then copied by different text-types. Ross, "Some Unnoticed Points," 62–63, argues that Mark never uses ἐμός in a possessive sense with a noun. Ross thus concludes on stylistic grounds that "λόγους was missing from the original text both here and in Luke." Care must be used here in drawing dogmatic conclusions on stylistic grounds since Mark uses ἐμός only twice (here and 10:40), and since one of these can be seen as a possessive use (here in 8:38). Ross continues, "An early copyist might easily have found the bare τοὺς ἐμούς unusual and added λόγους to supply the missing noun, on the analogy of 10:24 and 13:31; once the word had been added in Mark, copyists would add it in Luke also, in order to assimilate the two passages." Again, Ross fails to note that in 10:24 and 13:31, Mark uses the genitive personal pronoun, μου (13:31), or αὐτοῦ, and not ἐμός.

100. Metzger, *Textual Commentary,* 100, says the change "appears to have arisen from scribal inattentiveness, or from assimilation to the parallel in Luke 9.26."

101. Fitzmyer, *Luke (I–IX),* 789. The New Testament witness, however, is clear that angels frequently appear with Jesus in end-time and judgment references (Matt. 13:41; 25:31; John 1:51).

the idea found in αὐτοῦ ("here") in Luke 9:27. It may be an insertion to clarify the meaning of ὧδε ("here"). The deletion of ἄν αφτερ ἕως ("until") is inconsequential since Mark sometimes uses this construction with the subjunctive mood and sometimes does not.[102]

Mark 9:2–10: The Transfiguration

Mark 9:2. The insertion of ἐν τῷ προσεύχεσθαι αὐτούς (αὐτόν, Θ 28 *pc*, "while ~ they [he] pray[s]") is partly a harmonization with Luke 9:29, ἐν τῷ προσεύχεσθαι αὐτόν ("while he ~ prays"). That most of the manuscripts have αὐτούς ("they") instead of αὐτόν ("he"), though, shows that the scribes were not just blindly harmonizing to Luke. They knew the Lucan text and improved the Marcan text by *making it clearer*: it was not just Jesus praying (thus the plural pronoun) but also the three disciples.[103] The plural pronoun makes more sense in Mark given the prepositional phrase with the plural that soon follows this insertion, ἔμπροσθεν αὐτῶν ("before them").

Mark 9:6. Various words (all indicative mood) are substituted for the aorist subjunctive ἀποκριθῇ ("he answered"): (1) ἐλάλει ("he was saying," Θ d; Or^pt, an imperfect tense); (2) λαλεῖ ("he says," 𝔓^45 W sa, a present tense); (3) λαλήσει ("he will say," A C^3 D *f*^13 𝔐, a future tense); (4) ἀπεκρίθη ("he answered," 𝔐; Or^pt, an aorist tense). The Nestle-Aland^27 text is much more in conformity with *Marcan style*, since Mark almost always follows τί ("what") with an aorist subjunctive verb (11x, sometimes by both an indicative and then the subjunctive [3x]). It is probable that the grammatical difficulty concerning which tense to use in an indirect question led scribes to alter the tense and mood. Verbs in indirect questions often carried the tenses used in the original saying.[104] The mood also may have changed because the answer had already been given (9:5), so the doubtfulness of the subjunctive mood would not be needed (i.e., a *grammatical refinement*). Most of the uses of τί in Mark contain the element of doubt because they are questions referring to future time. The use here, however, does not fit into the normal pattern.

Some manuscripts replace ἔκφοβοι γάρ ἐγένοντο ("for ~ terrified they

---

102. Mark uses the ἕως plus subjunctive verb 4x; 3x with ἄν (6:10; 9:1; 12:36); 1x without ἄν (not counting variant readings): 14:32. See also Zerwick, *Biblical Greek*, §336.

103. See C. H. Turner's data on the oscillation of the singular and plural in "Marcan Usage" when referring to Jesus and His disciples, 26:225–26.

104. See BDF, §368, and Zerwick, *Biblical Greek*, §347–49. Zerwick concludes that the "moods of direct speech are retained when it passes into indirect."

were") with ἦσαν γὰρ ἔκφοβοι ("for ~ they were terrified"), an insignificant *synonym change.*

Mark 9:7. The word αὐτοῖς ("them") is replaced by either αὐτῷ ("him") or αὐτούς ("them," a *harmonization* with Matt. 17:5 and Luke 9:34). The change to the singular pronoun emphasizes Jesus rather than the entire group.[105]

One manuscript, 0131, inserts ὃν ἐξελεξάμην ("whom I have chosen") after ὁ ἀγαπητός ("the beloved"), which seems to be a *harmonization* with Luke 9:35, οὗτός ἐστιν ὁ υἱός μου ὁ ἐκλελεγμένος, αὐτοῦ ἀκούετε ("this is the son of me the one having been chosen, to him listen"). Others insert ἐν ᾧ εὐδόκησα ("in whom I am well pleased"), which is a *harmonization* with Matthew 17:5. On the other hand, if ὃν ἐξελεξάμην were original, it may have been deleted due to an *orthodox improvement* that would eliminate texts that seem to suggest an adoptionistic construal.[106]

Mark 9:8. The phrase ἀλλὰ τὸν Ἰησοῦν μόνον μεθ᾽ ἑαυτῶν ("but Jesus alone with themselves") is replaced in many manuscripts (ℵ [∫ B 33. 579. 2427] D N Ψ 892. 1241. 1424 lat syʰ) by εἰ μὴ τὸν Ἰησοῦν μόνον μεθ᾽ ἑαυτῶν ("except Jesus alone with themselves") and in a few manuscripts (0131 *pc* a k l syˢ) by εἰ μὴ τὸν Ἰησοῦν μόνον ("except Jesus alone"). The change from ἀλλα ("but") to εἰ μή ("except") is a *grammatical improvement* since ἀλλα ("but") is not the best lexical choice to show exception (note that Matt. also reads εἰ μή, "except").[107] It is difficult to know whether Marcan scribes made this change independently of Matthean *harmonization* (Matt. 17:8 has εἰ μὴ αὐτὸν Ἰησοῦν μόνον, "except Jesus himself alone"). It does appear, though, to be independent considering that the majority of manuscripts with this change keep μεθ᾽ ἑαυτῶν ("with themselves") at the end of the clause, which is exclusively Marcan.

Mark 9:9. The words καὶ καταβαινόντων ("and they were coming down") are changed to καταβαινόντων δέ ("and ~ they were coming down," A W Θ *f*^1.13 𝔐 f syʰ sa). The conjunction καί ("and") is used much more often than δέ ("and/but") in Mark.[108] Mark uses the genitive absolute construction twenty-one

---

105. See C. H. Turner, "Marcan Usage," 26:225–26.

106. So, Ehrman, *Orthodox Corruption of Scripture,* 67–68, 108 n. 106.

107. C. H. Turner, "Marcan Usage," 29:279, says, "It is in the last degree unlikely that any scribe should have altered εἰ μή to the ungrammatical ἀλλά, while the converse change, supported by the parallel in Matthew, would be easy enough." Moulton, *Prolegomena,* 1:241–42, concludes from Tb. P. 104 (*Tebtunis Papyri,* part i.) that ἀλλά can be synonymous with εἰ μή. N. Turner, *Syntax,* 3:13, says "In Aramaic the conjunction *'illâ (but)* has both exceptive and adversative force, which may . . . account for the textual variants in [Mark] 9⁸." BDF, §448(8), says "ἀλλά = εἰ μή 'except.'" See also Zerwick, *Biblical Greek,* §470.

108. According to N. Turner, *Syntax,* 3:332, Mark has a 5:1 ratio between the number of uses of καί and δέ.

times. In every single instance, he uses the conjunction καί, never δέ.[109] It can only be surmised that a scribe has mistakenly *assimilated* to the δέ in Luke 9:37, which is a close parallel to Mark 9:9.

The substitution of ἀπό ("from") for ἐκ ("of/from") is a *synonym* change (א A C L W Θ *f*[1.13] 𝔐). Besides here, both prepositions are used twice in the Synoptic Gospels to refer to coming down from a mountain.[110] It is possible that the change is due to a *harmonization* to the use of ἀπό ("from") in Luke 9:37 since this verse, though not a direct parallel with Mark 9:9, is the next verse after Luke 9:28–36, which parallels Mark 9:2–10. It also might be a *grammatical improvement*.[111]

Mark 9:10. The substitution of ὅταν ἐκ νεκρῶν ἀναστῇ ("when from [the] dead should arise") for τὸ ἐκ νεκρῶν ἀναστῆναι ("from [the] dead to rise") is an *assimilation* with Mark 9:9. The Nestle-Aland[27] reading is the *more difficult* since it is easy to understand why later scribes would assimilate to the wording of 9:9 but difficult to understand why they would change the parallel wording to different wording.[112]

Mark 12:1–12: The Parable of the Wicked Husbandmen

Mark 12:1. The word order of ἀμπελῶνα ἄνθρωπος ἐφύτευσεν ("a vineyard a man planted") is either changed to ἀμπελῶνα ἐφύτευσεν ἄνθρωπος ("a vineyard planted a man") or ἄνθρωπος ἐφύτευσεν ἀμπελῶνα ("a man planted a vineyard," which is the identical word order of Luke 20:9), or is replaced by ἄνθρωπος τίς ἐφύτευσεν ἀμπελῶνα ("a certain ~ man planted a vineyard"). The first change in word order merely changes the order to object-verb-subject rather than object-subject-verb. This change is to a *more "typical" Marcan* (and New Testament) *order*.[113] The insertion of τίς ("certain") is not Marcan style. Luke, however, normally introduces parables with the phrase ἄνθρωπος τίς ("a certain ~ man," 9x; John is the only other New Testament author to use it, 1x). It is questionable, however, whether or not it is used in the original of Luke

---

109. Mark 5:2, 18, 21; 6:2, 21, 22, 47, 54; 9:9, 28; 10:46; 13:1, 3; 14:3, 17, 18, 22, 66; 15:33, 42; 16:1.

110. The preposition ἀπό is used in Matthew 8:1 and Luke 9:37; ἐκ is used in Matthew 17:9 and 18:12.

111. C. H. Turner, "Marcan Usage," 29:282, says, "Of course ἀπό is the natural preposition to use with καταβαίνειν." This fact may explain the scribal change.

112. Taylor, *Mark*, 394, says just the opposite. He thinks ὅταν ἐκ νεκρῶν ἀναστῇ is original and was changed to a "smoother" reading. If he were correct, however, he would need to offer some valid explanations for why a scribe would change the parallel wording of 9:9–10 in 9:10 but not change it in 9:9, which Taylor fails to do. He says only that τὸ ἐκ νεκρῶν ἀναστῆναι is "more formal," whatever that means. Lane, *Mark*, 322 n. 26 again follows Taylor's conclusion (cf. Mark 8:17 above, where Lane also follows Taylor).

113. N. Turner, *Style*, 4:18–19.

20:9, the parallel to Mark 12:1. Thus, this is either a *harmonization* with Luke or is a scribal *insertion of typical Lucan parabolic style.*

Mark 12:3. The change to οἱ δέ ("but those") from καί ("and") is probably a *harmonization* with the wording of Luke 20:10, although it could be an independent scribal change of conjunction, which is common. It can be seen how an adversative conjunction would better fit this context since there is a change from verse 2 to verse 3 in that the servant is captured and killed in verse 3. So this change could be seen as a slight *grammatical improvement.*

Mark 12:4. Some manuscripts (A C Θ f^{13} 𝔐 sy$^{p.h}$) insert λιθοβολήσαντες ("stoning") after κἀκεῖνον ("and that one"). Most of these same manuscripts inserted this word in verse 3 after κενόν ("empty"), although the Nestle-Aland[27] apparatus does not cite this variant.[114] These insertions seem to be *harmonizations* with the idea of Matthew 21:35, where ἐλιθοβόλησαν ("they stoned") is used. They may also be independent *improvements in textual clarity* due to the uncertainty in meaning of κεφαλαιόω. While its meaning is normally "to sum up," NRSV translates it here as "they beat over the head."[115] Due to this uncertainty of meaning for κεφαλαιόω, scribes inserted λιθοβολήσαντες ("stoning") *to make it clear* that physical injury was implied.

Some manuscripts change ἠτίμασαν ("insulted") to either ἀπέστειλαν ἠτίμωμενον ("they sent having been disgraced") or to ἀπέστειλαν ἠτιμασμενον ("they sent having been disgraced"). The verb ἠτίμωμενον is a perfect passive from ἀτιμόω, which is a synonym for ἀτιμάζω and ἀτιμάω ("be disgraced or dishonored" in the passive voice).[116] These changes *assimilate* the meaning of this verse to verse 3, where ἀπέστειλαν ("sent away") was also used, and to verse 5, where more people are sent.

Mark 12:6. The words ἔτι οὖν ("still therefore") are substituted for ἔτι ("still") by A C D 𝔐 l q vg sy^h. "Therefore" is added to make the text a *little clearer.* Since

---

114. See Aland, *Synopsis Quattuor Evangeliorum,* 378.

115. BAGD, 430. BDF, §108 (1) says "κεφαλαιοῦν is usually taken to mean 'to strike on the head, treat brutally (with reference to the head),' but as such is entirely unattested." C. H. Turner, "Marcan Usage," 29:277, says, "I do not see that to 'knock on the head' even if we could get that sense out of the Greek word, which is all but impossible, satisfies this condition: and I see no alternative but conjectural emendation." He continues, "Very tentatively I suggest, that a metathesis of the syllables κε and φα has taken place, such as might occur with an unfamiliar word, and that we should read ἐφακελίωσαν (or ἐφακέλωσαν), 'trussed him up in a bundle.'" Taylor, *Mark,* 474, agrees: "Either, then, Mark used κεφαλαιόω in a sense otherwise unknown, or the reading is corrupt." He hypothesizes that "ἐκεφαλίωσαν may be a palaeographical blunder for ἐκολάφισαν, 'they buffeted.'" Cf. Mann, *Mark,* 465, who pulls a "Streeter" by hypothesizing that the original reading was lost very early; he thinks "there was an original scribal blunder and what was originally written was *ekolaphisan,* 'to knock in the head.'"

116. BAGD, 120.

all had died or been beaten or bound in verse 5, "therefore" he had only one left. Other manuscripts substitute ὕστερον δέ ("and ~ finally"), which is a *harmonization* with Matthew 21:37.

Manuscripts substitute ἔχων υἱόν ("having a son," A Cᵛ D Θ *pc*) or υἱὸν ἔχων ("a son having," 𝔐) or υἱὸν ἔχων, τόν ("a son having, who," W *f*¹·¹³ 28. 2542 *pc*) for εἶχεν υἱόν ("he had a son"). The Marcan wording in this clause is clumsy (with two finite verbs in close succession). The changes *improve the clarity and smoothes* out the wording. The change from the finite aorist verb to an adverbial participle allows the first clause of the sentence to flow more easily into the second by denoting an adverbial relationship, "since he had a beloved son, he sent him to them." The addition of the definite article, τόν ("the") may be a scribal attempt to *make it clearer* that this parable is symbolically speaking of God's Son, who is beloved of the Father (Mark 1:11; 9:7: both texts use the definite article with "beloved").

The insertion of αὐτου ("of him") may be a *harmonization* with Matthew 21:37. On the other hand, it may be an independent Marcan scribal addition to *make clear* the familial relationship between the father and the son in this parable. There are three alternative substitutions for αὐτόν ("him"): (1) καὶ αὐτόν ("even him"); (2) κακεινον ("even that one"); (3) deleted. The first substitution is an improvement since it *makes clear* the length to which the landowner goes by the addition of an ascensive καί, "even." Thus, "he even sent him (his beloved son)!" The second substitution would include this same idea. The change from the personal pronoun to the demonstrative pronoun is due to *assimilation* to the next verse, verse 7. The *deletion of the personal pronoun* would be a stylistic change of no consequence.

Some manuscripts change ἔσχατον πρὸς αὐτούς ("finally to them") to either πρὸς αὐτοὺς ἔσχατον ("to them finally"), an *insignificant stylistic change*, or πρὸς αὐτούς ("to them," 63 *pc* syˢ) or ἔσχατον ("finally," D it). While the deletion of πρὸς αὐτούς ("to them") is probably due to *assimilation* to the similar wording in 12:5, the deletion of ἔσχατον ("finally") is probably a *scribal error*.[117]

Mark 12:8. Many manuscripts change the word order of ἀπέκτειναν αὐτόν ("they killed him") to αὐτὸν ἀπέκτειναν ("him they killed"), which is an improvement to *make the meaning clearer*: "the son" is taken and then killed.

Other manuscripts omit the second αὐτόν ("him") after ἐξέβαλον ("threw

---

117. It may also be assimilation to the context since there are no time indicators in the text until here in 12:6.

out"). While this may be due to *harmonization* with Matthew 21:39, the *elimination of a personal pronoun* is a common scribal change.

Mark 12:9. The omission of οὖν ("then") is found in some manuscripts (B L 892*. 2427 *pc* k sy^s sa^mss bo). It is difficult to determine whether this was in the original manuscript or not. On the one hand, it is easy to see why later scribes would have added it to the document: first, it is both a harmonization with Matthew and Luke, and, second, the context requires a consequential idea in verse 9. On the other hand, if it were in the original document, why would scribes have eliminated it? No likely reason can be offered except that an error was made. For this reason, it is concluded (against the Nestle-Aland^27 text, which includes it in brackets) that οὖν was not in the original text and that scribes added it to *make the text smoother.*[118]

Mark 12:13–17: On Paying Tribute to Caesar

Mark 12:13. A few manuscripts (D it sa^ms) omit πρὸς αὐτόν ("to him") after ἀποστέλλουσιν ("they send"). Perhaps this omission is due to the presence of both a direct object, τινας ("some"), and a purpose clause, ἵνα ("in order that"). Some scribes may have thought the presence of the prepositional phrase made the sentence too verbose and *eliminated the redundancy* (although redundancy is typical Marcan style). Besides, it is already clear from the αὐτόν ("him") in ἵνα αὐτὸν ἀγρεύσωσιν ("in order that him they might catch") that Jesus is the object.

Mark 12:14. The replacement of καί ("and") with οἱ δέ ("but those") is the same change found above in 12:3. It may have been changed in order to eliminate the impersonal verb, λέγουσιν ("they say"), by *adding a subject* (notice that the next variation-unit shows the same improvement by directly providing a subject, οἱ Φαρισαῖοι ["the Pharisees"]). This change also may be due to *assimilation* to the abundant use of δέ ("and/but") in this pericope (4x in 12:15–17).

While some manuscripts merely change the word order of δοῦναι κῆνσον Καίσαρι ("to give a tax to Caesar") to κῆνσον Καίσαρι δοῦναι ("a tax to Caesar to give," A *f*^1.13 [28] 𝔐 it), other manuscripts replace these words with δοῦναι ἐπικεφάλαιον Καίσαρι ("to give the poll tax to Caesar," D Θ 565 k sy^s.p). Ἐπικεφάλαιον ("poll tax") normally refers specifically to the poll tax

---

118. C. H. Turner, "Marcan Usage," 26:17, 20, agrees with the conclusion of this current study. "In Mark [12:9] only B L (syr-sin sah) give the shorter reading without οὖν: but they are certainly right."

rather than to any other taxes.[119] Thus, this substitution of a near synonym, moving from the general to the specific, serves to *make the text more explicit* by restricting the meaning of the question. The question now does not deal with general taxes but specifically with the poll tax.

Mark 12:15. Some manuscripts replace εἰδώς ("having seen"), a perfect participle, with ἰδών ("seeing"), an aorist participle. This is probably a scribal improvement to bring this text into line with *Marcan style.* Mark normally uses ἰδών, and only uses εἰδώς twice (here and in 6:20). It also could be a change to show that Jesus did not know intuitively (εἰδώς) but knew by witnessing (ἰδών) that they were hypocrites. Such a change could possibly be motivated by *orthodox improvements* in that it emphasizes Jesus' human nature more than the original reading does.[120] The insertion of ὑποκριταί ("hypocrites") is a *harmonization* with Matthew 22:18.[121]

Mark 12:17. The opening words, ὁ δὲ Ἰησοῦς εἶπεν ("and Jesus said") are replaced by either καὶ ἀποκριθεὶς ὁ Ἰησοῦς εἶπεν ("and having answered Jesus said," A D f[1.13] 𝔐 lat sy[s.h]), or καὶ ἀποκριθεὶς εἶπεν ("and having answered he said," W Θ 565), or by καὶ λέγει ("and says," 1424). The final variant is probably an *assimilation* to the wording in Mark 12:16, καὶ λέγει αὐτοῖς ("and he says to them"). The previous two changes are basically *synonym changes.* The phrase ὁ δὲ Ἰησοῦς εἶπεν ("and Jesus said") is found 10x in Mark, all in chapters 9–14. The phrase ἀποκριθεὶς εἶπεν ("having answered he said") is found only 4x in Mark. Thus, either would have been familiar to scribes. The deletion of αὐτοῖς ("to them") is an example of the *deletion of a personal pronoun.*

Mark 12:18–27: The Question About the Resurrection

Mark 12:19. Some manuscripts change the word order of μὴ ἀφῇ τέκνον ("not leave a child") to τέκνον μὴ ἀφῇ ("a child not leave," W Θ f[1] 700. 2542 *pc* a c k), while others substitute in τέκνα μὴ ἀφῇ ("children not leave," A D f[13] 𝔐 lat sy[p.h]). The substitution of the plural τέκνα ("children") is for *harmonization* with Matthew 22:24. The change in word order, which brings τέκνον ("child")

119. Moulton and Milligan, *Vocabulary*, 240. The change to ἐπικεφάλαιον may have been made simply as an alternative to avoid the use of a Latin loanword, since κῆνσον is a transliteration of the Latin *census.* The word ἐπικεφάλαιον does not occur in the New Testament; κῆνσον occurs four times, twice in the Matthean parallel.

120. Ehrman, *Orthodox Corruption of Scripture*, shows that "orthodox" changes move both toward emphasizing Jesus' deity and Jesus' humanity since heretical views emphasized one or the other side of Jesus' nature.

121. Taylor, *Mark*, 479; and Lane, *Mark*, 422, think the inclusion was original due to its compliance with Marcan style (ὑπόκρισιν does occur earlier in the verse).

forward, may be the result of a desire to *emphasize this word*. On the other hand, it may have been a *harmonization* with the Hebrew word order in Deuteronomy 25:5, וּבֵן אֵין־לֹו ("and son to him there is no") = "a child not leave" (Gk.). The insertion of αὐτοῦ ("of him") after γυναῖκα ("wife") is due either to *harmonization* with Matthew 22:24 or to *assimilation* to the immediate context since αὐτοῦ ("of him") is used twice in this verse, after both ἀδελφός ("brother") and ἀδελφῷ ("[for] brother").

Mark 12:21. Many manuscripts substitute καὶ οὐδὲ αὐτὸς ἀφῆκεν ("and neither did he leave") for μὴ καταλιπών ("not having left behind"). This change may be for *assimilation* to the previous parallel wording found in both verse 20 and verse 22, οὐκ ἀφῆκεν σπέρμα ("did not leave a descendant"). If καὶ οὐδὲ αὐτὸς ἀφῆκεν ("and neither did he leave") were original, it would be *more difficult* to explain why a scribe would change similar or parallel wording to a different style, namely μὴ καταλιπών ("not having left behind").

Mark 12:22. Many manuscripts change ἔσχατον πάντων ("last of all") to ἔσχατον δὲ πάντων ("but last of all," G Δ Θ *f*[1.13] 28. 33. 565. 700. 2542 *al* q co), while a few change it to ἐσχάτη πάντων ("last of all," A Γ 1241. 1424 *pm* l vg sy[h]) or eliminate it altogether (D c sa[ms]). The insertion of δέ may be a scribal attempt to *make the text clearer* by differentiating the woman from the seven sons. Without this inclusion, one could misunderstand the modifier of the phrase ἔσχατον πάντων. Other scribes deleted the entire phrase in order to eliminate the possible misunderstanding. Concerning the change of gender, ἔσχατον is from the adjective, ἔσχατος ("last"), which is used here as an adverb.[122] Since this use of an adjective as an adverb was not very common in the New Testament, some scribes *improved the grammar* (at least they thought it was an improvement) by changing the gender of the adjective to agree with the feminine noun that it modifies, γυνή ("woman").

The change of word order from καὶ ἡ γυνὴ ἀπέθανεν ("and the woman died") to ἀπέθανεν καὶ ἡ γυνή ("died and the woman") may be for *harmonization* with Matthew 22:27. On the other hand, the change may have been made independently in order to *eliminate any misunderstanding* as to how to interpret Mark 12:22b. Some of the possible misunderstandings concerning ἔσχατον were discussed above. A second difficulty is the meaning of καί; is it a connective ("and") or an ascensive use ("even")? By placing καί after the verb, it is more likely an ascensive conjunction in this context, "last of all, even the woman died."

---

122. N. Turner, *Style*, 4:225–226.

Mark 12:23. The deletion of the bracketed ὅταν ἀναστῶσιν ("when they are raised") by ℵ B C D L W Δ Ψ 33. 579. 892. 2427 *pc* c r¹ k syᵖ co is either a *harmonization* with Matthew 22:28 and Luke 20:33 or an independent scribal *elimination of* Mark's typical *pleonastic style*.

Mark 12:25. Some manuscripts substitute the following for ἄγγελοι ("angels"): (1) οἱ ἄγγελοι οἱ ("the angels those," B [W] Θ [892]. 2427); (2) ἄγγελοι οἱ ("angels those," A Γ Ψ 565 *pm*); (3) ἄγγελοι Θεοῦ οἱ ("angels of God those," *f*¹³ [33] *pc* l vgˢ boᵐˢ). Mark uses the style article-noun-article only once, in Mark 3:22, οἱ γραμματεῖς οἱ ἀπὸ Ἱεροσολύμων ("the scribes those from Jerusalem"). The insertion of the first article serves to give definiteness to the noun, which *makes the text clearer*. The article οἱ used as a relative pronoun followed by a form of οὐρανός ("heaven") is found 13x in Matthew and 2x in Mark (11:25; 13:25). If the article used as a relative pronoun were originally present, it is *more difficult* to see why later scribes would have eliminated it, given that Mark uses this style in other places. On the other hand, it is easier to see why later scribes would inadvertently insert the article, considering their familiarity with this use from Matthew.

Mark 12:26. Some manuscripts delete the article in ὁ θεὸς Ἀβραάμ ("the God of Abraham"), and others delete both articles in [ὁ] θεὸς Ἰσαὰκ καὶ [ὁ] θεὸς Ἰακώβ ("[the] God of Isaac and [the] God of Jacob"; note that both D and W omit all three articles). All of these changes are similar to the LXX readings, in which the articles are not present. According to Semitic grammar, the first article is not needed since (1) the names are proper nouns, which are always definite and (2) any noun in construct with a proper noun is automatically definite. Ehrman discusses the alternate possibility that the article(s) were dropped due to "anti-Patripassianist" *orthodox corruptions*.¹²³

Mark 12:27. The insertion of ὁ ("the") before Θεός ("God") is either an *assimilation* to the previous verse, in which the article was used, or is an insertion to *make the text clearer* that "the" God is in mind here. In the same location, some manuscripts insert ὁ Θεός ("the God"; an arthrous *theos*), which is another change that tries to *make the text clearer by providing an explicit subject*. The insertion of Θεός in the predicate before ζώντων ("of living") is an attempt to *make the text clearer by providing an explicit object*.

Some manuscripts insert ὑμεῖς οὖν ("you therefore") before πολὺ πλανᾶσθε ("you are mistaken ~ greatly"). This insertion also *makes the text clearer* by pro-

---

123. Ehrman, *Orthodox Corruption of Scripture*, 266.

viding the explicit consequential relationship between Mark 12:27a and verse 27b. It also serves to make the text *flow more easily* into the final clause.

Mark 13:3–8: Signs Before the End

Mark 13:3. Many manuscripts change the singular ἐπηρώτα ("were questioning") to the plural ἐπηρώτων ("[they] were questioning"). This change is a *grammatical refinement* since the subject is technically plural. It is typical New Testament usage, however, to have a singular verb with a coordinate subject when the first term is singular, as we have here in verse 3.[124]

Some manuscripts insert the definite article, ὁ ("the"), before Πέτρος ("Peter"). Πέτρος is used 9x in Mark. This verse is the only instance where the definite article is not found. Scribes may have inserted the article in order to *"correct" to typical Marcan style.* The article is not found in this verse since a listing of names appears without the article.

Mark 13:4. Some manuscripts replace εἰπόν ("tell") with an alternate spelling of the same verb form, εἰπέ ("tell"), in *harmonization* with Matthew 24:3.[125]

Mark 13:5. Some manuscripts replace ὁ δὲ Ἰησοῦς ἤρξατο λέγειν αὐτοῖς ("and Jesus began to say to them") with (1) ὁ δὲ Ἰησοῦς ἀποκριθεὶς αὐτοῖς ἤρξατο λέγειν ("and Jesus answering to them began to say," A 𝔐 syʰ saᵐˢˢ); (2) καὶ ἀποκριθεὶς ὁ Ἰησοῦς εἶπεν αὐτοῖς ("and answering Jesus said to them," D Θ 565. 700. [1424]. 2542 *pc*); or (3) καὶ ἀποκριθεὶς αὐτοῖς ὁ Ἰησοῦς ἤρξατο λέγειν ("and answering to them Jesus began to say," W f¹·[13] 28 *pc*). The second alternative is a *harmonization* with the text of Matthew 24:4. Concerning alternatives 1 and 3, in six of the eight uses in Mark, the infinitive λέγειν ("to say") is followed by a dative personal pronoun. Thus, it is Marcan style to follow λέγειν with αὐτοῖς ("to them"), which is not found in these two alternatives. In addition, all fourteen uses of ἀποκριθεὶς ("answering") in Mark are followed by a form of λέγω ("to say"), never by ἤρξατο ("began"), which is found in these two alternatives (against Marcan style). Thus, these two alternatives are conflated forms of Mark's original text and Matthean *harmonizations.*

Mark 13:6. The insertion of γάρ ("for") is a *harmonization* to Matthew 24:5, which serves to make the *text clearer.*[126]

---

124. See a discussion in N. Turner, *Syntax*, 3:313–14.
125. Matthew uses εἰπέ 6x, Mark 0x; Matthew uses εἰπόν 7x, Mark 1x.
126. Lane, *Mark*, 455 n. 6, follows Gaston, *No Stone on Another*, 14, 52–53, in concluding that the γάρ is original. He says, "Logically, the γάρ is necessary in these verses, for it indicates the reason for the warnings expressed in verse 5 and verse 7a." It is precisely for this reason that we disagree with Lane's conclusion that γάρ is original. The absence of γάρ is the more difficult reading.

Mark 13:7. Following ὅταν δέ ("but ~ when"), two manuscripts (B 2542) substitute the present subjunctive ἀκούητε ("you hear") for the aorist subjunctive ἀκούσητε ("you hear"); others substitute the present indicative ἀκούετε ("you hear"). It is clear from the context that the action had not yet occurred. Thus, it is more likely that Mark used an aorist subjunctive, which is more grammatically correct, and later scribes substituted in the present tense, which emphasizes more clearly the future time element than the aorist tense.[127] Although the subjunctive mood is normally used after ὅταν ("when"), there are a few instances in the New Testament in which the indicative mood is used with the present tense (including Mark 11:25). Burton says that this construction is used in the New Testament "to express a future supposition with more probability."[128] Thus, this reading can also be seen as a later *grammatical improvement* to the original reading.

D and *pc* replace θροεῖσθε, "to be inwardly aroused, disturbed, frightened," with θορυβεῖσθε, "to be troubled, distressed, aroused."[129] The Matthean parallel has θροεῖσθε. Louw and Nida differentiate the two synonyms by stating that the former refers "to being in a state of fear associated with surprise," while the latter refers "to be emotionally upset by a concern or anxiety."[130] θροέω is used three times in the New Testament. All three contexts are related to the eschatological parousia or the end of the age. θορυβέω is used 4x in the New Testament, never in an eschatological context. Thus, it is concluded that θροεῖσθε is original (the Nestle-Aland[27] reading). The change to θορυβεῖσθε was either an innocent (although incorrect) *synonym change* or was a *scribal mistake* based on the similar sound of the two words (with θ-ο-ρ-εισθε as identical letters between the two words).

Mark 13:8. Some insert a καί ("and") before the second ἔσονται ("there will be," A *f*[1.13] 33 𝔐 q sy[p.h] sa[ms]), others replace it with just καί ("and," D Θ 565. 700 lat sa[mss]), and others delete it altogether (W sy[s]). The addition of the καί would

---

127. N. Turner, *Syntax,* 3:112–13, notes the following differences in meaning between the present and aorist subjunctive: present indicates "iterative action, indefinite, in the past or future," or "of a definite action occurring in the future," while the aorist indicates "most commonly of a definite action taking place in the future but concluded before the action of the main verb," and "much rarer are the instances when the action is indefinite or iterative." See Porter, *Idioms of the Greek New Testament,* 56–57; idem, *Verbal Aspect,* chap. 7; and Fanning, *Verbal Aspect in New Testament Greek,* chap. 6, for a discussion of the differences between the present and aorist subjunctive from the verbal aspect theory.

128. Burton, *Syntax,* §306.

129. BAGD, 364, 362, respectively.

130. Louw and Nida, *Greek-English Lexicon,* 2:25.262; 2:25.234.

be for the same reasons as stated above for the first occurrence of ἔσονται. The replacement of ἔσονται by καί would be an attempt to *improve the awkward sense* of having two uses of ἔσονται in such a short space with no connective conjunction. The deletion of ἔσονται altogether would be another attempt to deal with two uses of ἔσονται; however, this creates its own awkwardness since two nouns are placed together with no conjunction.

Following λιμοί ("famines"), three different variant readings are inserted: (1) καὶ ταραχαί ("and disorder," A [W, Θ] $f^{1.13}$ 33 𝔐 q sy sa[mss]); (2) καὶ λοιμοὶ καὶ ταραχαί ("and famines and disorder," Σ *pc*); (3) καὶ λοιμοί ("and famines," 2542 *pc*). The addition of καὶ λοιμοί ("and famines") in variants two and three is for harmonization with Luke 21:11 (Matt. 24:7 also has this as a variant reading). Given that the book of Acts mentions, "disturbances broke out concerning the Way" (Acts 19:23; cf. 12:18), the addition of καὶ ταραχαί ("and disorder") seems to be one by later scribes because of their desire to show that Jesus' prophecy was fulfilled in the early church.[131] If ταραχαί ("disorders") were original, though, it is possible that scribes *mistakenly deleted* it in copying (homoioteleuton) because of its similarity with the word that follows it, ἀρχή ("beginning").[132]

The replacement of ἀρχή ("beginning") by ἀρχαί ("beginnings") or the elimination of ἀρχή are later scribal attempts to *"improve" the grammar* by bringing numeral agreement with the plural predicate nominative, ταῦτα ("these things"). It could, however, be an *aural error* due to the similarity in sound, in essence, itacism.[133]

Mark 13:14–20: The Desolating Sacrilege

Mark 13:15. Many manuscripts insert εἰς τὴν οἰκίαν ("into the house") after καταβάτω ("let come down"). This seems to be an *assimilation* with the next phrase, εἰσελθάτω ἆραί τι ἐκ τῆς οἰκίας αὐτοῦ ("let him enter to take anything from the house of him"), which makes the sentence clearer and smoother.[134]

---

131. Beasley-Murray, *Mark Thirteen*, 36, follows Westcott and Hort in thinking that ταραχαί was inserted by scribes "for the sake of rhythm."

132. So, Metzger, *Textual Commentary*, 112; and D. Wenham, *Rediscovery of Jesus' Eschatological Discourse*, 298.

133. See Metzger and Ehrman, *Text of the New Testament*, 190–92.

134. Beasley-Murray, *Mark Thirteen*, 74, says this insertion "removes the ambiguity of the saying and possibly improves its flow."

Mark 13:18. Four different variant readings exist for γένηται χειμῶνος ("may come in winter"): (1) χειμῶνος γένωνται ("in winter may come," D); (2) γένηται ταῦτα χειμῶνος ("may come these things in winter," [∫ Θ] *f*¹³ 28. 565 *pc* [a b n* q vgᵐˢˢ]); (3) χειμῶνος ταῦτα γίνεται ἢ σαββάτου ("in winter these things may come or on Sabbath," L [*al* nᶜ saᵐˢ boᵐˢ]); (4) γένηται ἡ φυγὴ ὑμῶν χειμῶνος ("may come the escape of you in winter," ℵ² A Ψ *f*¹ 𝔐 [k] syᵖ·ʰ co). The first reading *improves the grammar* by changing the singular verb to a plural for the purpose of including all of the signs listed in verses 14–17. The second alternative includes the plural pronoun ταῦτα ("these things"), again to indicate all of the signs in verses 14–17 (another *grammatical improvement*). This reading, though, keeps the singular verb, as expected *(schema atticum)*. The third reading includes the idea of "Sabbath," perhaps in *harmonization* with Matthew 24:20. It also changes the subjunctive verb to the indicative mood. The ἵνα followed by the indicative mood is found only in passages where the subjunctive mood is also attested in the manuscripts.[135] The fourth reading is a direct *harmonization* with Matthew 24:20 (without the inclusion of μηδὲ σαββάτῳ, "nor on Sabbath").

Mark 13:19. A few manuscripts delete ἣν ἔκτισεν ὁ θεός ("which created God"), either in *harmonization* with Matthew 24:21 or as an independent *deletion of a redundant expression.* Lane notes that this clause would be needed for Mark's Gentile audience, who would not necessarily know or assume that God created the world.[136]

Mark 13:20. Three different readings exist for ἐκολόβωσεν κύριος ("shortens Lord"): (1) κύριος ἐκολόβωσεν ("Lord shortens," A C D *f*¹ 𝔐 a aur q syᵖ·ʰ), the reversal of word order; (2) ἐκολόβωσεν ("shortens," W 1241 *pc*); (3) ὁ θεὸς ἐκολόβωσεν ("God shortens," Θ [∫ Ψ] *f*¹³ 28. 565. 2542 *pc* [b c ff² k]). The first reading merely locates the emphasis upon the "Lord" by placing the subject before the verb.[137] The second reading *eliminates possible misunderstandings* by deleting "Lord," perhaps due to the possible confusion this word would present following the use of θεὸς ("God") in 13:19. Does κύριος ("Lord") refer to God the Father or Jesus? This also may be the reason for the third reading, which uses θεός instead of κύριος.

---

135. BAGD, 377.3 says that the change here in Mark 13:18 is due to "corruption of the text"; cf. BDF, §369; and N. Turner, *Syntax*, 3:100–101.

136. Lane, *Mark*, 465 n. 71.

137. The "normal" word order places the verb before the subject due to Hebraic influence ("normal" is in quotes because word order is highly flexible); see N. Turner, *Style*, 4:18.

Mark 13:21–23: False Christs and False Prophets

Mark 13:21. The insertion of either καί ("and") or ἤ ("or") *eliminates the* apparent *awkwardness* of the ἴδε . . . ἴδε ("look . . . look") construction. The insertion of ἤ ("or") is a *harmonization* with Matthew 24:23.

Mark 13:22. The deletion of ψευδόχριστοι καί ("false Christs and," D *pc* i k) may be an *orthodox deletion* resulting from the desire to eliminate the idea that false christs may appear. Perhaps the joining of these two words ("false" and "christ") together was too threatening.[138]

Some manuscripts insert ποιήσουσιν ("they will do") for δώσουσιν ("they will give"). The New Testament uses both words in reference to "signs and wonders." "Giving signs" is used by Matthew (16:4; 24:24; 26:48), Luke (11:29), Acts (14:3), and Revelation (13:14). "Doing signs" is used by John (14x), Acts (5x) and Revelation (4x). Metzger says that "giving" signs is more Semitic and thus more original.[139] It has, however, been determined in the analysis of text-critical criteria (see chap. 2) that the presence or absence of Semitisms is not a valid criterion for determining originality. It is necessary, therefore, to disagree with the Nestle-Aland[27] reading here. It is highly likely that ποιήσουσιν ("they will do") was the original reading, which was then *harmonized* with Matthew 24:24, δώσουσιν ("they will give"). It should be noted that ποιήσουσιν ("they will do") was the reading found in Nestle-Aland[25].

Mark 13:28–32: The Time of the Coming: The Parable of the Fig Tree

Mark 13:28. Normally, ὅταν ("when") with an aorist subjunctive indicates an event that will occur in the future,[140] while ἤδη indicates an event that is taking place "now, already, by this time."[141] In order to eliminate this apparent temporal conflict, one variant reading deletes ἤδη and reads αὐτῆς ὁ κλάδος ("by that time, the branch ~ of it"). The other variant reading changes the word order so that the two time indicators are not directly together, αὐτῆς ἤδη ὁ κλάδος ("of it by that time the branch"). These changes *eliminate the apparent grammatical discrepancy.*

---

138. Swete, *Mark*, 309, thinks that this title was "probably a creation of the Evangelists or their Greek source." If this is true, a misunderstanding of its meaning would be easy. Lane, *Mark*, 466 n. 73, thinks the omission of the reference to "false Christs" was "perhaps due to the pressure of Deuteronomy 13:2."

139. Metzger, *Textual Commentary*, 112.

140. N. Turner, *Style*, 4:112.

141. BAGD, 344.

Many manuscripts change the active, second person plural γινώσκετε ("you know") to the passive, third person singular γινώσκεται ("is known"). The textual apparatus questions whether this change is due to *iotacism,* "the substitution of letters with the same phonetic value."[142] Such seems to be the case, since a third singular verb makes no sense in this context, unless it is assumed that the fig tree is taking on the characteristic of "knowing."[143] Iotacism was a common problem since many manuscripts were copied *en masse* as one person read the original manuscript.

Mark 13:29. Some manuscripts alter the word order of ἴδητε ταῦτα ("you see these things") to ταῦτα ἴδητε ("these things you see"); others change the text to ἴδητε πάντα ταῦτα ("you see all these things"), in *harmonization* with Matthew 24:33. Perhaps the difficulty in determining the meaning of this phrase led some scribes to change the word order so that γινόμενα ("knowing") would be understood as a supplemental adverbial participle, which advances the meaning of ἴδητε ("you see"), instead of an adjectival participle modifying ταῦτα ("these things"). Little, of course, if any overall change is effected in formal meaning.

Mark 13:30. Different manuscripts change ταῦτα πάντα γένηται ("these things all happen") to πάντα ταῦτα γένηται ("all these things happen," A D W *f*[1] 𝔐 sy[h]), πάντα γένηται ("all happen," 579. 1424. 2542 *pc* a [c] k·), or πάντα γένηται ταῦτα ("all happen these things," 28 *pc*). The first and second readings are direct *harmonizations* with Matthew 24:33 and Luke 21:32, respectively. The third reading is both a *harmonization* with Matthew 24:33 and an *assimilation* to the word order found in Mark 13:4, at the beginning of this entire discussion, ταῦτα συντελεῖσθαι πάντα ("these things to be complete all"), which places the verb in the middle of the phrase.

Mark 13:31. B and D· delete μή ("no") after οὐ ("no"; note: this was the reading found in Nestle-Aland[25]). The parallels in Matthew 24:34 and Luke 21:32 have οὐ μή ("by no means"). Whenever the Gospels speak of Jesus' words not passing away, the construction with both οὐ and μή is used to indicate emphatic negation.[144] The construction οὐ μή followed by a subjunctive verb is used forty-one times in the Gospels, while οὐ μή followed by a future indicative verb is used only 6x (twice in this parallel; the only undisputed example is Matt. 16:22).[145] Perhaps because of the rarity of οὐ μή followed by a future indicative verb, later scribes deleted μή. This represents a change to more *typical New Testament style.*

---

142. The definition is from the introduction to Nestle-Aland[27] (57*).
143. Taylor, *Mark,* 521, thinks that γινώσκεται is original because it is the more difficult reading. It must be remembered, however, that sometimes a reading is more difficult because it is wrong.
144. Matthew 5:18; 24:35; Mark 13:31.
145. BDF, §365.

Mark 13:32. The deletion of the phrase οὐδὲ ὁ υἱός ("nor the son") by a few manuscripts (X *pc* vg^ms; note that many manuscripts omit this phrase in Matt. 24:36) may be an example of a later *orthodox improvement* to the text. "At the time of the Arian controversy the saying was naturally an embarrassment for the orthodox. Ambrose actually declared that οὐδὲ ὁ υἱός ("nor the Son") was an Arian interpolation."[146] Ehrman notes Metzger's comment that grammatically this phrase must be in the text to conclude the first οὐδέ ("nor") construction. Without this phrase, the οὐδὲ οἱ ἄγγελοι ("nor the angels") "stands oddly alone." He thinks the phrase was deleted by orthodox scribes who tried to prevent a heretical misuse of this verse to show that Jesus was not divine because he did not know the time, while the Father did know.[147]

CONCLUDING SUMMARY

The preceding analysis of variation-units seeks to determine whether the seven text-critical criteria from chapter 2 were also found in textual variants of Mark's gospel. With this goal in mind, the preceding examination of numerous examples of variation-units from Mark chapters 1, 2, 4, 6, 8, 9, 12, and 13, yields a summary conclusive discussion of our findings.[148] The reader will find in appendix A a comprehensive listing of every text-critical change by type.

Disagreements with the Nestle–Aland^27 Text

It was mentioned in the summary of chapter 1 that one of the presuppositions of this study was the use of the Nestle-Aland^27 text as a convenient and reliable guide that facilitates comparison of textual variation-units. It can be concluded from the preceding text-critical analysis, however, that some Nestle-Aland^27 readings are secondary.[149] For these variation-units, it can be accepted that a reading from the textual apparatus is original: Mark 1:41; 6:22, 41; 12:9; and 13:22.[150]

---

146. Cranfield, *Mark*, 410. Taylor, *Mark*, 522, states that it may have been eliminated "for doctrinal reasons."

147. Ehrman, *Orthodox Corruption of Scripture*, 91–92.

148. Similar conclusions of the types of scribal changes made to Mark's gospel can be found in Linton, "Second Century Revised Edition of St Mark," 321–55.

149. As Elliott, "L'importance de la Critique Textuelle pour le Problème Synoptique," 69, says, "Aucune édition du Nouveau Testament grec ni aucune Synopse ne présentera jamais un texte qui serait à cent pour cent un reflet du texte original."

150. The reader may examine the previous discussions in order to find the full discussions for all of these decisions. It should be added that this current study disagrees in *only* five locations. Considering the hundreds of textual variants that were examined, this is a very small percentage.

Discussion of Text-Critical Criteria

Using the seven text-critical criteria from chapter 2, the findings of this chapter will now be summarized in order to categorize typical scribal changes to gospel texts. In some cases these criteria have been divided into smaller units in order to increase precision.

1. The first criterion is the *source variant,* which states that the more original variant is that which best explains the existence of all the others and cannot itself be explained by the others. While this is the main criterion used by most textual critics today, this term was not often used in the preceding discussion because of the way the criteria was devised. The source variant was usually determined in this study by using other criteria. The source variant, though, is always in the background, even though it is not often explicitly mentioned.

In Mark 4:19, for example, it was found that three different substitutions exist for ἡ ἀπάτη τοῦ πλούτου ("the allurement of wealth"): (1) ἀπάται τοῦ πλούτου ("allurements of wealth"); (2) ἀπάται τοῦ κόσμου ("allurements of the world"); (3) ἡ ἀγάπη τοῦ πλούτου ("the love of wealth"). All three of these changes can be explained as improvements to the original text, ἡ ἀπάτη τοῦ πλούτου ("the allurement of wealth"), which could then be called the "source variant." On the other hand, if it were concluded that any of these three substitutions were original, it would be nearly impossible to explain the other readings. Thus, none of these textual variants could be the source variant from which the other readings were produced.

2. The second criterion says that the *more difficult reading* is more original. The textual variants in Mark 4:8 are an example of the more-difficult reading criterion. The text reads καὶ ἄλλα ἔπεσεν εἰς τὴν γῆν τὴν καλὴν καὶ ἐδίδου καρπὸν ἀναβαίνοντα καὶ αὐξανόμενα καὶ ἔφερεν ἓν τριάκοντα καὶ ἓν ἐξήκοντα καὶ ἓν ἑκατόν ("and others fell into the soil good and it was giving fruit rising up and growing and it was bearing [fruit], one thirty and one sixty and one one hundred"). The textual variants substitute different options with the letters ε-ν and ε-ι-ς, either as prepositions (ἐν, εἰς, "in, to, into") or numerals (ἓν, εἷς, "one"). It was concluded that it is less difficult to believe that the original reading was a thrice repeated numeral, ἓν, "one." Scribes then substituted various alternatives due to harmonization or assimilation tendencies, or apparent difficulties in using ἓν.

A second example of the more-difficult criterion is found in Mark 6:45. A geographical difficulty results in saying that Bethsaida is εἰς τὸ πέραν ("to the other side") because the feeding of the five thousand took place in Bethsaida, according to the Lukan parallel in 9:10. How, then, could they be going to "the other side" of the lake if they were on their way to Bethsaida? Due to this apparent geographical difficulty, scribes deleted εἰς τὸ πέραν ("to the other side") from the text. This deletion is much less difficult than the original reading.

Since "more difficult" is a rather broad criterion, in the preceding analysis this criterion was delineated into two subpoints: those readings that (2A) *"eliminate awkward expressions"*; those that (2B) *"eliminate possible misunderstandings or problems."*

2A. Perhaps the best example of a textual variant that *eliminates an awkward expression* is found in Mark 2:23, καὶ οἱ μαθηταὶ αὐτοῦ ἤρξαντο ὁδὸν ποιεῖν τίλλοντες τοὺς στάχυας ("and the disciples of him began to make ~ a way picking the heads of grain"). The difficult or awkward expression here is ὁδὸν ποιεῖν, "a way/road to make." Does it refer to making a kind of road as they traveled along? How does one make a road by plucking grain? Does it merely refer to traveling? Because of the awkwardness of this expression, scribes altered the wording.

2B. Many examples were found of scribal changes to *eliminate possible misunderstandings*. Scribes eliminated a difficult reference to the Pharisees in Mark 2:17 since it is doubtful that Jesus was speaking directly to the Pharisees, as the text implies. Perhaps the possible misunderstanding concerning who receives the "mysteries of the kingdom" led scribes to alter the obtuse wording of 4:10. Mark 8:14 seems to disagree with Mark 8:16 as to the amount of bread the disciples had with them. Because of this apparent disagreement, scribes changed the text to eliminate perceived difficulties.

3. The third criterion states, the reading that *is more in conformity with the author's usage* elsewhere is more original. Sometimes scribes made changes to Mark's text contrary to *Mark's typical style*. In Mark 9:6, for example, a plethora of moods and tenses are used in an indirect question. Based on Mark's almost always using an aorist subjunctive in indirect address, it can be concluded that the aorist subjunctive reading was original. In Mark 4:1, it can be concluded that πρός ("to") was original, based on the precise nuances that Mark has for his connotation of πρός ("to") compared to πέραν ("on the other side").

On numerous occasions, however, it was determined that a reading *not* typical Marcan style was original. This discrepancy led scribes to alter the original reading to conform with Mark's typical style. In Mark 6:32, for example, it was seen that scribes, in order to conform the reading to typical Marcan style, inserted immediately after the verb the location to which the people had departed. In 12:15, it was seen that scribes replaced εἰδώς ("having seen") with ἰδών ("seeing"), a much more typical Marcan word. A final example, Mark 13:3, shows that scribes inserted the definite article before Πέτρος ("Peter") in order to bring the reading into alignment with typical Marcan style.

Thus, sometimes a text that is in Marcan style is more original, but sometimes a text is more original that is *not* in Marcan style. Given these two opposing scribal tendencies, this conformity-with-author's-usage criterion must be used with utmost caution.

4A, 4B. Criterion four is that (A) the *less refined grammatical form* or (B) the less elegant *lexical expression* is more original. It is obvious from the analysis performed in this chapter that scribes tended to improve Mark's incorrect or less refined grammatical forms. In Mark 2:5, for example, scribes altered a present passive verb to a perfect passive verb in order to give a more refined nuance, namely to express the perfective nature of Jesus' forgiveness of the paralytic. To suggest the opposite direction of change, from a perfect with its excellent connotation, to a present tense, would be ridiculous.

4C. A final subset of the fourth criteria is *grammatical improvements,* which are found frequently in scribal changes. This does not mean that Mark has made grammatical "errors" that were then corrected by scribes. Rather, scribes have improved Mark's colloquial or awkward grammar with more refined and typical grammar.[151] A grammatical improvement is found, for example, in Mark 13:8, where some scribes replaced the singular ἀρχή ("beginning") with a plural, ἀρχαί ("beginnings"), so that it would agree numerically with the word it modifies, ταῦτα ("these things").

5. The fifth criterion is that the text that is *less smooth* is more original. In the discussion of textual variants in Mark, however, this criterion was divided into four categories: 5A, that reading that *makes the text clearer;* 5B, that reading that makes the text clearer by *adding a subject or object;* 5C, that reading that makes the *text flow more easily* (i.e., smoother); and 5D, that reading that *eliminates redundancy* are the later readings.

5A. Scribes often added words or altered the wording in order to *make Mark's text clearer.* In Mark 2:12, καὶ ἠγέρθη καὶ εὐθὺς ἄρας τὸν κράβαττον ἐξῆλθεν ἔμπροσθεν πάντων, ὥστε ἐξίστασθαι πάντας καὶ δοξάζειν τὸν θεὸν λέγοντας ὅτι οὕτως οὐδέποτε εἴδομεν ("and he arose and immediately taking the mattress went outside in front of everyone, so as to aston-

---

151. Hurtado, *Text-Critical Methodology,* 73, commented that the types of "grammatical improvements" that were made by the scribe of W "appear to be the small changes a high school composition teacher might make in a pupil's paper work."

ish everyone and to glorify [the] God saying, [that] thus never have we seen"), some scribes deleted λέγοντας ("saying") either because it was unclear that it modified πάντας ("everyone"), which occurred four words previously, or because the scribes thought that ὅτι ("that") should be understood as causal rather than as introducing an indirect statement. In Mark 12:4, some scribes inserted λιθοβολήσαντες ("they stoned") after κἀκεῖνον ("and that one") in order to make the meaning clearer since there is some debate as to whether κεφαλαιόω retains its normal meaning ("to sum up") or a unique reading ("to beat over the head").

5B. Since Mark was fond of impersonal verbs, scribes often *inserted subjects* in order to make the text clearer.

5C. In other places, scribes altered Mark's text in order to make it *flow more easily*. In Mark 4:16, for example, some scribes inserted ὁμοίως ("in the same way") in order to make the text smoother by showing its precise relationship to an earlier parable at verse 5. In 12:6, scribes inserted οὖν ("therefore") after ἔτι ("still") in order to make the text flow more easily by making explicit the consequential relationship between verses 5 and 6.

5D. A final subcategory of this fifth criterion is the readings that *eliminate Mark's typical redundancy* (pleonasm).[152] Mark 12:23 reads ἐν τῇ ἀναστάσει [ὅταν ἀναστῶσιν] τίνος αὐτῶν ἔσται γυνή; οἱ γὰρ ἑπτὰ ἔσχον αὐτὴν γυναῖκα ("in the resurrection [when they are raised] of which of them will she be [the] wife?—for [the] seven had her [as] wife"). It can readily be sees that in Greek the bracketed terms are pleonastic and thus were deleted by many scribes.

6. The reader who has waded through the preceding pages does not need a summary in order to agree that *harmonization* plays a huge role in Marcan textual criticism. Many times the Marcan text is harmonized to the Matthean text and sometimes to the Lucan text. At other times, Mark's text is assimilated to a similar expression found either in the immediate context or in another text in Mark.

7. The final criterion that was defined in the preceding chapter is that the reading that is *less orthodox* is more original. Perhaps the best example is found in Mark 1:41, where orthodox scribes have likely inserted σπλαγχνισθείς ("being filled with compassion") for ὀργισθείς ("having been angry"). In Mark 13:32, some manuscripts delete οὐδὲ ὁ υἱός ("nor the son") from περὶ δὲ τῆς

---

152. The term "pleonasm" is used to describe Mark's tendency, *contra* Neirynck, *Duality in Mark*, 71, who prefers the term *duality*. His book is an excellent resource for the various categories of pleonasm in Mark's gospel.

ἡμέρας ἐκείνης ἢ τῆς ὥρας οὐδεὶς οἶδεν, οὐδὲ οἱ ἄγγελοι ἐν οὐρανῷ οὐδὲ ὁ υἱός, εἰ μὴ ὁ πατήρ ("but ~ concerning that day or the hour no one knows, neither the angels in heaven nor the Son, except the Father"). This deletion would eliminate the idea that Jesus did not know the time of the Parousia while the Father knew, making it impossible for heretics to deny Jesus' deity from this verse.

Although chapter 2 delineated only seven text-critical criteria, an eighth category was added in the course of the investigation. It includes miscellaneous criteria: 8A, *scribal errors;* 8B, *addition or deletion of personal pronouns;* 8C, *insignificant stylistic or synonym changes;* 8D, *theologically motivated changes.*

8A. While generally the Nestle-Aland[27] textual apparatus has eliminated variant readings that are the result of *scribal error,* some still remain. In Mark 1:40, καὶ ἔρχεται πρὸς αὐτὸν λεπρὸς παρακαλῶν αὐτὸν [καὶ γονυπετῶν] καὶ λέγων αὐτῷ ὅτι ἐὰν θέλῃς δύνασαί με καθαρίσαι ("and comes to him a leper begging him [and kneeling down] and saying to him—if you are willing you are able to cleanse ~ me"), the phrase καὶ γονυπετῶν ("and kneeling down") is deleted by some manuscripts. It is probable that these words were deleted due to a scribal error since this phrase fills one entire line in some manuscripts. Thus, a scribe may have skipped to the second καί ("and") and accidentally omitted the entire line (homoeoteleuton).

8B. C. H. Turner noted in his extensive studies of Mark's textual history that scribes often *added or omitted personal pronouns* for no apparent reason.[153] The same phenomena were found in this present study.

8C. In some locations, *arbitrary stylistic or synonym changes* are found that cannot be explained. For example, in Mark 9:6, ἦσαν ("they were") replaces ἐγένοντο ("they were"). These two words have the identical meaning in this context. Larry Hurtado found vocabulary preferences used by the copyist of codex W that "apparently reflect the personal tastes of the scribe."[154]

8D. The final delineation is those changes that are *theologically motivated.* In Mark 8:38, for example, ὃς γὰρ ἐὰν ἐπαισχυνθῇ με καὶ τοὺς ἐμοὺς λόγους ἐν τῇ γενεᾷ ταύτῃ τῇ μοιχαλίδι καὶ ἁμαρτωλῷ, καὶ ὁ υἱὸς τοῦ ἀνθρώπου ἐπαισχυνθήσεται αὐτόν, ὅταν ἔλθῃ ἐν τῇ δόξῃ τοῦ πατρὸς αὐτοῦ μετὰ τῶν ἀγγέλων τῶν ἁγίων ("for ~ whoever is ashamed of me and the words of me in this generation adulterous and sinful, also the son of man will be ashamed of him, when he comes in the glory of the father of him with

153. C. H. Turner, "Marcan Usage," 157.
154. Hurtado, *Text-Critical Methodology,* 71–73.

the angels holy"), some manuscripts replace μετὰ ("with") with καί ("and"). Could this change have been motivated by a desire to theologically emphasize Jesus, whom the angels will witness returning to earth at the Parousia?

Criteria for the Analysis of Matthew's and Mark's Gospels

Similar to the conclusion of chapter 2, the following text-critical criteria explicated from this study of Mark's textual apparatus will be used in the next chapter as Matthew and Mark are examined for evidence of originality. These criteria are the text-critical criteria from chapter 2, which have now been further defined by means of the text-critical studies in this current chapter.[155]

1. Source Variant: that variant which best explains the existence of all the others and cannot itself be explained by the others is more original
2. The More Difficult Reading Is More Original
    2A. Readings that eliminate awkward expressions are later
    2B. Readings that eliminate possible misunderstandings or problems are later
3. Author's Style: that variant which is most in conformity with the author's style and usage elsewhere is more original
4. Less Refined Expressions Are More Original
    4A. The less refined grammatical form is more original
    4B. The less elegant lexical expression is more original
    4C. Grammatical improvements are later readings
5. Smoother Texts Are Later Readings
    5A. Readings that make the text clearer are later
    5B. Readings that make the text clearer by adding an explicit subject or object are later

---

155. Linton, "Second Century Revised Edition of St Mark's Gospel," 351–52, after a thorough examination of textual variants in Mark, concluded that the "reviser [of Mark] had some thoroughgoing principles": (1) "to produce a clear and reasonable text"; (2) eliminate "the most evident offences against Greek style and grammar"; (3) "introduce small grammatical amendments"; (4) "make it clear what the subject of a sentence is"; (5) delete "repetitions and superfluous words"; (6) infrequently, to make "amendments which concern logic and matter more than language." Notice that many of his conclusions are similar to the criteria of this current study.

Hurtado, *Text-Critical Methodology*, 67–84, listed the following types of scribal changes after surveying the types of scribal changes made in codex W: harmonizations, vocabulary preferences, grammatical improvements, changes toward concise expression, additions for clarification, significant sense changes, and word-order changes.

5C. Readings that make the text flow more easily, i.e., make the text smoother are later

5D. Readings that eliminate redundancy or pleonasm are later

6. Harmonization and Assimilation: that reading which is not a harmonization and/or assimilation is more original

7. Orthodoxy and Later Christian Community Changes

8. Others: other matters that indicate a later reading

8A. Scribal errors

8B. Addition or deletion of personal pronouns

8C. Insignificant stylistic or synonym changes

8D. Theologically motivated changes

— 4 —

EXAMINING THE TEXTUAL DIFFERENCES
BETWEEN MATTHEW AND MARK

CHAPTER SUMMARY

The previous chapter examined the types of changes that scribes typically made to Mark's gospel, using text-critical criteria to categorize
these changes. These same text-critical criteria will now be used in
this chapter to analyze the differences between the texts of Matthew
and Mark. The goal is to determine whether or not evidence can be
determined, based upon these criteria, that one Evangelist used the
other as a literary source when composing his own gospel.

EXAMINATION OF MATTHEW AND MARK

NOW THAT THE TYPES OF changes that scribes made to gospel texts have been
examined and categorized, these text-critical criteria from the previous chapter
will be used to examine the textual differences between Matthew and Mark. Doing so will determine whether or not text-critical evidence is present, indicating
that one of these Evangelists used the other as a literary source.

While almost every textual variation-unit in Mark's apparatus was commented
upon in the previous chapter for the passages we examined, comment will not
be made on every textual difference between Matthew and Mark. This is so
because not every difference falls within the focus of this study, which focus is
a text-critical explanation.[1]

---

1. While it might be "less boring" to have overall themes under which these examples are analyzed, it is
necessary to examine, as Gordon Fee requested, the texts verse by verse, pericope by pericope, in order
to provide detailed evidence for solving the Synoptic Problem. A summarizing conclusion can be found
at the end of this chapter for those who do not want to wade through the following discussions.

Mark 1:40–45 (Matt. 8:1–4): The Cleansing of the Leper

The context of the Marcan pericope 1:40–45 is found in verse 39: καὶ ἦλθεν κηρύσσων εἰς τὰς συναγωγὰς αὐτῶν εἰς ὅλην τὴν Γαλιλαίαν καὶ τὰ δαιμόνια ἐκβάλλων ("And he came preaching in the synagogues of them in [the] whole [region of]—Galilee and the demons casting out").[2] The context of the Matthean parallel, 8:1–4, is different. While Matthew earlier located Jesus in Galilee as an itinerant preacher (4:23), he then records one of his five discourse sections immediately after this (Matthew 5–7, the Sermon on the Mount). The location of this sermon is on a mountainside, ἰδὼν δὲ τοὺς ὄχλους ἀνέβη εἰς τὸ ὄρος, καὶ καθίσαντος αὐτοῦ προσῆλθαν αὐτῷ οἱ μαθηταὶ αὐτοῦ ("and ~ having seen the crowds he went up to the mountain, and [when] he sat down came to him the disciples of him").

Because of these slightly different contexts, Matthew and Mark's pericopae begin differently. Mark can immediately begin by introducing the "man with leprosy" since it follows directly upon his Galilean location. Matthew, on the other hand, has to bring Jesus down from the mountain before his introduction, καταβάντος δὲ αὐτοῦ ἀπὸ τοῦ ὄρους ἠκολούθησαν αὐτῷ ὄχλοι πολλοί ("and ~ [when] he came down from the mountain followed him many crowds"). This introduction to the Matthean pericope is in *typical Matthean style*.[3]

Mark 1:40. Matthew's text begins with a *characteristic Matthean* ἰδού ("behold," Matthew 62x; Mark 7x). While Mark's text reads ἔρχεται πρὸς αὐτόν ("comes to him"), Matthew has an introductory adverbial participle, προσελθών ("having approached"), which is *less redundant,* since αὐτὸν ("him") occurs 3x in only nine words in Mark, πρὸς αὐτὸν λεπρὸς παρακαλῶν αὐτὸν [καὶ

---

2. Davies and Allison, *Matthew,* 2:7, think that the Marcan text of this pericope is slightly more difficult due to the presence of ὀργισθείς, ἐμβριμησάμενος, and the leper's disobedient response to Jesus' command in 1:45. Bonnard, *L'Évangile selon Saint Matthieu,* 112, states, "Ici comme ailleurs, nous préférons cette troisième hypothèse [the possibility of an oral influence], qui n'exclut nullement une influence de la tradition orale, non seulement a l'origine de Mc. mais tout au long du processus de fixation littéraire."

3. The phrase ὄχλοι πολλοί occurs 6x in Matthew (4:25; 8:1; 12:15; 13:2; 15:30; 19:2), 0x in Mark. While ὄχλος occurs 38x in Mark, the plural form, ὄχλοι, is used only 1x. Matthew, though, uses ὄχλος 50x and the plural form, ὄχλοι, 14x. In terms of consistency of redactional activity in referring to the crowds, a consistent usage is seen in Matthew's wording, ὄχλοι πολλοί, but an inconsistency in Mark's. For these six occurrences of ὄχλοι πολλοί in Matthew, we find the following phrases in Mark: πολὺ πλῆθος (Matt. 4:25; 12:15 = Mark 3:7); no parallel (Matt. 8:1); ὄχλος πλεῖστος (Matt. 13:2 = Mark 4:1); no parallel (Matt. 15:30); ὄχλοι (Matt. 19:2 = Mark 10:1). It seems more probable that Matthew has brought a consistent redactional phraseology to Mark's various alternatives. Of these six uses of ὄχλοι πολλοί, four have the exact same wording as Matthew 8:1, ἠκολούθησαν αὐτῷ ὄχλοι πολλοι (4:25; 8:1; 12:15; 19:2).

γονυπετῶν] καὶ λέγων αὐτῷ ("to him a leper begging him [and kneeling down] and saying to him").

Matthew's more characteristic προσεκύνει αὐτῷ ("[he] worshiped him")[4] is *less pleonastic* than Mark's text, παρακαλῶν αὐτὸν [καὶ γονυπετῶν] ("begging him [and kneeling down]").[5] Matthew and Mark differ concerning which verb is indicative and which is participial: Matthew's text reads προσελθὼν προσεκύνει ("having approached he worshiped"), while Mark reads ἔρχεται . . . παρακαλῶν ("[he] comes . . . begging").[6] Matthew's reading is probably *more grammatically refined*, since he is correctly emphasizing the "worshiping" rather than the "coming."[7]

We also find that Matthew's text contains κύριε ("Lord"), which is a *characteristic Matthean* vocative.[8] No text-critical decision can be made since κύριε ("Lord") may have been consistently inserted by Matthew or deleted by Mark.

Mark 1:41. While Mark's text reads καὶ σπλαγχνισθεὶς ("and being filled with compassion"), Matthew simply has καὶ ("and"). Recall, though, from the text-critical study that a disagreement was found with Nestle-Aland[27]'s reading of σπλαγχνισθεὶς ("being filled with compassion").[9] The variant reading ὀργισθείς ("being angry") was instead chosen.[10] If this is the correct reading, Mark's reference to Jesus' anger is a *more difficult* reading for two reasons. First, it is not clear why Jesus would have been angry in this particular context.[11]

---

4. Neville, *Mark's Gospel*, 220–21, notes that this construction is typically Matthean.

5. For a discussion of Mark's pleonastic style in relation to the Synoptic Problem, see Tuckett, *Revival of the Griesbach Hypothesis*, 16–21.

6. Grundmann, *Das Evangelium nach Matthäus*, 247–48, notes that "der Ausdruck προσεκύνει ist dem Matthäus eigen (vgl. 2,2.II; 9,18; 15,25)."

7. See Zerwick, *Biblical Greek*, §376–77; Moulton, *Prolegomena*, 1:222; and Moule, *Idiom Book*, 99, for discussions of the normally subordinate nature of participles to indicative verbs. Moule says, "The ruling consideration in interpreting participles is that they express something which is dependent on the main verb, or a pendant to it; and one is sometimes given a clue to the interpretation of a participle not by its own tense but by the main verb, or the context in general."

8. Matthew uses κύριε 34x to Mark's 1x (7:28); κύριος is used 80x in Matthew, 18x in Mark. See Bornkamm, Barth, and Held, *Überlieferung und Auslegung im Matthäusevangelium*, 41–44, for a discussion of κύριε, "a term of Majesty." Abbott, *Diatessarica—Part 2*, suggested that the differences between Mark's αὐτῷ ὅτι and Matthew's κύριε are because Matthew used of a different translation of a Hebrew text behind Mark. Abbott lists 18 pages of corrections to Mark's text that can be found in Matthew and Luke. On the whole, as his appendix II states, "They presuppose in the Synoptic Gospels a frequency of translational error unparalleled in the LXX and unwarrantable even on the hypothesis of translation" (325).

9. Elliott, "Eclectic Textual Commentary," 53; and Marcus, *Mark*, 206, noted that if σπλαγχνισθεὶς were original, Matthew certainly would have retained it since he was fond of the theme of Jesus' compassion (4x: 9:36; 14:14; 15:32; 20:34; and possibly 18:27).

10. Garland, *NIV Application Commentary*, 75, tentatively agrees.

11. France, *Mark*, 118, suggests that the anger may not have been directed against the leper but rather against the "suffering caused by the disease" or perhaps to the "insensitivity of the social taboo" of leprosy.

Second, text-critically, the emotion of anger attributed to Jesus is more likely to be deleted than to be added. This absence of a reference to anger is similar to a scribal *orthodox improvement*.[12]

Instead of Mark's αὐτοῦ ἥψατο ("of him he touched") reading, Matthew has ἥψατο αὐτοῦ ("he touched him").[13] Given the placement of Mark's genitive personal pronoun, αὐτοῦ ("of him"), it is difficult to know whether it serves as a possessive pronoun with τήν χεῖρα ("the hand") or as the direct object of ἥψατο ("he touched"). Matthew, though, placed αὐτοῦ ("him") after ἥψατο ("he touched"), where it functions as a direct object.[14] Thus, Matthew's wording is *more clear* and *less problematic* in its interpretation.

Mark reads καὶ λέγει αὐτῷ ("and says to him"), while Matthew has simply λέγων ("saying"). Since Matthew's reading—because of the presence of a subordinate adverbial participle, λέγων ("saying") instead of a second indicative verb—places greater emphasis on ἥψατο ("he touched"), Matthew seems to be a *more refined grammatical expression*. Matthew's reading is also *less paratactic*, which is an *insignificant stylistic change*.[15] Third, Matthew's reading is *less redundant* since it *lacks the repetition of the personal pronoun*.[16]

Mark 1:42. While Mark begins with his *typical* εὐθύς ("immediately"), Matthew has his *typical* εὐθέως ("immediately").[17] No text-critical conclusion can be drawn since these changes could go either way.[18]

Mark then reads ἀπῆλθεν ἀπ᾽ αὐτοῦ ἡ λέπρα, καὶ ἐκαθαρίσθη ("went away from him the leprosy, and he was cleansed"), while Matthew has ἐκαθαρίσθη αὐτοῦ ἡ λέπαρα ("he was cleansed his ~ leprosy"), which is *less*

---

12. See also Davies and Allison, *Matthew*, 1:104; and Bonnard, *L'Évangile selon Saint Matthieu*, 112–13.

13. For a discussion of various textual variants in Mark's reading, and the resulting confusion with regard to solving the Synoptic Problem, see Wheeler, *Textual Criticism and the Synoptic Problem*, 94–100.

14. For Matthew, τήν functions as a possessive pronoun.

15. While it is true that both Matthew and Mark are fond of parataxis, Matthew has fewer occurrences than Mark (610 in Matthew; 828 in Mark). N. Turner, *Style*, 4:34, says "Generally, Matthew reduces the Semitic nature of Mark's style in this respect: Luke on 23 occasions, and Matthew on 19, have eliminated Mark's parataxis by the substitution of the participle." See Sanders, *Tendencies of the Synoptic Tradition*, 249–51, for the conclusion that "the mere fact of their being less paratactic than Mark does not prove that they are later."

16. Many scribes eliminated αὐτῷ from Mark's text due to its redundancy. Such a deletion was a common scribal tendency (see C. H. Turner, "Marcan Usage," 28:157).

17. While εὐθύς occurs 41x in Mark, it appears just 5x in Matthew; εὐθέως occurs 1x in Mark, 13x in Matthew. Mark has εὐθύς in 9 places where Matthew has εὐθέως 9x (Matt. 4:20, 22; 8:3; 13:5; 14:22; 20:34; 21:2; 26:49, 74).

18. Stein, *Synoptic Problem*, 81–82, though, gives good statistical reasons for concluding that Matthew's use of εὐθέως is redactional and dependent on Mark's gospel.

pleonastic.[19] In Matthew αὐτοῦ ("his/him") is not the object of ἀπ᾽ ("from"), as in Mark, but functions as a possessive pronoun with λέπρα ("leprosy"), a use that is unique in the Gospels and probably points to Mark's text as the *source of the variant.*[20]

Mark 1:43. Matthew does not have a parallel to this verse.[21] Is it more likely that Matthew deleted this verse from Mark or that Mark added it to Matthew? It seems that Mark's reading is *more difficult* considering both the negative connotation of anger in ἐμβριμησάμενος ("having sternly warned"), an *orthodox improvement*, and the *redundancy* and *thematic awkwardness* of Mark's reading in this context.[22] It is redundant because verse 44 contains the same idea as this verse. It is awkward because, if we take verse 43 literally, the leper was "cast out immediately" (apparently from Jesus' presence). Yet we find Jesus still talking to the leper in 1:44, so it is obvious that the leper was *not* immediately sent away. In addition, Mark's "anger" brings an awkward change in the demeanor of Jesus. It thus appears more likely from text-critical criteria that Mark is the source of Matthew, rather than vice versa.

Mark 1:44. While Mark begins this verse with an impersonal verb, λέγει ("says"), Matthew's text reads λέγει αὐτῷ ὁ Ἰησοῦς ("says to him—Jesus"). The presence of the subject in Matthew lessens the probability of a *possible misunderstanding* concerning the subject. It is clear that it is Jesus who speaks in Matthew 8:4 rather than the leper (the closest antecedent in Mark's text).[23]

---

19. Nowhere in the Gospels, except here in Mark and in Luke's parallel 5:13, is leprosy said to "come out" (ἀπῆλθεν) of a person. In every other occurrence, the leprosy is "cleansed" (ἐκαθαρίσθη: Matt. 10:8; 11:5; Luke 7:22). Despite this difficulty, Peabody, Cope, and McNicol, *One Gospel from Two*, 99, merely state that Mark's text is "another instance of alternating agreement in wording with Matthew and Luke."

20. In the three other instances of lepers being cleansed in the Gospels, a possessive pronoun is not attached to the "leprosy." In other words, leprosy is not viewed as the possession of a person. It is more likely that this unique use of Matthew was the result of an alteration of Mark's text rather than an independent use, which differs from every other New Testament use. This conclusion is based on the supposition that Matthew eliminated Mark's preposition, ἀπ᾽, which then led to this unique use of αὐτοῦ.

21. Taylor, *Mark*, 189, says, "It is not surprising that both Matthew and Luke omit the verse.... There can be no doubt of its genuineness and primitive character." Matthew does, though, have an apparent parallel to this verse at the end of his collection of miracles, at 9:30–31.

22. Guelich, *Mark 1–8:26*, 1:72–73, notes the structural awkwardness of this verse. He says that while ἐμβριμησάμενος and ἐξέβαλεν would fit nicely into an exorcism setting, they do not fit structurally into the present healing.

23. Recall from the text-critical discussion that scribes often inserted subjects in order to make it clearer who the subject was, since Marcan style often used impersonal verbs and left subjects unnamed. Matthew's text, then, is clearly a text-critical improvement. C. H. Turner, "Marcan Usage," 26:226 n. 1, notes that "Matthew adds ὁ Ἰησοῦς not less than some forty times, especially at the beginning of a paragraph."

Matthew's text is *less pleonastic* than Mark's since it does not contain μηδέν ("nothing") after μηδενί ("to no one").[24] Matthew has προσένεγκον ("offer") rather than Mark's προσένεγκε ("offer"), which is an *alternate spelling.*

Mark's text contains an *awkward* προσένεγκε περὶ τοῦ καθαρισμοῦ σου ἃ ("offer [the sacrifices] for the cleansing of you which"). As can be seen, Mark did not cite exactly the Leviticus text. As a result, his phrase is awkward.[25] Matthew's text reads τὸ δῶρον ("the gift"), which is a *smoother and less awkward reading.*[26]

Mark 1:45. Matthew does not have a parallel to this verse.[27] Mark's verse contains an awkward change of subject from the leper (ὁ δέ, "but he") to Jesus (αὐτόν, "him"),[28] and a unique use of λόγον ("word"), which is always a "technical term" in Mark for the "primitive Christian missionary preaching."[29] Thus, it is more likely that Matthew deleted the verse in order to *eliminate possible misunderstandings.* The absence of this verse also *eliminates a problem* in

---

24. For a comparison of the Matthean and Marcan use of the double negative, see Allen, *Matthew,* xxv.

25. Mann, *Mark,* 220, thinks that Mark's version "has all the indications of a clarification" of Matthew's and Luke's versions. It is all but impossible to understand how Mann thinks Mark's text is a "clarification" since Mark 1:44 is nearly identical to Matthew and Luke. It is unfortunate that Mann cites no particulars as to how Mark is a "clarification."

    Hagner, *Matthew 1–13,* 1:197, correctly notes that περὶ τοῦ καθαρισμοῦ σου was eliminated by Matthew in order to "emphasize that it was Jesus who had cleansed the leper; the priests could only certify the cleansing." This elimination is certainly a *Matthean improvement.* Cf. Cave, "The Leper," 249.

26. The word δῶρον is used elsewhere in the New Testament to refer to the offering that is brought to the priest, for example, Hebrews 8:3–4. Davies and Allison, *Matthew,* 2:15, note that the construction of προσφέρω + δῶρον is a favorite of Matthew.

27. Mann, *Mark,* 218–19, says that Mark's version, with its inclusion of these details, "may owe far more to an original oral reminiscence than to the other evangelists." Elliott, "Healing of the Leper," 175–76, shows that Matthew was dependent on Mark for this material. He concludes that the reason Matthew deleted this verse is because he interpreted it as referring not to the leper but to Jesus. "Matthew recognised that Mark i 35–39 plus 45 were separable from i 40–44, and thus felt able to delete these verses from his gospel." This explanation of why Mark 1:45 is not found in Matthew makes much more sense than Mann's explanation.

    Grundmann, *Das Evangelium nach Matthäus,* 247, states, "Matthäus hat die Erzählung gegenüber Markus gekürzt und sie auf das Zwiegespräch konzentriert."

28. *Contra* Allen, *Mark,* 64, who thinks "the whole verse refers to Christ" due to the similar wording that is used to describe Jesus elsewhere in Mark (e.g., 1:7, 14, 38, 39; 5:20). Likewise, Elliott, "Conclusion of the Pericope," 153–57, argues that since Jesus was the subject of the last main verb (λέγει in v. 44) he must be the subject of ἤρξατο in verse 45.

29. Guelich, *Mark 1–8:26,* 1:84. This unique use of λόγον here is one of the reasons that some think that Jesus is the subject of this entire verse. See also Peabody, Cope, and McNicol, *One Gospel from Two,* 40–41, 100, who think that "the Word used absolutely" is "a clear indication of Markan editorial activity." One wonders why Matthew and Luke could not have eliminated these absolute uses to emphasize that it is not just a "word," but "Jesus' words" that are of interest. Without clear criteria for deciding this, the conclusion that this is a "clear indication" of Marcan redaction remains unconvincing.

that (1) Mark 1:45 says that Jesus "could not enter into a city openly," while 2:1 has Jesus entering into Capernaum, and (2) the leper in 1:45 is not obedient to Jesus' command in verse 44. These latter two differences may be classified as *orthodox improvements*.[30]

Mark 2:1–12 (Matt. 9:1–8): The Healing of the Paralytic

Mark 2:1–2. While Mark says that Jesus καὶ εἰσελθὼν πάλιν εἰς Καφαρναούμ ("and having entered again into Capernaum"), Matthew says καὶ ἦλθεν εἰς τὴν ἰδίαν πόλιν ("and coming into the [his] own city").[31] While Matthew 8:5 (the verse that follows consecutively the preceding Marcan pericope) also places Jesus in Capernaum, Matthew then has Jesus get into a boat (v. 23) and cross to the other side of the sea to the "country of the Gadarenes" (v. 28). Here in Matthew 9:1—the parallel to Mark 2:1—Jesus gets back into the boat and "came to his own city." The name of this city cannot be known for certain.[32] The only similar words in Mark 2:1–2 and Matthew 9:1 are καὶ εἰσελθών ("and having entered," Mark 2:1) and καὶ ἦλθεν ("and came," Matt. 9:1). The latter is a more *refined grammatical expression* since Matthew lacks Mark's anacoluthon (a grammatical non sequitur).[33]

The rest of Mark 2:1–2 is entirely different in Matthew.[34] The only text-critically significant phrase is ἐν οἴκῳ ἐστίν, which may be translated "his [i.e., Jesus'] house."[35] This phrase is a *more difficult* reading since it potentially conflicts with Matthew 8:20, καὶ λέγει αὐτῷ ὁ Ἰησοῦς· αἱ ἀλώπεκες φωλεοὺς ἔχουσιν καὶ τὰ πετεινὰ τοῦ οὐρανοῦ κατασκηνώσεις, ὁ δὲ υἱὸς τοῦ ἀνθρώπου οὐκ ἔχει ποῦ τὴν κεφαλὴν κλίνῃ ("and says to him—Jesus, the foxes have ~ holes and the birds ~ of heaven, nests, but ~ the son ~ of man does not have [a place] where the [his] head he may lay").[36]

---

30. Orthodox scribes often deleted references to inability or apparent failure on Jesus' part. See Allen, *Matthew*, 76.

31. Sand, *Das Evangelium nach Matthäus*, 192, notes, "die Kürzung... dient der Hervorhebung des Wortes Jesu und der christologischen Aussage; dadurch rücket bei Matthew das Gespräch über Sündenvergebung noch stärker in den Vordergrund." So also, Dupont, "Le paralytique pardonné (Matt. 9,1–8)," 944; and Morris, *Matthew*, 213.

32. One possible method for identifying τὴν ἰδίαν πόλιν in Matthew 9:1 as Καφαρναούμ would be to translate Mark's ἐν οἴκῳ (2:1) as the idiomatic "at home"; so, for example, Swete, *Mark*, 32.

33. So, Taylor, *Mark*, 192.

34. Schlatter, *Der Evangelist Matthäus*, 297, thinks that Matthew's version is more original given its brevity and lack of details, which Mark contains, such as the mention of the "four men" (τεσσάρων).

35. So, Swete, *Mark*, 32. Certainly ἐν οἴκῳ, though, does not have to be translated with this meaning and probably should not be.

36. Cf. Harrington, *Matthew*, 1:121.

Mark 2:3–4. Matthew's parallel begins with his *characteristic* ἰδού ("behold," see above on Mark 1:40) and does not contain Mark's *impersonal third person verb,* ἔρχονται ("they come"). Matthew uses his *characteristically Matthean* dative personal pronoun, αὐτῷ ("to him"), where Mark's preposition is followed by an accusative object, πρὸς αὐτόν ("to him").[37] The wording of the remainder of these verses is entirely distinct.[38] Mark's αἰρόμενον ὑπὸ τεσσάρων ("being carried along by four [men]") is not found in Matthew, which reads ἐπὶ κλίνης βεβλημένον ("upon a stretcher lying"). While there are no text-critical grounds for this change, a possible *theological reason* for Matthew's reading might be to place emphasis upon the paralytic and not upon the other four men.[39] This explanation also could be the reason that Matthew does not contain verse 4, since its focus is again upon the other four, rather than the paralytic who was healed.

Mark 2:5. Matthew's wording is identical to the first clause of Mark, καὶ ἰδὼν ὁ Ἰησοῦς τὴν πίστιν αὐτῶν ("and having seen—Jesus the faith of them"). Within Mark's context, the reader immediately knows the actions that exhibited faith. In the Matthean context, however, "seeing their faith" does not make as much sense.[40] One could argue that the simple act of the presentation of the paralytic to Jesus might have elicited this response from Jesus, that is, they showed faith in believing that Jesus could heal. It seems more likely, however, that Mark is the *source variant,* and that Matthew has abbreviated Mark's account with the result that Matthew lacks pertinent information. The Matthean reader is left wondering exactly what actions occurred that elicited this comment. This lack of information in this particular Matthean healing is atypical of Matthean style. Elsewhere, Jesus sees faith exhibited through the doing of specific actions in those whom he heals. Matthew, therefore, shows dependency upon Mark's account.[41]

---

37. Since Hellenistic Greek prefers the preposition followed by the dative case, it is possible that this is an Atticistic improvement. Whether or not this theory is true, it is true that Matthean style is to prefer αὐτῷ instead of πρὸς αὐτόν. He uses αὐτῷ instead of πρὸς αὐτόν 8x out of 10 parallels with Mark (1:32, 40; 2:3; 3:31; 10:1; 11:27; 12:13, 18). This change seems to be a consistent Matthean redaction of Mark's text. Mark, on the other hand, does not consistently change Matthew's αὐτῷ to πρὸς αὐτόν. Matthew uses αὐτῷ 170x to Mark's 121x.

38. Hill, *Matthew,* 169, says that "the economy of description in the Matthean account (as elsewhere in the miracle stories) is such as to make it necessary to presuppose for its understanding a fuller version such as Mark preserves." See Bornkamm, Barth, and Held, *Überlieferung und Auslegung im Matthäusevangelium,* 175–77, for a description of the details found in Mark that are absent in Matthew.

39. So, Davies and Allison, *Matthew,* 2:87.

40. It makes even less sense given that it is the "four men" whose faith is in view here in Matthew, even though he has not specifically mentioned them; so, Sand, *Das Evangelium nach Matthäus,* 193.

41. Of course, an argument could be offered from exactly the opposite direction. It could be said that Mark has made Matthew's text clearer by supplying the missing information regarding the actions of the paralytic's friends. Such is not likely the case because of the *typical Matthean pattern,* which

Matthew uses an aorist εἶπεν ("said"), while Mark contains an *historical present* λέγει ("says"). No conclusive text-critical decisions can be made, although the likelihood favors Marcan priority due to the overall Matthean and Marcan usage of the historical present.[42]

Mark 2:6. Mark begins this verse with his *typical* ἦσαν δέ ("and there were," 5x in Mark compared to Matthew's 2x), while Matthew has his *characteristic* καὶ ἰδού ("and behold").[43] Mark's καὶ διαλογιζόμενοι ἐν ταῖς καρδίαις αὐτῶν ("and thinking about [these things] in the hearts of them") appears in Matthew's gospel in a more *typical Matthean* phrase, εἶπαν ἐν ἑαυτοῖς ("said among themselves"). While Matthew consistently uses the phrase ἐν ἑαυτοῖς ("among themselves") after verbs of speaking, Mark uses a variety of phrases to refer to this same idea.[44] It seems more likely that the author (Matthew) who has written in a *unified style* (ἐν ἑαυτοῖς) is less original than the author (Mark) who has written in an arbitrary style.

Mark 2:7. Matthew's οὗτος βλασφημεῖ ("this one he blasphemes") is *less redundant* than Mark's τί οὗτος οὕτως λαλεῖ; βλασφημεῖ ("why [is] this one speaking ~ thus. He blasphemes") since οὕτως λαλεῖ ("thus ~ speaking") and βλασφημεῖ ("he blasphemes") are similar ideas.

Matthew does not have a parallel for Mark's *unnecessary* τίς δύναται ἀφιέναι

---

always indicates some type of prolonged action, pleading, or perseverance on the part of those in whom Jesus saw faith: the centurion came from a distance and then believed that Jesus could heal without even seeing his daughter (8:5–13); the woman suffering from hemorrhages touched Jesus' cloak, believing that a mere touch would heal her (9:20–22); two blind men continued to follow and cry out to Jesus for healing (9:27–31); the Canaanite woman whose daughter was healed persevered in her request of Jesus even after his initial denial (15:21–28).

42. Sanders, *Tendencies of the Synoptic Tradition*, 246, says that Matthew changes Mark's historical present 78 times. Tuckett, *Revival of the Griesbach Hypothesis*, 22–25, concludes, "This tiny piece of evidence suggests that the theory of Marcan priority gives a more coherent and self-consistent picture of what must have been the redactional activity of the secondary evangelists than does the Griesbach Hypothesis." Farmer, *Synoptic Problem*, 135–37, though, thinks that it is unlikely that Matthew would change Mark's historic present on so many occasions when he himself uses it "no less than 50 times elsewhere in his Gospel." Farmer, though, underestimates the number of times that Matthew is said to have "corrected" Mark's historical present; he thinks he did this only 20 times. It seems, though, that, as Tuckett said, it is more consistent (although still not entirely consistent) to suggest that Matthew, who used the historical present 93x, altered Mark's historical present 78x, than to suggest that Mark, who used the historical present 151x in a shorter Gospel, did not retain Matthew's historical present in some forty instances (Farmer's data). Cf. Hawkins, *Horae Synopticae*, 144–49, for a listing of historical presents in Matthew and Mark.

43. See the discussion at Mark 1:40 (cf. Mark 2:3). For a list of typical Matthean vocabulary in this passage, see Luz, *Matthew 8–20*, 27 n. 6.

44. While Matthew uses ἐν ἑαυτοῖς 6x after verbs of speaking, Mark uses it only 1x (2:8). Mark instead uses a variety of phrases to refer to the same idea: ἐν καρδίαις (2:6, 8); πρὸς ἀλλήλους (4:41; 8:16; 9:34; 15:31); and πρὸς ἑαυτούς (1:27; 9:10; 10:26; 11:31; 14:4). Matthew does not use any of these various phrases.

ἁμαρτίας εἰ μὴ εἰς ὁ θεός ("who is able to forgive sins except [the] one—God?"). No text-critical decision can be made since Matthew may have deleted this sentence because his Jewish audience already would have known this fact, or Mark may have added this sentence to Matthew since his Gentile audience may not have known this. The absence of the reading in Matthew may also be an *orthodox improvement* that avoided the possible conflict with Matthew 9:8, which indicates that humans do have the authority to forgive sins.

Mark 2:8. While Matthew contains nearly the identical idea as Mark, the wording is almost entirely different.[45] Matthew's *typical* πονηρά ("evil," 26x to Mark's 2x) is *more explicit and clear* than Mark's more general ταῦτα ("these things"). Another possibility is that the absence of τῷ πνεύματι αὐτοῦ ("in the spirit of him") in Matthew was an *orthodox improvement* in order to avoid docetic tendencies.

Mark 2:9. Matthew inserts γάρ ("for") after τί ("which," Mark's reading) to *make the causal relationship clearer* between the verses (Mark 2:8–9; Matt. 9:4–5).[46] Mark's *unnecessary indirect object*, τῷ παραλυτικῷ ("to the paralytic") is not found in Matthew's text.[47] Nor is found in Matthew, Mark's *awkward command* to the paralytic, καὶ ἆρον τὸν κράβαττόν σου ("and pick up the mattress of you"). There seems to be no reason for the paralytic to take his bed with him. In addition, the absence of this clause serves to emphasize the "rising" and "walking" of the paralytic, which is logical. It seems more likely that, because of its awkwardness, Matthew deleted this clause from Mark, rather than vice versa, since awkwardness is rare among scribal additions.[48]

---

45. The most likely and most sensible reason for the difference in the two accounts is that Matthew is condensing the Marcan account in order to preserve room for his additions. See Stein, *Synoptic Problem*, 50, for a table of the actual number of words in the various parallel pericopae.

46. Aland, *Synopsis Quattuor Evangeliorum*, 61, indicates a few Marcan scribes added γάρ (W 1424 sa).

47. Riley, *Making of Mark*, 24, thinks that the presence of τῷ παραλυτικῷ is evidence for Matthean priority. He does not, though, give reasons for this conclusion. Since this study will be interacting with Riley throughout the discussion, it will help to give an overall evaluation of his work at this point. Though Riley sets his goal high (to show that Mark conflates Matthew and Luke), he fails to provide the necessary evidence. Instead, he merely makes assertions of priority rather than giving evidence or criteria for determining priority. His overall lack of footnotes and bibliography (he cites only thirty-eight titles in his entire bibliography), coupled with his lack of detailed comments on the specific differences between the Greek texts of the Gospels, combine to make his work accomplish less than what he desired. Only by glossing over major differences between the Gospels throughout his entire study can Riley conclude that his analysis has proven his theory of Matthean priority (p. 209).

48. Damm, *"Ornatus,"* 345, concludes that improvements to Mark's *elocutio* are good evidence that Matthew is deleting this phrase from Mark. He states, 347, "that many ancient authors wrote in a fashion that is similar to Matthew and Luke."

Mark 2:10. Matthew and Mark are identical except for word order and Matthew's inclusion of τότε ("then") before λέγει ("he says"). The τότε ("then") *makes the verse smoother* since indeed a break in the thought occurs between ἀμαρτίας ("sin") and λέγει ("he says"). The addition of τότε ("then") alerts the reader to this break.[49] Text-critically, it would be *more difficult* to explain why this word, which makes the text clearer, would have been deleted (if Mark used Matthew as his source).

Mark 2:11. Matthew's text is somewhat *less pleonastic* in that it does not contain Mark's redundant σοὶ λέγω ("to you I say"). After all, that Jesus was speaking to the paralytic already was made clear in the immediately preceding clause.

While Mark contains a present imperative active, ἔγειρε ("stand"), Matthew has an aorist passive participle, ἐγερθείς ("rising up"), which is the same form used in Matthew 9:7. It seems unlikely that Mark would have changed Matthew's *more consistent style* into two different forms, ἔγειρε ("stand") and ἠγέρθη ("he arose," 2:12).

Matthew's τὴν κλίνην ("the stretcher") is a *synonym* for Mark's τὸν κράβαττόν ("the mattress").[50] While some scholars think this is a *grammatical improvement* to a better word, the evidence for this does not seem conclusive.[51]

---

49. Even with the addition of τότε, though, there remains a conceptual break in the Matthean text (though less of a break than in Mark). The fact that Matthew and Mark both have an unexpected break here is good evidence either that they are recording the actual words of Jesus as he spoke them, or that one or the other is dependent on the other Gospel as a literary source.

   Lane, *Mark,* 97, thinks that "Mark is responsible for verse 10 in its entirety. The awkward syntactical structure is deliberate and functional." Duplacy, "Marc, 2, 10: Note de Syntaxe," 420, concludes "La syntaxe de ce verset [Mc, 2,10] est en effet assez étrange." Duplacy further gives three explanations for the anacolouthon in this verse (424–26). Mann, *Mark,* 222, though, says, "The phrase *he turned to the paralytic man* has all the marks of an editorial and copied interjection." Not only does Mann provide no evidence for this assertion, but he also fails to see the absurdity of this claim, considering that the texts of Matthew and Mark have the *identical* phrase.

50. Peabody, Cope, and McNicol, *One Gospel from Two,* 101, state, "It is easier to explain . . . Mark's imposing a unity on his text with the use of the Latin loanword, κράβαττος, than it is to explain them as a result of Matthew and Luke independently editing Mark's text in different ways but agreeing to omit or change every single usage of κράβαττος." Why is it easier? Matthew changes the word to the synonym once and does not have a parallel for the other three uses of the term in Mark 2, while Luke uses a different word in the two parallels that he has. If κράβαττος had negative connotations (see the following footnotes), it is easy to explain why the word may have been changed and not so easy to see this as conclusive evidence for Marcan redaction.

   In addition, if Mark's goal to "impose unity" upon the texts of Matthew and Luke, it must be admitted that he did a poor job in other places (see, for example, Mark 4:4–7 and the use of ἄλλο). See appendix B of this book for examples of where Matthew "Changes Arbitrary Style into Unified Style."

51. So, for example, D. A. Black, "R. Stein's *The Synoptic Problem* and Markan 'Errors,'" 96–97. Keener, *Matthew,* 291, suggests that Matthew "used an earlier version of Mark."

Streeter says that κλίνη ("stretcher") is a correction for the "apparent vulgarism κράββατον ("mattress")."[52] While these precise nuances may have been true in classical Greek (and it is difficult to conclusively support such a claim), the New Testament usage of these two words shows that New Testament authors attached no stigma to κράβαττος ("mattress").[53]

Mark 2:12. Matthew, again (cf. 9:5), does not mention "taking the mat." Matthew then says that the paralytic ἀπῆλθεν εἰς τὸν οἶκον αὐτοῦ ("he went away to the house of him"). Notably εἰς τὸν οἶκόν αὐτοῦ ("to the house of him") is the same wording used in the command by Jesus to the paralytic in Matthew 9:6 and Mark 2:11. Thus, Matthew's εἰς τὸν οἶκόν αὐτοῦ ("to the house of him") makes the paralytic's actions perfectly conform with Jesus' command. Mark, on the other hand, has the paralytic departing ἔμπροσθεν πάντων ("in front of everyone"), which is not exactly obedience to Jesus' command. Therefore, Matthew's text might be an *orthodox improvement* that shows total obedience on the part of the "faithful" paralytic, thus making Mark's text as more likely the source.

Matthew's *characteristic* οἱ ὄχλοι ("the crowds") is *clearer* than Mark's vague πάντας ("everyone"). It is possible that Matthew is showing his dependence on Mark by noting the presence of the crowd, which he has not mentioned previously, but Mark has in 2:2.[54]

The ending of this pericope in Matthew and Mark is totally different. Matthew writes τὸν θεὸν τὸν δόντα ἐξουσίαν τοιαύτην τοῖς ἀνθρώποις ("God the one having given such ~ authority ~ to men") while Mark has τὸν θεὸν λέγοντας ὅτι οὕτως οὐδέποτε εἴδομεν ("God saying—thus never have we seen"). It seems, though, that Matthew's text is dependent on, and is an addition to, Mark's because of the usage of the term ἐξουσία ("authority") in

---

52. Streeter, *Four Gospels,* 299, who was perhaps influenced by Hawkins, *Horae Synopticae,* 132. Streeter used an alternate spelling of κράβαττος, κράββατος (cf. BAGD, 447). So also Hill, *Matthew,* 170, who says that κράβαττος is a "colloquial term"; also Allen, *Matthew,* 87, who calls it a "vernacular and dialectic" word; and Stein, *Synoptic Problem,* 53, who calls it a "slang expression." Cf. Davies and Allison, *Matthew,* 1:105–6.

53. The word κράβαττος is used 11x (Mark 5x; John 4x; Acts 2x), while κλίνη is used 9x in the New Testament (Matt.: 2x; Mark: 3x; Luke: 3x; Rev: 1x) and κλινάριον 1x (Acts). If it is agreed that Luke, a highly sophisticated author, wrote both the Gospel of Luke and Acts, it is obvious that he does not think that κράβαττος is a "vulgar" word. In fact, he uses both words together in Acts 5:15, ὥστε καὶ εἰς τὰς πλατείας ἐκφέρειν τοὺς ἀσθενεῖς καὶ τιθέναι ἐπὶ κλιναρίων καὶ κραβάττων. Cf. Farmer, *Synoptic Problem,* 130. Metzger, *Text of the New Testament,* 196, though, cites an example from the fourth century that implies that κράββαττος was seen as a colloquial Koine word. Nevertheless, evidence must be sought primarily from the New Testament rather than from the fourth century. Murray, "Five Gospel Miracles," 83, suggests that Mark used τὸν κράβαττόν, a Latin (*grabatus*) loanword, since it "might be more familiar" to Mark's Roman audience.

54. See Davies and Allison, *Matthew,* 2:95.

the two gospels.[55] Given the importance of the "authority" theme to Mark, it is *more difficult* to surmise why Mark would have eliminated this clause if he were using Matthew as his source.

Mark 2:13–17 (Matt. 9:9–13): The Call of Levi (Matthew)[56]

Mark 2:13. Matthew does not have a parallel to this verse.[57] The inclusion of the verse in Mark's text appears to be the *most difficult* because of the *apparent difficulty* in Jesus' leaving Capernaum in order to go to the sea (v. 13), only to reappear in the same city again in verse 14.[58]

Mark 2:14. Matthew's ὁ Ἰησοῦς ("Jesus") *makes the subject clearer* than Mark's text does. While Mark names the tax collector as Λευὶν τὸν τοῦ Ἀλφαίου ("Levi the [son]—of Alphaeus"), Matthew has ἄνθρωπον . . . Μαθθαῖον λεγόμενον ("a man . . . being called ~ Matthew"). While it is beyond the scope of this study to do a thorough examination of this difference, some text-critical

---

55. Mark mentions ἐξουσία being given to Jesus (1:22, 27; 2:10; 11:28, 29, 33), to the Twelve (3:15; 6:7), and possibly to all Christians (13:34). Matthew mentions ἐξουσία being given to Jesus (7:29; 9:6; 21:23, 24, 27; 28:18) and to the Twelve (10:1).

56. Hill, *Matthew,* 172, lists five Matthean "improvements" to Mark's text in this pericope: "(a) he omits Mark 2.13, which is awkward and inappropriate to the context; (b) he simplifies the name of the tax-collector to Matthew; (c) he has abbreviated and improved the description of Jesus eating with sinners (Mark 2.15b is suppressed); (d) he has made concise and direct the attack by the Pharisees on Jesus' behaviour; and (e) he has supported Jesus' important word in verse 13 by a fitting quotation from the Old Testament." Hill does not, though, give criteria by which he has judged that these are Matthean improvements.

57. Harrington, *Matthew,* 1:126, thinks that Matthew deleted this verse because it contains *superfluous information.* Riley, *Making of Mark,* 26, makes the confusing (considering his conclusion that Mark is a redaction of Matt.) assertion that Mark's text is "rather more ambiguous." Peabody, Cope, and McNicol, *One Gospel from Two,* 104, state, "Every word or phrase in this verse that does not stand in verbatim agreement with either Matthew, Luke, or both is characteristic of Mark, and none of the words and phrases in Mark that are paralleled in the other Gospels is characteristic of Mark. What other explanation is there for such a consistent pattern of positive and negative correlations than that Mark has freely recomposed the loosely parallel texts of Matthew and Luke . . . ?" Since, though, only two words are paralleled in Luke, and none in Matthew, this statement actually says very little. Matthew has not "omitted only what is characteristic to Mark," he has eliminated the entire verse. And, since the "most difficult text" is a criterion that Peabody himself uses, it remains more likely that Mark's text is more difficult and thus prior, given that it is indeed repetitive and a bit awkward.

58. See Lane, *Mark,* 99–100, who concludes that 2:14 took place in the city because cities are the usual location for toll booths, although Guelich, *Mark 1–8:26,* 1:127, thinks the toll booth was "located on a commercial road along the sea for the purpose of taxing goods in transport." Crum, *Mark's Gospel,* 55–56, sees evidence of a second stage of Marcan redaction beginning in this verse. He concludes that this geographical difficulty in Mark 2:13 is due to a later redaction of the original Mark. Hard evidence for such suggestions, though, are always difficult. As Crum admits, "Every step in the delicate operation of making this separation is, of course, conjecture" (2).

comments can be made.[59] The use of the name "Levi, the son of Alphaeus" is *more difficult* in this context than "Matthew." Recall from above that some Marcan scribes changed the name from Levi to James in order to harmonize it with Mark 3:18 (Matt. 10:3), Ἰάκωβον τὸν τοῦ Ἀλφαίου ("James the son of Alphaeus"). In the same way, the name Matthew is a less difficult name since it *harmonizes* Matthew 9:9 with 10:3, Μαθθαῖος ὁ τελώνης ("Matthew the tax collector"). If Matthew were first, it would be very difficult to understand from text-critical criteria why Mark would have changed Matthew's "Matthew" to "Levi," given that Matthew is named both as a tax collector (v. 3) and an apostle.

Mark 2:15. In the location of Mark's adverbial infinitive clause, κατακεῖσθαι αὐτόν ("[that] he reclined"), Matthew has an introductory genitive absolute construction, αὐτοῦ ἀνακειμένου ("he was reclining at table"). Since both Matthew and Mark use both of these constructions, no text-critical evidence exists for priority.

Matthew does not have αὐτοῦ ("his") after ἐν τῇ οἰκίᾳ ("in the house"), as Mark does. Mark's text is *more difficult* in that it contains a *possible misunderstanding*. The αὐτοῦ ("his") could infer that Jesus owned the house, since its antecedent may be either Levi (Matthew) or Jesus.[60] The absence of the pronoun in Matthew could be taken as an *orthodox improvement* since it harmonizes this text with Matthew 8:20, καὶ λέγει αὐτῷ ὁ Ἰησοῦς· αἱ ἀλώπεκες φωλεοὺς ἔχουσιν καὶ τὰ πετεινὰ τοῦ οὐρανοῦ κατασκηνώσεις, ὁ δὲ υἱὸς τοῦ ἀνθρώπου οὐκ ἔχει ποῦ τὴν κεφαλὴν κλίνῃ ("and says to him—Jesus, the foxes have ~ holes and the birds—of heaven, nests, but ~ the son of man does

---

59. See Davies and Allison, *Matthew*, 2:98–99, for a brief survey of possible reasons for the name change from Levi to Matthew.

   Both Sabourin, *Matthew*, 2:483–84; and Pesch, "Levi-Matthäus (Mc 2:14/Mt 9:9; 10:3)," 50–53, note that Matthew limits the use of the term *disciple* to the Twelve. Thus, Matthew must use one of these twelve names for the calling of the disciple here in Matthew 9:9–13, whereas Mark and Luke can use Levi since they have not restricted *disciple* to only the Twelve. They are followed by Schweizer, *Matthew*, 226. Kiley, "Why 'Matthew' in Matt 9, 9–13?" 347–51, suggests that Matthew was chosen because of the "etymological link" between Μαθθαῖος and Matthew's theological foci in this passage, namely, discipleship and learning, μαθητής and μάθετε.

60. Although most scholars think that the house belonged to Levi, Malbon, "ΤΗ ΟΙΚΙΑ ΑΥΤΟΥ: Mark 2.15 in Context," 282–92, thinks that the house belonged to Jesus. One of the reasons she holds to this argument is the use of the personal pronoun in Mark 2:14–15. A form of αὐτός is used five times in these two verses: four of the five definitely refer to Jesus. The only questionable referent is in the phrase in question, ἐν τῇ οἰκίᾳ αὐτοῦ. Thus, she argues, it would make more sense for this pronoun to also refer to Jesus. Such reasoning, though, implies the characteristics of consistency and clarity on the part of Mark as a composer, which is not always the case.

   Grundmann, *Das Evangelium nach Matthäus*, 270, is unsure of whose house it is: "Welches Haus es ist, in dem es stattfindet, wird nicht gesagt; man wird zuerst an das Haus des Zollpächters denken, aber auch das des Simon oder Jesu selbst ist nicht auszuschließen."

not have [a place] where the (his) head he may lay").[61] Matthew contains ἰδού ("behold"), a *typically Matthean word* (62x vs. Mark's 7x). The end of Mark's verse is not found in Matthew, ἦσαν γὰρ πολλοὶ καὶ ἠκολούθουν αὐτῷ ("for ~ there were many and they were following him"). Matthew's text is *less redundant* since πολλοὶ ("many") has already been used earlier in the verse to describe this group. Mark's text is also *more difficult* due to the ambiguity of its meaning: did πολλοὶ refer to the "disciples" or the "sinners?"

Mark 2:16. Mark's unique and conceptually difficult οἱ γραμματεῖς τῶν Φαρισαίων ("the scribes of the Pharisees") is a *more difficult* expression than Matthew's more normal οἱ Φαρισαῖοι ("the Pharisees").[62] It is more likely that Mark has the primary reading here. Matthew's text is *less redundant* than Mark because it does not contain ὅτι ἐσθίει μετὰ τῶν ἁμαρτωλῶν καὶ τελωνῶν ("that he eats with—sinners and tax collectors"), which occurs a second time later in this same verse.[63]

Mark's text has a ὅτι ("why?/that") while Matthew has διὰ τί ("why"). It is probable that both authors are seeking to ask a question. Thus, Matthew's text is *more clear* since Mark's ὅτι ("why?/that") may also be interpreted as recitative and would pose an interpretative *difficulty*.[64] The presence of ὁ διδάσκαλος ὑμῶν ("the teacher of you") in Matthew *makes the subject* of the impersonal verb (ἐσθίει, "eats") *clearer* than it is in Mark's text.

Mark 2:17. Mark begins the verse by making the subject clear, ὁ Ἰησοῦς ("Jesus"). Matthew does not contain this reading, but no text-critical conclusion may be reached since it would have been redundant for Matthew to contain this reading since the word "Jesus" appeared just two verses before. Matthew's text does not contain *the indirect object,* αὐτοῖς ("to them"), a typical scribal change that was seen in the previous chapter. Matthew contains a quote from Hosea 6:6, which is not found in Mark, πορευθέντες δὲ μάθετε τί ἐστιν· ἔλεος θέλω καὶ οὐ θυσίαν ("but ~ going learn what is [the meaning of this]: I desire ~ mercy and not sacrifice"). Matthew uses the quote again at 12:7. Is it more likely

---

61. Recall from the text-critical study in chapter 2 that some Marcan scribes made the same deletion.

62. Recall from the text-critical study that similar improvements were made by Marcan scribes to this unique expression. Carlston, *Parables of the Triple Tradition,* 10, thinks the change may have been motivated by Matthew's "generally favorable attitude toward 'scribes,' whom he elsewhere removes from unfavorable situations (Matt. 12:24; 17:14; 21:23; 22:35, 41; 26:3, 47; 27:1), and by his understanding of 'Pharisees' as a kind of negative ideal (9:34; 12:24, 38)." France, *Mark,* 134, says that the phrase, although unusual, "correctly represents the fact that within the larger Pharisaic party there were professional scribes." Marcus, *Mark,* 519–24, contains an "Appendix: the Scribes and the Pharisees," which tries to make sense of this expression.

63. So, Hurtado, *Text-Critical Methodology,* 74.

64. Allen, *Matthew,* 90, calls this a *"grammatical correction."*

that Matthew added this Old Testament quote, or that Mark deleted this quote? It is *more difficult* to understand why Mark would have deleted it, given the causal relationship both authors imply in the last phrase (Matt. 9:13; Mark 2:17), οὐ γὰρ ἦλθον καλέσαι δικαίους ἀλλὰ ἁμαρτωλούς ("for ~ I have not come to call [the] righteous but sinners."). Matthew has made this causal relationship *clearer* by the inclusion of γάρ ("for"). Without the Old Testament quote, the causal relationship is a little awkward. This addition also may be a *theologically motivated change* since it fits in with Matthew's emphasis on the Law.[65]

Mark 2:18–22 (Matt. 9:14–17): The Question About Fasting

Mark 2:18. While many minor differences in this verse appear between Matthew and Mark, three main changes are text-critically important. First, Matthew does not contain Mark's introductory sentence, καὶ ἦσαν οἱ μαθηταὶ Ἰωάννου καὶ οἱ Φαρισαῖοι νηστεύοντες ("and came the disciples of John and the Pharisees fasting"). Matthew, therefore, is *less redundant,* since both Matthew and Mark repeat the same idea later in the verse. Second, Matthew's genitive possessive pronoun in οἱ δὲ μαθηταὶ σου οὐ νηστεύουσιν ("but ~ the disciples of you do not fast") is *less awkward* and *clearer* than Mark's dative pronoun, οἱ δὲ σοὶ μαθηταὶ οὐ νηστεύουσιν ("but your disciples do not fast"). Third, Matthew's reading of οἱ Φαρισαῖοι ("the Pharisees") is *less problematic and less difficult* than Mark's οἱ μαθηταὶ τῶν Φαρισαίων ("the disciples of the Pharisees"). Mark's wording is problematic because the "Pharisees were a religious party and technically did not have 'disciples.'"[66]

Mark 2:19. Mark's νηστεύειν ("to fast") and Matthew's πενθεῖν ("to mourn") are basically *synonyms.*[67] Matthew's ἐφ' ὅσον ("as long as") *clearly* emphasizes the duration of the fast ("in so far as the bridegroom is with them"),[68] while the exact meaning of Mark's ἐν ᾧ . . . ὅσον ("while the . . . as long as") is *less clear* since ἐν ᾧ is used with various meanings.[69] Matthew is *less pleonastic* considering

---

65. So, Blomberg, *Interpreting the Parables,* 106.

66. Guelich, *Mark 1–8:26,* 1:110, concludes that this "may only be a loose usage of μαθητής." See the similar uses in Matthew 22:16 (τοὺς μαθητὰς αὐτῶν) and 12:27 (οἱ υἱοὶ ὑμῶν). But, cf. K. H. Rengstorf, "μαθητής," in Kittel, *TDNT,* 4:443, who says, after surveying the construction οἱ μαθηταὶ τῶν Φαρισαίων in its first century-context, "Thus there is no reason to suspect the difficult οἱ μαθηταὶ τῶν Φαρισαίων in terms of contemporary usage." Rengstorf, though, is not able to cite any evidence for his conclusion other than New Testament evidence.

67. Sabourin, *Matthew,* 490, thinks that "'mourn' and 'fast' seem to be different renderings of the Aramaic 'ith'annê.'"

68. BAGD, 289.3.2.b.

69. Ibid., 261; for example, duration or circumstantial.

the absence of Mark's redundant χρόνον ἔχουσιν τὸν νυμφίον μετ᾽ αὐτῶν οὐ δύνανται νηστεύειν ("time they have the groom with them they are not able to fast").[70] This clause is not necessary since both Matthew and Mark had just used it.

Mark 2:20. Matthew is identical to Mark except for omitting Mark's final phrase, ἐν ἐκείνῃ τῇ ἡμέρᾳ ("in that day"). Again, Matthew is *less redundant* since the time has already been indicated in Matthew and Mark (ὅταν and τότε, "when" and "then").[71] Matthew's text would also be *less difficult* since, by the time the Gospels were written, the time of fasting had lasted longer than a day (in fact, well over 10,000 days!).

Mark 2:21. Matthew's ἐπιβάλλει ("sews") is a *more common synonym* than Mark's ἐπιράπτει ("sews"; 18 uses vs. 1 use in the New Testament). It is possible that the more uncommon word is the *more difficult reading* since it is more likely that a redactor would change an uncommon word to a more common word.[72] While Mark has αἴρει τὸ πλήρωμα ἀπ᾽ αὐτοῦ τὸ καινὸν τοῦ παλαιοῦ ("will pull away the patch from it the new from the old"), Matthew's wording, αἴρει γὰρ τὸ πλήρωμα αὐτοῦ ἀπὸ τοῦ ἱματίου ("for ~ it takes away the fullness of it from the garment"), is *more precise and clear* through the presence of τοῦ ἱματίου ("the garment") instead of αὐτοῦ ("it"). Text-critically, it is *more difficult* to understand why Mark would alter Matthew's text to a more awkward text.

Mark 2:22. Mark's ῥήξει ὁ οἶνος τοὺς ἀσκούς ("will tear the wine the wineskins") is paralleled by ῥήγνυνται οἱ ἀσκοί ("are torn the wineskins") in Matthew. The Matthean reading is a *less difficult expression,* given the theological significance of these words. Matthew makes it clear that it is not the new wine (i.e., Jesus' teachings) that bursts the wineskins (i.e., Judaism). Rather, the wineskins (i.e., Judaism) burst because of their own incapability of expanding to accept the new wine (i.e., Jesus as Messiah).[73] If this is the case, Matthew's precise wording could be *theologically motivated.* While Mark has a future tense, ῥήξει ("will tear"), Matthew has a present tense, ῥήγνυνται ("are torn"), perhaps an

---

70. Dodd, *Parables of the Kingdom,* 87, suggests that Mark 2:19b is a post-Marcan gloss, which was added to make the transition to the next verse easier. Gundry, *Mark,* 136, and *Matthew,* 169–70, though, shows that the idea of Mark 2:19b is included in Matthew 9:15 and therefore cannot be a post-Marcan gloss (note that this is an argument from a Marcan priority commitment).

71. Philippe Rolland cited in Neirynck, "Les Expressions Doubles chez Marc et le Problème Synoptique," 306, concludes, "Le texte simple de Mt. se recommande comme plus originel." Neirynck, though, shows that "simplicity" is not so easily defined in the Gospels (307).

72. So, Davies and Allison, *Matthew,* 1:105–6. Streeter, *Four Gospels,* 310, says, "The noun ἐπίβλημα almost shouts out to an editor to alter the verb to ἐπιβάλλει."

73. So, Davies and Allison, *Matthew,* 2:113–14.

assimilation to the present tenses that follow, ἐκχεῖται ("is poured out") and ἀπόλλυνται ("are ruined"). Perhaps, though, Matthew is *theologically motivated* to indicate that these concepts are presently occurring in Jesus' ministry.

Matthew's καὶ ὁ οἶνος ἐκχεῖται καὶ οἱ ἀσκοὶ ἀπόλλυνται ("and the wine is poured out and the wineskins are ruined") is *less awkward* than *Mark's* καὶ ὁ οἶνος ἀπόλλυται καὶ οἱ ἀσκοί ("and the wine is ruined and the wineskins"). In Mark, both the wine and the wineskins are "destroyed"; in Matthew the wine is "poured out," and the wineskins are "destroyed." Since the wine, technically, is not "destroyed" but spilled—and thereby lost due to the destruction of the wineskins—Matthew's reading is *more precise*. Given Matthew's better and smoother wording, it would be *difficult* to understand why Mark would change this wording into more difficult wording if Mark used Matthew as his source.

Matthew then *makes explicit* Mark's understood verb by inserting βάλλουσιν ("puts"). Καὶ ἀμφότεροι συντηροῦνται ("and both are preserved") is present in Matthew but not found in Mark. This is a *typical Matthean theme*, namely, the fulfillment of the old in the new, rather than Mark's replacement of the old by the new.[74] Text-critically, though, it is just as likely that Matthew, because of his thematic preferences, added this clause as it is that Mark deleted it, since it is not one of his themes.

Mark 2:23–28 (Matt. 12:1–8): Plucking Grain on the Sabbath[75]

Mark 2:23. Mark's καὶ οἱ μαθηταὶ αὐτοῦ ἤρξαντο ὁδὸν ποιεῖν τίλλοντες τοὺς στάχυας ("and the disciples of him began to make [their] way picking the heads of grain") is *more difficult* and more easily *misunderstood* than Matthew's οἱ δὲ μαθηταὶ αὐτοῦ ἐπείνασαν καὶ ἤρξαντο τίλλειν στάχυας καὶ ἐσθίειν ("and ~ the disciples of him hungered and they began to pick [the]

---

74. So, C. H. Turner, *Mark*, 19, and Johnson, *Griesbach Hypothesis*, 45–46.

75. Mann, *Mark*, 237, says that Mark's text in this pericope is "a very good example of the conflation methods of the evangelist. All the essential elements are present, but the colorful details of Matthew and Luke are absent." He does not, though, give further definition of what is "essential" or "colorful." For example, is Matthew 12:5–7 deleted by Mark because it is deemed "colorful" rather than "essential"? Is not Luke's ψώχοντες ταῖς χερσίν "essential" since it indicates that the reaping was done by hand, which *was* allowed by the law (Deut. 23:25), whereas reaping with an instrument was *not* allowed? See Snodgrass, *Parable of the Wicked Tenants*, 55–71, for an argument for Matthean priority. See Shin, *Textual Criticism and the Synoptic Problem*, 221–40, for an examination of this pericope. He concludes (ibid., 264) that 18 of the 42 differences that are evidenced between Matthew and Mark support the priority of Mark. Matthew has zero evidence for priority in the pericope.

heads of wheat and to eat").[76] Mark's ambiguous "began to make a way plucking the grain" is *much clearer* in Matthew's text.[77] Recall from the text-critical study that some scholars think that the disciples were making a road for the coming king.[78] With Matthew's precise wording, no misunderstanding is possible. They were plucking and eating the grain because "they were hungry."

Mark 2:24. Matthew includes ἰδόντες ("seeing [this]"), which is a *clearer* reading than in Mark because it gives the precise reason why the Pharisees said these things, namely, because they witnessed the disciples' behavior. In addition, if Mark were later than Matthew, he would have had no reason to delete this word since he uses it 5x elsewhere in his gospel.[79] Mark's ἴδε ("look") is found in Matthew as the *more typically Matthean* ἰδού ("behold"). It is more probable that Mark is original here given the data on their respective word choices. Mark uses ἴδε 9x and ἰδού 7x. He thus has no real preference. Matthew, on the other hand, uses ἴδε only 4x and ἰδού 62x. It is much more probable that Matthew would have changed Mark's original ἴδε to his more typical ἰδού than for Mark to have changed Matthew's ἰδού to ἴδε.[80] Matthew's οἱ μαθηταί σου ("the disciples of you") *makes the subject clearer* than Mark's impersonal verb. Matthew's text also contains the infinitive ποιεῖν ("to do, make"), which *makes the object of* ἔξεστιν ("is permitted") *clearer.*

Mark 2:26. Mark's *problematic* ἐπὶ Ἀβιαθὰρ ἀρχιερέως ("during [the days of] Abiathar [the] high priest") is certainly the *more difficult reading.* The absence of it in Matthew is perhaps an *orthodox improvement.* Recall that, depending upon the interpretation of ἐπί, this phrase could be seen as a historical error since Abiathar was not the high priest when David entered the house of God to eat the bread of the presence.[81]

---

76. Mann, *Mark,* 237, makes the concessive declaration that "the manuscript evidence is in confusion—evidence of the difficulty experienced by copyists with Mark's style." We must ask Mann, though, why Mark changed Matthew and Luke's easier text to a *more difficult* text? Hawkins, *Horae Synopticae,* 122, includes this verse in his list of seventeen passages that "might cause offence or difficulty."

77. So, Shin, *Textual Criticism and the Synoptic Problem,* 248.

78. See footnote 36 in chapter 3 on Mark 2:23.

79. So, Shin, *Textual Criticism and the Synoptic Problem,* 250.

80. Davies and Allison, *Matthew,* 2:306, note similar changes at 12:49 (Mark 3:34) and 24:23 (Mark 13:21).

81. McNeile, *Matthew,* 168, suggests that the phrase ἐπὶ Ἀβιαθὰρ ἀρχιερέως "was perhaps a later erroneous gloss in Mark." He is followed by Bundy, *Jesus and the First Three Gospels,* 178. No evidence for this claim, though, has been found.

Talbert and McKnight, "Can the Griesbach Hypothesis Be Falsified?" 355–56, list evidence that Mark was prior. One piece of evidence "consists of the agreement of Matthew and Luke in their omission of the phrase ἐπὶ Ἀβιαθὰρ ἀρχιερέως in Mark 2:26. Inclusion of this phrase is a Marcan error since at that time, according to 1 Samuel 21:1; 22:20, Abiathar's father, Ahimelech, held office."

Matthew's singular verb εἰσῆλθεν ("he entered") followed by a plural ἔφαγον ("ate") is grammatically odd. Perhaps the clue to Matthew's numerical change can be found in the previous verse, καὶ οἱ μετ᾽ αὐτοῦ ("and the ones with him"). This text implies that David (singular) entered the house of God, passed out the bread of the presence to those with him, and they (plural) all ate. Matthew also has the plural τοὺς ἄρτους τῆς προθέσεως ("the bread[s] of the presentation") followed by a singular relative pronoun, ὅ. While it is certainly grammatically permissible to refer to a plural with a singular relative pronoun, Mark has a more *grammatically refined* consistency: the singular εἰσῆλθεν ("he entered") is followed by the singular ἔφαγεν ("ate"), while the plural τοὺς ἄρτους τῆς προθέσεως ("the loaves of the presentation") is followed by the plural relative pronoun οὓς ("which"). Matthew also contains the superfluous ὃ οὐκ ἐξὸν ἦν αὐτῷ φαγεῖν οὐδὲ τοῖς μετ᾽ αὐτοῦ ("which was ~ not permissible for him to eat nor for the ones with him"), in comparison to Mark's more compact οὓς οὐκ ἔξεστιν φαγεῖν ("which is not permitted to be eaten"). One could say that Mark has *eliminated* Matthew's *redundancy* here. According to text-critical principles, these changes point to Matthean priority.

Matthew's dative τοῖς ἱερεῦσιν μόνοις ("for the priests alone") following Mark's ἔξεστιν φαγεῖν εἰ μὴ ("it is not permissible to eat except") is *more grammatically refined* than Mark's accusative τοὺς ἱερεῖς ("by the priests") since normally ἔξεστιν takes the dative case.[82] The end of Mark 2:26, καὶ ἔδωκεν καὶ τοῖς σὺν αὐτῷ οὖσιν ("and he gave [some] also to the ones with him being") is not found in Matthew's text. Matthew's text is *less redundant* since it is already clear from verse 25 (Matt. 12:3) that David's men also ate the bread of the presence.

Buchanan, however, in "Has the Griesbach Hypothesis Been Falsified?" 562, replied to Talbert, "The suggestion that Matthew and Luke have omitted the reference to Abiathar because Ahimelech was really the priest in charge is not certain. According to the LXX, well known to all three Evangelists, the priest who gave David the Bread of the Presence was Abiathar. It is not likely that either Matthew or Luke would have omitted the LXX account just because it did not agree with the MT." Buchanan seems to have satisfactorily answered the problem.

Unfortunately for Matthean priorists, that was not the end of the story. Morgan, "When Abiathar Was High Priest," 409, examined available LXX versions for Buchanan's claim that the evangelists read "Abiathar" in their LXX text. She could find no LXX version with this reading, not even in variant readings. She concluded, "This investigation reveals emphatically that no text of the LXX reads 'Abiathar' in 1 Kgdms 21:1(2) or 21:6(7)." "Matthew (12:4) and Luke (6:4) . . . simply corrected the error by omission."

82. Davies and Allison, *Matthew*, 2:310. Swete, *Mark*, 49, says this is a change to the more usual style, namely the dative case after ἔξεστιν. Cf. footnote number 38 in chapter 3.

Matthew also contains another illustration between Mark 2:26 and 2:27, ἢ οὐκ ἀνέγνωτε ἐν τῷ νόμῳ ὅτι τοῖς σάββασιν οἱ ἱερεῖς ἐν τῷ ἱερῷ τὸ σάββατον βεβηλοῦσιν καὶ ἀναίτιοί εἰσιν; λέγω δὲ ὑμῖν ὅτι τοῦ ἱεροῦ μεῖζόν ἐστιν ὧδε. εἰ δὲ ἐγνώκειτε τί ἐστιν· ἔλεος θέλω καὶ οὐ θυσίαν, οὐκ ἂν κατεδικάσατε τοὺς ἀναιτίους ("or have you not read in the law that on the sabbaths the priests in the temple the sabbath desecrate and innocent are? But ~ I say to you that the temple [something] greater than is here. But if you had known what this means, 'I desire ~ mercy and not sacrifice' you would not have condemned the innocent"). Most of this text *contains typical Matthean theological themes,* including the "one greater than . . . is here."[83] No text-critical conclusions, though, can be made since it is just as plausible that Matthew added this text to Mark as it is that Mark deleted this text from Matthew.[84]

Mark 2:27. Matthew does not have a parallel to this verse, possibly because it takes the emphasis away from Jesus, which emphasis is the *Matthean goal* in this pericope, as seen in the insertion of Matthew 12:5–7. Mark's reading is also the *more difficult* reading given its apparent awkwardness with the next verse.[85]

---

83. See, for example, Matthew 12:6, 41, and 42, where Jesus is said to be greater than the temple, Jonah, and Solomon.

84. So, Shin, *Textual Criticism and the Synoptic Problem,* 262.

85. Manson, "Mark ii. 27f," 138, states, "Verse 28 does not seem to flow very naturally from the premise laid down in verse 27." Beare, "The Sabbath Was Made for Man?" 134, says, "It is not hard to see why the two later evangelists have eliminated the saying: 'The sabbath was made for man, not man for the sabbath.' As it stands in the Greek text of Mark which was before them, they could hardly fail to take it as affirming that man is the measure of all things, and that the observance of God's law is to be subordinated to the passing needs of the individual." Beare thinks that "man" in verse 27 and "Son of man" in verse 28 are both translations of the one phrase *bar nasha.* Davies and Allison, *Matthew,* 2:315, though, think that the phrase was eliminated from Matthew for the simple reason that it "stands in tension with the Christological conclusion in the next verse: the Son of man, not man in general, is Lord of the sabbath." Cf. Hübner, *Das Gesetz in der synoptischen Tradition,* 120–21, who says that Mark 2:27 was added in a later addition of Mark and was not included in the Q parallel. Aichinger, "Quellenkritische Untersuchung der Perikope vom Ährenraufen am Sabbat," 128, concludes, "Es ist möglich, wie G. Barth andeutet, daß Matthew und Luke in ihrer Mark-Vorlage dieses Logion gar nicht gelesen haben." Guelich, *Mark 1–8:26,* 1:126, has a different explanation for why Matthew may have deleted Mark 2:27 based on the meaning of "Son of Man" in 2:28 and "man" in 2:27: "If, however, Son of man (ὁ υἱὸς τοῦ ἀνθρώπου) literally renders the Aramaic (בר נשא) behind 2:28 and "man" (ἄνθρωπος) literally renders an Aramaic expression behind 2:27, we would have the possibility of a wordplay in Aramaic not unlike Psalm 8:4 (i.e., "man"/"son of man."). "The play on words is lost in Greek, which may help explain why Matthew 12 and Luke 6 have dropped 2:27."

Riley, *Making of Mark,* 30–31, makes the confusing statement that, although Mark's text "has been a problem for the commentators, both as regards its precise meaning and with regard to its coherence with the words that follow," and although it "obscures the logic of the story as Matthew and Luke have presented it," he still claims that Mark has inserted this text into his sources (i.e., Matt. and Luke). Such contradictory logic defies understanding.

Mark 4:1–9 (Matt. 13:1–9): The Parable of the Sower[86]

Mark 4:1. Although both Matthew and Mark place the parable of the sower after the pericope concerning Jesus' "true kindred," they begin this parable slightly differently. Mark gives a generic introduction, καὶ πάλιν ἤρξατο διδάσκειν ("and again he began to teach"), while Matthew *makes it explicit* that this parable occurred on the same day as the preceding pericope, ἐν τῇ ἡμέρᾳ ἐκείνῃ ἐξελθὼν ὁ Ἰησοῦς τῆς οἰκίας ("on—that day having gone out—Jesus of the house").[87] Mark contains a *historical present*, συνάγεται ("gathers together"), where Matthew has an aorist, συνήχθησαν ("gathered together"). No conclusive text-critical decisions can be made.[88] Matthew's reading, which does not contain Mark's ἐν τῇ θαλάσσῃ ("in the lake"), is *less redundant* since it is obvious that Jesus was on the sea given that he was in a boat.[89]

Mark 4:2. Matthew's πᾶς ὁ ὄχλος ἐπὶ τὸν αἰγιαλὸν εἱστήκει ("the ~ entire crowd along the shore stood") is a *less awkward expression* than Mark's πᾶς ὁ ὄχλος πρὸς τὴν θάλασσαν ἐπὶ τῆς γῆς ἦσαν ("all the crowd near the lake on the land were"). We see that Matthew has the same type of reading that may be found in Mark's textual apparatus, as scribes attempted to improve Mark's awkwardness.[90] It is *more difficult,* if not nearly impossible, to suggest that Mark changed Matthew's "standing on the beach" to the *obtuse and redundant* "they were alongside the sea upon the land." Obviously they were "upon the land" if they were "alongside the sea." While Mark reads that Jesus ἐδίδασκεν ("he was teaching"), Matthew wrote that Jesus ἐλάλησεν ("he told"). This change seems odd given the theological emphasis in Matthew's gospel on Jesus as teacher.[91] In studying every occurrence, however, of διδάσκω ("[I] teach") in passages that are parallel in Matthew and Mark, it is found that Matthew

---

86. Davies and Allison, *Matthew,* 2:373, state, "All of the differences between Matthew 13.1–23 and its Markan parallel can without difficulty be explained in terms of Matthean redaction, as the verse-by-verse analysis shows." Hagner, *Matthew,* 1:367, concludes, "These changes and omissions do not affect the substance of Mark and amount to *improvements of Mark's Greek* and an economy of style." For a detailed exegetical discussion of the redaction-critical changes from a Marcan priority perspective, see Kingsbury, *Parables of Jesus in Matthew 13.*

87. Schweizer, *Matthew,* 296, makes the insightful comment that Matthew shows his dependency on Mark here in that he has Jesus departing the house in 4:1, even though Matthew never recorded Jesus' entry into the house (which Mark recorded at 3:20–21).

88. See the data concerning the use of historical presents in footnote 42 above on Mark 2:5.

89. C. H. Turner, *Mark,* 24, says, "It is not surprising that neither Matthew nor Luke retain this naive description of Mark's."

90. See the scribal changes above in chapter 3.

91. Recall that France titled his book on Matthean theology *Matthew: Evangelist and Teacher.*

seldom uses διδάσκω ("[I] teach") in these parallel readings.[92] Since, however, "the verb 'taught' (ἐδίδασκεν) as well as the noun διδαχή, 'teaching' (both in v. 2), [are] perhaps less appropriate for parables than for the interpretation of the law,"[93] Mark's reading would be *more difficult*.

Mark 4:3. Matthew does not contain the *superfluous* ἀκούετε ("listen"), probably because it is followed by ἰδού ("behold"), another word that would demand attention. Matthew, similar to what is found in Mark's textual apparatus, has τοῦ before the purpose infinitive σπείρειν ("to sow [seeds]"). Matthew also has a present tense infinitive while Mark has an aorist. It is possible that Matthew is emphasizing the present nature of Jesus' sowing.

Mark 4:4. Mark's singular relative pronoun, ὅ ("some"), is found as a plural in Matthew, ἅ ("these"). While it can be said that the singular is a collective, it is probably *more grammatically refined* to use the plural here since there was obviously more than one seed.[94] Mark's *paratactic* καὶ ἦλθεν ("and came") is subordinated in Matthew, as an adverbial participle, καὶ ἐλθόντα ("and having come"). This *"stylistic improvement"* emphasizes κατέφαγεν ("devoured"), where the attention should be focused.[95]

Mark 4:5. Matthew's plural ἄλλα ("others") and τὰ πετρώδη ("the rocky places") have *more parallelism* with the precise wording found in the interpretation of this parable (found in Matt. 13:20; Mark 4:16) than does Mark's singular ἄλλο ("other") and τὸ πετρῶδες ("the rocky place"). Mark's typical εὐθύς ("immediately") is found in Matthew as his *typical* εὐθέως ("immediately").[96]

Mark 4:6. The only difference in this verse and Matthew 13:6 is an insignificant stylistic difference between Mark's subordinate clause, καὶ ὅτε ἀνέτειλεν ὁ ἥλιος ("and when rose the sun"), and Matthew's genitive absolute construction,

---

92. Matthew uses διδάσκω in parallels to Mark 6:2, 6; 14:49 but uses a different word or does not have a parallel at Mark 4:1, 2; 6:34; 8:31; 9:31; 10:1; 11:17; and 12:35. If it is assumed that Matthew is original, we find that Mark retains Matthew's διδάσκω at Matthew 7:29; 9:35; 13:54; 22:16; and 26:55; and changes the word at 4:23 and 21:23. Thus, one cannot make any conclusions concerning originality based upon διδάσκω word usage.

93. Hagner, *Matthew*, 1:368, followed by Dupont, "Le Point de Vue de Matthieu dans le Chapitre des Paraboles," 233. Carson, "Matthew," 301, cites, but disagrees with, Kingsbury, *Parables of Jesus in Matthew 13*, 28–31, who "holds that the change from 'taught' to 'told' owes everything to the structure of Matthew's Gospel. After Matthew 12 Jesus never teaches or preaches to the Jews." See also Sabourin, *Matthew*, 2:637; and Rist, *Independence of Matthew and Mark*, 41, who says that the phrase "in his teaching" is "clumsy and unnecessary in Mark."

94. We will see that Matthew uses the plural in a *consistent style*, whereas Mark switches arbitrarily from singular to plural. Gundry, *Matthew*, 253, says "Mark refers to the seed in the singular till he comes to the seed that falls on good soil. This inconsistency looks original." Kingsbury, *Parables of Jesus in Matthew 13*, 33, says that Matthew prefers "the plural with its connotation of plenty."

95. So, McNeile, *Matthew*, 187.

96. See above on Mark 1:42 for data on usage of these two terms.

ἡλίου δὲ ἀνατείλαντος ("and ~ [the] sun having arisen"). The genitive absolute is a more *typical Matthean style*.[97] On the other hand, Matthew may be seen
as a more *grammatically refined* reading since the genitive absolute construction
lessens the emphasis on the sun and places more emphasis on the seed, which,
after all, is the emphasis in this parable.

Mark 4:7. Besides the singular/plural differences (see above), Mark's preposition in εἰς τὰς ἀκάνθας ("into the thorn bushes") occurs in Matthew as ἐπὶ
τὰς ἀκάνθας ("among the thorn bushes"), perhaps due to *assimilation* with
the parallel construction in Matthew 13:5 (Mark 4:5).

Matthew does not have a parallel for the end of the verse in Mark, καὶ καρπὸν
οὐκ ἔδωκεν ("and fruit it did not give").[98] Matthew's text, perhaps, is *less redundant* since it is already obvious that if the thorn plants choked the seeds they
could not produce any fruit.

Mark 4:8. Mark's ἀναβαίνοντα καὶ αὐξανόμενα καὶ ἔφερεν ("rising up
and growing and it was bearing") is *redundant* since it is already obvious from
ἐδίδου καρπόν ("it was giving fruit") that the seed is growing and producing
fruit.[99] Matthew has the opposite order in his text concerning the amount of fruit
produced, going from one hundred to sixty to thirty, rather than Mark's thirty
to sixty to one hundred. No text-critical conclusions can be drawn. Matthew's
ὃ μέν . . . ὃ δέ . . . ὃ δέ ("the one . . . the other . . . the other") "is simpler and
more literary" than Mark's ἕν . . . καὶ ἕν . . . καὶ ἕν ("one . . . and one . . .
and one").[100]

Mark 4:9. Matthew's version reads ὁ ἔχων ὦτα ἀκουέτω ("the one having
ears let that one hear"), which is his *typical Matthean style*, whereas Mark reads
ὃς ἔχει ὦτα ἀκούειν ἀκουέτω ("who has ears to hear let him hear"). Since
Matthew uses this same construction 3x, it is text-critically more likely that he
has introduced a *unified style* onto Mark's various formulas than to conclude that
Mark has changed Matthew's unified expressions into various formulas.[101]

---

97. So, Gundry, *Matthew*, 253.
98. McNeile, *Matthew*, 188, suggests that καὶ καρπὸν οὐκ ἔδωκεν was a "gloss later than Matthew
    and Luke" that was added to Mark. He does not, though, give any evidence for this conclusion.
99. So, Davies and Allison, *Matthew*, 2:384, who calls these participles "redundant and awkward."
100. So, Gundry, *Matthew*, 254.
101. Matthew uses this identical formula in 11:15; 13:9; and 13:43, whereas Mark uses a slightly different
    wording in his two uses: Mark 4:9: ὃς ἔχει ὦτα ἀκούειν ἀκουέτω; Mark 4:23: εἴ τις ἔχει ὦτα
    ἀκούειν ἀκουέτω.

Mark 4:10–12 (Matt. 13:10–17): The Reason for Speaking in Parables[102]

Mark 4:10. Matthew and Mark differ almost entirely in this verse. Matthew's text is written using his *typical vocabulary*.[103] Matthew's οἱ μαθηταὶ ("the disciples") is much *clearer* than Mark's *awkward* οἱ περὶ αὐτὸν σὺν τοῖς δώδεκα ("the ones around him with the twelve").[104] This difference in wording resulted in a *clearer and more precise* text in that Matthew states exactly who receives the mysteries; it is not merely those who are "around Jesus," but those who are followers of Jesus, that is, "disciples." This precision *eliminates the possible misunderstanding* that, for example, the Pharisees might receive the mysteries because they were physically around Jesus. On the other hand, as mentioned in the textual criticism study, this difference might have been made in order to expand the giving of the mysteries to other than just those who were living in Jesus' day. Thus, it is possible that this is an *improvement by the later Christian community,* who continued to receive the "mysteries" of the kingdom.

The wording of the question in Mark is *obtuse* and is the *more difficult* reading, ἠρώτων αὐτὸν … τὰς παραβολάς ("were asking him … the [meaning of the] parables"). It is difficult to know exactly how the accusative παραβολάς ("parables") functions grammatically. Matthew's text, however, διὰ τί ἐν παραβολαῖς λαλεῖς αὐτοῖς ("why in parables are you speaking to them"), does not contain this grammatical difficulty since παραβολαῖς ("parables") is now the object of a preposition.[105]

Mark 4:11.[106] Since Matthew has the disciples asking a question in the previous

---

102. Hagner, *Matthew,* 1:371, concludes that Matthew is dependent on Mark but also uses a variety of sources in the composition of this pericope.

103. Davies and Allison, *Matthew,* 2:387, list προσέρχομαι (51x to Mark's 5x), διὰ τί, and λαλέω.

104. Carlston, *Parables of the Triple Tradition,* 4, says this Matthean change is "the obvious way to simplify Mark's complex expression." Cf. Harrington, *Matthew,* 1:195.

105. C. A. Evans, *To See and Not Perceive,* 108, says that "Matthew sensed the awkwardness of Mark's text, and has attempted to smooth it out."

106. Ambrozic, *Hidden Kingdom,* 86–92, thinks that the Matthean version of this verse may be prior to Mark's because Mark's account admits "understanding" on the part of the disciples, which is not admitted anywhere else in Mark's Gospel. Thus, he argues, Mark must be dependent on Matthew here. Yet, contrary to Ambrozic, Mark's text does not follow Matthew's in retaining γνῶναι. Thus, Mark does *not* say that the disciples "know" or "understand." He says only that the "mysteries have been given" to them. In fact, the remainder of the pericope makes it clear that the disciples do *not* understand, especially in Mark 4:13: καὶ λέγει αὐτοῖς· οὐκ οἴδατε τὴν παραβολὴν ταύτην, καὶ πῶς πάσας τὰς παραβολὰς γνώσεσθε. It seems that Matthew is dependent on Mark and has inserted γνῶναι in order to emphasize his typical theme of understanding on the part of the disciples (cf. the similar changes in Matt. 10:26 and Mark 4:22; Matt. 12:7 and Mark 2:23–28; Matt. 16:3 and Mark 8:11–12). Cf. Wilkins, *Following the Master,* 180. Gundry, *Matthew,* 255–57, replies to Ambrozic. Cf. Luz, "Disciples in the Gospel," 102–5; and Dupont, "Le Point de Vue de Matthieu dans le Chapitre des Paraboles," 245.

verse, he begins with ὁ δὲ ἀποκριθεὶς εἶπεν αὐτοῖς ("and having answered he said to them") rather than Mark's more general reading, καὶ ἔλεγεν αὐτοῖς ("and he was saying to them"). Matthew includes a causal ὅτι ("because"), which serves to *make clearer* the causal relationship between the two clauses. Mark's typical τῆς βασιλείας τοῦ θεοῦ ("the kingdom of God") is found in Matthew as his *typically Matthean* τῆς βασιλείας τῶν οὐρανῶν ("of the kingdom of the heavens").[107] Matthew (ἐκείνοις δὲ οὐ δέδοται, "but ~ to those it has not been granted") has a different account at the end of this verse in comparison to Mark's ἐκείνοις δὲ τοῖς ἔξω ἐν παραβολαῖς τὰ πάντα γίνεται ("but ~ to those—outside in parables—everything comes"). This difference may have been written by Matthew to avoid the *possible misunderstanding* that "those out-side" are merely those who are not physically present (see discussion above on Mark 4:10).[108] Matthew also includes a verse that is paralleled later in Mark 4:25 (Matt. 13:12). Is it more likely that Matthew moved this verse forward from the location of Mark 4:25 or that Mark moved this verse backward from Matthew 13:12? Since the overall theme of Mark 4:10–12 (Matt. 13:10–17) is to give the reason for speaking in parables, it seems more likely that Matthew has moved this verse forward due to the thematic ties between these two verses, since Matthew 13:12 (Mark 4:25) is also about the reason that Jesus speaks in parables. Thus, it appears that Mark's text is the *source variant*.

Mark 4:12. Mark 4:12 appears to be an allusion to Isaiah 6:9. Matthew's parallel (13:13) is shorter, but he also quotes nearly the entirety of Isaiah 6:9–10 in Matthew 13:14–15.[109] As New says, it is more probable that Mark is original here because he only alludes to Isaiah 6:9–10 in Mark 4:12 and does not follow

---

107. Matthew uses a construction similar to τῆς βασιλείας τῶν οὐρανων 32x, while Mark never uses this construction. Matthew uses a construction similar to τῆς βασιλείας τοῦ θεοῦ 5x to Mark's 14x. No text-critical conclusions can be reached since Matthew may have changed Mark's "God" to avoid using the divine name, or Mark may have changed Matthew's phrase so that his Gentile audi-ence would understand it.

108. Cerfaux, "La Connaissance des Secrets du Royaume D'Apres Matt. XIII.11 et Parallèles," 242, states, "Nous nous demandons si on ne retrouverait pas la vraie phrase primitive en combinant Matthieu et Luc et en lisant: τοῖς δὲ λοιποῖς οὐ δέδοται." McNeile, *Matthew,* 189, suggests that "it is possible that Mark's semi-technical τοῖς ἔξω . . . for which Matthew has ἐκείνοις . . . is a later touch." He does not, though, cite any reasons for this conclusion. See also D. Wenham, "The Synoptic Problem Revisited," 17–20, 28, for various suggestions that Mark may be dependent on another source, perhaps Matthew.

109. Davies and Allison, *Matthew,* 2:394, along with other scholars (see 2:394 n. 80), think that Matthew 13:14–15 was not in the original Matthew but was a very early post-Matthean interpolation. For a defense of the originality of the verses, see Gundry, *Use of the Old Testament,* 116–18. Cerfaux, "La Connaissance des Secrets du Royaume D'Apres Matt. XIII.11 et Parallèles," 248, thinks that Matthew's version points to "une rédaction antérieure qui serait à la source des deux" [i.e., Matt. and Mark].

Matthew's direct quotation of these verses.[110] Matthew *makes the text more explicit* by quoting the entirety of the allusion. Mark's ἵνα ("in order that") and μήποτε ("lest") clauses are much *more difficult* than Matthew's ὅτι ("for") clause because Mark implies that it was Jesus' purpose to dumbfound "those outside."[111]

Mark 4:13–20 (Matt. 13:18–23): Interpretation of the Parable of the Sower[112]

Mark 4:13. The only words Matthew and Mark have in common in this verse are τὴν παραβολήν ("the parable"). The remainder of v. 13 gives the reason Jesus is explaining the meaning of this parable to the disciples, namely, because even they do not understand it, οὐκ οἴδατε τὴν παραβολὴν ταύτην ("do you not know [the meaning of]—this ~ parable"). As a result of their failure to understand, Jesus further explains its meaning in the remainder of the pericope, Mark 4:14–20 (Matt. 13:19–23). Matthew, though, does not contain this information concerning the lack of understanding on the part of the disciples due to *Matthean theological emphases.*[113] This absence may have been because of a desire

---

110. New, *Old Testament Quotations,* 110. For a more cautious view of such changes, see Cope, "Review of *Old Testament Quotations in the Synoptic Gospels,*" 516–17.

111. For a discussion of the various interpretations of the difficult ἵνα clause, see Guelich, *Mark 1–8:26,* 1:209–15. Mann, *Mark,* 264, after surveying three options for lessening the difficulty of the ἵνα clause, admits that "no suggestion adequately mitigates the force of the Markan saying." It is precisely because of this difficult reading that the majority of scholars believe that Mark was the original reading. M. Black, *Aramaic Approach to the Gospels and Acts,* 212–14; and Rist, *Independence of Matthew and Mark,* 44, seek to show that the same Aramaic particle lies behind both prepositions. Even if this were true, though, it fails to solve the difficulty of the present Matthew and Mark texts.

112. Hagner, *Matthew,* 1:378, concludes that the various modifications of Mark's text by Matthew "can be explained as resulting from Matthew's customary abbreviation of Mark, improvement of Mark's Greek style, and alterations in keeping with Matthew's special interests." Schweizer, *Matthew,* 210, shows that Matthew condenses Mark's miracle stories by about 55 percent, controversy narratives by 20 percent, and Christological narratives by 10 percent. D. Wenham, "Interpretation of the Parable of the Sower," 299–319; and idem, "The Synoptic Problem Revisited: 3–38, based on a subjective re-creation of a pre-Marcan source, concludes that both Matthew and Mark are dependent on this source. Wenham is partially followed by Carson, "Matthew," 312.

113. For the argument that Matthew redacts Mark in order to emphasize the "understanding" of the disciples, see Bornkamm, Barth, and Held, *Überlieferung und Auslegung im Matthäusevangelium,* 109–10; and Wilkins, *Following the Master,* 180. C. A. Evans, *To See and Not Perceive,* 113, says, "Matthew is careful (1) to avoid any implication that the disciples are obdurate, or (2) that Jesus' word produces obduracy." Cf. Hawkins, *Horae Synopticae,* 121. Kingsbury, *Parables of Jesus in Matthew 13,* 41, thinks that Matthew 13:10–17 is the best example of Matthew altering Mark's text in order to cast the disciples in a favorable light as the recipients of special insight and revelation. On the other hand, see McKnight, "Role of the Disciples," who concludes that while "Matthew on 17 occasions has made a negative picture [of the disciples] in Mark less negative" (112), "Matthew does not always 'idealize' the disciples. In fact, he occasionally [6x] makes them more blind in his editorial work" (114).

to avoid negative descriptions of the disciples, in essence, an *orthodox improve-ment*. Matthew's own gospel, however, seems to contain a logistical problem in that the reason for Jesus explaining the parable is missing. Matthew here presents Jesus explaining the parable to the disciples; but this seems to contradict Matthew 13:10–17, especially verses 16–17, which implies that the disciples are not hard of hearing and should understand the parables. Yet, they do not understand, and Jesus has to explain it to them. As a result, one could argue that it appears that Mark is improving Matthew by providing explicit information on the disciples' lack of understanding. Mark seems to be making Matthew's gospel flow more easily. On the other hand, we may be reading too much into the text to expect that the disciples should understand the parable without an explanation.[114] No text-critical conclusions can be made.

Mark 4:15. In this verse, Matthew and Mark have very different wording but the same basic content. Matthew contains the explanatory τῆς βασιλείας ("of the kingdom") after τὸν λόγον ("the word"), which *makes it clearer* what the "word" or "seed" symbolizes.[115] Matthew contains a statement concerning those who hear the word, μὴ συνιέντος ("not understanding [it]"), which makes the text *clearer* than Mark's reading concerning the reason that Satan is able to snatch the word away. This statement also thematically links this parable's interpretation with what Jesus said before in this parable and with the later parables in Matthew 13.[116] Matthew uses a more *typical Matthean word*, ὁ πονηρός ("the evil one")

---

114. Davies and Allison, *Matthew*, 2:399, say that it is precisely because the disciples can see and hear that Jesus explains the parable to them. As Gundry, *Mark*, 197, says, Mark only says that the mysteries have been "given" to the disciples; it does not say that an understanding of the parable is given. "'Has been given' instead of the expected 'has been revealed' states privilege but stops short of implying that the disciples understand the mystery and thereby leaves the way open to their non-understanding and Jesus' explanation. Hence, there is no contradiction between Mark 4:11–12 and 13–20." Thus, the apparent "problem" is not really a problem at all. Matthew can delete this information in Mark 4:13 with no problematic gap of information. Guelich agrees, *Mark 1–8:26*, 1:206–7, saying, "This divine disclosure of the 'mystery' came through Jesus' private instruction, his interpretation of the παραβολάς (so 4:14–20; cf. v. 34b), for 'those around him' (v. 10a)." Another explanation, by Carlston, *Parables of the Triple Tradition*, 22–23, that eliminates this apparent problem is the interpretation of the word *understand* as "soteriological (and perhaps also ethical), not primarily intellectual." In this way, the disciples may not intellectually understand, but they do understand the Christian message in a soteriological sense; and thus, may be said to be "understanding."

115. Kingsbury, *Parables of Jesus in Matthew 13*, 53, shows that while Mark's text confuses the referent to the seed (sometimes the Word [Mark 4:14f.] and sometimes the people who hear the word [vv. 15, 16, 18, 20]), Matthew makes changes that consistently make the seed refer to the hearers; *contra* D. Wenham, "Interpretation of the Parable of the Sower," 304.

116. Matthew uses συνίημι only 9x in his Gospel but 6x in this chapter, verses 13, 14, 15, 19, 23, and 51. In passages that are parallel to Matthew, though, Mark uses the word only at 4:12. It is clear that Matthew has *imposed a Matthean theme* onto Mark's text here, namely, that the disciples *do* understand, while the outsiders do not understand. It is much easier to suggest that Matthew has *imposed this unified theme* on Mark's text.

where Mark has ὁ Σατανᾶς ("[the] Satan"). No text-critical conclusions can be drawn from this difference.[117]

Mark 4:16. While Mark has an indicative, λαμβάνουσιν ("receive"), in οἳ ὅταν ἀκούσωσιν τὸν λόγον εὐθὺς μετὰ χαρᾶς λαμβάνουσιν αὐτόν ("who when they hear the word immediately with joy receive it"), Matthew has a participle, λαμβάνων ("receiving it"), in the parallel clause, ὁ τὸν λόγον ἀκούων καὶ εὐθὺς μετὰ χαρᾶς λαμβάνων αὐτόν ("the one the word listening to and immediately with joy receiving it"). This difference may simply be an *assimilation* to the mood of ἀκούων ("listening"). More likely, though, this difference may be called a *grammatical refinement* since it subordinates the "receiving" (participle) so that the "not having roots" (indicative) in the following verse may be properly emphasized.

Mark 4:17. Matthew continues to use plurals where Mark has singulars (although this has no text-critical ramification). The rest of this verse is identical in Matthew and Mark except that both Mark's καί ("and," at the beginning of the verse) and εἶτα ("then," in the middle of the verse) appear in Matthew as δέ ("but"). The latter is *more grammatically refined* since there is a conversive idea between the verses. The latter difference is probably a use of a *more typical Matthean style,* since Matthew normally uses δέ in genitive absolute constructions.[118]

Mark 4:18. While Mark reads καὶ ἄλλοι εἰσὶν οἱ εἰς τὰς ἀκάνθας σπειρόμενοι ("and others are the ones among the thorns being sown"), Matthew has ὁ δὲ εἰς τὰς ἀκάνθας σπαρείς, οὗτός ἐστιν ("and ~ the [seed] among the thorns being sown, this one is"). This is the same formula Matthew uses throughout this pericope (at 13:20, 22, 23—only verse 19 uses a different construction, οὗτός ἐστιν ὁ παρὰ τὴν ὁδὸν σπαρείς, "this one is [like] the [seed] along the path being sown"). Mark, on the other hand, uses a variety of constructions in this pericope: verse 15, οὗτοι δέ εἰσιν οἱ παρὰ τὴν ὁδόν ("and ~ these are the ones beside the road"); verse 16, καὶ οὗτοί εἰσιν οἱ ἐπὶ τὰ πετρώδη σπειρόμενοι ("and these are the ones upon the rocky places being sown"); verse 18, καὶ ἄλλοι εἰσὶν οἱ εἰς τὰς ἀκάνθας σπειρόμενοι ("and others are the ones among the thorns being sown"); verse 20, καὶ ἐκεῖνοί εἰσιν οἱ ἐπὶ τὴν γῆν τὴν καλὴν σπαρέντες ("and those are the ones upon the soil—good having been sown"). Notice that none of Mark's four constructions

---

117. It could be said that Matthew has changed Mark's word to a more Matthean word (Matt. uses πονηρός 26x to Mark's 2x), or it could be said that Mark has made Matthew's ὁ πονηρός more explicit.

118. Matthew has 48 genitive absolute constructions; 29 of them begin with δέ, and none of them begin with εἶτα. Mark, on the other hand, uses δέ and εἶτα only 1x each; he normally uses καί (in 25 of 30 genitive absolute constructions).

are identical. Text-critically, it is more likely that Matthew *imposed a unified style* upon Mark's arbitrary style, rather than vice versa.[119]

Mark 4:19. Matthew does not have a parallel to Mark's καὶ αἱ περὶ τὰ λοιπὰ ἐπιθυμίαι εἰσπορευόμεναι ("and the for the remaining things desires coming in"). Certainly Mark's reading is *more awkward,* especially the difficult περὶ τὰ λοιπά ("for the remaining things").

Mark 4:20. While Mark has παραδέχονται ("receive [it]"), Matthew has συνιείς ("understanding [it]"). It seems that Matthew's reading is a *more refined grammatical construction* since it forms an antithetical *inclusio* with 13:19 (μὴ συνιέντος, "not understanding [it]").

Mark 6:17–29 (Matt. 14:3–12): The Death of John the Baptist[120]

Mark 6:17. Matthew does not contain Mark's slightly *awkward* ἀποστείλας ("having sent"). Mark's reading is *more difficult* considering the absence of an object of this participle. Matthew's reading contains καὶ ἀπέθετο ("and he put [him] away"), which is not present in Mark's text. This phrase *makes it clearer* that Herod had John the Baptist bound before placing him into prison, which brings Matthew's text more into alignment with Josephus's version of this story.[121] Thus, Matthew's text has John arrested, then bound, and then thrown into prison; Mark has John arrested and then bound in prison. Matthew's text does not contain Mark's ὅτι αὐτὴν ἐγάμησεν ("for he married ~ her"). This sentence is *superfluous* since the remainder of the pericope explains the relationship between Herod and Herodias.

Mark 6:18. Matthew has a personal pronoun, αὐτῷ ("to him"), while Mark has a more clear τῷ Ἡρῴδῃ ("to Herod"). No text-critical decision can be made since Matthew may have thought it superfluous to repeat Herod's name

---

119. This is exactly the same type of change found in Mark's textual apparatus on this verse. D. Wenham, "Interpretation of the Parable of the Sower," 301 n. 1, thinks that three of Mark's four constructions are awkward.

120. While Mark has 248 words, Matthew has a mere 138. It is due to such drastic reduction that Matthew, according to Davies and Allison, *Matthew,* 2:463–64, has apparent discrepancies that point to his knowledge of the fuller Marcan text. Cf. Styler, "Priority of Mark," 293–94, and a reply in Orchard and Riley, *Order of the Synoptics,* 100; and Cope, "Argument Revolves," 148–50, who makes the insightful claim that "Matthew's version . . . is more correct grammatically" (149). Although this conclusion leads to Marcan priority based on text-critical criteria, Cope himself argues for Matthean priority by assuming that "Mark's less than sophisticated command of Greek is likely to have led him to stumble at the parenthesis in Matthew."

121. Josephus, *Ant.* 18.119, says that John the Baptist was "brought in chains to Machaerus," a fortress-palace.

again since it is clear that John was speaking to him. Matthew does not contain Mark's *superfluous* ὅτι ("that").

Mark 6:19–20. Matthew has three main differences from Mark's text.[122] First, Matthew makes Herod the one who wants to kill John, not Herodias, as in Mark. Matthew also does not contain Mark's description of Herod's opinion of John: καὶ συνετήρει αὐτόν, καὶ ἀκούσας αὐτοῦ πολλὰ ἠπόρει, καὶ ἡδέως αὐτοῦ ἤκουεν ("and he was protecting him, and having heard him he was disturbed ~ greatly, and [yet] gladly he was listening ~ to him"). Because of these differences, Matthew 14:9 is *more difficult* to understand. Why would Herod be grieved if he was the one who wanted to kill John in the first place? It apparently makes sense only if it is postulated that the Marcan text is behind the Matthean text. In Matthew's abbreviation of the text, he has eliminated Marcan material that he needs in his story for it to make perfect sense.[123] Some suggest that Matthew has *corrected* the story in light of Josephus's account, which states that Herod wanted to kill John.[124] Second, While Mark states that Herod feared John, ἐφοβεῖτο τὸν Ἰωάννην ("[he] feared—John"), Matthew states that the object of Herod's fear was the crowd, ἐφοβήθη τὸν ὄχλον ("he feared the crowd"). This difference brings Matthew 14:5 into *harmonization* with the Jewish leaders' fear of the crowd concerning John the Baptist in Matthew 21:26, and in regard to arresting Jesus in verse 46. Third, Matthew states that John the Baptist was considered a προφήτην ("a prophet"), while Mark referred to John as ἄνδρα δίκαιον καὶ ἅγιον ("a man righteous and holy"). Matthew's text is more in *alignment* with both Matthew and Mark's description of John (Matt. 11:9; 21:26; Mark 11:32: ἐφοβοῦντο τὸν ὄχλον· ἅπαντες γὰρ εἶχον τὸν Ἰωάννην ὄντως ὅτι προφήτης ἦν, "they were afraid of the crowd. For ~ everyone was considering—John really that he was ~ a prophet").

Mark 6:21. In the location of Mark's καὶ γενομένης ἡμέρας εὐκαίρου ὅτε Ἡρῴδης τοῖς γενεσίοις αὐτοῦ δεῖπνον ἐποίησεν ("and having come about a suitable ~ day when Herod on the birthday celebrations of him made ~ a dinner"), Matthew has the *much simpler* and shorter γενεσίοις δὲ γενομένοις τοῦ Ἡρῴδου ("now ~ at the birthday celebration it came about [that]—of Herod"). Mark's text also might be *more difficult* in that he refers to Herod's chance to kill John as εὐκαίρου ("suitable"). It is more likely that Matthew deleted this word

---

122. See Davies and Allison, *Matthew,* 1:107, 2:471; and Gundry, *Matthew,* 286–87.

123. Hill, *Matthew,* 244, says the texts of Mark and Matthew are "contrary" and cannot be harmonized. Gundry, *Matthew,* 287, though, has plausibly suggested that Herod is "grieved" not because he must kill John, but "because he wanted to kill John under better circumstances (cf. v 5)."

124. Josephus, *Ant.* 18.116–119.

than that Mark added it. Matthew does not have a parallel for the remainder of verse 21 concerning who attended the party.[125]

Mark 6:22–23. Matthew's ὠρχήσατο ἡ θυγάτηρ τῆς Ἡρῳδιάδος ἐν τῷ μέσῳ καὶ ἤρεσεν ("danced the daughter of Herodias in the midst [of them] and it pleased") is a *less pleonastic* reading than what we find in Mark, with his καὶ εἰσελθούσης ("and having entered") in καὶ εἰσελθούσης τῆς θυγατρὸς αὐτοῦ Ἡρῳδιάδος καὶ ὀρχησαμένης ἤρεσεν ("and having entered the daughter of him, Herodias, and having danced she pleased"). The name of the girl in Mark is also *more difficult,* τῆς θυγατρὸς αὐτοῦ Ἡρῳδιάδος ("the daughter of him, Herodias"). Matthew's ἡ θυγάτηρ τῆς Ἡρῳδιάδος ("the daughter of Herodias") perfectly *harmonizes* with Mark 6:24, τῇ μητρὶ αὐτῆς ("to the mother of her"), and *eliminates possible historical problems.*[126] Matthew's text does not contain *the unnecessary repetition* of Herod's oath, which is found in Mark, εἶπεν ὁ βασιλεὺς τῷ κορασίῳ· αἴτησόν με ὃ ἐὰν θέλῃς, καὶ δώσω σοι· καὶ ὤμοσεν αὐτῇ [πολλὰ] ὅ τι ἐάν με αἰτήσῃς δώσω σοι ἕως ἡμίσους τῆς βασιλείας μου ("said the king to the young girl, ask me whatever you wish and I will give [it] to you. And he made a promise to her solemnly, whatever you ask ~ me I will give to you up to half of the kingdom of me"). Matthew simply says, ὅθεν μεθ᾽ ὅρκου ὡμολόγησεν αὐτῇ δοῦναι ὃ ἐὰν αἰτήσηται ("and so with an oath he promised to her to give whatever she asked").

Mark 6:24–25. Whereas Mark recites the conversation between the girl and her mother and then recounts the same conversation between the king and the girl, Matthew is *less redundant.* He cites only the conversation between the girl and the king. He refers to the entire former conversation with the word προβιβασθεῖσα ("having been prompted"). The basic content of the request for John the Baptist's head, though, is the same in both Matthew and Mark (Matthew reads, δός μοι, φησίν, ὧδε ἐπὶ πίνακι τὴν κεφαλὴν Ἰωάννου τοῦ βαπτιστοῦ, "give to me she said here upon a platter the head of John the Baptist"), with a few inconsequential differences.

Mark 6:26. Mark uses an intensive, περίλυπος ("very sad"), perhaps because Mark originally said that Herodias wanted John dead and that Herod enjoyed listening to John. Matthew, though, uses a less emphatic λυπηθείς ("grieving"),

---

125. Davies and Allison, *Matthew,* 2:463, see this deletion as evidence that Matthew used Mark as his source, because this information is presupposed in Matthew 14:6–8, even though Matthew himself had not mentioned it.

126. See the discussion of the identity of this girl above in our discussion of Mark 6:22–23 in chapter 3. Marcus, *Mark,* 396, thinks that there are "a number of historical inaccuracies in this passage."

since he earlier said that Herod wanted John the Baptist dead (14:5). Matthew's text could be called the *more difficult* reading since it is a little awkward that Herod is grieved when John is killed. Nevertheless, that Herod had put John into prison shows us that both Matthew and Mark presented a Herod who was not entirely fond of John. So, Matthew's reading is not impossible.

Both Matthew and Mark called Herod ὁ βασιλεὺς ("the king"). This is interesting because Matthew *"correctly"* used the title "tetrarch" at Matthew 14:1, where Mark had called Herod "king." Mark's use of "king" in both places is *more difficult* than Matthew. One might postulate that Matthew was dependent on Mark here at 6:26 and copied Mark's less accurate title for Herod.[127] It is very difficult to understand why Mark would change Matthew's more accurate title for a less accurate title if he were using Matthew as a source.[128] Mark, then, is the *source variant*.

Matthew uses the plural τοὺς ὅρκους ("the promises"), even though he originally used the singular form in 14:7, ὅρκου ("promise"). This plural makes little sense unless one concludes that Matthew is using Mark as his source and copied the plural in this instance.

Mark 6:27.[129] Matthew does not have a parallel for Mark's *more redundant* καὶ εὐθὺς ἀποστείλας ὁ βασιλεὺς σπεκουλάτορα ἐπέταξεν ἐνέγκαι τὴν κεφαλὴν αὐτοῦ ("and immediately having sent the king an executioner he commanded to bring the head of him"). Mark basically repeats this in vv. 27b–28. Matthew has τὸν Ἰωάννην ("John"), where Mark has the personal pronoun αὐτὸν ("him"). While this change makes little difference, it does make the *text a little clearer by making the object explicit.*

Mark 6:28. This verse is almost identical to Matthew 14:11 except that Matthew uses passive voice verb forms (due to the absence of the σπεκουλάτορα,

---

127. So, Davies and Allison, *Matthew,* 2:463, 2:466, and 2:474. Mann, *Mark,* 295, agrees that "tetrarch" is the correct title, but justifies Mark's change from a more correct title to "king" by suggesting that "Mark's use of *king* here may represent local popular usage." He fails, though, to provide any evidence that "king" may have been a local title for Herod. Hooker, *Mark,* 159, reminds us, "It was Herod's request to Rome for the title of king which led to his deposition and banishment." She adds, though, "Mark's mistake may reflect popular usage, which was unconcerned with the niceties of Roman officialdom." Keener, *Matthew,* 398, thinks that Mark may have ironically given Herod the title "king." Cf. Rolland, "La Question Synoptique Demande-t-elle une Réponse Compliquée?" 218–19.

128. So, Tuckett, *Revival of the Griesbach Hypothesis,* 65–66, who says that if Mark were using Matthew as his source, "there is no reason why Mark should alter the concurrent testimony of his sources incorrectly." Hagner, *Matthew,* 2:410, suggests that Matthew changed Mark to "tetrarch" in order to "distinguish him clearly from Herod the Great, who figured so largely in chap. 2."

129. P. Parker, "Posteriority of Mark," 68, lists Mark 6:27 as one of the many examples of Marcan ignorance. He says that John the Baptist was imprisoned in Machaerus (per Josephus, *Ant.* 18.5.2) while the birthday celebration took place in Tiberias in Galilee (v. 21), "a good 100 miles" away.

"executioner" from Mark 6:27) rather than the active voice, as Mark has. In addition, Matthew's text is *less superfluous* because he does not have parallels to Mark's αὐτὴν ("her"), τὸ κοράσιον ("the girl"), and, again, αὐτήν ("her").[130]

Mark 6:29. Matthew's text, καὶ προσελθόντες οἱ μαθηταὶ αὐτοῦ ("and having approached the disciples of him"), is (again) *less redundant* than Mark's καὶ ἀκούσαντες οἱ μαθηταὶ αὐτοῦ ἦλθον ("and having heard [this] the disciples of him came").

Matthew's ἔθαψαν αὐτόν ("buried him") is a *more refined lexical expression* since it is "more precise and descriptive"[131] than Mark's text, ἔθηκαν αὐτὸ ἐν μνημείῳ ("placed it in a tomb"). Matthew contains καὶ ἐλθόντες ἀπήγγειλαν τῷ Ἰησοῦ ("and having come they reported [it] to Jesus") at the end of the verse, which is not paralleled in Mark. This Matthean clause *makes the text flow smoother* into the context of the next verse. Mark, though, has a rather loose connection with the next verse. Even Mann, who holds to Matthean priority, agrees that Mark's text is the *more difficult* here.[132]

Mark 6:32–44 (Matt. 14:13–21): Five Thousand Are Fed

Mark 6:32. After unique introductions, Matthew and Mark are identical, except for the absence of the article in τῷ πλοίῳ ("the boat") in Matthew. Mark's text has a *possible misunderstanding* in that the article could point to one specific boat that Jesus and the disciples used for their travels.[133]

Mark 6:33. Mark's καὶ εἶδον αὐτοὺς ὑπάγοντας καὶ ἐπέγνωσαν ("and saw them going and knew [where they were going]") is a more *awkward expression* than Matthew's simpler καὶ ἀκούσαντες ("and having heard [this]"). The latter is also *more refined* since it is an introductory subordinate clause, rather than Mark's paratactic, pleonastic expression. Mark's generic πολλοί ("many") occurs in Matthew in a *more characteristic Matthean* οἱ ὄχλοι ("the crowds"). Mark's συνέδραμον ἐκεῖ καὶ προῆλθον αὐτούς ("they ran there and they arrived ahead of them") is *more difficult* than Matthew's simple ἠκολούθησαν

---

130. It, again, could be argued in the opposite direction, of course, by saying that Mark is making the text more explicit by adding these words. If this were the case, however, he would have used a proper noun instead of αὐτήν. Also, this is not the type of addition that would make a text clearer.

131. So, Davies and Allison, *Matthew*, 2:475.

132. Mann, *Mark*, 298, says, "We think that Matthew is inherently more plausible."

133. Davies and Allison, *Matthew*, 2:478, indicate that the very fact of Matthew's mentioning the boat at all is an indication that he is dependent on Mark since Matthew's "narrative would seem to have him at Nazareth, which is not a coastal village (cf. 13.53–8)."

αὐτῷ ("[they] followed him"). Recall from the text-critical discussion that it would be more difficult to have the crowds arriving before Jesus since they had to travel around the sea by foot.[134] Notice that Matthew has the crowds "follow," which is a *typical Matthean emphasis*.[135]

Mark 6:34. While Matthew and Mark are identical for the first nine words, they have very different endings. Mark has ὅτι ἦσαν ὡς πρόβατα μὴ ἔχοντα ποιμένα, καὶ ἤρξατο διδάσκειν αὐτοὺς πολλά ("for they were like sheep not having a shepherd, and he began to teach them many things"), while Matthew has καὶ ἐθεράπευσεν τοὺς ἀρρώστους αὐτῶν ("and healed their ~ sick"). Matthew has a similar idea to Mark's text earlier in his gospel, at 9:36, ἰδὼν δὲ τοὺς ὄχλους ἐσπλαγχνίσθη περὶ αὐτῶν, ὅτι ἦσαν ἐσκυλμένοι καὶ ἐρριμμένοι ὡσεὶ πρόβατα μὴ ἔχοντα ποιμένα ("and ~ having seen the crowds he felt sympathy for them, for they were distressed and weary as sheep not having a shepherd").[136] Matthew's ἐθεράπευσεν ("[he] healed") is a *more typical Matthean word* (16x to Mark's 5x).

Mark 6:35. Mark's καὶ ἤδη ὥρας πολλῆς γενομένης ("and already a late hour was coming") is a *grammatically awkward* clause. Matthew has his *more characteristic* ὀψίας δὲ γενομένης ("now ~ [when] evening having come," 6x in Matthew). Matthew does not have a genitive personal pronoun αὐτοῦ ("of him") in connection with the disciples, as Mark does. This may show a later reading (i.e., *a later Christian community change*) since "his disciples" could be referred to later simply as "the disciples."

Mark 6:36. Mark's personal pronoun αὐτούς ("them") is found in Matthew's text as a *clearer* (by making *explicit the object*) *and more stylistically Matthean* τοὺς ὄχλους ("the crowds"). Mark's εἰς τοὺς κύκλῳ ἀγροὺς καὶ κώμας ("to the surrounding farms and villages") is *more pleonastic* than Matthew's εἰς τὰς κώμας ("into the villages").

---

134. This is even more difficult given Mark 6:34 (Matt. 14:14), which implies that Jesus was there alone and only when he "came out" (ἐξελθών) did he see the crowds. If the crowd were there before Jesus, this would not have been the case, especially given the large size of the crowd. Even if it were possible for the crowds to arrive before Jesus and the disciples (so, e.g., Guelich, *Mark 1–8:26*, 1:340, and Swete, *Mark*, 130: "If there was little wind, it would be easy to get to the place before a sailing boat."), Mark is still the more difficult reading. Yes, Jesus and the disciples may have had to travel around a cove that stretched far into the sea while the crowd had merely to run a short distance. But, usually, traveling by boat was faster than traveling by foot, and because of this usual speed, the reading that says the crowds arrived first remains the more difficult reading. Pettem, "Le premier récit de la multiplication des pains et le problème synoptique," 76, though, concludes, "La leçon de Matthieu est un peu difficile"; but he gives little sound reasoning for this conclusion.

135. In Matthew 7x (4:25; 8:1; 12:15; 14:13; 19:2; 20:29; 21:9) to Mark's 1x (5:24). So, Gundry, *Matthew*, 290.

136. See also footnote 92 above for word statistics on Matthew's retention of διδάσκω from Mark.

Mark's τί φάγωσιν ("what they may eat") is found in Matthew as βρώματα ("food"). Mark's text is *more difficult* because he has an interrogative pronoun as the object of the verb, ἀγοράσωσιν ("they may buy"). Matthew's accusative noun is more *grammatically refined* and what one would expect to find here. Text-critically, it would be difficult to explain why Mark would change Matthew's good grammatical expression into a very awkward expression.

Mark 6:37–38. Matthew's text is *clearer* due to his inclusion of the subject, Ἰησοῦς ("Jesus").[137] Matthew's text contains οὐ χρείαν ἔχουσιν ἀπελθεῖν ("they have no need to go out"), which *makes the text clearer* but also may be seen as superfluous. Matthew does not have a parallel to Mark's καὶ λέγουσιν αὐτῷ· ἀπελθόντες ἀγοράσωμεν δηναρίων διακοσίων ἄρτους καὶ δώσομεν αὐτοῖς φαγεῖν; ὁ δὲ λέγει αὐτοῖς· πόσους ἄρτους ἔχετε; ὑπάγετε ἴδετε. καὶ γνόντες λέγουσιν· πέντε, καὶ δύο ἰχθύας ("and they say to him having departed may we buy for two hundred ~ denarii loaves and will we give to them to eat?—and he says to them how many loaves do you have? Go [and] see and having known they say five and two fish").[138] It is difficult to explain this text-critically. Perhaps Mark is *more redundant.* Or, perhaps Matthew could be understood as a *more orthodox* reading since Mark's text implies that Jesus does not have the knowledge of how many loaves the disciples have.[139]

Matthew's text includes a superfluous detail, ὁ δὲ εἶπεν· φέρετέ μοι ὧδε αὐτούς ("but ~ he said bring to me here them"). This is his second addition of superfluous details in this pericope, which seems to contradict Matthew's overall strategy here, namely, shortness. This text may have been included, however, for *theological reasons* since it has Christological emphases, which is a Matthean theme in this pericope.[140]

Mark 6:39–40. Mark's *typical* ἐπέταξεν ("he commanded," 4x in Mark, 0x in Matt) appears in Matthew as a more *typically Matthean* κελεύσας ("having commanded," 0x in Mark, 7x in Matt.), an insignificant *synonym difference.* Mark's less specific personal pronoun αὐτοῖς ("to them") is found in Matthew

---

137. Gundry, *Matthew,* 290, thinks that the insertion of Ἰησοῦς in Matthew is made for "Christological emphasis" (80x to Mark's 12x).

138. See the reply to H. J. Held, "Matthew as Interpreter of the Miracle Stories," in Bornkamm, Barth, and Held, *Überlieferung und Auslegung im Matthäusevangelium,* 181–83. See Carson, "Matthew," 341–42, on the theological meaning of this omission. Gundry, *Matthew,* 292, states that Matthew makes this omission because he wants to portray the disciples as understanding. This, however, extends the Matthean theme of the disciples' understanding too far. Their failure to know the amount of bread they had with them would not be theologically significant.

139. So, Davies and Allison, *Matthew.*

140. See footnote 137 above and 141 and 142 below.

as his *typical Matthean* τοὺς ὄχλους ("the crowds"). Matthew's text is *clearer* in that he names specifically who is to recline. In Mark's text, the αὐτοῖς ("to them") is initially unclear as to whether it is the disciples or the crowds who are to recline. Notice also that Matthew has Jesus himself command the people, rather than his disciples, as in Mark.[141]

While, as seen above, Matthew has included specific details in this pericope that Mark does not have, his more general tendency is to lack specific details that Mark includes. In these two Marcan verses can be seen a few specific details that are not found in the Matthean account: the manner in which the people were divided in 6:39, συμπόσια συμπόσια ("group by group"); all of verse 40, καὶ ἀνέπεσαν πρασιαὶ πρασιαὶ κατὰ ἑκατὸν καὶ κατὰ πεντήκοντα ("and they reclined group by group in hundreds and in fifties"); the color of the grass, χλωρῷ ("green").[142] No text-critical conclusions may be drawn based on the presence or absence of specific details.[143]

Mark 6:41. Two minor differences can be found in the first half of this verse in Matthew and Mark. An *insignificant stylistic difference* occurs where Matthew has the aorist ἔδωκεν ("he gave") while Mark has an imperfect, ἐδίδου ("he was giving"). The end of the verse, though, differs drastically. Mark's telic clause, ἵνα παρατιθῶσιν αὐτοῖς ("in order that they might set before them") occurs in Matthew as a somewhat redundant (although with *typical Matthean words*), οἱ δὲ μαθηταὶ τοῖς ὄχλοις ("and ~ the disciples to the crowds"). Mark's version seems to be more grammatically refined and *less redundant*. Matthew also lacks the reference to the dividing of the fish. Given that the early church probably saw this miracle of Jesus as symbolic of the later Lord's Supper (cf. John 6), it seems more likely that Mark is the *source variant* in this instance because it is more likely that Matthew omitted the reference to the fish than that Mark added the reference to the fish.[144]

Mark 6:43. It was seen in the previous chapter that scribes improved Mark's *awkward expression* concerning the baskets, ἦραν κλάσματα δώδεκα κοφίνων

---

141. This may be an assimilation to Jesus' directions to the crowds in Matthew 15:35 and Mark 8:6, and is a *Christological emphasis*.

142. Gundry, *Matthew*, 294, thinks that this omission would "further concentrate attention on Jesus as the host at this Lord's Supper."

143. The Synoptic Problem literature offers many reasons for these differences in the amount of details in Matthew and Mark: Matthew may be omitting details in order to save room for his special material, or Mark may be adding details to Matthew's incomplete account based on specific Petrine information.

144. The opposite could, of course, be said—that Mark has added the reference to the fish to make the text more historically accurate.

πληρώματα ("they picked up fragments twelve full ~ baskets"). Matthew's text, ἦραν τὸ περισσεῦον τῶν κλασμάτων δώδεκα κοφίνους πλήρεις ("they carried up the leftovers of the fragments twelve baskets full"), has the same types of differences.[145] Matthew *makes it clear* that there are twelve baskets full of fragments of bread; Mark's grammar can lead to different interpretations.[146] Matthew again (cf. Mark 6:41) lacks the reference to the fish, which may be a *later Christian community change.*[147]

Mark 6:44. Matthew lacks the reference to τοὺς ἄρτους ("the loaves"), which is a bracketed reading in Mark.[148] Matthew's reading might *eliminate a slight problem* since the crowd ate bread and fish. Matthew contains χωρὶς γυναικῶν καὶ παιδίων ("apart from [the] women and children") after ἄνδρες ὡσεὶ πεντακισχίλιοι ("men about five thousand"), which makes the text *more explicit* by stating that this count did not include the women and children.

Mark 6:45–52 (Matt. 14:22–33): Walking on the Water[149]

Mark 6:45. Mark's εὐθύς ("immediately") is found in Matthew in his *more typical* εὐθέως ("immediately"). Here, too, is another *absence of the personal pronoun,* αὐτοῦ ("of him"), with τοὺς μαθητάς ("the disciples," cf. Mark 6:41), possibly a *later Christian community change.* Matthew's text lacks πρὸς Βηθσαϊδάν ("to Bethsaida"), which could be seen as a *correction of a possible geographical problem* in light of the parallel in Luke 9:10.[150] Mark's ἕως αὐτὸς ἀπολύει τὸν ὄχλον ("until he dismisses the crowd") occurs in Matthew as his *typical style,* ἕως οὗ ἀπολύσῃ τοὺς ὄχλους ("until he might send away the

---

145. Gundry, *Matthew,* 294, thinks the insertion of τὸ περισσεῦον suggests the "inexhaustibility of supply. The bread of the Lord's Supper will never run out. All nations may come and eat."

146. Grammatically, one could translate Mark's clause as the awkward "they took up fragments full of twelve baskets."

147. Davies and Allison, *Matthew,* 2:492, suggest that the deletion of the references to fish are made because fish are not present in 26:26–29, the account of the Last Supper.

148. Wheeler, *Textual Criticism and the Synoptic Problem,* 157, concludes that τοὺς ἄρτους "is to be read in Mark."

149. A good text-critical discussion of the Matthean text is available in Sibinga, "Matthew 14:22–33—Text and Composition," 156–57, who gives six reasons why Matthew is later to and based upon Mark in this passage.

150. So, McKnight, "Role of the Disciples," 157. Recall from the text-critical study in this current volume that, according to Luke 9:10, the feeding of the five thousand took place in Bethsaida. How, then, could Jesus and the disciples now be going "to the other side" of the sea "to Bethsaida?" Further, according to Mark 6:53 (Matt. 14:34), the boat lands in Gennesaret. See the discussion of the location of the miracle in Sabourin, *Matthew,* 2:638–40. Riley, *Making of Mark,* 81, admits that the Marcan geography here is "confusing," and his arguments for Marcan posteriority are weak.

crowds"). Matthew uses a *more uniform style* than Mark's arbitrary style, ἕως οὗ ("until"). This arbitrary style suggests that Mark is prior.[151]

Mark 6:46. Matthew uses a *more common* ἀπολύσας ("having sent away") (Matthew: 19x; Mark: 12x) where Mark uses the *hapax legomenon* ἀποταξά-μενος ("having said farewell"). If Matthew were original, it is doubtful that Mark would have changed this common word, given that scribes generally changed to more common words and that Mark and Matthew both use the same word in eleven other passages. Matthew, again, uses his *typical style,* τοὺς ὄχλους ("the crowds," cf. Mark 6:36, 40), where Mark has a personal pronoun αὐτοῖς ("to them"). In place of Mark's ἀπῆλθεν εἰς τὸ ὄρος ("he departed to the mountain"), Matthew uses a *more refined and precise lexical expression,* ἀνέβη εἰς τὸ ὄρος ("he went up to the mountain"). Matthew's version is more refined since Jesus actually must "go up" the mountain, whereas Mark merely wrote that Jesus "went" to the mountain. Perhaps, also, Matthew used this phrase in order to emphasize the *Matthean theological theme* of Jesus as the greater Moses.[152]

Mark 6:47–48. Matthew and Mark differ as to the location of their descriptions of Jesus. Mark has καὶ αὐτὸς μόνος ἐπὶ τῆς γῆς ("and he was alone on the land") at the end of verse 47 after mentioning the ship; Matthew has it at the beginning (Matt. 14:23) before speaking of the ship. Perhaps Matthew placed this reference earlier in order to place all references to Jesus in one location. Now, when Matthew discusses the boat, he can discuss it all in one place, whereas Mark interrupts his description of the disciples in the boat to remind the reader that Jesus was still on the land. Thus, Matthew's text is a *smoother* reading. Matthew's τὸ δὲ πλοῖον ἤδη σταδίους πολλοὺς ἀπὸ τῆς γῆς ἀπεῖχεν ("now ~ the boat by this time many ~ stadia from the land was distant") is *more explicit* than Mark's description of the boat, ἦν τὸ πλοῖον ἐν μέσῳ τῆς θαλάσσης ("was the boat in [the] middle of the lake").[153] Matthew also notes that the object of the waves' battering is the boat, βασανιζόμενον ὑπὸ τῶν κυμάτων ("being tossed by the waves"), whereas in Mark, the waves are battering the disciples, αὐτοὺς βασανιζομένους ἐν τῷ ἐλαύνειν ("them straining in the rowing"). Mark's

---

151. This construction appears in Matthew's 6x to Mark's 0x. Mark uses various constructions (6:45; 14:32: ἕως; Mark 9:9: εἰ μὴ ὅταν). In the three Matthew-Mark parallels where Matthew uses this construction, Mark has a different construction in each place. Thus, *Matthew has imposed a unified style to Mark's arbitrary style.* Hurtado, *Text-Critical Methodology,* 73, found the same change to the subjunctive mood in codex W: "The indefiniteness of the statement no doubt seemed to the scribe to demand the proper subjunctive construction" (i.e., a *grammatical refinement*).

152. So, Gundry, *Matthew,* 297.

153. Matthew's text, though, is disputed. Davies and Allison, *Matthew,* 2:502 n. 26, think the original Matthean text read τὸ δὲ πλοῖον ἤδη μέσον τῆς θαλάσσης ἦν.

text is *more difficult* here since it says the disciples themselves were tormented (a very strong word) by the waves.[154] While Mark has a *historical present*, ἔρχεται ("he comes"), Matthew has an aorist, ἦλθεν ("he came").[155] The end of Mark 6:48, καὶ ἤθελεν παρελθεῖν αὐτούς ("and he wanted to go by them") is a *problematic* text. Why would Jesus have intended to pass by the "tormented" disciples, especially given that the reason Jesus walked out on the water was to go help the disciples (ἔρχεται πρὸς αὐτούς, "he comes to them")?[156] Matthew's text, which does not contain a parallel to this clause, is much easier and, therefore, more likely to be secondary.

Mark 6:49–50. Matthew's μαθηταί ("disciples") *makes the subject clearer* and also *emphasizes the Matthean discipleship theme.* Matthew locates ἐταράχθησαν ("were troubled") immediately after the statement that the disciples saw Jesus walking on the sea. Mark, though, uses this same word later, after a redundant 6:50a. Matthew's text is *less pleonastic* since all of Mark 6:50a already has been noted by both Matthew and Mark. Matthew's ὁ Ἰησοῦς ("Jesus") *makes the subject clear.*[157] In the location of Mark's μετ᾽ αὐτῶν . . . αὐτοῖς ("with them . . . to them"), Matthew simply has αὐτοῖς ("to them"), which is *less pleonastic.* Between Mark 6:50 and 6:51, Matthew inserts a long section about Peter walking on the water. The account contains many *Matthean words:* ὀλιγόπιστος, "one of little faith" (4x to Mark's none); κύριος "lord" (34x to Mark's one); κελεύω, "command" (7x to Mark's zero); διστάζω, "doubt" (2x to Mark's

---

154. βασανίζω is used in Matthew 3x and Mark 2x to describe tormented demons (Mark 5:7; Matt. 8:29) and a tormented paralytic (Matt. 8:6). Thus, this is not the best word to describe the disciples' experience in the boat. Blomberg, *Matthew*, 234, goes too far, though, in stating that the word suggests "an occult element at work" in this text. Sabourin, *Matthew*, 2:647, suggests that Matthew's change to "boat" was made for theological reasons, since "Matthew sees in the boat a figure of the church." He is followed by Schweizer, *Matthew*, 323, but few other scholars.

155. N. Turner, *Style*, 35, says that Matthew changes Mark's historical present 78x. See the footnote on Mark 2:5 above.

156. Mann, *Mark*, 305, says, "The phrase is peculiar to Mark, and it is not without difficulty in the Greek." Yet Mann does not explain why Mark changed Matthew to a *more difficult reading*, a move that seems to counter text-critical criteria. Davies and Allison, *Matthew*, 2:504–5, state, "This strange notice, whose meaning is elusive, has been neglected by the First Evangelist because it seemingly states that Jesus was unable to do something he wished to do." C. H. Turner, *Mark*, 23–24, lists this verse and five others as instances in which Matthew deletes Mark's phrases that "seem to suggest unfulfilled intentions of Christ" (i.e., *orthodox improvements*). As to the difficulty of this phrase, Cory, "Aloofness of Jesus in Mark," says that it fits the overall picture of Jesus in Mark. In Mark's version Jesus is "aloof, uncaring, rude, withdrawn, and cold." Fleddermann, "He Wanted to Pass by Them," 394, concludes that the text "functions both in the sea-rescue miracle and in the epiphany." An exhaustive survey of interpretations of Mark 6:48 can be found in T. Snoy, "Marc 6,48: '. . . et il voulait les dépasser'," 352–60, cited in Fleddermann, "He Wanted to Pass By Them," 390.

157. See also above on 6:37–38, where it is stated that the inclusion of ὁ Ἰησοῦς in Matthew has a Christological emphasis.

none).[158] If Matthew were original, it is almost impossible to understand why Mark would have omitted these verses, especially given Mark's tendency to portray the disciples in a negative fashion (cf. Mark's addition at 6:52). Certainly Peter's failure here would have been good material for this theme.[159] Thus, Mark is the *source variant*.

Mark 6:51–52. Mark's paratactic ἀνέβη ("he went up") is found in Matthew as an introductory, subordinate, genitive absolute construction, ἀναβάντων ("as they ~ were going up.") No text-critical conclusion can be reached on this difference.[160] Mark 6:51b–52 is totally different from Matthew 14:33.[161] Mark reads καὶ λίαν [ἐκ περισσοῦ] ἐν ἑαυτοῖς ἐξίσταντο· οὐ γὰρ συνῆκαν ἐπὶ τοῖς ἄρτοις, ἀλλ᾽ ἦν αὐτῶν ἡ καρδία πεπωρωμένη ("and very much [exceedingly] in themselves they were amazed. For ~ they did not understand concerning the loaves, but had been their heart hardened"), while Matthew has οἱ δὲ ἐν τῷ πλοίῳ προσεκύνησαν αὐτῷ λέγοντες· ἀληθῶς θεοῦ υἱὸς εἶ ("and the ones in the boat worshiped him saying, truly God's Son you are"). Matthew's text is written in *more typical Matthean style* with Matthean *theological emphases.*[162] Mark ends this pericope with the disciples still lacking understanding (6:52, which has no Matthean parallel). In Matthew, though, the

---

158. Davies and Allison, *Matthew,* 2:497, add the following Matthean vocabulary: δράζω + λέγων, καταποντίζομαι, and ἐκτείνας τὴν χεῖρα.

159. Mann, *Mark,* 306, says, "At this point the matter of priority in sources is of some difficulty; . . . It is difficult—both on an assumption of Petrine reminiscences as a source for the Gospel of Mark, and also on any assumption of Marcan dependence on Matthew—to see why Mark should have omitted this story. Moreover, since it is commonly said that Matthew and Luke treat the disciples with more respect than Mark, it is worth noting that the Matthean narrative casts Peter in anything but a favorable light." Mann does not suggest, however, a solution to this difficulty.

   C. H. Turner, *Mark,* 33, though, says, "No sort of argument can be founded on its absence from Mark's narrative, for that would be quite of a piece with Peter's general self-suppression in the Gospel; cf. for instance the references to Peter in Matthew 17:24–27; Luke 22:31–32; John 13:24, none of which have any parallel in Mark."

   Peabody, Cope, and McNicol, *One Gospel from Two,* 166–67, surmise that the story was eliminated by Mark because it emphasizes the disciples and not Jesus. They conclude, "The reader of Mark's Gospel is led to focus more on the power of Jesus and, in contrast, the incapacity of the disciples to understand who he is." It seems, though, that *including* the story of Peter would serve to highlight this supposed purpose of Mark in that Peter did not understand and only through the powerful Jesus is Peter saved from the water.

160. Concerning the use of parataxis in Matthew and Mark, see footnote 15 above on Mark 1:41.

161. See Carson, "Matthew," 345–46; and Blomberg, *Matthew,* 236, who explain the differences between Matthew and Mark in such a way as to leave both of them historically accurate to the actual event.

162. This is seen in the use of προσκυνέω (Matt. 13x; Mark 2x) and υἱὸς Θεοῦ. Mark uses υἱὸς Θεοῦ as a declaration on the lips of humans only after the crucifixion. Before this time, only demons are able to recognize the nature of Jesus as the Son of God. Matthew, though, has the disciples (14:33), Peter (16:16), and then the centurion (27:54) recognize Jesus as the Son of God, while the high priest wonders if Jesus is the Son of God (26:63) and the crowds mock Jesus as the Son of God (27:40).

disciples are "worshiping" and calling Jesus the "Son of God."[163] No text-critical conclusions may be reached.[164]

Mark 6:53–56 (Matt. 14:34–36): Healings at Gennesaret[165]

Mark 6:53. Matthew and Mark are the same except that Matthew lacks the *superfluous ending* found in Mark, καὶ προσωρμίσθησαν ("and anchored [there]").

Mark 6:54. Matthew does not contain Mark's *redundant* beginning of this verse, καὶ ἐξελθόντων αὐτῶν ἐκ τοῦ πλοίου εὐθὺς ("and they ~ having come out from the boat immediately"). Matthew contains οἱ ἄνδρες τοῦ τόπου ἐκείνου ("the men—of that ~ region around"), which *makes the subject clearer.*

Mark 6:55. Mark's *obtuse* καὶ ἤρξαντο ἐπὶ τοῖς κραβάττοις τοὺς κακῶς ἔχοντας περιφέρειν ὅπου ἤκουον ὅτι ἐστίν ("and they began upon—mattresses the one illness having to carry where they heard that he is") is much shorter and *clearer* in Matthew's parallel, καὶ προσήνεγκαν αὐτῷ πάντας τοὺς κακῶς ἔχοντας ("and they brought to him all the ones having ~ illness").[166]

Mark 6:56. Matthew does not have a parallel to Mark's beginning of this verse, καὶ ὅπου ἂν εἰσεπορεύετο εἰς κώμας ἢ εἰς πόλεις ἢ εἰς ἀγρούς, ἐν ταῖς ἀγοραῖς ἐτίθεσαν τοὺς ἀσθενοῦντας ("and wherever he was entering into villages or into cities or into countryside, in the marketplaces they were putting the ones having sickness"). It might be said that Mark is *more superfluous* since these words do not add anything substantive to the context. Matthew 14:36, though, is nearly identical to the rest of the verse. Matthew's text includes μόνον ("only") before ἄψωνται ("they might touch"), perhaps to *emphasize the heal-*

---

163. Again, see Bornkamm, Barth, and Held, *Überlieferung und Auslegung im Matthäusevangelium*, 105–12. This is the first time in Matthew's gospel that the disciples make the confession that Jesus is the Son of God.

164. No conclusion can be reached because one could argue that Mark has eliminated this reference to the disciples' understanding in Matthew because of his theme of lack of understanding in the disciples; or it could be argued that Matthew has added this reference to Mark's text because of his theme of understanding on the part of the disciples.

165. Concerning this pericope, Mann, *Mark*, 309, says, "For all the distinctive Markan phraseology, the evangelist has heightened the impact of the shorter and stylized Matt 14:34–36, especially in verse 56." In other words, Mann is saying that Mark has changed Matthew's better style to a more crude style. It is precisely such arguments that scholars have used in the so-called text-critical argument for Marcan priority, and Mann himself has seen it in this pericope, though with opposite conclusions.

166. Hagner, *Matthew*, 2:426, calls Mark's wording "rough syntax."

ing power of Jesus.[167] Although Matthew has the compound διεσώθησαν ("they were cured") in the location of Mark's ἐσῴζοντο ("they were being healed"), these two words are *synonyms.*[168]

Mark 8:14–21 (Matt. 16:5–12): The Leaven of the Pharisees[169]

Mark 8:14. While Mark says that the disciples brought one loaf of bread, καὶ ἐπελάθοντο λαβεῖν ἄρτους καὶ εἰ μὴ ἕνα ἄρτον οὐκ εἶχον ("and they forgot to take loaves and except one loaf they did not have [anything]"), Matthew's ἐπελάθοντο ἄρτους λαβεῖν ("they forgot to take ~ loaves") states that they brought no bread (which is the same type of change found in Mark's textual apparatus).[170] Mark's text is the *more difficult* text since it seems to contradict Mark 8:16, which says that the disciples had "no bread."[171] Mark is also *more awkward* than Matthew's text since Mark says they forgot to take bread, except one loaf. Literally, if one forgets to take bread, one has *no* bread.

Matthew's text contains οἱ μαθηταί ("the disciples"), which *makes the subject clearer.* Matthew's καὶ ἐλθόντες οἱ μαθηταὶ εἰς τὸ πέραν ("and having come the disciples to the other side") makes the location a little *more precise* than Mark's μεθ᾽ ἑαυτῶν ἐν τῷ πλοίῳ ("with themselves in the boat"), given that they are no longer "in the boat" but have already crossed over.

Mark 8:15. While Mark has διεστέλλετο ("he was giving orders"), Matthew has εἶπεν ("said"). Mark's term is *more difficult* because neither Matthew nor Mark use διεστέλλετο in a context outside of the messianic secret, except here. Thus, Matthew's term is more *contextually appropriate.* Matthew's ὁ Ἰησοῦς ("Jesus") *makes the subject explicit.*

---

167. Perhaps this change is also an assimilation to Matthew 9:21, μόνον ἅψωμαι τοῦ ἱματίου αὐτοῦ, per Davies and Allison, *Matthew,* 2:512.

168. Mounce, *Matthew,* 147, says the compound διεσώθησαν emphasizes a complete healing. BAGD, 189, though, defines the word as "save, rescue without special feeling for the meaning of διά."

169. After a survey of several difficulties in interpreting Mark 8:14–21, Davies and Allison, *Matthew,* 2:586, conclude that "given the very real perplexities of Mark 8.14–21 as compared with the clarity of Matthew 16.5–12, it makes more sense to think of the latter as an improvement upon the former. What could have possessed a man to turn the perfectly intelligible Matthew 16.5–12 into a riddle? To what end, on the Griesbach hypothesis, could he have been working?" Luz, *Matthew 8–20,* 349–50, gives a list of seven Matthean changes to Mark's text. He does not, however, give objective reasons for concluding that these changes are Matthean changes to Mark rather than the reverse.

170. See chapter 3 above for a discussion of scribal changes to this verse.

171. Guelich, *Mark 1–8:26,* 1:420, calls this phrase "awkward" and "stylistically clumsy." Manek, "Mark viii 14–21," 10–11, thinks that Matthew may have omitted this reference "in connection with his inclination to ignore all traces of human limitation in Jesus. Whereas Mark taken literally intends to say that. . . . Jesus can multiply this one loaf, Matthew's narrative intends to say that Jesus is able to change nothing into much."

Mark's *pleonastic* βλέπετε ("you see") is not found in Matthew's parallel. Instead, Matthew has a more *typical Matthean word*, προσέχετε ("beware," 6x to Mark's 0x). Matthew also contains a conjunction, καί ("and"), before προσέχετε. Davies and Allison call the presence of καί between consecutive verbs a *"stylistic improvement."*[172] Mark's τῆς ζύμης Ἡρῴδου ("the leaven of Herod") is definitely more difficult and rare than Matthew's τῆς ζύμης . . . Σαδδουκαίων ("the leaven . . . of the Sadducees"). The meaning of Mark's τῆς ζύμης Ἡρῴδου ("the leaven of Herod") is uncertain.[173]

Mark 8:16. Similar to the types of differences found at Mark 2:6, Mark's καὶ διελογίζοντο πρὸς ἀλλήλους ("and they were arguing among themselves") appears as οἱ δὲ διελογίζοντο ἐν ἑαυτοῖς ("but they were reasoning/arguing among themselves") in Matthew.[174] Matthew's unified expression after verbs of speaking gives precedence to Mark's arbitrary style.[175] Following οἱ δὲ διελογίζοντο ἐν ἑαυτοῖς, Matthew reads λέγοντες ("saying"), which makes the meaning of ὅτι ("that") in Mark clearer.[176] Mann, who holds to Matthean priority, admits that Mark 8:15–16 points to Marcan priority because of the improvements Matthew has made. He says, "It must be freely admitted that this is one instance where the two-document hypothesis is on the face of it more convincing as an explanation of the relationship between Matthew and Mark."[177]

---

172. Davies and Allison, *Matthew*, 2:586.

173. Mann, *Mark*, 333, says, "The reference to Herod in Mark is odd, indeed so odd that we must conclude that it has all the marks of authenticity." Even Mann concludes that Mark's text is original!

     Commentators have various interpretations of Mark's "leaven." For example, Cole, *Mark*, 198, defines the leaven of the Pharisees as "hypocrisy" and the leaven of Herod as "procrastinating time-serving which had led Herod first to imprison John the Baptist, then to execute him, though fighting his own conscience all the time." He then defines what the leaven of the Herodians and of the Sadducees might have meant. If, however, "leaven" is equated with teaching, per Davies and Allison, *Matthew*, 2:588, one must ask the appropriate question, what did Herod teach? Therein lies the difficulty with Mark's text. Sabourin, *Matthew*, 666 n. 75, suggests that the Aramaic word for "teaching" sounds identical to that for "leaven," implying that the disciples misunderstood.

174. Matthew's three uses of διαλογίζομαι are all found in verses parallel with Mark: Matthew 16:7, 8; 21:25. Mark, on the other hand, uses διαλογίζομαι 7x. A redactional tendency seems to be present here.

175. While Matthew uses ἐν ἑαυτοῖς 6x after a verb of speaking, Mark uses a variety of phrases: ἐν καρδίαις (2:6, 8); πρὸς ἀλλήλους (4:41; 8:16; 9:34; 15:31); ἐν ἑαυτοῖς (2:8); and πρὸς ἑαυτοὺς (1:27; 9:10; 10:26; 11:31; 14:4).

176. As Gundry, *Mark*, 408, shows, Mark's ὅτι could be epexegetic, indirectly interrogative, directly interrogative, recitative, or causal. This uncertainty in the meaning led Matthew to this insertion. Guelich, *Mark 1–8:26*, 1:418, adds that the addition of λέγοντες makes the "awkward construction smoother."

177. Mann, *Mark*, 334. As has been noted throughout the discussion in this volume, however, this is not the only place where Mann hints that Mark may be prior; he does it also in the previous verse, on the meaning of "the leaven of Herod."

Mark 8:17–18. Matthew inserts ὁ Ἰησοῦς ("Jesus") in order to make the subject explicit (cf. v. 15). Matthew also lacks the personal pronoun, αὐτοῖς ("to them"), and he has an aorist, εἶπεν ("said"), where Mark has a historical present, λέγει ("says"). Matthew's inclusion of ἐν ἑαυτοῖς ("among themselves") after διελογίζεσθε ("they were reasoning/arguing") seems to be an assimilation to Matthew 16:7. Matthew includes a favorite Matthean word, ὀλιγόπιστοι ("ones of little faith," four of five New Testament uses are in Matthew).

Matthew does not have a parallel to the end of Mark 8:17 and most of verse 18, οὐδὲ συνίετε; πεπωρωμένην ἔχετε τὴν καρδίαν ὑμῶν; ὀφθαλμοὺς ἔχοντες οὐ βλέπετε καὶ ὦτα ἔχοντες οὐκ ἀκούετε ("nor comprehend? Have you ~ having become hardened the heart of you? Having ~ eyes do you not see and having ~ ears do you not hear?"). One might say that Mark is the more difficult reading since this criticism is aimed toward the disciples. It is easily understood why a later author would omit it. Hagner says that such a harsh criticism is "reserved for those unreceptive of the kingdom; cf. 13:15–16."[178]

Mark 8:19–20. Matthew does not have parallels to the underlined words in Mark's text: ὅτε τοὺς πέντε ἄρτους[179]ἔκλασα εἰς τοὺς πεντακισχιλίους, πόσους κοφίνους κλασμάτων πλήρεις ἤρατε; λέγουσιν αὐτῷ· δώδεκα. ὅτε τοὺς ἑπτὰ εἰς τοὺς τετρακισχιλίους, πόσων σπυρίδων πληρώματα κλασμάτων ἤρατε; καὶ λέγουσιν [αὐτῷ]· ἑπτά ("When the five loaves I broke for the five thousand, how many baskets of pieces full you picked up? They say to him, twelve. When the seven for the four thousand, how many baskets full of pieces you picked up? And they say to him, seven."). It can readily be seen that these words are not needed for the sense to be conveyed. Thus, Matthew's text is *less superfluous.* He has *a stylistically unified summary* in his two sentences; whereas Mark has varying terms and different cases throughout. It appears that Mark is the *source variant* because it is hard to imagine Mark breaking up Matthew's unified style into his arbitrary and slightly awkward style.

---

178. Hagner, *Matthew*, 2:458. But, see Barth, "Matthew's Understanding of the Law," 114.

179. This is one of the differences in the overall theologies of Matthew and Mark. Mark is much harder on the disciples, and they never seem to understand. Matthew, though, lightens many of these hard statements. See Stein, *Synoptic Problem,* 64–65, for a listing of four examples of Mark's negative descriptions of the disciples that have been improved in Matthew. Meagher, "Die Form- und Redaktionsgeschichtliche Methoden," 469, says that Mark's version gets lost in that Mark never explains that the disciples understand. Meagher says, "In the effulgence of Mark's general indictment of their [the disciples'] insensitivity, there is no general direction." He adds, though, that Matthew's "treatment makes sense of the whole episode." Although Meagher gives some insights into the character of Mark as an author, he has failed to see the overall theological plan of Mark and thus misinterprets this pericope as a result. Carson, "Matthew," 362, reminds us that the disciples, even in Matthew, do not understand everything; rather, they are *"beginning* to understand, exactly as we might expect from their position in salvation history."

Mark 8:21. Whereas Mark's text leaves unclear the issue of whether or not the disciples understand, καὶ ἔλεγεν αὐτοῖς· οὔπω συνίετε ("and he was saying to them, do you not comprehend?"), Matthew writes a much longer πῶς οὐ νοεῖτε ὅτι οὐ περὶ ἄρτων εἶπον ὑμῖν; προσέχετε δὲ ἀπὸ τῆς ζύμης τῶν Φαρισαίων καὶ Σαδδουκαίων. τότε συνῆκαν ὅτι οὐκ εἶπεν προσέχειν ἀπὸ τῆς ζύμης τῶν ἄρτων ἀλλὰ ἀπὸ τῆς διδαχῆς τῶν Φαρισαίων καὶ Σαδδουκαίων ("How can you not understand that not concerning loaves I spoke to you? But ~ beware of the leaven of the Pharisees and Sadducees. Then they understood that he did not say to beware of the leaven of the loaves, but of the teaching of the Pharisees and Sadducees"). In Matthew's ending, Jesus is much more direct, and, as a result, the disciples finally understand (16:12).[180] Notice also that Matthew *makes the meaning* of ζύμης ("leaven") *clear.* His text defines it as the διδαχῆς ("teaching") of the Pharisees and Sadducees.

Mark 8:22–26: A Blind Man Is Healed at Bethsaida

Matthew does not have a parallel to this pericope. Is it more likely that Matthew omitted or that Mark added this pericope? Does this pericope suggest that Jesus is incapable of immediately recovering the sight of the blind man? Since this healing shows an apparent lack of power in Jesus, it seems more likely that Matthew would omit it as an *orthodox improvement.*[181]

Mark 8:27–30 (Matt. 16:13–20): Peter's Confession[182]

Mark 8:27. While Mark has a paratactic indicative ἐξῆλθεν ("went out"), Matthew has a subordinate genitive absolute construction, ἐλθών ("having

---

180. Mann, *Mark,* 333, says, "Mark leaves the enigmatic statement in this verse without explanation, presumably feeling that his own sources offered no interpretation and equally that Matthew's verse 12 was not very illuminating." It seems that Mann has failed to grasp the meaning of Matthew's text and just how "illuminating" it is to the overall meaning of these pericopes in Matthew and Mark.

181. So, for example, Hawkins, *Horae Synopticae,* 118 (a complete list is on 117–21); Hagner, *Matthew,* 2:464; and Held, "Matthew as Interpreter," 207. McNeile, *Matthew,* 237, suggests that this pericope was deleted "for three reasons: Jesus uses material means, saliva, for the cure; He asks the man a question; and the cure is not immediate but gradual." Farmer, *Synoptic Problem,* 166–67, though, thinks it is much easier to suggest that Mark added this miracle story to Matthew and Luke. He fails, though, to suggest any reasons for its addition. Farmer himself notes that the "use of saliva was a common feature in Hellenistic miracle stories." Could this not be a reason for omission by later Evangelists?

182. See Cullmann, "Πέτρος," in *TDNT,* 6:103–8, for an extensive discussion of this pericope. Cullmann concludes that "Mark is probably the original version of the story." Davies and Allison, *Matthew,* 2:602, suggest that Matthew may have known "a non-Markan version of Mark 8.27–30, one which included the blessing of Peter." As a result of this conjecture, they admit that "it must be conceded that Mark 8.27–30 could reasonably be regarded as secondary *vis-à-vis* its Matthean parallel."

come"). Since Matthew's text subordinates the "coming" and emphasizes the next indicative verb, "asking," it seems that Matthew's text is more *grammatically refined* than Mark's. Matthew does not have a parallel for Mark's καὶ οἱ μαθηταί ("and the disciples"). It could be said that Mark's text is *more redundant* since the disciples become the object later in this same verse. In addition, Matthew's omission of οἱ μαθηταὶ ("the disciples") may be for *theological reasons,* that is, to place the emphasis on Jesus.

Mark's κώμας ("villages") occurs in Matthew as the *"clearer"* and more accurate μέρη ("region").[183] Matthew's text also writes the construction in *typical Matthean and Marcan style,* where μέρη ("region") is followed by the name of a city or a region.[184]

Matthew does not have a parallel to Mark's *superfluous* αὐτοῖς ("to them"). The lack of this pronoun after λέγων ("saying") is also in more *typical Matthean and Marcan style.*[185] Mark's personal pronoun με ("me") occurs in Matthew as τὸν υἱὸν τοῦ ἀνθρώπου ("the son of man"). It seems, since Mark uses this term in reference to Jesus immediately after this pericope, in 8:31, besides fourteen other occurrences (to Matthew's thirty), that his text is the *source variant* and that Matthew changed Mark's pronoun into "the Son of Man." In other words, if Mark were using Matthew, he probably would have retained τὸν υἱὸν τοῦ ἀνθρώπου ("the son of man"), given his emphasis on this term in his gospel.

Mark 8:28. Mark's *personal pronoun,* αὐτῷ ("to him"), is not paralleled in Matthew's text, perhaps because it is *unnecessary* in the context. Matthew also does not have parallels for the *pleonastic* λέγοντες ὅτι ("saying that"), which is obviously redundant following εἶπαν ("they spoke").

In the answer to Jesus' question to the disciples about who people thought that he was, Matthew contains Ἰερεμίαν ("Jeremiah"), which is not in Mark's text. Matthew has references to Jeremiah in 2:17 and 27:9, which are also not paralleled in Mark.[186] No text-critical conclusion can be drawn from this since it could be argued that Matthew consistently redacts "Jeremiah" into Mark or that Mark consistently eliminates this term to from Matthew. Matthew also

---

183. Mann, *Mark,* 340, admits that "Matthew's 'the district of Caesarea Philippi' is much clearer" than Mark's version.

184. Mark uses κώμη 7x; Matthew uses it 4x. The only instance of these eleven uses in which the name of a town or region follows κώμη is here at Mark 8:27. On the other hand, μέρη, is used 1x in Mark and 3x in Matthew; all of them are immediately followed by the name of a city or region.

185. Of Matthew and Mark's sixty-seven occurrences of λέγων, Mark 8:27 is the only place where it is followed by αὐτοῖς.

186. See Davies and Allison, *Matthew,* 2:618–19, for possible reasons for the addition of "Jeremiah." See also Knowles, *Jeremiah in Matthew's Gospel,* esp. 81–95.

has a more grammatically correct text in that all of the names are in the same case, accusative, while Mark has "one [of the prophets]" in the nominative case. Thus, it is more likely that Matthew has improved Mark's text, rather than vice versa.[187] Scribes made the identical change to Mark's text by inserting ἕνα τῶν προφητῶν ("one [of the prophets]") for Mark's εἷς τῶν προφητῶν ("one [of the prophets]").[188]

Mark 8:29. Matthew's λέγει αὐτοῖς ("he says to them") is less redundant than Mark's καὶ αὐτὸς ἐπηρώτα αὐτούς ("and he questioned them"), but Mark's text is more specific and accurate than Matthew's generic λέγει ("he says") since a question does follow. Text-critically, Matthew seems to be the source variant here.

Tuckett points out that it is difficult to understand why Mark, if he were using Matthew as a source, would have omitted Matthew's reference to Jesus as the "Son of God," given that the title has immense theological significance in Marcan theology (Mark 1:1, 11; 9:7; 14:61f.; 15:39).[189]

Following Mark 8:29, Matthew contains a long section concerning Peter (Matt. 16:17–19).[190] It is hard to determine the more difficult text. One could say that Matthew added this material to Mark's text to give further information about Peter. Davies and Allison conclude, however, that Matthew's inclusion of 16:17–19 would be a more difficult reading in the early church due to the emotional debates concerning "Peter and his authority (Acts 11:1–3; 1 Cor. 1:12; Gal. 1:18–2:21) and the New Testament's otherwise unanimous verdict that the foundation of the church is Jesus, not Peter."[191]

Mark 8:30. Mark's ἐπετίμησεν ("he warned") is found in Matthew as a more contextually and stylistically appropriate διεστείλατο ("he gave orders").[192]

---

187. Allen, *Mark*, 117, calls Matthew's change from εἷς to ἕνα a "correction." Grundmann, *Das Evangelium nach Matthäus*, 386, calls this difference a "stilistischer Angleichung."

188. This scribal correction is found in A C Θ *f*[1.13] 33. 1006. 1506 (E F G H 205. 700. 1424. 2542) 𝔐 lat sy.

189. Tuckett, "Synoptic Problem," 6:265.

190. Luz, "Primacy Text," 46, concludes that "Matthew 16:18 originates in Syria in post-apostolic times." Cf. idem, "Das Primatwort Matthäus 16.17–19 aus Wirkungsgeschichtlicher Sicht," *NTS* 37 (1991): 415–33.

191. Davies and Allison, *Matthew*, 2:606. Mann, *Mark*, 341, explains the deletion of this material by Mark in this way: "We regard the Markan text as all of a piece with the tightly controlled narrative so characteristic of this gospel. Everything extraneous to the account of ministry in action is excluded, and certainly anything which would draw attention away from Jesus." While the latter reason may be true, the former certainly is not! Mark is full of redundant and unnecessary facts and details.

192. Cf. Mark 8:15 above. Mark uses ἐπιτιμάω for rebuking demons, winds, and little children. He uses it only here and in 3:12, though, in reference to the messianic secret. A better word choice would be διαστέλλω since it is normally used with reference to silencing people concerning the identity of Jesus (see Mark 5:43; 7:36; 9:9).

Mark's indefinite περὶ αὐτοῦ ("about him") is found in Matthew as a more precise and accurate ὅτι αὐτός ἐστιν ὁ χριστός ("that you are the Christ"). If Mark used Matthew as his source, why would he have changed the precise ὁ χριστός ("the Christ") to the generic αὐτοῦ ("him"), given that they both used χριστός ("Christ") earlier?

Mark 8:31–33 (Matt. 16:21–23): Jesus Foretells His Passion[193]

Mark 8:31. Since there is a definite turning point at Mark 8:31 (Matt. 16:21), Matthew's more time specific ἀπὸ τότε ("from that point") is grammatically more refined than Mark's simple καί ("and"). Mark's διδάσκειν ("to teach") is found in Matthew as δεικνύειν ("to explain"). As stated above (Mark 4:2), Matthew seldom parallels Mark's usage of διδάσκω ("teach").[194] No text-critical conclusions can be drawn from this. Matthew has a more specific τοῖς μαθηταῖς αὐτοῦ ("to the disciples of him") in his parallel to Mark's αὐτοὺς ("them").

Matthew parallels Mark's more specific τὸν υἱὸν τοῦ ἀνθρώπου ("the son of man") with a personal pronoun, αὐτόν ("for him"). While this change normally would point to Matthean priority from a text-critical standpoint, such a conclusion is unwarranted here since Matthew just used τὸν υἱὸν τοῦ ἀνθρώπου ("the son of man") at Matthew 16:13 (a redaction of Mark 8:27). Thus, it is possible that Matthew did not want to repeat this term. Matthew's text includes εἰς Ἱεροσόλυμα ἀπελθεῖν ("to Jerusalem to go"), which makes the text *more precise.* Matthew's τῇ τρίτῃ ἡμέρᾳ ("on the third day") is *more histori-cally precise* than Mark's μετὰ τρεῖς ἡμέρας ("after three days"). Matthew's reading clearly signifies "on the third day," whereas Mark's construction can also refer to "a short time later" or "after three days," which is not as accurate as Matthew's "on the third day" since Jesus was not actually in the tomb three entire days.[195] Mark's less accurate text is *more difficult.* Mark's ἀναστῆναι ("to

---

193. Davies and Allison, *Matthew*, 2:653, conclude that Mark is prior to Matthew here because "Mark's text lacks precisely those features of Matthew 16.21–3 which one must consider characteristic of the First Evangelist," i.e., characteristic Matthean vocabulary. This is, however, a circular argument.

194. See footnote 89 above. Gundry, *Matthew*, 337, sees a theological reason for the change from διδάσκειν to δεικνύειν. He states that Matthew uses the former for "public teaching"; the latter for "private instruction."

195. So Hooker, *Mark*, 206; Gundry, *Mark*, 244–45; Hurtado, *Mark*, 142; and Hagner, *Matthew*, 2:477. Mark also uses μετὰ τρεῖς ἡμέρας at 9:31 and 10:34.

All of the following scholars, however—C. H. Turner, *Mark*, 40–41; Taylor, *Mark*, 378; McNeile, *Matthew*, 244–45; Schlatter, *Der Evangelist Matthäus*, 525–26; and Sabourin, *Matthew*, 693–94; fol-lowed by France, *Gospel According to Matthew*, 259; and Riley, *Making of Mark*, 99—cite evidence

rise") is found in Matthew in a *more typical Matthean word* for the raising from the dead, ἐγερθῆναι ("to be raised").[196]

Mark 8:33. Since Peter alone, not the disciples, is being rebuked, Mark's καὶ ἰδὼν τοὺς μαθητὰς αὐτοῦ ("and having seen the disciples of him") is a little *awkward*. Why does Mark mention that Jesus looked at all of the disciples? Perhaps Jesus rebuked Peter as the representative of the other disciples. Mark's text, however, even with this explanation is *more difficult* than Matthew's. It is easier to imagine Matthew deleting this text than to imagine Mark adding to Matthew's text. Mark's harsh ἐπετίμησεν ("he rebuked") is found in Matthew as a kinder and gentler εἶπεν ("said," although the rest of Mark and Matthew is not so gentle toward Peter). Matthew does, however, have parallels for the rest of the harsh words toward Peter that are found in Mark's text. In addition, Matthew also contains σκάνδαλον εἶ ἐμοῦ ("you are ~ a stumbling block to me"), which is very harsh. None of these changes is text-critically significant.[197]

Mark 8:34–9:1 (Matt. 16:24–28): "If Any Man Would Come After Me . . ."

Mark 8:34. Matthew does not have a parallel to the beginning of Mark's verse, καὶ προσκαλεσάμενος τὸν ὄχλον ("and having called together the crowd"). Mark's is the *more difficult text* since it contains a *possible problem* in that the previous contexts appear to be private teaching of the disciples only, without the crowds present.[198] Mark 8:34, though, unexpectedly shifts to the crowds together

---

that μετὰ τρεῖς ἡμέρας and τῇ τρίτῃ ἡμέρᾳ are synonymous. Matthew himself, in fact, uses μετὰ τρεῖς ἡμέρας at 27:63. N. Walker, "After Three Days," 261–2, though, cites evidence that these two phrases are not equivalent. He shows, for example, that in Acts 28:13 the phrase μετὰ μίαν ἡμέραν in καὶ μετὰ μίαν ἡμέραν ἐπιγενομένου νότου δευτεραῖοι ἤλθομεν εἰς Ποτιόλους refers to the second day and not to the first day. Thus, "after three days" would be the equivalent of four days rather than three days.

196. Mark uses both ἐγείρω and ἀνίστημι to refer to rising from the dead (ἀνίστημι: 8x out of 17 uses: 8:31; 9:9, 10, 31; 10:34; 12:23, 25; 16:9; ἐγείρω: 6x out of 19 uses: 6:14, 16; 12:26; 14:28; 16:6, 14). Matthew, though, does not use ἀνίστημι to refer to one being raised from the dead; he uses ἐγείρω, though (11x out of 36), to refer to one being raised from the dead.

197. It is interesting that Farmer, *Gospel of Jesus*, 113–14, argues for Matthean priority in this pericope because "Mark's text can be construed as softening the more conflictive text of Matthew." He fails to see, though, that Matthew appears to soften Mark's text in other places in this pericope. The critical analyst must examine *all* of the data!

198. As McNeile, *Matthew*, 246, says, the reference to the crowds "is unexpected, and suggests that the passage belongs to a different context. Matthew avoids the difficulty by making it addressed only to the disciples."

Davies and Allison, *Matthew*, 2:670, note that it would be inappropriate for Jesus to address such hard demands on the "crowds, who have not decided for or against him, what he demands of his closest followers." See similar reasoning in Schweizer, *Matthew*, 346.

with the disciples. Matthew's text also has some *characteristically Matthean words*, τότε ("then," 90x to Mark's 6x) and ὁ Ἰησοῦς ("Jesus").

Mark 8:35. Only minor differences are found here. Mark has ἄν ("whoever") followed by an indicative construction, ἄν ἀπολέσει ("whoever loses"), where Matthew has ἄν plus subjunctive, ἄν ἀπολέσῃ ("whoever loses"). Matthew's text is a *more typical Marcan and Matthean style*.[199] It also might be an *assimilation* to the same construction earlier in the verse. Matthew does not have a parallel to Mark's καὶ τοῦ εὐαγγελίου ("and the good news") after ἕνεκεν ἐμοῦ ("for the sake of me"). Farmer thinks that Mark's addition is in accord with his "editorializing style as may be seen by a comparison with Mark 10:29."[200] Two texts, though, do not make a style. Further, one also could argue that it is Matthew's "editorializing style" to delete the phrase since Matthew deletes the phrase in both cases! It appears, then, that no text-critical decision can be made. In the parallel to Mark's σώσει ("will save"), Matthew has εὑρήσει ("will find"). Gundry thinks that this substitution points to Marcan priority since "find" is a more exact parallel to "lose" than Mark's "save,"[201] and thus a *grammatical refinement*.

Mark 8:36. Matthew's future, ὠφεληθήσεται ("will be benefited"), is a *more grammatically refined* tense than Mark's present tense, ὠφελεῖ ("does it benefit"), since the verse connotes a future idea. Matthew also has a *more grammatically refined* nominative, ἄνθρωπος ("man"), after ὠφεληθήσεται ("will be benefited," cf. the parallel in Luke 9:25) than Mark's accusative ἄνθρωπον ("a man").[202] Notice that Mark himself has the nominative case in the next verse, τί γὰρ δοῖ ἄνθρωπος ("for ~ what may give a man").

Mark 8:37. In the location of Mark's γάρ ("for"), Matthew has ἤ ("or"). Matthew's text *makes the text flow more smoothly*. Since Mark 8:37 (Matt. 16:26b) does not have a causal relationship with the previous sentence, Mark's text could present a slight interpretative *difficulty* due to the presence of γάρ ("for").

---

199. This same type of difference was seen in Mark's textual apparatus, discussed in the previous chapter, where Taylor called this change a "grammatical correction." Mark uses ἄν plus a future indicative only 2x but ἄν plus a subjunctive 17x; Matthew never uses a future indicative after ἄν, but the subjunctive follows it 36x. It would be nearly impossible to think that Mark would have changed Matthew's more typical text.

200. Farmer, *Synoptic Problem*, 142–43. He adds that the phrase is "secondary to the original form of the tradition since it reflects a usage of the term 'gospel' which is accepted as characteristic of the life situation of the church rather than that of Jesus." See also the text-critical discussion of this phrase earlier in chapter 3.

201. Gundry, *Matthew*, 201, 339; and idem, *Mark*, 454.

202. See N. Turner, *Syntax*, 3:291–92. Davies and Allison, *Matthew*, 2:672, call this change an "improvement."

Matthew, though, avoids this difficulty by showing the parallelism with the previous sentence by using ἤ ("or"). Matthew uses an indicative mood, δώσει ("will give"), while Mark uses a subjunctive, δοῖ ("may give"). Matthew appears to be an *assimilation* to the parallel construction earlier in this verse, τί γὰρ ὠφελεῖ ("for ~ what does it benefit").

Mark 8:38. Matthew does not have a parallel to the beginning of this verse, ὃς γὰρ ἐὰν ἐπαισχυνθῇ με καὶ τοὺς ἐμοὺς λόγους ἐν τῇ γενεᾷ ταύτῃ τῇ μοιχαλίδι καὶ ἁμαρτωλῷ ("for ~ whoever is ashamed of me and—my words in—generation this—adulterous and sinful"). At the end of the verse, Matthew (16:27) has a text that has no parallel in Mark, καὶ τότε ἀποδώσει ἑκάστῳ κατὰ τὴν πρᾶξιν αὐτοῦ ("and then he will recompense each one according to the actions of him").[203] It is difficult to make any text-critical conclusions. It could be said that Matthew certainly would have retained Mark's text if he were dependent on Mark because of the many Matthean themes that are present in 8:38a.[204] On the other hand, Matthew's unique ending broadens the concept that Mark was suggesting at the beginning of this verse and is also in typical Matthean words.[205] The remainder of the verse is identical except that Matthew writes τῶν ἀγγέλων αὐτοῦ ("the angels of him") instead of Mark's τῶν ἀγγέλων τῶν ἁγίων ("the angels holy"), probably for theological reasons (Christological), to bring less emphasis to the angels and more to Jesus.[206]

Mark 9:1. Matthew does not have a parallel to Mark's superfluous καὶ ἔλεγεν αὐτοῖς ("and he was saying to them") since it is immediately followed by λέγω ὑμῖν ("I say to you"). Matthew has a different ending for the verse; whereas Mark has "the kingdom of God has come in power," Matthew has, "the son of man coming in his kingdom." This difference may reflect Matthean *assimilation* to the same phrase, ὁ υἱὸς τοῦ ἀνθρώπου ("the son of man"), found in 16:27 (Mark 8:38). The change also may reflect a *Matthean theological* interpretation of this saying.[207] No text-critical conclusions can be drawn.

---

203. Matthew also has a partial parallel to Mark 8:38a at Matthew 10:33: ὅστις δ' ἂν ἀρνήσηταί με ἔμπροσθεν τῶν ἀνθρώπων, ἀρνήσομαι κἀγὼ αὐτὸν ἔμπροσθεν τοῦ πατρός μου τοῦ ἐν [τοῖς] οὐρανοῖς.

204. Matthew uses λόγος 33x; he uses it in the construction "my words" 3x (7:24, 26; 24:35); Matthew uses γενεά 13x, 2x with μοιχαλίς (12:39; 16:4).

205. Typical Matthean words include ἀποδίδωμι: 18x to Mark's 1x; τότε: 89x to Mark's 6x.

206. McNeile, *Matthew*, 247, followed by Gundry, *Matthew*, 340, note that the addition of αὐτοῦ "emphasizes the divine authority of the glorified Christ." See the similar phraseology in Matthew 13:41; 24:31; and 25:31.

207. Davies and Allison, *Matthew*, 2:677–79, conclude that "the substitution of 'the Son of man coming in his kingdom' for Mark's 'the kingdom of God has come in power' points to a definite understanding. Matthew has interpreted Mark." They think the reference may refer to either or both the Resurrection

Mark 9:2–10 (Matt. 17:1–9): The Transfiguration[208]

Mark 9:2. Matthew's μεθ᾽ ἡμέρας ἓξ ("after six ~ days") is written in *more typical Matthean (and New Testament) style* than Mark's μετὰ ἡμέρας ἓξ ("after six ~ days").[209] Matthew's reading contains τὸν ἀδελφὸν αὐτοῦ ("the brother of him") after Ἰωάννην ("John"), which does not occur in Mark's text.[210] Text-critically, it is slightly more plausible that Mark is the *source variant* here. While it can definitely be said that Matthew would have altered Mark's text to his normal style, it is not certain that Mark would have deleted τὸν ἀδελφὸν αὐτοῦ ("the brother of him") from Matthew's text since Mark has both types of constructions in his gospel. Matthew does not have a parallel to Mark's μόνους ("alone") at the end of the verse. Mark's text is *pleonastic* since κατ᾽ ἰδίαν ("privately") already suggests this idea. Matthew's text contains καὶ ἔλαμψεν τὸ πρόσωπον αὐτοῦ ὡς ὁ ἥλιος ("and shone the face of him like the sun"), which was probably written for a *Matthean theological reason,* namely, to suggest similarities between Moses and Jesus.[211] From a text-critical angle, though, it is best to avoid dogmatic conclusions since it is almost as plausible to say that Mark deleted these Mosaic themes as it is to say that Matthew added them.[212]

---

and the Parousia, which are "two halves of one event, the eschatological glorification and vindication of the Son of Man."

208. Dabrowski, *La Transfiguration de Jésus,* 85:22, does not think a determination of the most ancient text can be reached using internal criteria. He comments, "Il faut donc s'en rapporter uniquement aux témoignages externes. Et puisque la tradition historique nous dit que S. Matthieu, le premier, a écrit l'évangile en hébreu, le texte de S. Matthieu doit être tenu pour la plus ancienne forme du récit de la Transfiguration."

209. The preposition μετά is followed by the letter "η" 2x in Matthew (Matt.: 1:23; 17:1), both of which change the preposition to μεθ᾽. In the New Testament, μετά is normally changed to μεθ᾽ when followed by a vowel (11x: Matt. 1:23; 17:1; Luke 9:49; 24:29; John 20:26; 2 Thess. 1:7; 1 John 1:3; 2:19; 4:17; 2 John 2–3); it remains as μετά only 4x: Mark 9:2; Luke 2:46; Acts 28:17; and 2 Thessalonians 3:12.

210. When he mentions both James and John, Matthew always includes the descriptive phrase τὸν ἀδελφὸν αὐτοῦ (3x); Mark, though, includes the phrase 4x and does not include it 6x.

211. So, Feuillet, "Les Perspectives Propres à Chaque Évangéliste dans les Récits de la Transfiguration," 293, who anticipates the title of Allison's monograph when he asks, "Jésus n'est-il pas un nouveau Moïse?" Allison, *New Moses,* 317, states, "I have argued above not only that many items in chapters 1–8 recall the story of Moses but that the structure of the entire section was shaped by a desire to make the new exodus and new redeemer resemble the first exodus and the first redeemer. If so, the Moses Christology was very much near the center of Matthew's concern." Cf. Davies and Allison, *Matthew,* 2:686–87, 696. Streeter, *Four Gospels,* 315–16, followed by Taylor, *Mark,* 389, think that the reference to the "face" of Jesus was originally in the Marcan text but dropped out by mistake at a very early stage. There is, though, no manuscript evidence for this hypothesis.

212. At the same time, since Mark does have some emphasis on Moses in his gospel (8x), it seems more likely that if Matthew were prior, Mark would have retained these emphases. Thus, it is concluded that slightly more evidence can be found for Marcan priority in these passages.

Mark 9:3. Mark's στίλβοντα λευκὰ λίαν, οἷα γναφεὺς ἐπὶ τῆς γῆς οὐ δύναται οὕτως λευκᾶναι ("shining exceedingly ~ white of such a kind a bleacher on—earth is not able thus to whiten") is more *pleonastic* than Matthew's λευκὰ ὡς τὸ φῶς ("brilliant as the light").[213] It is also possible that Matthew has *assimilated* to the parallel construction of the previous line, τὸ πρόσωπον αὐτοῦ ὡς ὁ ἥλιος ("the face of him like the sun").

Mark 9:4. Matthew's text contains *his typical* ἰδού ("behold," 62x to Mark's 7x). While Mark has the order of names as Ἠλίας καὶ Μωϋσεῖ ("Elijah and Moses"), Matthew has the reverse order, Μωϋσῆς καὶ Ἠλίας ("Moses and Elijah"). Matthew's order emphasizes Moses, about whom he has been hinting throughout this passage.[214] This is a *theologically motivated* difference. Mark's text should be seen as the *source variant* since many reasons could be cited for Moses' appearing first (importance, chronological) but no reasons can be presented for placing Elijah first.[215] Matthew does not have a parallel to Mark's καὶ ἦσαν ("and they were"). Thus, Matthew's text does not have the periphrastic participial phrase. "Though [periphrastic tenses] proliferate in Mark, they were not favoured in vernacular Greek, nor by subsequent copiers and correctors of the New Testament text, for there are variant readings at Mark 1:39; 2:4; 3:1; 5:11, 40; 9:4; 13:25; 14:4; 15:26."[216] This change should therefore be seen as a *grammatical refinement*. Matthew's text has the same type of change that we find in scribal changes to Mark.

Mark 9:5. Mark's *historical present,* λέγει ("says"), is found as an aorist in Matthew's text, εἶπεν ("said").[217] Matthew's text has κύριε ("lord") in the parallel to Mark's ῥαββί ("rabbi/teacher"). As Davies and Allison say, "Because ῥαββί is strange in a context where Jesus is transfigured into a divine being, the independent alterations of Matthew and Luke are natural *improvements*."[218]

---

213. Riley, *Making of Mark,* 102, claims that Mark's longer text is "an expansion [of Matthew's text] that is certainly due to Mark's gift for dramatic storytelling, secondary to Matthew's wording." Why, though, would this text have to be secondary? Mark certainly could have creatively written this verse prior to Matthew. Such claims by Riley show that his arguments are not based on objective evidence but the result of a presupposition of Matthean priority.

214. Allison, *New Moses,* 244: "Matthew rescripted Mark in order to push thought toward Moses. Thus the lawgiver now comes first, and no priority of significance is given to Elijah."

215. Hooker, *Mark,* 216, overstates the case when she calls this switch in order a "correction." Allen, *Matthew,* 184, sees this change simply as effecting a more natural chronological order.

216. N. Turner, *Style,* 4:20.

217. See above on Mark 2:5 concerning historical presents.

218. Davies and Allison, *Matthew,* 2:699. Lane, *Mark,* 320 n. 24, agrees: "Peter's use of the title 'Rabbi' is surprising, almost as if no discovery of Jesus' messianic dignity had been made among the villages of Caesarea Philippi." Gundry, *Mark,* 458, though, says the title is "honorific." "It does not signal a retreat from Peter's confessing Jesus as 'the Christ' (8:29)."

Mark 9:6. Matthew does not have a parallel to this verse.[219] Mark's inclusion of this text is *more difficult* due to the harsh picture of the disciples. Matthew's absence of this verse may be a *theologically motivated difference.*

Mark 9:7. Mark's generic καὶ ἐγένετο ("and there came") is found in Matthew as a *more time specific* ἔτι αὐτοῦ λαλοῦντος ἰδοὺ ("while he is speaking behold").[220] Matthew's text contains ἐν ᾧ εὐδόκησα ("in whom I am well pleased"), which is an *assimilation* to the voice from heaven at Jesus' baptism at Matthew 3:17, οὗτός ἐστιν ὁ υἱός μου ὁ ἀγαπητός, ἐν ᾧ εὐδόκησα ("this is the son of me the beloved, in whom I am well pleased," cf. 12:18).[221] Given that Mark also has this statement in his account of Jesus' baptism (Mark 1:11), it is doubtful, then, if Mark were using Matthew, that Mark would have deleted this statement.[222] Following Mark 9:7, Matthew 17:6–7 has some unique material, which is filled with *typical Matthean vocabulary.*[223] Mark has a partial parallel to the idea of "fear" in Mark 9:6, ἔκφοβοι γὰρ ἐγένοντο ("for ~ terrified they were"). Because of this, it is highly unlikely that Mark would have deleted these verses from Matthew if Matthew were his source. Thus, Mark is the *source variant,* and Matthew seems to have added these verses from his own material.

Mark 9:8. Matthew's parallel to Mark's ἐξάπινα περιβλεψάμενοι ("suddenly having looked around") is an *insignificant synonym difference,* ἐπάραντες τοὺς ὀφθαλμοὺς ("having lifted the eyes").[224] Matthew does not have a parallel for Mark's *pleonastic* οὐκέτι ("no longer") nor μεθ᾽ ἑαυτῶν ("with themselves"). The reading in Matthew, εἰ μή ("except"), is a *grammatically more refined* reading than Mark's ἀλλά ("but"), since the idea here is exception, rather than contrast.

Mark 9:9. Matthew's (ἐνετείλατο, "commanded") and Mark's (διεστείλατο, "he gave orders") again have an *insignificant synonym difference.*[225] As seen many

---

219. Dabrowski, *La Transfiguration de Jésus,* 21, notes that Matthew may have a parallel to Mark's ἔκφοβοι in verse 7, ἐφοβήθησαν σφόδρα. Dabrowski concludes that, because of this different location, Matthew is not dependent on Mark's text as a source.

220. The expression καὶ ἐγένετο is a Semitic construction and does not indicate a time, as seen in the other Marcan uses: 1:9; 2:23; 4:4, 39; 9:26.

221. So, Feuillet, "Les Perspectives Propres à Chaque Évangéliste dans les Récits de la Transfiguration," 300.

222. So, Taylor, *Mark,* 392.

223. Gundry, *Matthew,* 345, lists "μαθηταί (31,5 [i.e., 31x in Matt.; 5x in Mark]), ἔπεσαν (5,3), πρόσωπον (3,2), ἐφοβήθησαν (8,2), σφόδρα (5,2), προσῆλθεν (38, 6), Ἰησοῦς (80,12), ἐγέρθητε (11,8), and μὴ φοβεῖσθε (4,1)."

224. The word ἐξάπινα is a hapax legomenon. While περιβλεψάμενοι is used by Mark 6x, Matthew does not use the term. Matthew uses ἐπάραντες only here, and Mark does not use it at all.

225. Louw and Nida, *Greek-English Lexicon,* 2:33.323, 33.329, give basically the same definition for these two words. They define διαστέλλομαι as "to state with force and/or authority what others must do—'to order, to command,'" while they define ἐντέλλομαι as "to give definite orders, implying authority or official sanction—'to command.'" Matthew uses the former 1x, the latter 4x, while Mark uses them 2x and 5x, respectively.

times, Matthew includes ὁ Ἰησοῦς ("Jesus") in order to *make the subject explicit* and possibly for *Christological emphases.* The remainder of the verse is very different for the two authors. Matthew's ἕως οὗ ("until") is *more grammatically correct* than Mark's *awkward and rare* εἰ μὴ ὅταν ("except when," only once in the New Testament). Matthew's reading is more correct because the phrase is connoting a time sense. Mark's text combines an exceptive idea (εἰ μή, "except") with a time idea (ὅταν, "when"), which is very awkward. Matthew again uses ἐγερθῇ ("has been raised") in the location of Mark's ἀναστῆναι ("to rise"), just as he had done at Mark 8:31.[226]

Mark 9:10. Matthew does not have a parallel to this entire verse, probably for *theological reasons* since the verse shows that the disciples still lack understanding (a typical Marcan theme, but not a Matthean theme).

Mark 12:1–12 (Matt. 21:33–46): The Parable of the Wicked Husbandmen[227]

Mark 12:1. Matthew and Mark have different contexts for this pericope. While both of them are preceded by the pericope titled, "The Question about Authority" (Mark 11:27–33; Matt. 21:23–27), Matthew has placed another parable just before this parable, "The Parable of the Two Sons" (21:28–32). As a result of this addition, Matthew has a different introduction than Mark to this, the second parable he includes. While Mark indicates that this is the beginning of the parables that he includes, καὶ ἤρξατο αὐτοῖς ἐν παραβολαῖς λαλεῖν ("and he began to them in parables to speak"), Matthew notes that Jesus is continuing his teaching

---

226. See above at Mark 8:31 for a discussion of the use of these two words by Matthew and Mark.
227. Blomberg, "Tendencies of the Tradition in the Parables of the Gospel of Thomas," 82–90, 123–30; and D. Wenham, "Tradition and Redaction," 189–90, examine the textual differences between the Gospels and the gospel of Thomas's account of this parable and conclude that the gospel of Thomas is a later work. Snodgrass, "Parable of the Wicked Husbandmen," 142–44, thinks that the gospel of Thomas was tampered with. Because of this tampering, the gospel of Thomas appears to be earlier than Mark's version. See also Snodgrass, *Parable of the Wicked Tenants,* in which he concludes that Matthew's version shows the greatest signs of originality (52–71), although he is "not arguing for the priority of Matthew as a whole" (61). For a response to his arguments, see Gundry, *Mark,* 682–83; and Sibinga, "Review of *The Parable of the Wicked Tenants,*" 383–84, who say that his "case for the originality of Matthew's version seems to be much overstated." Robinson, "Parable of the Wicked Husbandmen," 451, concludes that "Thomas is likely to be the most primitive" and is "not dependent on any of the Synoptic gospels." He further makes decisions regarding how primitive is each word in Matthew, Mark, and Luke. He concludes that Mark is overall the most primitive. Some words in Matthew and Luke, though, appear to be more primitive than Mark. He finally concludes that there is an "Ur-gospel" that lies behind our Gospels, which should be called "Ur-Marcus" since Mark is the nearest to its wording (455–56).

by parables, ἄλλην παραβολὴν ἀκούσατε ("another parable listen to").[228]
Matthew contains ἦν οἰκοδεσπότης ("a house master"),[229] which was probably
added by Matthew for *theological reasons* because it emphasizes the relationship
between the authority of the man in this parable and the overall context of the
Jewish leaders' question about Jesus' authority (Matt. 21:23).

Mark 12:2. In place of Mark's generic τῷ καιρῷ ("in the season"), Matthew
has a *clearer and more specific* (with *typical Matthean vocabulary*) ὅτε δὲ ἤγγισεν
ὁ καιρὸς τῶν καρπῶν ("and ~ when came near the time of the fruits").[230]
Two differences in Matthew's text *make it clearer* that Jesus is speaking of one
with authority, in order to emphasize that the one with authority is none other
than God, Jesus' Father.[231] First, Mark's singular δοῦλον ("slave") is found in
Matthew as a plural τοὺς δούλους αὐτοῦ ("the slaves of him"). Notice also
that a possessive genitive personal pronoun is included in order to emphasize
that the servants were the landowner's. Second, Matthew's text has λαβεῖν τοὺς
καρποὺς αὐτοῦ ("to receive the fruits of it") where Mark has ἵνα ... λάβῃ
ἀπὸ τῶν καρπῶν τοῦ ἀμπελῶνος ("in order that ... he might receive from
the fruits of the vineyard"). This change is similar to the first change in that it
emphasizes that the fruit is the landowner's possession. These differences both
make clearer the connection in Matthew's text between the authority of the landowner and the one who is symbolized by the landowner, namely, God.

Mark 12:3. Matthew's οἱ γεωργοί ("the farmers"), which is not found in
Mark's text, *makes the subject explicit.* One can see that Mark's text is a little
ambiguous. Is the subject of λαβόντες ("having taken") the landowner or the
servant? The subject is unclear because in the previous sentence the servant was
the subject of the same verbal root, λάβῃ ("he might receive"). In this sentence,
the tenants are the subject of λαβόντες ("having taken"). It is left to the reader
to infer this change of subject through the overall context. The two differences
in Matthew's text make the text *much clearer and smoother.* Mark's personal pronoun αὐτόν ("him") is found in Matthew as the *clearer and more specific* τοὺς
δούλους αὐτοῦ ("the slaves of him"). Mark 12:3b, ἔδειραν καὶ ἀπέστειλαν

---

228. P. Parker, "Posteriority of Mark," 99, thinks that Mark may be a summary of Matthew's more extended,
because the plural παραβολαῖς, is followed by only one parable.

229. The term οἰκοδεσπότης is used 7x in Matthew (10:25; 13:27, 52; 20:1, 11; 21:33; 24:43) compared
to 1x in Mark (14:14).

230. Matthew typically uses ἐγγίζω (Matt. 3:2; 4:17; 10:7), καρπός (3:8, 10; 7:16–20; 12:33; 21:41, 43),
and καιρός (8:29; 13:30; 21:41; 26:18) to refer to events that directly relate to the coming of the
kingdom or the end of the age. Thus, he has made it clear that this "reaping" did not occur just "at
some time" (as in Mark), but is a specific reaping at a specific time, namely, the end of the age. Cf.
Hill, *Matthew*, 299.

231. So, for example, Hagner, *Matthew*, 2:617–18.

κενόν ("they beat [him] and sent [him] away empty"), is found in Matthew in *more typical Matthean themes.*[232] He speaks of three different ways that the tenants treated the slaves: ὃν μὲν ἔδειραν, ὃν δὲ ἀπέκτειναν, ὃν δὲ ἐλιθοβόλησαν ("this one they beat, another they killed, and another they stoned").

Mark 12:4–5. Matthew again has the plural ἄλλους δούλους ("other slaves," cf. v. 2) where Mark has the singular ἄλλον δοῦλον ("another slave"), but Mark also adds a further descriptive, πλείονας τῶν πρώτων ("more than the first ones"). Mark then gives an extensive list of what the tenants did to each successive servant who was sent by the landowner: "beat," "insulted," "killed." Matthew, on the other hand, has already written these ideas above, in 21:35.[233] As a result, Matthew substitutes a summary statement, καὶ ἐποίησαν αὐτοῖς ὡσαύτως ("and they did to them similarly").

Mark 12:6. Matthew uses a *more typical Matthean style* by writing ὕστερον ("finally") in the parallel to Mark's ἔτι ... ἔσχατον ("still ... finally"). Ἔσχατον "never occurs as an adverb in the first gospel." Text-critically, this difference is insignificant.[234] Matthew has τὸν υἱόν αὐτοῦ ("the son of him") in the location of Mark's ἕνα υἱὸν ἀγαπητόν ("one beloved ~ son"), which is probably due to *assimilation* with the expression used just nine words later in verse 6, τὸν υἱον μου ("the son of me"), but also may be a move to *more typical Matthean style.*[235]

Mark 12:7. Since there is only one group of tenants, Mark's *superfluous* demonstrative pronoun, ἐκεῖνοι ("those"), is not needed. Matthew's text does not contain this word. Matthew uses ἰδόντες ("having seen") in order to *make it clear* that the tenants said these things only after they saw the son. Mark's πρὸς ἑαυτοὺς ("to themselves") occurs in Matthew in his *typical Matthean* ἐν ἑαυτοῖς ("among themselves"). We saw above that Mark's arbitrary style is found in Matthew in a *unified style.*[236] Matthew *assimilates* Mark's ἡμῶν ἔσται ἡ κληρονομία ("ours will be the inheritance") to the same grammatical con-

---

232. In the background of Matthew's text appears the actual history of Judaism, which includes God's sending a number of servants to Israel and Judah. Thus, Matthew's text is more historically oriented. In addition, it should be noted that the ill treatment of God's servants is an emphasized theme in Matthew. Cf. Matthew 23:37.

233. Gundry, *Mark*, 683, says that Matthew is "smoothing out the roughness in Mark 12:5b."

234. *Contra* Robinson, "Parable of the Wicked Husbandmen," 453–54.

235. All three of Matthew's uses τὸν υἱόν μου are direct quotes where God is speaking. Nowhere does Matthew himself refer to Jesus with this expression. Matthew's text also notes that the landowner (i.e., God) has only one son.

236. See Mark 2:6 above for a discussion of ἐν ἑαυτοῖς in Matthew. It was seen there that Matthew typically changes Mark's various constructions to this unified style.

struction used immediately preceding the conjunction, καί ("and"), a hortatory subjunctive (ἀποκτείνωμεν αὐτόν, "let us kill him"). Thus, Matthew writes σχῶμεν τὴν κληρονομίαν αὐτοῦ ("let us take possession of the inheritance of him"—notice again the possessive pronoun).

Mark 12:8. Matthew and Mark have the same words, but Matthew's order is different. Mark's "take—kill—throw out of vineyard" occurs in Matthew as "take—throw out of vineyard—kill."[237] The usual order is to throw them out before killing in order to keep the produce ritually clean. Thus, it is probable that Matthew (and Luke) changed Mark's *more difficult* word order to a more normal order of events.[238]

Mark 12:9. Matthew's inclusion of ὅταν ἔλθη ("when came"), which is not found in Mark, *makes it clear* that the time of the landowner's coming is indefinite. Matthew also contains τοῖς γεωργοῖς ἐκείνοις ("to those ~ farmers"), again to *make the object clear*.

Mark 12:9b is very *unclear*. Is Jesus or the disciples speaking? Matthew's text contains λέγουσιν αὐτῷ ("they say to him") in order to *make it clear* that the disciples are responding to Jesus' question. In other words, in Mark, the τί ("why") at the beginning of this verse introduced a rhetorical question. In Matthew, it introduced a real question, with a response from the disciples. Matthew's ἐκδώσεται ("he will lease") is a *more lexically refined* word choice for this context than Mark's δώσει ("will give") since δίδωμι is used in a general sense of "giving," but ἐκδίδωμι ("lease") is used more in commercial terms in the literature.[239] Matthew further defines and *makes clear* the types of tenants who are worthy of running the landowner's land, οἵτινες ἀποδώσουσιν αὐτῷ τοὺς καρποὺς ἐν τοῖς καιροῖς αὐτῶν ("who will give back to him the fruits in their ~ season").

---

237. Morris, *Matthew,* 542 n. 63, suggests that Mark's "they killed him" means only that they gave him a mortal wound. Thus, Matthew and Mark have the same basic meaning.

238. Peabody, Cope, and McNicol, *One Gospel from Two,* 250, upon seeing the potential problem in the Marcan text, ask, "Did [Mark] think that Golgotha was inside the city?" This "change" to a less likely chronological order is harder to understand under the Two-gospel hypothesis because Mark is changing a normal order to a more difficult order.

   Gundry, *Mark,* 687; Allen, *Matthew,* 231; C. H. Turner, *Mark,* 57; Taylor, *Mark,* 475; Sabourin, *Matthew,* 2:771; Hill, *Matthew,* 300; Carson, "Matthew," 453; Harrington, *Matthew,* 1:302; Robinson, "Parable of the Wicked Husbandmen," 454; and Hagner, *Matthew,* 2:618, think that Matthew and Luke changed the order as a result of the influence of the events of Jesus' death.

   Snodgrass, *The Parable of the Wicked Tenants,* 60–61, argues in precisely the opposite direction, saying that Mark changed Matthew's more original order of events in order to emphasize the cleanness of the produce (see Gundry's reply to Snodgrass in *Mark,* 687).

239. BAGD, 238, defines ἐκδίδωμι as "to let out for hire, lease." See also Moulton and Milligan, *Vocabulary,* 192. Both Matthew and Mark use the term ἐκδίδωμι at the beginning of the parable, Mark 12:1 and Matthew 21:33.

Mark 12:10. Because the disciples were speaking previous to this, Matthew must include λέγει αὐτοῖς ὁ Ἰησοῦς ("says to them Jesus") in order to *make it clear* that Jesus is now speaking. Recall that Mark does not need to do this since he has had Jesus speaking all along. Matthew has the plural ταῖς γραφαῖς ("the scriptures") in the location of Mark's singular τὴν γραφήν ("the scripture") perhaps because he has included another Old Testament quote in the following verses.

Mark 12:11. This verse is identical in Matthew and Mark. In Matthew, though, unique material follows in 21:43–45. Not only does this add another Old Testament quote (a *favorite Matthean theme*), but verse 45 helps to make Mark *flow more smoothly* by providing the background for why the chief priests and Pharisees wanted to arrest Jesus in Mark 12:12 (Matt. 21:46), namely, because they understood that the parable was about them.[240]

Mark 12:12. Matthew and Mark 12:12a are identical, except for minor changes. Mark's ἐζήτουν ("they were seeking") is found in Matthew as a subordinate participial phrase, ζητοῦντες ("seeking"), probably to emphasize the main verb in the sentence, ἐφοβήθησαν ("they were afraid"). Matthew's text is *clearer* due to his inclusion of the reason that the chief priests and Pharisees feared the crowds, ἐπεὶ εἰς προφήτην αὐτὸν εἶχον ("since as a prophet they considered ~ him"), which is not found in Mark's text.

Mark 12:13–17 (Matt. 22:15–22): On Paying Tribute to Caesar[241]

Mark 12:13. Prior to verse 13, Matthew contains 22:15, which is full of *typical Matthean vocabulary.*[242] The verse makes Mark 12:13 *clearer* by providing the needed background on what happened after the Pharisees and chief priests left Jesus (at v. 12). Mark does, though, provide a similar reason for the coming of the Pharisees and Herodians later in verse 13b, ἵνα αὐτὸν ἀγρεύσωσιν λόγῳ

---

240. *Contra* Farmer, *Synoptic Problem*, 248–49, who thinks that Mark, by omitting Matthew's insertions, "inadvertently recreated the parable in a form which in outward shape is closer to the original." In other words, Farmer is suggesting that Mark is more original, but it is only due to Mark's inadvertent action. This logic seems to defy objective criteria for determining originality.

241. Farmer, *Synoptic Problem*, 262, says, "The question concerning tribute to Caesar affords a clear-cut test of the Marcan hypothesis as over against that of Griesbach"; and "in this instance, the Griesbach hypothesis affords the most intelligible solution to otherwise difficult redactional problems." Tuckett, *Revival of the Griesbach Hypothesis*, 120–24, though, says concerning Farmer's conclusions, "The self-contradictory nature of Mark's redactional procedure according to the Griesbach Hypothesis here must put into question the validity of the whole theory."

242. Tuckett, *Revival of the Griesbach Hypothesis*, 124, lists τότε (Matt. 90x; Mark 6x), συμβούλιον (Matt. 5x; Mark 2x), λαμβάνω (Matt. 53x; Mark 20x), and ὅπως (Matt. 17x; Mark 1x).

("in order that they might catch ~ him in a word"). Mark's πρὸς αὐτόν ("to him") is paralleled in Matthew by his *typical* αὐτῷ ("to him").[243]

Mark 12:14. Matthew has three differences that *make the text flow more smoothly*. First, Mark's *pleonastic* καὶ ἐλθόντες λέγουσιν αὐτῷ ("and having come they say to him") occurs in Matthew as an introductory λέγοντες ("saying"). Mark's καὶ ἐλθόντες . . . αὐτῷ ("and having come . . . to him") is redundant since he just said the same thing in the previous verse, ἀποστέλλουσιν πρὸς αὐτόν ("they send to him," v. 13a). Second, Matthew differs in the location of the clause ἀλλ᾽ ἐπ᾽ ἀληθείας τὴν ὁδὸν τοῦ θεοῦ διδάσκεις ("but rather on the basis of truth the way—of God you teach"), with the result that it is placed directly next to the statement with a similar theme, οἴδαμεν ὅτι ἀληθὴς εἶ ("we know that you are ~ truthful"). This difference allows Matthew's entire *clause to run smoothly together.*[244] Third, he *deletes the pleonastic* δῶμεν ἢ μὴ δῶμεν ("should we give or should we not give"). Mark's restatement is not needed since it is already included in δοῦναι ("to give").

Mark 12:15. Matthew's text again contains ὁ Ἰησοῦς ("Jesus"). Matthew differs from Mark in that, while Mark has τὴν ὑπόκρισιν ("hypocrisy") as the object of what Jesus knew, Matthew has a *more typical Matthean* τὴν πονηρίαν ("the evil," 26x to Mark's 2x). Matthew, though, includes Mark's "hypocrisy" theme by the use of his *typical Matthean* vocative ὑποκριταί ("hypocrites") in the next clause (13x to Mark's 1x). Text-critically, though, this is not decisive as to priority. Matthew does not have a parallel for Mark's *personal pronoun* αὐτοῖς ("to them"). Matthew's ἐπιδείξατέ ("show") is slightly *more refined* and *less awkward* than Mark's φέρετέ . . . ἵνα ἔδω ("bring . . . in order that I may look"). Matthew also uses a more general term for coin, τὸ νόμισμα τοῦ κήνσου ("the coin of the poll tax") than Mark's δηνάριον ("denarius"). This difference may be an *assimilation* to the use of κῆνσον ("poll tax") in Matthew 22:17 (Mark 12:14). Since the question technically was about paying "taxes," Matthew has used a *better lexical term* since he mentions the coin of the "taxes," rather than Mark's denarius.[245]

---

243. See Mark 2:4 above concerning the Matthean use of personal pronouns and the possible Atticistic tendencies here.

244. Against the view of this current study that Matthew's text is an improvement, Farmer, *Synoptic Problem*, 263, says, "There is no obvious explanation for Matthew's changing the order of Mark's phrasing, or for his slightly altering the wording of one phrase after copying three faithfully." But, see Gundry, *Matthew*, 441–42, for a response to Farmer through the listing of reasons for Matthew's redaction.

245. The denarius was the specific coin used to pay this tax. See, for example, Sabourin, *Matthew*, 2:781.

Mark 12:16. Mark's οἱ δὲ ἤνεγκαν ("and they brought [one]") is very *awkward*. Mark uses a transitive verb here without a direct object. Matthew's text is *more grammatically refined* since he includes an object, δηνάριον ("a denarius"). Notice also that, though Matthew used τὸ νόμισμα τοῦ κήνσου ("the coin of the poll tax") in 22:19a, he now uses the technical name of the coin, δηνάριον ("a denarius"). Matthew then has an atypical difference from Mark's text. Matthew parallels Mark's aorist εἶπαν ("he said") with a historical present λέγουσιν ("they say"). This is probably an insignificant change, though it could probably be concluded that Matthew is not the original source here. Why? Because if Mark were using Matthew, it would be quite strange that he does not copy Matthew's historical present tense given his fancy for it.[246] It is probably *more difficult* to say that Mark failed to copy Matthew's historical present, given his abundance of them, than to say that Matthew changed Mark's aorist to a historical present.

Mark 12:17. Matthew again has a historical present, λέγει ("he says"), in parallel to Mark's aorist εἶπεν ("he said"). Matthew also does not contain the subject ὁ Ἰησοῦς ("Jesus"), as Mark does, which also seems to be against Matthew's style (note, though, that Matthew contains ὁ Ἰησοῦς ["Jesus"] in his parallel to Mark 12:15).[247] Matthew's reading of οὖν ("therefore") *makes the text flow more easily* than Mark's text, which lacks the conjunction. It clearly shows that the following statement is a consequence of the previous. In the last part of the verse Mark's καὶ ἐξεθαύμαζον ἐπ᾽ αὐτῷ ("and they were amazed at him") is paralleled in Matthew by καὶ ἀκούσαντες ἐθαύμασαν, καὶ ἀφέντες αὐτὸν ἀπῆλθαν ("and having heard [this] they were amazed, and having left him they went away"). This difference *makes Matthew's text clearer* (by inserting "having heard [this]") and *makes the text flow more easily* into the next pericope (by inserting "and having left him they went away"). Notice that καὶ ἀφέντες αὐτὸν ἀπῆλθαν ("and leaving him they went away") is the identical clause that Mark had at 12:12b! While this clause could fit into the

---

246. N. Turner, *Style*, 4:35, notes that while Matthew changed Mark's historical present 78x, he himself uses the historical present independently 23x. Thus, it cannot be claimed that Matthew is grammatically concerned about the use of the historical present. It should not be seen as impossible for him to use a historical present even though Mark has not. Matthew has, in fact, just retained Mark's historical present, λέγει, earlier in this same verse. In addition, Gundry, *Matthew*, 443, shows that Matthew often used the historical present λέγει αὐτοῖς "for emphasis" (in fact, 21x).

247. This explicit subject could be an example of a Marcan improvement to the Matthean text, since it could be said that Mark is making Matthew's text clearer by adding an explicit subject. Matthew, though, does not need ὁ Ἰησοῦς here since he has already substituted this explicit subject at Mark 12:15 (Matt. 21:18). Thus, Matthew may have chosen not to repeat "Jesus" here because of redundancy. As a result, no text-critical conclusion can be made.

context at 12:12b, it makes much more sense here where Matthew has placed it. Why? Because the location does not change from Mark 12:12 to verse 13. All of the characters remain, in fact, the same (Pharisees, chief priests, Jesus, disciples) in both of these pericopae. The clause makes perfect sense, however, after Mark 12:17, where Matthew has placed it. There is a definite change in characters after this point. The Pharisees leave and do not come back. Now, beginning at Mark 12:18 (Matt. 22:23), the Sadducees enter the scene. Thus, Mark's placement of this clause is *more difficult* and *awkward*.

Mark 12:18–27 (Matt. 22:23–33): The Question About the Resurrection

Mark 12:18. Matthew's ἐν ἐκείνῃ τῇ ἡμέρᾳ ("in that—day") *makes the time of this event clearer* than Mark's text. Mark's πρὸς αὐτόν ("to him") occurs in Matthew as a simple dative αὐτῷ ("to him," cf. Mark 12:13).[248] Mark's πρὸς αὐτόν ("to him") is followed by an indefinite relative pronoun, οἵτινες λέγουσιν ("who say"). This is grammatically awkward since the indefinite relative pronoun, οἵτινες, follows another pronoun, αὐτόν, rather than Σαδδουκαῖοι ("Sadducees"), its antecedent. Matthew's text uses a participle, λέγοντες ("saying"). This participle is a *more refined grammatical expression*.

Mark 12:19. Matthew has an insignificant *synonym* difference εἶπεν ("said") instead of Mark's ἔγραψεν ("wrote").[249] He does not have parallels for Mark's *two superfluous words,* a personal pronoun, ἡμῖν ("to us"), and an indirect ὅτι ("that"). As a result of this difference, Matthew's text is *less awkward* than Mark and *flows more easily*.[250] Mark's τινος ἀδελφός ("of someone a brother") is found in Matthew simply as τις ("which"), which is *less awkward* since it is clear from the context that this "someone" has a brother. Matthew does not have a parallel to Mark's καὶ καταλίπῃ γυναῖκα ("and leave behind a wife"), possibly in *assimilation* to the wording of Deuteronomy 25:5.[251] Further, this clause is not

---

248. See Mark 2:4 above concerning the Matthean use of personal pronouns.

249. Gundry, *Matthew*, 444, says that Matthew changed ἔγραψεν to εἶπεν so that it would parallel Jesus' speaking as recorded by Matthew in 22:29, ὁ Ἰησοῦς εἶπεν. See also Gundry's list of Matthean-Moses parallels in his topical index, under "Moses Parallel Jesus," 683.

250. Allen, *Matthew*, 238, says, "Mark's Greek is awkward. In ἔγραψεν ὅτι-ἵνα there is a confusion of two constructions, and the threefold ἀδελφός obscures the meaning. Matthew substitutes τις for τινος ἀδελφός, thus getting rid of one ἀδελφός, omits the superfluous ἵνα, omits the unnecessary καὶ καταλίπῃ γυναῖκα, and substitutes the technical ἐπιγαμβρεύειν for λάβῃ." Allen is followed by Gundry, *Matthew*, 444, who calls Mark's ὅτι "awkward." Even Mann, *Mark*, 474, admits that Mark's Greek in this verse is "less elegant."

251. So Gundry, *Matthew*, 444.

needed in the context since the whole idea concerns the wife who is left due to the death of her husband. Mark's awkward ἵνα λάβῃ ("in order that [he] may take") is found in Matthew as ἐπιγαμβρεύσει ("marry/raise up offspring"), perhaps an allusion to Genesis 38:8 (LXX), εἴσελθε πρὸς τὴν γυναῖκα τοῦ ἀδελφοῦ σου καὶ γάμβρευσαι αὐτὴν καὶ ἀνάστησον σπέρμα τῷ ἀδελ-φοῦ σου ("go in to the wife of the brother of you and raise up offspring/marry her and raise up offspring for the brother of you"). R. T. France mentions that ἐπιγαμβρεύσει ("shall marry/ raise up offspring") "is not the normal Greek word, but a technical term for the performance of the levirate duty."[252] Thus, Matthew's expression is a *more refined lexical expression* since he uses the more precise term.

Mark 12:20. Mark's *asyndeton* is not found in Matthew due to the presence of δέ ("and"). No text-critical conclusions, though, can be drawn from this since both Matthew and Mark use asyndeton.[253]

Mark 12:22. Matthew again *avoids the asyndeton* that is found in Mark's text by inserting δέ ("and") before πάντων ("of all," cf. v. 20 and its footnote). Matthew uses a *more typical Matthean style* by writing ὕστερον ("last") in the parallel to Mark's ἔσχατον ("last") since ἔσχατον "never occurs as an adverb in the first gospel."[254]

Mark 12:23. Mark's *pleonastic* ὅταν ἀναστῶσιν ("when they are released") is not found in Matthew's text (many Marcan scribes also deleted it). Matthew also contains a more appropriate οὖν ("therefore"), which *makes the text clearer* by correctly providing a consequential relationship between these two verses. Matthew's *text is clearer* due to the presence of an *explicit object*, τῶν ἑπτά ("of the seven"), where Mark has the pronoun αὐτῶν ("of them"). In the next clause, though, Matthew's text has the reverse; Mark has the explicit οἱ ἑπτά ("the seven"), while Matthew has the pronoun. Overall, though, Matthew's text is *clearer*. Mark's *pleonastic* γυναῖκα ("a wife") is not paralleled by Matthew at the end of the verse.

---

252. France, *Gospel According to Matthew*, 317.

253. See N. Turner, *Style*, 4:31, for a listing of the thirty occasions on which Matthew eliminates Mark's asyndetons. While Hawkins, *Horae Synopticae*, 137, calls asyndeton "harsh" due to its "abruptness of construction," Turner notes that Matthew also contains asyndetons in twenty-one Matthew-Mark parallels where Mark does not (31). Overall, though, Matthew contains less asyndetons than Mark, so we may conclude that the absence of asyndetons in Matthew is a Matthean stylistic trait; so Duplacy, "Marc, 2, 10: Note de Syntaxe," 426.

254. So, Gundry, *Matthew*, 445. Matthew 21:37 (Mark 12:6) has the same difference as this text in regard to these two words. The term ὕστερον occurs 7x in Matthew.

Mark 12:24. Matthew uses a *more typical Matthean style* in ἀποκριθεὶς ...
εἶπεν ("having answered ... said") for Mark's ἔφη ("said").[255] Matthew does
not have a parallel for Mark's οὐ διὰ τοῦτο ("not for this") at the beginning of
Jesus' response to the Sadducees. Certainly Mark's reading is *more difficult,* as it
is hard to know the referent for Mark's τοῦτο ("this").[256]

Mark 12:25. Mark's ὅταν γὰρ ἐκ νεκρῶν ἀναστῶσιν ("for ~ when from
[the] dead they rise") occurs in Matthew as ἐν γὰρ τῇ ἀναστάσει ("for ~
in the resurrection"), in *assimilation* with the occurrence of this same phrase at
verse 23 (Matt. 22:28).

Mark 12:26. Mark's slightly *awkward* περὶ δὲ τῶν νεκρῶν ὅτι ἐγείρονται
("but ~ concerning the dead that they are raised") is found in Matthew as περὶ
δὲ τῆς ἀναστάσεως τῶν νεκρῶν ("but ~ concerning the resurrection of the
dead"), possibly also in *assimilation* with the earlier uses of ἀνάστασις ("resurrection," Matt. 22:23, 28, 30).[257] After a similar οὐκ ἀνέγνωτε ("have you
not read"), Matthew has a simpler text than Mark's ἐν τῇ βίβλῳ Μωϋσέως
ἐπὶ τοῦ βάτου πῶς εἶπεν αὐτῷ ὁ θεὸς λέγων ("in the book of Moses
at the thornbush how spoke to him—God saying"), namely, τὸ ῥηθὲν ὑμῖν
ὑπὸ τοῦ θεοῦ λέγοντος ("the thing spoken to you by—God saying"). This
difference may be *theologically motivated* since one of Matthew's themes is the
condemnation of Jewish leaders.[258] We can see that Matthew's accusation of the
Sadducees is even stronger because the word is not spoken "to Moses," but "to
you." Mark's Old Testament quote of Exodus 3:6 is identical in Matthew except
for the presence of εἰμι ("I am") after ἐγώ ("I") in order to bring it more into
harmonization with the wording of the Old Testament.[259] It is doubtful that Mark
would have eliminated εἰμι ("I am") from Matthew's text since it is identical to
the Old Testament quote, but very possible for Matthew to add it to Mark's text.
Thus, Mark's text appears to be the *source variant.*[260]

Mark 12:27. Matthew is identical to Mark for the first six words but lacks a
parallel to the last two, πολὺ πλανᾶσθε ("greatly mistaken"). These words
are slightly *redundant* (cf. v. 24; Matt. 22:29) and anticlimactic after the Old

---

255. Matthew uses ἀποκριθείς followed by some form of λέγω 43x to Mark's 14x.

256. As Hooker, *Mark,* 283, says, "The Greek is obscure."

257. Gundry, *Matthew,* 446, also says this change was made to *make the text smoother.*

258. See, for example, France, *Matthew: Evangelist and Teacher,* 218–23.

259. Stendahl, *School of St. Matthew,* 71, suggests, "Matthew's greater measure of agreement with the LXX
    may even depend upon the improvement of Mark's Greek." He does not elaborate, though, on his
    meaning of improvement.

260. So, New, *Old Testament Quotations,* 69, who says, "It is unlikely that this verb [εἰμί] would be removed
    if it appeared in the source of an evangelist, but it might be added."

Testament quote. Following this verse, Matthew contains 22:33, καὶ ἀκού σαντες οἱ ὄχλοι ἐξεπλήσσοντο ἐπὶ τῇ διδαχῇ αὐτοῦ ("and having heard [this] the crowds were being amazed at the teaching of him"). If Mark were using Matthew as his source, it is *difficult* to believe that he would have deleted this verse, given that Mark records the same idea on five other occasions (1:22; 6:2; 7:37; 10:26; 11:18).

Mark 13:3–8 (Matt. 24:3–8): Signs Before the End[261]

Mark 13:3. Matthew's ἐπί ("on") is a *more refined lexical expression* than Mark's εἰς ("in") since one sits "on" a mountain rather than "in" one.[262] *Mark's unnecessary geographical reference,* κατέναντι τοῦ ἱεροῦ ("opposite the temple"), is not paralleled in Matthew. No text-critical conclusion can be reached. Either Matthew could delete this reference from Mark because his Jewish readers would know the location of the temple, or Mark could have added it to Matthew's text for his Gentile readers.[263]

Mark 13:4. Mark's general ταῦτα ... πάντα ("these things ... all") is *more specific and clear* in Matthew's τῆς σῆς παρουσίας καὶ συντελείας τοῦ αἰῶνος ("of your coming and [the] closing of the age").[264] It seems that συντελείας τοῦ αἰῶνος ("closing of the age") is at least included in Mark's ταῦτα ... πάντα ("these things ... all"), but Matthew's τῆς σῆς παρουσίας ("of your coming") is much more specific.[265]

---

261. No comment will be made here on the allusions and quotations from the Old Testament found in Mark 13 (Matt. 24). Rather, the reader can turn to Mann, *Mark*, 500–504, for a quick listing of possible parallels; Gundry, *Use of the Old Testament*, 46–56; and France, *Jesus and the Old Testament*, 254–57. Concerning the literary relationships between Matthew and Mark in this pericope, Farmer, *Synoptic Problem*, 271, says that it is "one of the most interesting and complicated redactional problems in the whole of Synoptic criticism."

262. Although prepositions were, of course, very fluid in the Hellenistic period. See M. J. Harris, "Prepositions and Theology," in NIDNTT 3:1171–1215. Gundry, *Matthew*, 476, says this change is "more natural with 'sitting.'"

263. Gundry, *Matthew*, 476, says that Matthew deletes this reference "because Jesus has now forsaken the temple and no longer relates to it," i.e., this is a *theologically motivated change.*

264. That Matthew's text is "clearer" is admitted by Mann, *Mark*, 513, who holds to Matthean priority. Thus, Mann admits here that Mark has taken Matthew's "clearer" text and made it more obscure, an odd move for an author according to text-critical criteria. Beare, "Synoptic Apocalypse," 120, calls this change "a distinctive Matthean recasting of the vague words of Mark."

265. While Mark never uses παρουσία, Matthew uses the term 4x (24:3, 27, 37, and 39). McNeile, *Matthew*, 344, says that Matthew, writing after A.D. 70, used this discourse "to encourage readers who were disappointed that although the city had fallen the Parousia was still delayed."

Mark 13:5. Mark's ἤρξατο λέγειν ("began to say")[266] is paralleled by Matthew in a more *typical Matthean style,* ἀποκριθεὶς . . . εἶπεν ("having answered . . . said").[267] Matthew's text contains ὁ χριστός ("the Christ") after ἐγώ εἰμι ("I am"), presumably in an effort to *make the text clearer* as to the meaning of "I am."[268]

Mark 13:6. Matthew's text contains γάρ ("for"), which, more than does Mark's reading, *makes the text flow more smoothly* with the preceding verse.[269] This conjunction supplies the proper consequential force between these two verses. Mark's *superfluous* recitative ὅτι is not paralleled in Matthew. Matthew again contains ὁ χριστός ("the Christ") after ἐγώ εἰμι ("I am"), which *makes the text clearer* (by making explicit what the claim was). Given the use of ὁ χριστός ("the Christ") at Mark 13:21 in a parallel context, it is difficult to know why Mark, if he were using Matthew here, would not have cited it here.[270]

Mark 13:7. Mark's ὅταν δὲ ἀκούσητε ("but ~ when you hear") is found in Matthew as μελλήσετε δὲ ἀκούειν ("but ~ you are about to hear"). While Mark's construction can refer to an indefinite future action,[271] Matthew's construction refers to "imminence."[272] The presence in Matthew of ὁρᾶτε ("see to it"), which is not found in Mark, also adds to the closeness of the action by exhorting the hearer (reader) to be watchful. Is it possible that Matthew has these different readings because he wants to emphasize that the readers of Matthew are even nearer to the fulfillment of Jesus' words than the earlier readers of Mark's gospel? If so, these are *theologically motivated changes.*[273] Matthew's text again contains γάρ ("for," cf. v. 6 [Matt. 24:5]), which *makes the text flow more easily* by supplying the consequential relationship between the two clauses.

---

266. N. Turner, *Style,* 4:20, notes that Mark "is fond of the redundant auxiliary *began to;* it occurs 26 times, and a further three times in text D, easily seen in the concordance, and evenly distributed throughout the Gospel. Matthew reduces these instances to six." Turner, though, concludes that "in view of [all] the evidence it cannot be urged that Matthew was trying to improve the style of Mark by eliminating the auxiliary *begin to.*" He notes that Matthew himself used the term 13x. Yet, of these thirteen, nine were redactional.

267. See the same difference at Mark 12:24 and the word statistics on ἀποκριθείς above.

268. Cf. Swete, *Mark,* 503.

269. So, Hagner, *Matthew,* 2:690.

270. McNicol, "Eschatological Discourse," 187, thinks that Mark deleted this subject from Matthew 24:5 "because, for his non-Palestinian audience, it is a proper name for Jesus rather than a general term for the Messiah." This explanation, though, fails to account for Mark's seven uses of the title elsewhere in his gospel.

271. N. Turner, *Style,* 4:112–13.

272. BDF, §356. BAGD, 501, defines Matthew's construction as "be about to, be on the point of."

273. *Contra,* Beare, "Synoptic Apocalypse," 125, who concludes there is no significant difference between Matthew and Mark.

Mark 13:8. Mark's elided ἐπ᾽ ἔθνος ("against nation") appears in Matthew as ἐπὶ ἔθνος ("against nation"), which is a *more typical Matthean and Marcan style.*[274] It seems more likely that Mark would have maintained Matthew's reading, if he were using Matthew as a source. Mark's *redundant* repetition of ἔσονται ("there will be") is avoided in Matthew's text by the use of καί ("and") in place of its second occurrence. This difference also results in the avoidance of *Mark's asyndeton* (cf. 12:20, 22). In the final clause, Matthew contains πάντα δέ ("but ~ all"), which is not found in Mark's text, again *avoiding Mark's asyndeton.*

Mark 13:14–20 (Matt. 24:15–22): The Desolating Sacrilege[275]

Mark 13:14. Mark's vague ἑστηκότα ὅπου οὐ δεῖ ("having stood where it ought not") is found in Matthew as a *more specific* and *grammatically correct* τὸ ῥηθὲν διὰ Δανιὴλ τοῦ προφήτου ἑστὸς ἐν τόπῳ ἁγίῳ ("the thing spoken through Daniel the prophet, having stood in [the] holy ~ place"). Mark's text is *more grammatically difficult* since ἑστηκότα ("having stood") does not agree with its modifying noun, τὸ βδέλυγμα ("the abomination").[276] Matthew is *more specific* and *less difficult* since he gives more information than Mark's veiled reference. In other words, there is less for the "reader to understand" in Matthew than in Mark.[277] Mark's "vague reference" is now a "specific indication of a place

---

274. This is the only location in either Matthew or Mark where ἐπί is not elided to ἐπ᾽ before the vowel "ε." Five times it is elided (Mark 1:45; 8:4; 13:8; Matthew 18:26, 29). A non-elided ἐπί is followed by the vowel "ε" 11x in the New Testament.

275. For an explanation of Mark 13:14–32 from the viewpoint of the Two-gospel hypothesis, see McNicol, "Eschatological Discourse," 193–97. D. Wenham, *Rediscovery of Jesus' Eschatological Discourse,* 175–218, after a thorough study, concludes that there is a pre-Synoptic sayings tradition, and Matthew and Mark have equal claims to originality (194). Cf. the Matthean redactional emphases in the excellent study by G. N. Stanton, *Gospel for a New People,* 192–206; and the response by Wong, "Matthaean Understanding of the Sabbath," 3–18.

276. The change from the masculine ἑστηκότα to the neuter ἑστός is a "grammatical correction" so that it agrees with its noun, τὸ βδέλυγμα, per McNeile, *Matthew,* 348; Wenham, *Rediscovery of Jesus' Eschatological Discourse,* 193; Gundry, *Matthew,* 482; and Hagner, *Matthew,* 2:698. Rist, *Independence of Matthew and Mark,* 81, thinks that "Mark's version is probably somehow corrupt," though he offers no evidence.

277. The fact that both Matthew and Mark have this reference to the reader, ὁ ἀναγινώσκων νοείτω, is strong evidence for a direct literary relationship between the two; so Hawkins, *Horae Synopticae,* 56; and Stein, *Synoptic Problem,* 37–38. It seems that Matthew has filled in some of the information concerning the "abomination that causes desolation," about which Mark only hints from references to Daniel 9:27; 11:31; and 12:11. Matthew notes that this abomination will take place ἐν τόπῳ ἁγίῳ, based on Daniel's writings (LXX): 9:27: ἐπὶ τὸ ἱερόν; 11:31: τὸ ἁγιου τοῦ φόβου. As Cranfield, *Mark,* 403, says, "Mark's mysterious phrase [ὅπου οὐ δεῖ] is no doubt correctly glossed by Matthew xxiv. 15, ἐν τόπῳ ἁγίῳ."

of worship."[278] Thus, Matthew *eliminates some of the possible misunderstandings from Mark's more difficult text.*

Mark 13:16. Mark's εἰς ("in/to/into") in the phrase εἰς τὸν ἀγρόν ("in the field") is found in Matthew as ἐν ("in"), which is technically a *more refined lexical expression* since "in the field" is technically more correct in this context than "into the field."[279] Matthew does not have a parallel to Mark's εἰς τά ("to the things") before ὀπίσω ("behind"), either because of *assimilation* to the similar pattern in the previous verse,[280] or simply because it is *superfluous.*

Mark 13:18. Matthew's ἡ φυγὴ ὑμῶν ("the escape of you") *makes the text clearer by adding an explicit subject,* though it also may have been written by Matthew to include Matthew's reader in the exhortation, which is a different meaning than Mark's more general exhortation.[281] Matthew also contains μηδὲ σαββάτῳ ("nor on [the] sabbath") after χειμῶνος ("in winter"), probably a *theologically motivated change* to give further instructions to the Matthean community.[282]

Mark 13:19. Mark's ἔσονται γὰρ αἱ ἡμέραι ἐκεῖναι θλῖψις ("will be for—days in those tribulation") is *awkward* to understand because of the interpretative *difficulty* with θλῖψις ("tribulation") as a predicate nominative.[283] Matthew's parallel is ἔσται γὰρ τότε θλῖψις μεγάλη ("for ~ will be then great ~ tribulation").[284] Mark's *redundant* τοιαύτη ("of such kind") is not paralleled in

---

278. Gundry, *Matthew*, 482. So also Fee, "A Text-Critical Look at the Synoptic Problem," 19.

279. Recall, though, from above, that prepositions are fluid in the Hellenistic period. It still must be explained, however, why, if one assumes Matthean priority, Mark would change the preposition to a less precise word. So, Fee, "A Text-Critical Look at the Synoptic Problem," 20–21.

280. So, Gundry, *Matthew*, 483.

281. So, G. N. Stanton, *Gospel for a New People*, 198–203.

282. Contrary to Filson, *Matthew*, 255; Harrington, *Matthew*, 1:337; and Hummel, *Die Auseinandersetzung zwischen Kirche und Judentum im Matthäusevangelium*, 41, who think that the addition of μηδὲ σαββάτῳ by Matthew indicates that the Matthean community kept the Sabbath strictly; Gundry, *Matthew*, 483, surmises that it is not because traveling on the Sabbath is prohibitive for the Christian disciple but rather because the flight would be hampered by rabbinic restrictions and by Jews who do not recognize the mortal danger, who would therefore make the purchasing of supplies and traveling more difficult. See the restrictions in Nehemiah 13:19–22. France, *Gospel According to Matthew*, 341, notes that "gates would be shut and provisions unobtainable" on a Sabbath. Cf. Barth, "Matthew's Understanding of the Law," 91–92, who thinks that Matthew made the addition so that his community would not "give offence" to Jews. For a longer study, see Stanton, *Gospel for a New People*, 192–206, who concludes that the Christian disciples would face hostility from Jewish leaders if the flight were on the Sabbath.

283. So, Hawkins, *Horae Synopticae*, 133. The difficulty of Mark's wording is seen, for example, in the way the NRSV translates it: "For in those days there will be suffering." Notice that they have made the subject, αἱ ἡμέραι ἐκεῖναι, into an introductory adverbial clause. The NIV translates it "because those will be days of distress," with θλῖψις translated like a genitive. Cf. Wenham, *Rediscovery of Jesus' Eschatological Discourse*, 199.

284. Matthew uses τότε 90x to Mark's 6x. Given Mark's tendency toward impersonal verbs (N. Turner, *Style*, 4:12), it would seem that, if Matthew were original, Mark would have retained the impersonal verb.

Matthew. Matthew's text does not contain ἣν ἔκτισεν ὁ θεὸς ("which created God"). This latter clause would not be needed for Matthew's Jewish audience as much as it would be for Mark's Gentile audience.[285] It is, however, impossible to determine priority from this difference since one can argue in either direction: Matthew deleted it since his Jewish audience would know this; Mark added it since his Gentile audience would need to know this.

Mark 13:20. Matthew does not contain κύριος ("lord"), perhaps because *typical Matthean style* used this term for Jesus rather than God the Father.[286] Perhaps as a result of the absence of κύριος ("lord") as the subject, τὰς ἡμέρας ("the days"), which was Mark's predicate, functions as the subject (αἱ ἡμέραι, "those days") in Matthew, and the active verb (ἐκολόβωσεν ("shortens")) is found as a divine passive (ἐκολοβώθησαν, "were cut short").[287] Mark's *pleonastic* οὓς ἐξελέξατο ("whom he chose") is not paralleled in Matthew. This is not needed since it is already clear that they are "elect" from noun, τοὺς ἐκλεκτούς ("the chosen").

Mark 13:21–23 (Matt. 24:23–28): False Christs and False Prophets

Mark 13:21. Mark's ἴδε ἐκεῖ ("look there") is found in Matthew as ἤ· ὧδε ("or here"), which may be an *assimilation* to the same word used in the previous clause.

Mark 13:22. Matthew contains μεγάλα ("great") after σημεῖα ("signs," cf. the same difference at Matt. 24:21 = Mark 13:19). Mark's πρὸς τό ("in order to") followed by an infinitive corresponds to Matthew's ὥστε ("so as") followed by an infinitive. While the former expresses purpose, the latter also could express result. This difference may simply be an *insignificant stylistic difference,* or it may be a Matthean use of a more *typical Matthean and Marcan style* of ὥστε ("so as") with the infinitive, since it is used much more often in these two gospels.[288] It seems that Mark's reading is the *source variant* due to the likelihood that, given his overall uses of these constructions, he would have retained Matthew's ὥστε ("so as") followed by the infinitive rather than changing it to a construction that he does not use anywhere else in his entire gospel.

---

285. Cf. Allen, *Matthew,* 256.

286. So, Gundry, *Matthew,* 484.

287. Matthew has the same difference at the end of the verse where Mark's ἐκολόβωσεν τὰς ἡμέρας occurs as κολοβωθήσονται αἱ ἡμέραι ἐκεῖναι.

288. The construction of πρὸς τό followed by an infinitive is used 5x in Matthew, 1x in Mark; ὥστε followed by an infinitive is used 13x in Matthew, 11x in Mark.

Mark 13:23. Mark's βλέπετε ("beware") is found in Matthew as a *more typical Matthean style,* ἰδού ("behold," 62x to Mark's 7x, which Matthew parallels every time). Matthew does not have a parallel for Mark's πάντα ("all things"), perhaps to *eliminate possible misunderstandings.* After all, Jesus really had not told them "all things," as is obvious from the veiled reference in verse 14 (Matt. 24:15), ὁ ἀναγινώσκων νοείτω ("the one reading take note").[289]

Mark 13:24–27 (Matt. 24:29–31): The Coming of the Son of Man

Mark 13:24. Matthew's δέ ("but") is a *grammatically more refined* reading than Mark's strong adversative ἀλλά ("but") since there is not a strong adversative relationship between vv. 23 and 24 (Matt. 24:28–29). Mark's ἐκείνην ("that") after θλῖψιν ("tribulation") is not paralleled in Matthew. Mark's text is *more pleonastic and "clumsy"* since he has ἐκείναις ... ἐκείνην ("those ... that").[290]

Mark 13:25. Mark's periphrastic participle, ἔσονται πίπτοντες ("will be falling"), is found in Matthew as a simple future indicative πεσοῦνται ("will fall"). Periphrastic tenses, which are common in Mark, "were not favoured in vernacular Greek, nor by subsequent copiers and correctors of the New Testament text."[291] This difference, therefore, should be seen as a *grammatical refinement.* Matthew's text is the same type of change found in scribal changes to Mark. Matthew's genitival phrase, αἱ δυνάμεις τῶν οὐρανῶν ("the powers of the heavens"), is an *insignificant stylistic difference* from Mark's relative pronoun plus locative dative, αἱ δυνάμεις αἱ ἐν τοῖς οὐρανοῖς ("the ones in the heavens will be shaken").

Mark 13:26. Prior to this verse, Matthew contains καὶ τότε φανήσεται τὸ σημεῖον τοῦ υἱοῦ τοῦ ἀνθρώπου ἐν οὐρανῷ, καὶ τότε κόψονται πᾶσαι αἱ φυλαὶ τῆς γῆς ("and then will appear the sign of the son—of man in heaven, and then will mourn all the tribes of the earth"). No text-critical decision can be rendered on this difference. One could say that Matthew is making Mark more explicit or that Mark is deleting superfluous material from Matthew. Matthew has a different location for πολλῆς ("great"). In Mark it modifies δυνάμεως ("power"), but in Matthew it modifies δόξης ("glory").

---

289. So, Hagner, *Matthew,* 2:705.
290. Riley, *Making of Mark,* 157, admits that Mark's text "reads like a rather clumsy rendering of Matthew's." While it is certainly possible for a writer to change a more refined text to a clumsy text, such arguments break every rule of textual criticism.
291. N. Turner, *Style,* 4:20. Cf. the similar difference at Mark 9:4.

This may be an insignificant difference, or it may be a *theologically motivated change* to emphasize Jesus' glory.[292]

Mark 13:27. Matthew does not have a parallel for Mark's *unnecessary* τότε ("then"). It is unneeded since Mark used it in the previous verse. Matthew contains the possessive genitive pronoun, αὐτοῦ ("of him"), in order to *make the text clearer* that the angels answer to the Son of Man.[293] Matthew contains μετὰ σάλπιγγος μεγάλης ("with a loud ~ trumpet call"). "Loud" is the type of detail that Mark is fond of using in his gospel. Thus, if Matthew were original, why would Mark have eliminated this detail?[294] Mark's singular ἐπισυνάξει ("he will gather together") is found in Matthew as a plural, ἐπισυναξουσιν ("they will gather together"), which is a *grammatically more correct reading* since the text actually says that it is the angels who will gather, rather than Jesus himself (unless one classifies the plural "angels" as a collective noun, which would take a singular verb).

Concluding Summary

The previous chapter concluded with an overall summary of the types of changes that scribes made to Mark's text. In light of the eight criteria that were established from the previous two chapters, a survey can now be presented of the types of differences between Matthew's and Mark's texts. A complete picture can be gained by referring to the preceding numerous examples. In addition, appendix B contains a comprehensive list of every difference, categorized by text-critical criteria.

1. Criterion one: The first criterion, as determined in the last two chapters, is to delineate what a source variant is rather than merely state that one variant reading is the source variant without further explanation. Thus, much of the analysis in this current chapter has concentrated on other, more narrowly focused, criteria. This criterion was, however, used on occasion in the preceding pages.

2. Criterion two: The second criterion is that the more difficult reading is more original (generally). Since this is also a broad criterion, it was, in chapter 3, divided into two parts: readings that eliminate awkward expressions; readings that eliminate possible misunderstandings or problems. Mark 2:14 (Matt. 9:9) is

---

292. Matthew seems to have slightly more interest in Jesus' glory (Matt. 16:27; 19:28; 24:30; 25:31) than does Mark (8:38; 10:37; 13:26).

293. Recall the same types of changes in the parable of the wicked husbandmen (Mark 12:1–12).

294. *Contra* McNicol, "Eschatological Discourse," 196, who concludes that Mark deleted Matthew's reference because it is a "Jewish 'apocalyptic' detail."

an example of a more difficult reading, using the name of Levi for the tax collector who became a disciple of Jesus. Matthew, though, has a less difficult "Matthew" harmonizing the text with 10:3, where Matthew the tax collector is named as one of the twelve apostles. Another example is found in Mark 12:8 (Matt. 21:39), in which Mark's order of events has the son of the landowner "seized, killed, thrown out," λαβόντες—ἀπέκτειναν—ἐξέβαλον. Matthew, though, has the order in a less difficult "seized, thrown out, killed," λαβόντες—ἐξέβαλον—ἀπέκτειναν. This order is less difficult for two reasons: first, it harmonizes exactly with the historical order of the events of Jesus' own passion, which is alluded to in this parable; second, it is the more normal order of events to take a victim out of the vineyard before killing him so as not to make the vineyard ritually unclean. Mark's gospel is filled with awkward readings. One example of Matthew's containing a less awkward reading than Mark will suffice.[295] Mark 4:1 contains the awkward πᾶς ὁ ὄχλος πρὸς τὴν θάλασσαν ἐπὶ τῆς γῆς ἦσαν ("all the crowd near the lake on the land were"), while Matthew 13:2 has πᾶς ὁ ὄχλος ἐπὶ τὸν αἰγιαλὸν εἱστήκει ("all the crowd along the shore stood"). Matthew's "standing on the beach" is a much less awkward text than the obtuse and redundant "they were alongside the sea upon the land." The second part of this criterion is those readings that eliminate possible misunderstandings or problems are the later. One example is found in Matthew 14:6, where it has ἡ θυγάτηρ τῆς Ἡρῳδιάδος ("the daughter of Herodias"), while Mark 6:22 has τῆς θυγατρὸς αὐτοῦ Ἡρῳδιάδος ("the daughter of him Herodias"). Mark's reading is a more problematic text since it seemingly contradicts Mark 6:24 and possibly raises moral problems.

3. Criterion three: The third criterion suggested is that the reading that is more in conformity with the author's usage elsewhere is more original. The criterion was further delineated in chapter 3 to include changes from arbitrary style into a more unified style. While this is a less objective criterion for doing text criticism, it is valid for analyzing Matthew-Mark differences. Why? Typical Matthean vocabulary and style can be determined with assurance from portions of his gospel that are text-critically certain. This known vocabulary and style can then be used as a grid through which to analyze the differences in style and vocabulary between Matthew and Mark. Over and over again it has been seen that Matthew writes his parallels to Mark's sentences in his own vocabulary

---

295. An interesting but fruitless theory for explaining why Mark's gospel is filled with awkward readings is found in Crum, *Mark's Gospel*, 1–2, who concludes that our present Mark "is a second writing, amplifying and interrupting and working over [a] first writing." As a result of this rework, Mark's text became filled with awkward readings.

and style. Following are some of the typical Matthean words and phrases (with Marcan parallel):

- ἰδού ("behold"): Mark 1:40; 2:3–4, 6, 15, 24; 9:4; 13:23
- κύριε ("lord"), Mark 1:40; 6:50
- εὐθέως ("immediately"): Mark 1:42; 4:5; 6:45
- οἱ ὄχλοι ("the crowds"): Mark 2:12; 6:33, 36, 39–40, 46
- προσέρχομαι ("come to"): Mark 4:10
- διὰ τί ("why"): Mark 4:10
- λαλέω ("speak"): Mark 4:10
- τῆς βασιλείας τῶν οὐρανῶν ("the kingdom of—heaven"): Mark 4:11
- ὁ πονηρός ("the evil one"): Mark 4:15
- ἐθεράπευσεν ("heal"): Mark 6:34
- κελεύω ("command"): Mark 6:39–40, 50
- ὀλιγόπιστος ("one of little faith"): Mark 6:50; 8:17–18
- διστάζω ("doubt"): Mark 6:50
- προσκυνέω ("worship"): Mark 6:51–52
- προσέχετε ("be warned"): Mark 8:15
- ἀποδίδωμι ("give"): Mark 8:38
- τότε ("then"): Mark 8:38; 13:26
- πρᾶξις ("actions"): Mark 8:38
- ὑποκριτής ("hypocrites"): Mark 12:15.

Matthew also uses typical Matthean style in his parallels to Mark:
- αὐτῷ ("to him"): Mark 2:3–4
- Matthew lacks impersonal verb: Mark 2:3–4, 24
- Matthew lacks parataxis: Mark 1:41; 6:51–52
- Matthew lacks historical present: Mark 2:5; 4:1; 6:47–48; 9:5
- Matthew lacks asyndeton: Mark 12:20, 22; 13:8 (2x)
- δέ ("but") in genitive absolute constructions: Mark 4:17
- ἕως οὗ construction: Mark 6:45
- μέρη ("region") followed by the name of a city or region: Mark 8:27
- ἐγείρω ("raised") used for one being raised from the dead: Mark 8:31
- ἄν followed by subjunctive: Mark 8:35
- Ἰωάννην ("John") followed by τὸν ἀδελφὸν αὐτοῦ ("the brother of him"): Mark 9:2
- ὕστερον ("last") as an adverb: Mark 12:22
- ἀποκριθεὶς ... εἶπεν ("having answered ... said"): Mark 12:24; 13:5

The other category of stylistic differences between Matthew's and Mark's texts is Matthew's unified style in his parallels to Mark in contrast to Mark's various constructions. In 2:6 and 8:16, for example, Mark uses a variety of phrases after διαλογίζόμαι ("to argue about"): ἐν ἑαυτοῖς ("among themselves"), πρὸς ἀλλήλους ("to one another"), ἐν καρδίαις ("in their hearts"), and πρὸς ἑαυτούς ("to themselves"). Matthew, though, consistently uses the same expression, ἐν ἑαυτοῖς ("among themselves"). Text-critically, it is more likely that Matthew has changed Mark's arbitrary style into a consistent style, rather than vice versa.

4. Criterion four: Criterion four states that the less refined grammatical form or less elegant lexical expression is more original. Thus, more refined grammatical forms, more refined lexical expressions, and grammatical improvements indicate later readings. The gospel that has the better grammatical form is, in general, later. Especially given the number of grammatical differences found, it is nearly impossible to think that Mark was this grammatically imprecise if he had Matthew's text before him. It is much more likely that Matthew has improved the grammar of Mark's text.[296] In Mark 8:28 (Matt. 16:14), for example, is a nominative case, εἷς ("one"), as a direct object. Matthew, though, uses a more grammatically correct accusative case, ἕνα ("one"). Another example is found in Mark 13:14, in which Mark uses the masculine ἑστηκότα ("set/establish"), which does not agree with the neuter noun it modifies, βδέλυγμα ("desecration"). Matthew (24:15) though, uses the contextually correct neuter gender, ἑστὸς ("set/establish"). It is extremely unlikely, if Mark were using Matthew as his source, that he would have changed a grammatically correct gender to an incorrect gender. It is likely, though, if Matthew were using Mark as his source, that Matthew would improve the grammar by changing the gender to the correct neuter.

5. Criterion five: This criterion was defined in the text-critical study as "that text that is less smooth is more original." In chapter 3, it was further divided into four categories, which will now be examined.

5A: *Readings that make the text clearer are later.* Forty-six instances were found where Matthew's text is clearer or more explicit than Mark's text. Matthew 9:5, for example, contains γάρ in order to make the causal relationship clearer. This γάρ is not found between Mark 2:8 and 2:9. It would be difficult to explain why Mark, if he were using Matthew as his source, would have deleted such a word. Another example is found in Mark 13:4, where Matthew's parallel to Mark's

---

296. So, e.g., Duplacy, "Marc, 2, 10: Note de Syntaxe," 426: "Ils [Matthew and Luke] corrigent généralement avec grand soin les défauts de grammaire ou de style de Marc."

general ταῦτα . . . πάντα ("these . . . all") is clearer. Matthew's text reads τῆς σῆς παρουσίας καὶ συντελείας τοῦ αἰῶνος ("of your coming and [the] closing of the age"). Even C. S. Mann, who holds to Matthean priority, admits that Matthew's text is clearer here. Thus, he must concede that Mark has taken a clear text and made it less clear. This is possible, but almost ridiculous, according to text-critical criteria. "What could have possessed a man to turn the perfectly intelligible [Matthew] into a riddle? To what end, on the Griesbach hypothesis, could he have been working?"[297]

5B: *Readings that make the text clearer by adding an explicit subject or object are later.* We see this repeatedly in Matthew. His gospel contains, to name just a few examples, ὁ διδάσκαλος ὑμῶν ("the teacher of you") in his parallel to Mark 2:16; ὁ Ἰησοῦς ("Jesus") in his parallels to Mark (1:44; 2:14, 17; 6:37, 50; 8:15, 17, 34; 9:9; 12:10, and 15); ἡ φυγὴ ὑμῶν ("the escape of you") in his parallel to 13:18.

5C: *Readings that make the text flow more easily, that is, make the text smoother, are later.* Matthew, for example, contains a clause that is not paralleled in Mark 6:29, καὶ ἐλθόντες ἀπήγγειλαν τῷ Ἰησοῦ ("and having come they reported [it] to Jesus"), which makes his text flow more easily into the next pericope. Mark's text, as is, has a very loose connection with the next pericope.

5D: *Readings that eliminate redundancy or pleonasm are later.* Mark has been classified as an extremely redundant author. The current study found this to be true. Matthew, though, continually carries less baggage. It is, of course, probable that Matthew worked even harder at eliminating the excess verbiage since he had so much extra material that he wanted to add that is not paralleled in Mark. Since the length of a document was fixed by the length of a scroll, Matthew had to write less redundantly than Mark. In approximately sixty places, in only 173 verses, Matthew's text is less redundant than Mark's text (see appendix B). One example will suffice. Most of Mark 2:16a is basically repeated in 2:16b: καὶ οἱ γραμματεῖς τῶν Φαρισαίων ἰδόντες ὅτι ἐσθίει μετὰ τῶν ἁμαρτωλῶν καὶ τελωνῶν ἔλεγον τοῖς μαθηταῖς αὐτοῦ· ὅτι μετὰ τῶν τελωνῶν καὶ ἁμαρτωλῶν ἐσθίει ("and the scribes of the Pharisees seeing that he eats with—sinners and tax collectors were saying to the disciples of him—with—tax collectors and sinners does he eat?"). Matthew's text does not contain this restatement.

6. Criterion six: Harmonization and assimilation are indicative of later readings. Matthew assimilates his wording to a construction of an immediate parallel in Mark 2:22; 4:7, 8, 16; 8:17-18, 35, 37; 9:1; 12:6, 7, 15, 25, 26, 31. In Mark 8:35, for

---

297. Davies and Allison, *Matthew*, 2:586.

example, ἄν is followed by an indicative, ἄν ἀπολέσει ("loses"). In Matthew, though, ἄν is followed by a subjunctive construction, ἄν ἀπολέσῃ ("loses"). While Matthew's text may only be a use of a more typical New Testament style, it is also an assimilation to the identical construction found earlier in this same verse. Matthew assimilates to an identical form that is used in a similar, though distant, context at Mark 2:11; 4:5; 6:20(2x), 22–23; 9:7; and 12:19. In his parallel to the wording of Mark 6:20, for example, Matthew says that Herod is afraid of "the crowd" rather than "of John" in order to create parallelism with Matthew 21:26, 46, where the Jewish leaders are afraid of "the crowd" at Jesus' trial.

7. Criterion seven: This criterion states that those readings that are more orthodox are less original. Greater orthodoxy is the result of later influences by the Christian community upon the formulation and transmission of the passage in question. Most of these "orthodox improvements" are Matthean attempts to avoid any kind of negative description of Jesus. Matthew, as many of the Marcan scribes did, avoided the use of ὀργισθείς ("being angry") in his parallel to Mark 1:41, desiring to eliminate the negative emotion of "anger" in this context, which would not seem to elicit such a response. Matthew also sought to avoid references to an apparent lack of total power in Jesus. Thus, in Mark 2:12, ἔμπροσθεν πάντων ("in front of everyone"), Matthew writes εἰς τὸν οἰκόν σου ("to the house of you"), which indicates that the paralytic perfectly obeyed Jesus' order from Mark 2:11, ὕπαγε εἰς τὸν οἰκόν σου ("go to the house of you"). Matthew's text shows total obedience of the paralytic to Jesus' command; Mark does not. Matthew also avoided many of the negative descriptions of the disciples. Matthew does not have, for example, the reference to the disciples' failure to understand the parable of the sower, which is found in the parallel in Mark 4:13.

8. Criterion eight actually includes (8A) miscellaneous criteria, including 8B, *the addition or deletion of personal pronouns.* Just as Marcan scribes sometimes added or deleted personal pronouns is a seemingly arbitrary way, Matthew's gospel contains the same tendency (add: 12:1; delete: Mark 2:17; 6:29, 56; 8:17–18, 28; and 12:15).

8C: *Insignificant stylistic or synonym changes.* While nearly all of the stylistic or vocabulary differences can be explained as Matthean tendencies or better lexical constructions, some differences nonetheless seem to be inexplicable. Mark 9:8, for example, has ἐξάπινα περιβλεψάμενοι ("suddenly having looked around"), while Matthew has ἐπάραντες τοὺς ὀφθαλμοὺς ("having lifted the eyes"). Both texts indicate a "looking around or up" and are basically synonymous. Another example is found in the very next verse where Matthew has an insignificant synonym difference, ἐνετείλατο ("command"), in parallel to Mark's διεστείλατο ("he gave orders"), which is an almost identical synonym.

8D: *Theologically motivated changes.* While this criterion could be found in many places, these types of changes were limited to only those locations that (a) could not be explained by other text-critical criteria, and (b) are clearly very important Matthean theological themes. Matthew is clearly seeking to show that Jesus is the fulfillment of the Old Testament. Thus, Mark 2:22 states, "no one puts new wine into old wineskins; otherwise, the wine will burst the skins, and the wine is lost, and so are the skins; but one puts new wine into fresh wineskins" (NRSV); Matthew 9:17 contains an additional comment at the end of the verse, "Neither is new wine put into old wineskins; otherwise, the skins burst, and the wine is spilled, and the skins are destroyed; but new wine is put into fresh wineskins, and *so both are preserved*" (NRSV). It is possible that Matthew added this clause to indicate the fulfillment of the old in the new, rather than the total destruction of the old.

Another of Matthew's main theological themes is the condemnation of the Jewish leaders.[298] Thus, Matthew has different wording than Mark 12:26, for example, which places the emphasis on Moses' contemporaries. Matthew, though, has Moses speaking to the Jewish leaders in Jesus' day, ὑμῖν ("you"). This difference focuses the condemnation on the leaders in Jesus' day. Another of Matthew's theological themes was the similarities of Jesus to Moses.[299] Thus, Matthew (17:2) contains a long phrase that is not paralleled in Mark 9:2, καὶ ἔλαμψεν τὸ πρόσωπον αὐτοῦ ὡς ὁ ἥλιος ("and shone the face of him like the sun"), which makes Jesus' transfiguration parallel Moses' Mount Sinai experience (Exod. 34:29). A similar difference is found just two verses later in Mark 9:4. Mark's text has "Elijah and Moses," while Matthew apparently has changed the word order to "Moses and Elijah," perhaps to emphasize Moses.

---

298. See, for example, France, *Matthew: Evangelist and Teacher*, 218–23.
299. See, for example, Allison, *New Moses*.

COMPARING MATTHEAN–MARCAN DIFFERENCES WITH SCRIBAL CHANGES

CHAPTER SUMMARY

Text-critical criteria were used in chapter 3 to examine Mark's textual apparatus in order to determine typical scribal tendencies. In chapter 4 these same text-critical criteria were used to examine the textual differences between Matthew and Mark. This chapter compares and contrasts the findings from these two chapters in order to determine which of the two Evangelists made changes to the other gospel, being changes that are similar to the types of changes that later scribes made to Mark's gospel. The chapter concludes with three observations based on this evidence.

MARK'S TEXTUAL APPARATUS HAS been examined in order to find typical scribal changes made to his gospel (chap. 3), and a detailed comparison has been made of the textual differences between Matthew and Mark (chap. 4). It now remains to compare the findings from these two analyses. In other words, which of the two Evangelists used the other as a source and made changes to that source that are similar to the types of changes that later scribes made to Mark's gospel?

The preceding pages of evidence has likely made the answer clear. Time and time again, the differences between the texts of Matthew and Mark, according to text-critical criteria, show that Matthew has secondary features in comparison to primary features in Mark's text. If a literary relationship exists between Matthew and Mark,[1] it can confidently be concluded that Matthew consistently

---

1. See M. C. Williams, "Case for the Markan Priority View," 24–34, for evidence of literary dependence between the Gospels.

made the same types of changes to Mark's gospel that scribes made when they were "copying" Mark. On the other hand, assuming that Mark had Matthew's text before him as he wrote, we cannot conclude that Mark consistently made the same types of changes to Matthew's text that scribes made to manuscripts; if Mark were using Matthew as his source, he used it in a manner that is unlike virtually anything that scribes did to texts.

It must also be noted, though, that not every "text-critical" difference that was examined in the previous chapter has led to the conclusion that Matthew is secondary while Mark is primary. While the evidence overwhelmingly points to Marcan priority, a few textual differences remain that are best explained as secondary features in Mark's gospel in comparison to primary features in Matthew's gospel.[2]

The issue to keep in mind, however, is which solution to the Synoptic Problem gives a better *overall* explanation for the differences between Matthew and Mark. Using text-critical criteria, it can confidently be concluded that the two-source hypothesis gives a consistently better explanation. This is not to say that no difficulties inhere in this solution or that the changes between Matthew's and Mark's gospels can be easily understood. Rather, the *cumulative* effect of the investigation of texts indicates that the two-source hypothesis is the better solution.

With this overall conclusion, now will be investigated (1) specific examples from the previous chapter that are near-definite Matthean text-critical secondary readings in comparison to Mark's gospel, (2) examples of likely Marcan text-critical secondary readings in comparison to Matthew's gospel, and (3) possible reasons for this somewhat mixed evidence.

Matthean Secondary Readings

This section summarizes examples of readings from the previous chapter. In doing so, the *best* examples are presented that clearly appear to be secondary

---

2. Similar conclusions have been reached by Léon-Dufour, "Interprétation des Évangiles et Problème Synoptique," 16, who concluded, "Mc ne représente pas nécessairement la tradition primitive, pas plus que Mt ou Lc. Il convient de refuser la priorité absolue de Mc comme un a priori de la critique"; cf. also W. O. Walker, *Relationships Among the Gospels*, 153: "It is thus not impossible both that Matthew could have influenced Mark and that Mark could have influenced our text of Matthew"; P. Parker, "Second Look at *The Gospel Before Mark*," 393, 408 (though he based his conclusions on a prior, common source used by both Matt. and Mark); Boismard, "Influences Matthéennes sur L'Ultime Rédaction de L'Évangile de Marc," 93; Peabody, "Pre-Markan Prophetic Sayings Tradition," 409; and Ellis, "Making of Narratives in the Synoptic Gospels," 310. Cf. Sanday, *Studies in the Synoptic Problem*, 9.

readings in Matthew's gospel in comparison to Mark, according to the principles of textual criticism.[3]

In Mark 1:42, Mark writes that the leprosy "came out" of the leper (ἀπῆλθεν, "went away"), which is a unique phrase in the New Testament. Matthew's reading, ἐκαθαρίσθη, is secondary since it is more precise and accurate in saying that leprosy is "cleansed." According to text-critical principles, it is difficult to think that Mark, if he were using Matthew as a source, would have changed Matthew's more accurate word to a less accurate word.

In Mark 2:6 is found διαλογιζόμενοι ἐν ταῖς καρδίαις αὐτῶν ("thinking about [these things] in the heart of them"); in Matthew's parallel is found εἶπαν ἐν ἑαυτοῖς ("said among themselves"). Matthew in his gospel consistently uses ἐν ἑαυτοῖς ("among themselves") after verbs of speaking (6x). Mark, though, uses a variety of phrases to refer to the same idea: ἐν καρδίαις ("in their hearts"), πρὸς ἀλλήλους ("with one another"), and πρὸς ἑαυτοὺς ("to themselves"). It seems more likely that Matthew has redacted a unified, consistent style onto Mark's arbitrary style, rather than vice versa. Why would Mark have changed Matthew's unified style into a variety of phrases, if Matthew were primary?

Matthew 9:8 mentions that God had given "authority" to human beings. Mark's parallel, 2:12, though, does not contain the word "authority." Given the emphasis on ἐξουσία ("authority") in Mark's gospel, it is difficult to understand why Mark would not have retained this word, if he were using Matthew as a source. It is much more likely that Mark is primary and Matthew is secondary.

Mark 2:14 calls the tax collector "Levi, the son of Alphaeus." Matthew's parallel, though, names the tax collector as Matthew, one of the apostles who was a tax collector (10:3). Mark's text is more difficult than Matthew's, its being easily understood why Matthew would change Mark's text to a more likely name, rather than the other way around. It was even found that Marcan scribes made the same type of change in the textual apparatus. Text-critically, Matthew is much more likely the secondary text.

Mark's οἱ γραμματεῖς τῶν Φαρισαίων ("the scribes of the Pharisees," 2:16) is a more difficult phrase than Matthew's more normal parallel (οἱ Φαρισαῖοι, "the Pharisees") since "scribes" and "Pharisees" were never joined in such a manner in the Gospels. The scribes and the Pharisees appear together nineteen times in the Gospels, but only in Mark 2:16 are the scribes said to be a part of the Pharisaic group.

---

3. Since a full discussion of each of these Matthew-Mark differences may be found in the preceding chapter, each example will be only briefly discussed here in the conclusion.

Mark's problematic ἐπὶ Ἀβιαθὰρ ἀρχιερέως ("during [the days of] Abiathar high priest") in 2:26 is not found in Matthew's parallel. Since it was probably not Abiathar but Abiathar's father (or son), Ahimelech, who was high priest when David ate the bread of the presence, Mark's text is no doubt primary and has been improved by Matthew's secondary text.

Mark 4:15 says that Satan takes away the seed from those who are like the seed sown on the path. Mark does not, though, give us the reason why Satan can snatch away the word. Matthew's fuller text seems to be secondary since it gives a much needed reason, namely, because these people were μὴ συνιέντος ("not understanding").

Mark names the girl who dances before Herod in 6:22 as τῆς θυγατρὸς αὐτοῦ Ἡρῳδιάδος ("the daughter of him, Herodias"). Matthew, though, has ἡ θυγάτηρ τῆς Ἡρῳδιάδος ("the daughter of Herodias"), which is a less difficult name, morally (since it is not Herod's own daughter who is pleasingly dancing before him), historically (since other historical accounts also name the girl as Herodias's daughter), and textually (since Matthew's account now harmonizes with Mark 6:24). It is difficult to imagine Mark altering Matthew's more correct description of the girl.

In Mark 6:14 and 6:26 Mark uses the title "king" for Herod (ὁ βασιλεὺς). Matthew, however, in his parallel to Mark 6:14 (Matt. 14:1), uses the more correct title "tetrarch." It seems that Mark's text is primary and that Matthew has improved the title. It is doubtful that Mark would have changed a more correct title to a less correct title if he were using Matthew as a source. Recall, that in solving the Synoptic Problem, the important matter is not merely which author uses more accurate titles. Rather, following the two-gospel hypothesis, the matter concerns the change of a less accurate title by an author, Mark, who is using a source that includes the more accurate title, Matthew. This type of change is, then, according to text-critical criteria, difficult to understand.

Mark 6:33 mentions that the crowd συνέδραμον ἐκεῖ καὶ προῆλθον αὐτούς ("they ran there and they arrived ahead of them"). Since it is more difficult to believe that the crowd could travel upon land (πεζῇ, "on foot") and arrive before Jesus, who was traveling by boat, it appears that Mark's text is primary and Matthew's secondary.[4]

Between Mark 6:50 and 51 Matthew has a long section about Peter walking

---

4. It should again be mentioned that this current discussion does not focus on what happened historically, but on a comparison of the two texts using text-critical criteria.

on the water (14:28–31). Since this section contains many Marcan themes, it is difficult to imagine Mark not retaining this section if Matthew were prior.[5]

Mark's ἐπελάθοντο λαβεῖν ἄρτους καὶ εἰ μὴ ἕνα ἄρτον ("they forgot to take loaves and except one loaf") of 8:14 seemingly contradicts verse 16, which says the disciples ἄρτους οὐκ ἔχουσιν ("loaves they do not have [any]"). Mark 8:14 is paralleled in Matthew by ἐπελάθοντο ἄρτους λαβεῖν ("they forgot to take ~ loaves"), which is an easier reading since it harmonizes the amount of bread in the two accounts. It seems that Matthew has improved the primary Marcan account. If Matthew were prior, why would Mark have destroyed Matthew's harmonized account by creating seemingly contradictory accounts?

Mark has a very odd reference to the τῆς ζύμης Ἡρῴδου ("the leaven of Herod") in 8:15. What did Mark mean? This statement is more conceptually difficult to understand than Matthew's parallel, τῆς ζύμης τῶν ... Σαδδουκαίων ("the leaven of the ... Sadducees"). There can be little question that Mark's reading is primary, and Matthew's is secondary. Even Mann, who holds to Matthean priority, admits that Mark's version "has all the marks of authenticity."[6] In fact, Mann admits that all of 8:15–16 points to Marcan priority because of the improvements Matthew has made. Such analyses and conclusions are exactly what this current study is trying to achieve: who has made improvements to whom? The evidence points to Matthew consistently and constantly improving Mark's text.

Mark 8:35 has an ἄν followed by an indicative construction, whereas Matthew's parallel has ἄν followed by a subjunctive. Since Matthew's version is both an assimilation to the same construction found earlier in the verse and a more typical Matthean and Marcan style, it is likely that Matthew has improved Mark's grammatical construction. It is unlikely that Mark would have changed a more typical form to an atypical form, especially given that Mark had just used the same form earlier in the verse (ἐὰν θέλῃ, "if desires").

Matthew's parallel to Mark 9:7 contains the addition of ἐν ᾧ εὐδόκησα ("in whom I am well pleased") after οὗτός ἐστιν ὁ υἱός μου ὁ ἀγαπητός ("this is the son of me the beloved"). Since Matthew's exact words are found in both Mark's and Matthew's baptismal account, it seems more likely that Matthew would have added these words to Mark's account in order to harmonize the two statements by God than to say that Mark deleted these words from Matthew's account.

---

5. Even Mann, *Mark*, 306, who holds to Matthean priority, agrees with this conclusion.

6. Ibid., 333.

Following Mark 12:27, Matthew's text contains an additional verse, 22:33, καὶ ἀκούσαντες οἱ ὄχλοι ἐξεπλήσσοντο ἐπὶ τῇ διδαχῇ αὐτοῦ ("and having heard [this] the crowds were being amazed at the teaching of him"). If Mark were using Matthew as a source, it is difficult to know why he would have deleted this verse given that Mark has recorded the same concept five times in his gospel (1:22; 6:2; 7:37; 10:26; 11:18). Thus, it is more plausible to conclude that Mark is primary and Matthew has added this verse to Mark's text.

Mark 13:4 uses a very general ὅταν μέλλῃ ταῦτα συντελεῖσθαι πάντα ("when are about these things to be complete all"). It is difficult to know what Mark means by these vague references (ταῦτα, "these things"). Matthew, on the other hand, has a more specific and clear τί τὸ σημεῖον τῆς σῆς παρουσίας καὶ συντελείας τοῦ αἰῶνος ("what the sign—of your coming and of [the] closing of the age"). Given the precision of Matthew's text and the vagueness of Mark's text, it seems more likely that Mark is prior and Matthew has improved Mark's text by making it clearer.[7] Using text-critical principles, it is doubtful that Mark would have taken a clear source, Matthew's text, and written a more obscure text.

Mark 13:14 gives a vague allusion (ἑστηκότα ὅπου οὐ δεῖ, "having stood where it ought not") that is more specific and grammatically correct in Matthew's parallel (τὸ ῥηθὲν διὰ Δανιὴλ τοῦ προφήτου ἑστὸς ἐν τόπῳ ἁγίῳ, "the thing spoken through Daniel the prophet having stood in [the] holy ~ place"). It is more specific in that Matthew states explicitly that the "desolating sacrilege" will be set up in the holy place, as was foretold in Daniel. Mark, though, has no specifics. He leaves all of it for "the reader to understand." Matthew's text also is more grammatically correct since Mark's masculine participle ἑστηκότα ("having stood"), does not agree with the neuter noun, τὸ βδέλυγμα ("the detestable"). It is much more likely that Matthew has improved Mark's text both grammatically and conceptually than that Mark has marred Matthew's text.

Marcan Secondary Readings

Other texts seem to show that Matthew has the primary reading and Mark has the secondary reading.[8] According to text-critical principles, however, there are far fewer occasions where Mark appears to be secondary. While only a few of the

---

7. That Matthew's text is clearer is admitted by Mann, *Mark*, 513.
8. See Sanders, *Tendencies of the Synoptic Tradition*, 290–93, for a list of thirty-four examples of Matthean texts that scholars think are primary readings.

Matthean readings that appear to be secondary have been reviewed, almost *all* of the Marcan readings that were found to be secondary in the previous chapter will be reviewed since there are not many of them.

In Matthew's parallel to Mark 2:26 (Matt. 12:4), Matthew has a grammatically awkward text, εἰσῆλθεν εἰς τὸν οἶκον τοῦ θεοῦ καὶ τοὺς ἄρτους τῆς προθέσεως ἔφαγον, ὃ: ("he entered into the house—of God and the bread of the presentation ate, which"). Εἰσῆλθεν ("he entered") is singular, and ἔφαγον ("they ate") is plural, while τοὺς ἄρτους ("the loaves of bread") is plural, and the relative pronoun, ὃ ("which"), is singular. Matthew's text is numerically mixed. Mark's text, on the other hand, has consistency, with singular verbs and plural nouns, εἰσῆλθεν εἰς τὸν οἶκον τοῦ θεοῦ ἐπὶ Ἀβιαθὰρ ἀρχιερέως καὶ τοὺς ἄρτους τῆς προθέσεως ἔφαγεν, οὓς ("he entered into the house—of God during [the days of] Abiathar high priest and the loaves of the presentation he ate, which"). It seems that Mark's text is grammatically more refined and consistent. If Matthew were using Mark as a source, why would he have altered the numbers? It seems that Mark is secondary to Matthew's primary text.

A difficult variation is found in Mark 4:13. Mark gives the reason for Jesus' explaining the meaning of the parable to his disciples, namely, the disciples do not understand, οὐκ οἴδατε τὴν παραβολὴν ταύτην, καὶ πῶς πάσας τὰς παραβολὰς γνώσεσθε ("do you not know [the meaning of]—this ~ parable, and how all the parables will you come to know"). In Matthew these words are not found. As a result, Matthew's text is a little awkward. Why is Jesus explaining the meaning of the parable to the disciples, especially given Matthew 13:16–17, which seems to imply that the disciples should understand the parable? Depending on how one explains the theological nuances of Matthew and Mark, priority is difficult to decide.[9] It is certainly possible that Mark is making Matthew's awkward text clearer.

Matthew 14:9 states that Herod is grieved when he hears that Herodias's daughter wants the head of John the Baptist on a platter. Yet, in the Matthean context of verse 5, which states that Herod wanted to kill John (θέλων αὐτὸν ἀποκτεῖναι, "desiring to kill ~ him"), this emotion does not make total sense. If Herod wanted John killed, why would he be grieved? Matthew's text is awkward. Mark's text, though, is consistent. Mark 6:20 states that Herod liked to listen to John the Baptist, even though he feared him, ὁ γὰρ Ἡρῴδης ἐφοβεῖτο τὸν Ἰωάννην, εἰδὼς αὐτὸν ἄνδρα δίκαιον καὶ ἅγιον, καὶ συνετήρει αὐτόν, καὶ ἀκούσας αὐτοῦ πολλὰ ἠπόρει, καὶ ἡδέως αὐτοῦ ἤκουεν ("—for

---

9. See the options and conclusions in chapter 4.

Herod feared—John, having known him [to be] man a righteous and holy, and he was protecting him, and having heard him, he was disturbed ~ greatly, and gladly he was listening ~ to him"). As a result of this, it makes sense that Herod would be "greatly grieved" when Herodias's daughter asks for John's head. It seems that Mark has cleared up a problem in Matthew's text. Thus, it appears that Matthew is primary, and Mark is secondary, according to text-critical criteria.

Between 8:29 and 30 Mark does not have a parallel for Matthew 16:17–19, the blessing of Peter following his confession of Jesus as the Messiah. Davies and Allison, who hold to Marcan priority, admit that this pericope may be an example of Matthean priority:

> Mark 8.27–30 could reasonably be regarded as secondary *vis-à-vis* its Matthean parallel; for we shall contend that the Markan text is a truncated version of what we find in Matthew. Hence the Griesbach hypothesis would here seem to work; that is, Matthew may indeed have here the more primitive text.[10]

This conclusion is reached because Matthew 16:17–19 would be a more difficult reading in the early church, considering the emotional debates about "Peter and his authority (Acts 11:1–3; 1 Cor. 1:12; Gal. 1:18–2:21) and the New Testament's otherwise unanimous verdict that the foundation of the church is Jesus, not Peter."[11] As a result of this difficulty, it is easy to see why Mark may have omitted this from Matthew's text.

Possible Reasons for Both Matthean and Marcan Secondary Readings

As seen above, many Matthean readings appear to be secondary while Mark's parallels appear to be primary. Nevertheless, a few places can be found where Mark appears to be secondary and the Matthean parallel appears to be primary. While text-critical criteria consistently point toward Marcan priority, why do a few texts apparently point toward Matthean priority? Is it not the case that either Matthew is dependent on Mark, or Mark is dependent on Matthew? Should not, therefore, either Matthew or Mark consistently show secondary readings?

In a perfect-case scenario, original readings would be found in only Matthew

---

10. Davies and Allison, *Matthew*, 2:602.
11. Ibid., 2:606.

or Mark. A perfect case, however, does not exist in regard to these two gospels. A variety of influences and a plethora of possible problems may have led to the current ambiguous situation. Some of those problems include continuing oral influence, lack of total objectivity in criteria, recensional texts, and Mark-Q overlaps.

Continuing Oral Influence

One possible reason for the apparently mixed state of originality is a continuing oral influence[12] even after the first gospel was written.[13] Thus, for example, if Mark wrote first, Matthew may have been dependent on Mark, but he also could have been dependent on oral sources, or even on his own memory since he was physically present for many of the events recorded in his gospel.[14] Therefore, Matthew may have a more original reading in his gospel because of his knowledge of the tradition in a different form than has Mark, that is, an oral form. It must be remembered that the influence of the oral tradition was very strong even as late as Papias, who wrote, "For I did not suppose that information from books would help me so much as the word of a living and surviving voice."[15] As a result, "it behoves [sic] investigators into the question of the synoptic problem to avoid too rigorous adherence to merely literary solutions."[16] This oral influence may be found both in the process of writing and in the later transmission, as scribes may have altered the manuscript due to oral influence in their copying. One fact that may have increased the Evangelists' and scribes' reliance upon oral

---

12. The following list of scholars who hold to the continuing oral influence is not, of course, complete: Collins, Review of *Oral Tradition and the Gospels*, 517–20; Hawkins, *Horae Synopticae*, 77; Bonnard, *L'Évangile selon Saint Matthieu*, 112; Kilpatrick, *Origins*, 38–44; Farmer, *Synoptic Problem*, 201; Rist, *Independence of Matthew and Mark*, 10; Keck, "Oral Tradition Literature and the Gospels," 122; Fitzmyer cited in Walker, *Relationships Among the Gospels*, 257; Sanders cited in W. O. Walker, *Relationships Among the Gospels*, 326 n. 1; Westcott cited in Styler, "Priority of Mark," 288; Gerhardsson, "Path of the Gospel Tradition," 93–94; Kelber, *Oral and Written Gospel;* Reicke cited in Walker, *Relationships Among the Gospels*, 316; Reicke, "The Synoptic Reports on the Healing of the Paralytic," 326, 328; Dunn, "Matthew's Awareness of Markan Redaction," 1349; Hagner, *Matthew*, 2:416; Mann, *Mark*, 218–19; G. N. Stanton, *Gospel for a New People*, 36–41; Fee, "A Text-Critical Look at the Synoptic Problem," 24, 28; and Robinson, "Parable of the Wicked Husbandmen," 457. See also the conference papers published in Wansborough, *Jesus and the Oral Gospel Tradition*.

13. Walker, *Relationships Among the Gospels*, 152, concludes that "the memory of oral teaching could be retained with considerable integrity over an extended period of time."

14. Dunn, "Jesus in Oral Memory," 302, says, "It is surely more plausible to deduce that Matthew and Luke knew their own (oral) version of the story and drew on them primarily or as well."

15. Cited in Eusebius, *H.E.* 3.39.3–4. Cf. Koester, "Written Gospels or Oral Tradition?" 293–97. For a recent survey of the importance of morality in antiquity, see Alexander, "The Living Voice," 221–47.

16. Elliott, "Review of *Jesus and the Oral Gospel Tradition*," 307.

reminiscences is the difficulty of writing on a scroll in antiquity.[17] The suggestion that the Evangelists may have examined a certain text in their source, then placed the source scroll down so that they could write their own document makes it more plausible to see the kind of similarity and differences that we find in many synoptic passages.[18]

Lack of Total Objectivity in the Criteria

It must be remembered that the criteria used in textual criticism were developed after the fact[19] to explain, from observations of scribal tendencies, the process of textual transmission. These criteria are not, therefore, hard-and-fast, totally objective rules. They are explanations from the outside. As a result, the criteria used in this study may lead to the conclusion that, in certain cases, a reading is original when, in fact, it is not. While this problem is not major, it may nonetheless influence some text-critical conclusions.

Recensional Texts

Because of the fluidity of textual transmission in the first few centuries, it is difficult to say that we presently have the exact original text that the Evangelists wrote.[20] There is little doubt that some of the original words of the Gospels have

---

17. See Metzger, "Furniture in the Scriptorium at Qumran," 513–14, who shows that there is an "almost total lack of evidence depicting ancient scribes at work on tables and desks." Thus, the ancient scribe wrote with the scroll laid across the knees. This posture certainly made it more difficult to examine written sources for incorporation into a later text. Sanday, *Studies in the Synoptic Problem*, 16–17, concluded that "it is not at all likely that the roll would be taken out and referred to more often than could be helped." Goodacre, "Fatigue in the Synoptics," 47, suggests that Matthew's relationship to Mark should be seen as "direct dependence rather than direct copying in minute detail." See also Crook, "Synoptic Parables of the Mustard Seed and the Leaven," 203. See the extended discussion in Neville, *Mark's Gospel*, 120–28.

18. See McIver and Carroll, "Experiments to Develop Criteria," 687: "These observations led to the formulation of criteria . . . 16 or more words that are exactly the same in two or more documents indicate that a process of copying has taken place." "Nevertheless, the majority of the parallels . . . are more typical of a process of transmission that involves memory rather than straight copying: the common vocabulary is found in short sequences of words; there are changes of mood, tense, and grammatical construction; synonyms are common; and the passages are of different length." Metzger, *Text of the New Testament*, 192–93, notes that scribes often substituted synonyms due to the nature of copying a text, namely that a scribe often forgot exactly what he had read "while a copyist was holding a clause or a sequence of letters in his (somewhat treacherous) memory between the glance at the manuscript and the writing down of what he saw there."

19. Cf. W. O. Walker, "Unexamined Presupposition," 43; and G. N. Stanton, *Gospel for a New People*, 36–41.

20. A partial list of scholars who think that the present gospel texts are the result of recension or cross-

been lost or altered in transmission. Thus, the "Mark" that "Matthew" used might, in some cases, actually be found in "Matthew" rather than in our present "Mark."

> Despite all the labours of the twentieth-century textual critics, we cannot claim to have in our hands a pristine Greek text; and because the earliest papyri and manuscripts attest a very fluid text tradition, the supposition—following Streeter—that Matthew and Luke had copies of Mark slightly different from what we have is far from impossible.[21]

Although overstated, Eldon Epp, at the end of a recent summary of issues in textual criticism concluded, "If the Gospels and other early Christian literature circulated as a free and 'living text' in the early centuries, is there an original text, or specifically a 'single original text,' to be recovered?"[22]

Mark-Q Overlaps

The explanation of Mark-Q overlaps[23] to account for apparent Matthean priority was a favorite of Streeter, who thought that about fifty verses overlapped.[24] While this explanation cannot explain all of the Matthean texts that appear

---

fertilization include Abbott, *Diatessarica—Part 2*, 52; Weisse cited in Stoldt, *Geschichte und Kritik der Markushypothese*, 62; Sanday, *Studies in the Synoptic Problem*, 21–22; C. H. Turner, "Marcan Usage," *JTS* 26:337; Colwell, *Methodology in Textual Criticism*, 150; J. P. Brown, "Early Revision of the Gospel of Mark," 215–27; Dodd, *Parables of the Kingdom*, 87; Jepsen, "Anmerkungen eines Aussenseiters zum Synoptikerproblem," 113–14; W. O. Walker, "Unexamined Presupposition," 41–52; Sanders cited in W. O. Walker, *Relationships Among the Gospels*, 326 n. 1; 94; Streeter, *Four Gospels*, 168, 315–16; Fee, "Modern Text Criticism," 217 n. 41; Robinson, *Redating the New Testament*, 75, 94; Luz, *Das Evangelium nach Matthäus (Mt 1–7)*, 30; Stanton, "J. C. Anderson's 'Life on the Mississippi,'" who said, "We will never know exactly what the Evangelist wrote"; idem, *Gospel for a New People*, 36–41; D. Wenham, *Rediscovery of Jesus' Eschatological Discourse*, 365, 369; Koester, "Text of the Synoptic Gospels," 37; Davies and Allison, *Matthew*, 2:602; Metzger, *Textual Commentary*, 92; Taylor, *Mark*, 328, 389. Cf. Boismard, "Théorie des Niveaux Multiples," 250, 253. Keener, *Matthew*, 191, suggests that Matthew may have "used an earlier version of Mark" at Matthew 9:8.

21. Davies and Allison, *Matthew*, 1:113. Luz, *Matthew 8–20*, 179, declares that "we have to assume the existence of a recension of Mark that is somewhat different from and presumably later than our text of Mark." Cf. Boismard, "Influences Matthéennes sur L'Ultimate Rédaction de L'Évangile de Marc," 93, who concluded, "Dans ce cas, ce serait la première rédaction marcienne qui aurait influencé Mt et l'ultime rédaction marcienne qui aurait subi l'influence de Mt"; and the reply to Boismard's theory in Neirynck, "Urmarcus redivivus?" 103–45, who shows that Boismard is not being logically consistent (104).

22. Epp, "Issues in New Testament Textual Criticism," 75. See also D. C. Parker, *Living Text*, 203–13.

23. See the discussion of recent research in Tuckett, "Mark and Q," 155–75.

24. Streeter, *Four Gospels*, 187, 242–43. Cf. his discussion in Sanday, *Studies in the Synoptic Problem*, 171, sometimes referred to as the *Oxford Studies;* so also Sanders, "Overlaps of Mark and Q," 453–65.

to be original, it nonetheless remains a possibility that Matthew used Q material that was very similar but slightly different from Mark's material. Because
of these minor differences, Matthew may contain a reading that appears to be
primary to Mark's text. It must be realized, however, that Matthew's text would
not be, in this instance, primary to Mark's gospel as a result of a direct redaction
of Mark's gospel. Rather, the differences are because of reliance on a different
source, namely Q.[25] This proposed overlap of Mark and Q has been dubbed the
"blessed overlap" by those who—because of the "magical" appearance of Q
passages that happen to parallel Mark in a more primitive form—hold to the
two-gospel hypothesis.[26]

CONCLUDING SUMMARY

As a result of all of these influences, it cannot be said that a simple one-stage
literary redaction was what historically took place.[27] The process seems to be
more complex than some would like to imagine. Nevertheless, some overall,
final conclusions may be made with a high degree of certainty:

1. The kinds of readings found in Matthew in comparison to Mark are the
    kinds of readings one finds in Mark's textual apparatus in comparison
    to Mark's text. In other words, Matthew made the same types of changes
    that Marcan scribes made to Mark's gospel. Is Matthew a scribe? Yes and
    no. His purported changes to Mark's gospel are "scribe-like" in their
    improvements. But this study has found that many of Matthew's changes
    to Mark's text are because of Matthew's being a theological re-writer of
    Mark's text and not just a copyist who makes minor changes or improve-
    ments, as scribes did in their "copying."[28] "Matthew and Luke, it must be
    realized, were not mere scribes commissioned to produce an accurate copy
    of a particular MS.; they were historians combining and freely rewriting
    their authorities."[29]

---

25. See Blomberg, *Jesus and the Gospels*, 376 n. 23.

26. For an alternate theory that relies on Aramaic sources for Mark's gospel, see Casey, *Aramaic Sources of Mark's Gospel*, 256.

27. So, Stanton, *Gospel for a New People*, 41.

28. So, Orton, *Understanding Scribe*.

29. Streeter, *Four Gospels*, 295. It should be reiterated that scribes were not mere "copiers" of texts, as my analysis in chapter 3 exemplified: countless scribal changes were made to the original text of Mark, most of which seem to be purposefully made.

2. Text-critical criteria clearly and consistently support Marcan priority and Matthean posteriority.[30] Nevertheless, sporadic instances of primary readings in Matthew are found.[31] Thus, just as the Nestle-Aland text should, with a few exceptions, be accepted as the original text,[32] Marcan priority should, with a few exceptions, be accepted as *the* solution to the Synoptic Problem.

3. Using the Nestle-Aland Greek New Testament and not agreeing with Marcan priority reveals inconsistency since the *same* text-critical arguments that were used to establish the present Nestle-Aland text also establish that Matthew has secondary readings and Mark has original readings. Text-critical criteria "so consistently move in the direction of Markan priority that one is compelled either to adopt the Oxford Hypothesis or jettison text-critical procedures in use by all scholars today."[33]

---

30. Recall Davies and Allison, *Matthew*, 2:586, who said, "What could have possessed a man to turn the perfectly intelligible Matthew 16.5–12 into a riddle? To what end, on the Griesbach hypothesis, could he have been working?" Peabody, Cope, and McNicol, *One Gospel from Two*, set out to give reasonable explanations for these changes but lack the details to be convincing.

31. Boismard, "Théorie des Niveaux Multiples," 232, is correct: "Le problème synoptique est complexe; il ne peut être résolu que par une solution complexe." Sanders concurs: "I rather suspect that when and if a new view of the Synoptic problem becomes accepted, it will be more flexible and complicated than the tidy two-document hypothesis. With all due respect for scientific preference for the simpler view, the evidence seems to require a more complicated one" (*Tendencies of the Synoptic Tradition*, 279).

32. In regard to this current study, disagreement with the Nestle-Aland text occurred only 5x in chapter 3 in an examination of a total of 173 verses of Mark's gospel: Mark 1:41; 6:22, 41; 12:9; and 13:22.

33. McKnight, "Source Criticism," 148.

Appendix A

SUMMARY OF TEXT-CRITICAL CHANGES TO MARK'S GOSPEL

1. Source Variant: Mark 4:8, 19; 6:48
2. More Difficult Reading: Mark 2:3, 16; 4:5, 8(2x); 6:20, 32, 33, 44; 8:15, 28, 35, 38; 9:10; 12:21, 25; 13:29
   2A. Eliminate awkward readings: Mark 2:23, 24; 13:8, 21
   2B. Eliminate possible misunderstandings or problems: Mark 2:1, 7, 17, 24, 26; 4:8, 10(2x); 6:45; 8:14; 12:22; 13:20, 28
3. Author's Style: Typical Style or Vocabulary: Mark 2:2, 7, 16, 23, 26; 4:1; 6:22, 23, 32, 45, 48, 50, 53, 55, 56; 8:20, 27, 28, 34; 9:6; 12:1, 14, 15; 13:3, 31
   Change arbitrary style into unified style: Mark 4:18
4. Less Refined Expressions
   4A. Less refined grammatical form: Mark 2:5, 9, 23; 6:20, 29; 13:3
   4B. Less elegant lexical expression: Mark 2:4(2x), 9, 16, 27–28; 4:11, 19; 6:33, 39; 12:21–22
   4C. Grammatical improvements: Mark 2:15, 16, 22, 26; 4:1, 6, 8, 18, 19; 6:27, 39, 45, 52; 8:20, 35; 9:8, 9; 12:3, 22; 13:7, 8, 18
5. Smoother Texts Are Later Readings
   5A. Make the text clearer: Mark 1:40; 2:7, 12, 15, 16(2x), 25, 26; 4:1, 10, 16, 24; 6:33, 47, 48, 55; 8:17, 27; 9:2; 12:4, 6, 7, 8, 14, 22, 25, 27; 13:6, 15
   5B. Adding explicit subject or object: Mark 1:41, 42–43; 2:4; 6:24, 33; 12:14, 27
   5C. Make the text smoother: Mark 1:42–43; 2:3; 4:1, 4, 16; 6:23, 24, 55; 8:15; 12:9, 27
   5D. Eliminate redundancy: Mark 1:42–43; 2:8; 4:3; 6:41, 49–50, 51, 56; 8:15, 28; 12:13, 23; 13:19

6. Harmonization and Assimilation: everywhere
7. Orthodox Readings and Later Christian Community Changes: Mark 1:41, 42–43; 2:10, 27–28; 4:10; 6:41, 45, 48, 49; 8:14, 38; 9:7; 12:15, 26; 13:22, 32
8. Others

    8A. Scribal errors: Mark 1:40; 2:22, 26; 4:19; 6:23, 35, 37, 40; 8:35; 12:6; 13:7, 8, 28

    8B. Add or delete personal pronouns: Mark 1:41; 2:8, 17; 6:37; 8:20; 12:6, 8, 17

    8C. Insignificant stylistic or synonym changes: Mark 2:3, 12; 4:11; 9:1, 6; 12:6, 17; 13:7

    8D. Theologically motivated changes: Mark 8:38

Appendix B

SUMMARY OF MATTHEAN-MARCAN DIFFERENCES

1. Source Variant: Mark 1:42; 2:3–4, 5; 4:11; 6:26, 41, 50; 8:19–20, 27, 29; 9:2, 4, 7; 12:26

2. More Difficult Reading: Mark 1:41, 43; 2:10, 12, 14, 15, 16, 17, 20, 21, 22, 26, 27; 4:2, 10, 12; 6:17, 19–20, 21, 23, 26, 29, 33(2x), 36, 47–48; 8:14, 15, 17–18, 29, 30, 31, 33, 34; 9:6; 12:8, 16, 17, 24, 27; 13:14

   2A. Eliminate awkward readings: Mark 1:44; 2:9, 18, 22(2x); 4:2, 19; 6:33, 35, 43; 8:14, 33; 12:15, 19

   2B. Eliminate possible misunderstandings or problems: Mark 1:41, 44, 45; 2:1–2, 13, 15, 16, 18, 23; 4:10, 11; 6:22–23, 32, 44, 45; 8:34; 13:14, 23

3. Author's Style: Typical Style or Vocabulary: Mark 1:40(3x), 42; 2:3–4(2x), 5, 6, 12, 15, 24; 4:5, 6, 10, 11, 15, 17; 6:33(2x), 34, 35, 36, 39–40, 41, 46(2x), 50; 8:15, 17–18, 27, 31, 34, 35, 38; 9:2, 4, 7; 12:6, 13, 15, 22, 24; 13:5, 8, 22, 23, 27

   Change arbitrary style into unified style: Mark 2:6; 4:9, 18; 6:45; 8:16, 20; 12:7; 13:20

4. Less Refined Expressions

   4A. Less refined grammatical form: Mark 1:40, 41; 2:1–2, 26; 4:4(2x), 8,16, 17, 20; 6:29, 36, 41; 8:27, 35, 36(2x); 9:4, 9; 13:24, 25

   4B. Less elegant lexical expression: Mark 2:11, 22(2x); 4:6; 6:33, 46; 8:30, 31; 9:5, 8; 12:15, 16, 18, 19; 13:3, 16

   4C. Grammatical improvements: Mark 8:28; 9:9; 13:14, 27

5. Smoother Texts Are Later Readings

   5A. Make the text clearer: Mark 1:41; 2:8, 9, 16, 17, 18, 19, 21, 22, 23, 24; 4:1, 10, 11, 12, 15; 6:17, 37–38, 39–40, 43, 44, 47–48, 49, 55; 8:14, 16,

21, 27(2x), 30, 31(2x); 9:7; 12:2, 3, 7, 9, 10, 12, 13, 17, 18, 23; 13:4, 5, 27

5B. Adding explicit subject or object: Mark 2:14, 16, 17, 24(2x); 6:27, 37–38, 49, 50, 54; 8:14, 15, 17–18; 9:9; 12:3, 9, 15; 13:6, 18

5C. Make the text smoother: Mark 1:44; 2:10; 6:29, 47–48; 8:37; 12:11, 14, 17(2x); 13:6(2x), 7

5D. Eliminate redundancy: Mark 1:40(3x), 41, 42, 44; 2:7(2x), 9, 11, 15, 16, 18, 19, 20, 25, 26(2x); 4:1, 2, 3, 7, 8; 6:17, 18, 22–23(2x), 24–25, 27, 28, 29, 36, 37–38, 49, 50, 53, 54, 56; 8:19, 27, 28, 29; 9:1, 2, 3; 12:7, 14, 19, 23(2x), 27; 13:6, 8, 16, 19, 20, 21, 24, 27

6. Harmonization and Assimilation: Mark 2:11, 14, 22; 4:5, 7, 8, 16; 6:20(2x), 22–23; 8:17–18, 35, 37; 9:1, 3, 7; 12:6, 7, 15, 19, 25, 26; 13:16, 21

7. Orthodox Readings and Later Christian Community Changes: Mark 1:41, 43, 45; 2:7, 8, 12, 15, 26; 4:10, 13; 6:35, 37–38, 43, 45; 8:22–26

8. Others

8A. Add or delete personal pronouns: Mark 2:9, 17; 6:29, 45, 56; 8:17–18, 28; 12:1, 15

8B. Insignificant stylistic or synonym changes: Mark 1:41, 44; 2:11, 19, 21; 4:6; 6:39–40, 41; 9:1, 8, 9; 12:19; 13:22, 25

8C. Theologically motivated change: Mark 2:3–4, 17, 22, 26; 4:13; 6:37–38, 46, 49, 51–52, 56; 8:27, 38; 9:1, 2, 4, 6, 9, 10; 12:1, 3, 11, 26; 13:7, 18, 26

Bibliography

Abbott, Edwin. *Diatessarica—Part 2: The Corrections of Mark Adopted by Matthew and Luke.* London: Adam and Charles Black, 1901.

Aichinger, Hermann. "Quellenkritische Untersuchung der Perikope vom Ährenraufen am Sabbat: Mark 2,23–28 par Matthew 12,1–8 par Luke 6,1–5." In *Jesus in der Verkündigung der Kirche,* edited by Albert Fuchs, 110–53. Linz: A. Fuchs, 1976.

Aland, Kurt. "Ein neuer Textus Receptus für das griechische Neue Testament?" *NTS* 28 (1982): 143–53.

———. *Synopsis Quattuor Evangeliorum.* 13th ed. Stuttgart: Deutsche Bibelgesellschaft, 1985.

———. "The Twentieth Century Interlude in New Testament Textual Criticism." In *Text and Interpretation: Studies in the New Testament Presented to Matthew Black,* edited by Ernest Best and Robert McL. Wilson, 1–14. Cambridge: Cambridge University Press, 1979.

Aland, Kurt, and Barbara Aland. *The Text of the New Testament: An Introduction to the Critical Editions and to the Theory and Practice of Modern Textual Criticism.* 2d rev. ed. Translated by E. R. Rhodes. Grand Rapids: Eerdmans; Leiden: Brill, 1989.

Alexander, Loveday. "The Living Voice: Scepticism Towards the Written Word in Early Christian and in Graeco-Roman Texts." In *The Bible in Three Dimensions,* edited by D. J. A. Clines, S. E. Fowl, and S. E. Porter, 221–47. Sheffield: JSOT Press, 1990.

Allen, Willoughby C. *A Critical and Exegetical Commentary on the Gospel According to S. Matthew.* 3d ed. ICC. Edinburgh: T. and T. Clark, 1912.

———. *The Gospel According to Saint Mark with Introduction and Notes.* OCBC. London: Rivingtons, 1915.

Allison, Dale C., Jr. *The New Moses: A Matthean Typology.* Minneapolis: Fortress, 1993.

————. "A Plea for Thoroughgoing Eschatology." *JBL* 113 (1994): 651–68.

Ambrozic, Aloysius M. *The Hidden Kingdom: A Redaction-Critical Study of the References to the Kingdom of God in Mark's Gospel.* CBQMS 25. Washington, D.C.: Catholic Biblical Association of America, 1972.

Barth, Gerhard. "Matthew's Understanding of the Law." In *Überlieferung und Auslegung im Matthäusevangelium* [Tradition and Interpretation in Matthew], by Günther Bornkamm, Gerhard Barth, and Heinz Joachim Held, 58–164. NTL. Philadelphia: Westminster, 1963.

Bauer, Walter, William Arndt, F. Wilbur Gingrich, and Frederick Danker. *A Greek-English Lexicon of the New Testament and Other Early Christian Literature.* 2d ed. University of Chicago Press, 1979. Cited as BAGD.

Beare, F. W. "The Sabbath Was Made for Man?" *JBL* 79 (1960): 130–36.

————. "The Synoptic Apocalypse: Matthean Version." In *Understanding the Sacred Text: Essays in Honor of Morton S. Enslin on the Hebrew Bible and Christian Beginnings,* edited by John Reumann, 115–33. Valley Forge, Pa.: Judson, 1972.

Beasley-Murray, G. R. *A Commentary on Mark Thirteen.* London: Macmillan, 1957.

Bellinzoni, Arthur J., Jr., ed. *The Two-Source Hypothesis: A Critical Appraisal.* Macon, Ga.: Mercer, 1985.

Bengel, John Albert. Η ΚΑΙΝΗ ΔΙΑΘΗΚΗ: *Novum Testamentum Graecum.* 2 vols. Amsterdam: Dommeriana, 1752. Reprint, Graz, Austria: Akademische Druck und Verlagsanstalt, 1962.

————. *Gnomon of the New Testament.* Translated and edited by Andrew R. Fausset. 5 vols. 3d ed. Edinburgh: T. and T. Clark, 1860.

Black, David Alan. "Discourse Analysis, Synoptic Criticism, and the Problem of Markan Grammar: Some Methodological Considerations." Kansas City, Kans.: Society of Biblical Literature, 1991. Photocopied.

————. *New Testament Textual Criticism: A Concise Guide.* Grand Rapids: Baker, 1994.

————, ed. *Rethinking New Testament Textual Criticism.* Grand Rapids: Baker, 2002.

————. "Some Dissenting Notes on R. Stein's *The Synoptic Problem* and Markan 'Errors.'" *FN* 1 (1988): 95–101.

————. "The Text of Mark 6.20." *NTS* 34 (1988): 143

Black, David Alan, and David R. Beck, eds. *Rethinking the Synoptic Problem.* Grand Rapids: Baker, 2001.

Black, M. *An Aramaic Approach to the Gospels and Acts.* 3d ed. Oxford: Clarendon, 1967.

Blass, F., A. Debrunner, and R. W. Funk. *A Grammar of the New Testament and Other Early Christian Literature.* Chicago: University of Chicago Press, 1961. Cited as BDF.

Blomberg, Craig L. *Interpreting the Parables.* Downers Grove, Ill.: InterVarsity, 1990.

————. *Jesus and the Gospels.* Nashville: Broadman and Holman, 1997.

————. *Matthew.* Vol. 22. NAC. Nashville: Broadman, 1992.

————. "The Synoptic Problem: Where Do We Stand at the Start of a New Century?" In *Rethinking the Synoptic Problem.* Edited by David Alan Black and David R. Beck. Grand Rapids: Baker, 2001.

————. "The Tendencies of the Tradition in the Parables of the Gospel of Thomas." M.A. thesis, Trinity Evangelical Divinity School, 1979.

Boismard, M.-É. "Influences Matthéennes sur L'Ultimate Rédaction de L'Évangile de Marc." In *L'Évangile selon Marc: Tradition et Rédaction,* edited by M. Sabbe, 93–101. BETL 34. Leuven: Leuven University Press, 1974.

————. "Théorie des Niveaux Multiples." In *The Interrelations of the Gospels: A Symposium Led by M.-É. Boismard, W. R. Farmer, F. Neirynck, Jerusalem 1984,* edited by David L. Dungan, 231–43. BETL 95. Macon, Ga.: Mercer; Leuven: Leuven University Press, 1990.

————. "The Two-Source Theory at an Impasse." *NTS* 26 (1979): 1–17.

Bonnard, Pierre. *L'Évangile selon Saint Matthieu.* 2d ed. Commentaire du Nouveau Testament 1. Paris: Delachaux et Niestlé, 1970.

Bornkamm, Günther, Gerhard Barth, and Heinz Joachim Held. *Überlieferung und Auslegung im Matthäusevangelium* [Tradition and Interpretation in Matthew]. NTL. Translated by Percy Scott. Philadelphia: Westminster, 1963.

Bristol, Lyle O. "New Testament Textual Criticism in the Eighteenth Century." *JBL* 69 (1950): 101–12.

————. "New Testament Textual Criticism in the Nineteenth Century." *RevExp* 49 (1952): 36–40.

Bromiley, G. W., ed. *International Standard Bible Encyclopedia.* 4 vols. Grand Rapids: Eerdmans, 1979–1988. Cited as *ISBE.*

Brooks, James A. *Mark.* Vol. 23. NAC. Nashville: Broadman, 1991.

Brown, John P. "Early Revision of the Gospel of Mark." *JBL* 78 (1959): 215–27.

Brown, Robert K., and Philip W. Comfort, trans. *The New Greek-English Interlinear New Testament.* Edited by J. D. Douglas. 4th ed. Wheaton, Ill.: Tyndale House, 1993.

Bruce, F. F. *The Books and the Parchments: Some Chapters in the Transmission of the Bible.* Westwood, N.J.: Revell, 1950.

Buchanan, G. W. "Has the Griesbach Hypothesis Been Falsified?" *JBL* 93 (1974): 550–72.

Bundy, W. E. *Jesus and the First Three Gospels.* Cambridge, Mass.: Harvard University Press, 1955.

Burkett, Delbert. *Rethinking Gospel Sources: From Proto-Mark to Mark.* New York: T. and T. Clark, 2004.

Burkitt, F. C. "Levi, Son of Alphaeus." *JTS* 28 (1927): 273–74.

Burton, Ernest De Witt. *Some Principles of Literary Criticism and Their Application to the Synoptic Problem.* Chicago: University of Chicago Press, 1904.

———. *Syntax of the Moods and Tenses in New Testament Greek.* 3d ed. Edinburgh: T. and T. Clark, 1898.

Butler, B. C. *The Originality of St. Matthew: A Critique of the Two-Document Hypothesis.* Cambridge: Cambridge University Press, 1951.

Buttrick, David G., ed. *Jesus and Man's Hope.* Vol. 1 of *A Perspective Book.* Pittsburgh: Pittsburgh Theological Seminary, 1970.

Carlston, Charles E. *The Parables of the Triple Tradition.* Philadelphia: Fortress, 1975.

Carson, Donald A. "Matthew." In *EBC.* Vol. 8, *Matthew, Mark, Luke,* edited by Frank E. Gaebelein, 1–599. Grand Rapids: Zondervan, 1984.

Casey, Maurice. *Aramaic Sources of Mark's Gospel.* Cambridge: Cambridge University Press, 1998.

Cave, C. H. "The Leper: Mark 1.40–45." *NTS* 25 (1978–79): 245–50.

Cerfaux, Lucien. "La Connaissance des Secrets du Royaume D'Apres Matt. XIII.11 et Parallèles." *NTS* 2 (1956): 238–49.

Cole, R. Alan. *The Gospel According to Mark: An Introduction and Commentary.* TNTC 2. 2d ed. Leicester: InterVarsity; Grand Rapids: Eerdmans, 1989.

Collins, A. Y. Review of Barry W. Henaut, *Oral Tradition and the Gospels: The Problem of Mark 4. JBL* 114 (1995): 517–20.

Colwell, Ernest C. "Scribal Habits in Early Papyri: A Study in the Corruption of the Text." In *The Bible in Modern Scholarship,* edited by J. P. Hyatt, 370–89. Nashville: Abingdon, 1965. Reprinted in *Studies in Methodology in Textual Criticism of the New Testament,* edited by Bruce M. Metzger, NTTS 9 (Leiden: Brill, 1969), 106–24.

———. *Studies in Methodology in Textual Criticism of the New Testament.* Edited by Bruce M. Metzger. NTTS 9. Leiden: Brill, 1969.

Cope, O. Lamar. "The Argument Revolves: The Pivotal Evidence for Markan Priority Is Reversing Itself." In *New Synoptic Studies: The Cambridge Gospel*

Conference and Beyond, edited by William R. Farmer, 143–59. Macon, Ga.: Mercer, 1983.

———. *Matthew: A Scribe Trained for the Kingdom of Heaven.* CBQMS 5. Washington, D.C.: The Catholic Biblical Association of America, 1976.

———. Review of David S. New, *Old Testament Quotations in the Synoptic Gospels, and the Two-Document Hypothesis. JBL* 114 (1995): 516–17.

Cory, Steven. "The Aloofness of Jesus in Mark." Paper presented at the annual meeting of the national SBL; Philadelphia, 1995.

Cranfield, C. E. B. *The Gospel According to Saint Mark: An Introduction and Commentary.* 2d impression with supplementary notes. Cambridge Greek Testament Commentary. Cambridge: Cambridge University Press, 1963.

Crook, Zeba Antonin. "The Synoptic Parables of the Mustard Seed and the Leaven: A Test-Case for the Two-Document, Two-Gospel, and Farrer-Goulder Hypotheses." *JSNT* 78 (2000): 23–48.

Crossley, James G. *The Date of Mark: Insight from the Law in Earliest Christianity.* JSNTSup 266. London: T. and T. Clark, 2004.

Crum, J. M. C. *St. Mark's Gospel: Two Stages of Its Making.* Cambridge: W. Heffer, 1936.

Cullmann, O. "Πέτρος." In *Theological Dictionary of the New Testament,* edited by G. Kittel and G. Friedrich, 6:103–8. Translated by G. W. Bromiley. 10 vols. Grand Rapids: Eerdmans, 1964–1976. Cited as TDNT.

Dabrowski, Eugène. *La Transfiguration de Jésus.* Scripta Pontificii Instituti Biblici 85. Rome: Institut Biblique Pontifical, 1939.

Damm, Alex. "*Ornatus:* An Application of Rhetoric to the Synoptic Problem." *NovT* 45.4 (2003): 338–64.

Davies, W. D., and D. C. Allison, Jr. *A Critical and Exegetical Commentary on the Gospel According to Saint Matthew.* Vol. 1, *Introduction and Commentary on Matthew I–VII.* Vol. 2, *Commentary on Matthew VIII–XVIII.* ICC. Edinburgh: T. and T. Clark, 1988, 1991.

Dehandschutter, B. "La Parabole des Vignerons Homicides (Mc., XII, 1–12) et L'Évangile selon Thomas." In *L'Évangile selon Marc: Tradition et Rédaction,* edited by M. Sabbe, 203–19. BETL 34. Leuven: Leuven University Press, 1974.

Demetrius. *Demetrius on Style.* Translated by W. R. Roberts. LCL. Cambridge, Mass.: Harvard University Press, 1953.

deWette, Wilhelm Martin Leberecht. *Lehrbuch der historisch kritischen Einleitung in die kanonischen Bücher des Neuen Testaments.* Berlin: G. Reimer, 1826.

Dewey, J. "The Literary Structure of the Controversy Narratives in Mark." *JBL* 92 (1973): 394–401.

Dodd, C. H. *The Parables of the Kingdom*. New York: Charles Scribner's, 1961.

Donahue, John R., and Daniel J. Harrington. *The Gospel of Mark*. Vol. 2. SP. Collegeville, Minn.: Liturgical Press, 2002.

Doudna, John Charles. *The Greek of the Gospel of Mark*. JBLMS 12. Philadelphia: Society of Biblical Literature and Exegesis, 1961.

Downing, F. G. "Compositional Conventions and the Synoptic Problem." *JBL* 107 (1988): 69–85.

———. *Doing Things with Words in the First Christian Century*. JSNTSup 200. Sheffield: Sheffield Academic Press, 2000.

———. "Redaction Criticism: Josephus' *Antiquities* and the Synoptic Gospels (I)." *JSNT* 8 (1980): 46–85.

———. "Word Processing in the Ancient World: The Social Production and Performance of Q," *JSNT* 64 (1996): 29–48. Reprinted in *Doing Things with Words in the First Christian Century*, JSNTSup 200 (Sheffield: Sheffield Academic Press, 2000), 75–94.

Dungan, David L. *A History of the Synoptic Problem: The Canon, the Text, the Composition, and the Interpretation of the Gospels*. Anchor Bible Reference Library. New York: Doubleday, 1999.

———, ed. *The Interrelations of the Gospels: A Symposium Led by M.-É. Boismard, W. R. Farmer, F. Neirynck, Jerusalem 1984*. BETL. Macon, Ga.: Mercer; Leuven: Leuven University Press, 1990.

———. "Mark: The Abridgement of Matthew and Luke." In *Jesus and Man's Hope*. Vol. 1 of *A Perspective Book*, edited by David G. Buttrick, 51–97. Pittsburgh: Pittsburgh Theological Seminary, 1970. Reprinted (partial) in *The Two-Source Hypothesis: A Critical Appraisal*, edited by Arthur J. Bellinzoni Jr. (Macon, Ga.: Mercer, 1985), 143–61.

———. "The Purpose and Provenance of the Gospel of Mark According to the Two-Gospel (Owen-Griesbach) Hypothesis." In *New Synoptic Studies. The Cambridge Gospel Conference and Beyond*, edited by William R. Farmer, 411–40. Macon, Ga.: Mercer, 1983.

Dungan, David L. and John S. Kloppenborg, "The Synoptic Problem: How Did We Get Our Gospels?" In *The International Bible Commentary: A Catholic and Ecumenical Commentary for the Twenty-First Century*, edited by William R. Farmer, 1231–40. Collegeville, Minn.: The Liturgical Press, 1998.

Dunn, James D. G. "Jesus in Oral Memory: The Initial Stages of the Jesus Tradition." In *SBLSP* 39. Atlanta: SBL, 2000.

———. "Matthew's Awareness of Markan Redaction." In *The Four Gospels, 1992: Festschrift Frans Neirynck*, edited by F. van Segbroeck, C. M. Tuckett,

G. Van Belle, and J. Verheyden, 1349–59. BETL 100. Leuven: Leuven University Press, 1992.

Duplacy, Jean. "Marc, 2, 10: Note de Syntaxe." In *Mélanges Bibliques Redigés en L'Honneur de Andre Robert*, 420–27. Travaux de L'Institut Catholique de Paris 4. Paris: Bloud and Gay, 1957.

Duplacy, Jean, and Jack Suggs. "Les Citations Grecques et la Critique du Texte du Nouveau Testament: Le passé, le Présent et l'Avenir." In *La Bible et les Pères*, edited by A. Benoit and P. Prigent, 187–213. Paris: Presses Universitaires de France, 1971.

Dupont, Jacques. "Le paralytique pardonné (Matt. 9,1–8)." *NRTh* 82 (1960): 940–58.

———. "Le Point de Vue de Matthieu dans le Chapitre des Paraboles." In *L'Évangile selon Matthieu: Rédaction et Théologie*, edited by M. Didier, 221–59. BETL 29. Leuven: Leuven University Press, 1972.

Dyer, Charles H. "Do the Synoptics Depend on Each Other?" *BSac* 138 (1981): 230–45.

Edwards, Elizabeth G. "On Using the Textual Apparatus of the UBS Greek New Testament." *BT* 28 (1977): 121–42.

Ehrman, Bart D. *The Orthodox Corruption of Scripture: The Effect of Early Christological Controversies on the Text of the New Testament*. New York: Oxford University, 1993.

———. "A Problem of Textual Circularity: The Alands on the Classification of New Testament Manuscripts." *Bib* 70 (1989): 377–88.

Ehrman, Bart D., and Michael W. Holmes, eds. *The Text of the New Testament in Contemporary Research: Essays on the Status Quaestionis. A Volume in Honor of Bruce M. Metzger*. Studies and Documents 46. Grand Rapids: Eerdmans, 1995.

Elliott, J. K. "The Atticist Grammarians." In *Essays and Studies in New Testament Textual Criticism*, 65–77. EFN. Cordoba: Ediciones El Almendro, 1990.

———. *A Bibliography of Greek New Testament Manuscripts*. SNTSMS 62. Cambridge: Cambridge University Press, 1989.

———. "Can We Recover the Original New Testament?" *Theology: A Monthly Review* 77 (1974): 338–53. Reprinted in *Essays and Studies in New Testament Textual Criticism*, EFN (Cordoba: Ediciones El Almendro, 1990), 17–44.

———. "The Conclusion of the Pericope of the Healing of the Leper and Mark 1,45." *JTS* 22 (1971): 153–57.

———. "An Eclectic Textual Commentary on the Greek Text of Mark's Gospel." In *New Testament Textual Criticism: Its Significance for Exegesis: Essays in*

Honour of Bruce M. Metzger, edited by Eldon Jay Epp and Gordon D. Fee, 47–60. Oxford: Clarendon, 1981. Reprinted in *The Language and Style of the Gospel of Mark: An Edition of C. H. Turner's "Notes on Marcan Usage," Together with Other Comparable Studies,* NovTSup 71 (Leiden: Brill, 1993), 189–202. Also reprinted in *Essays and Studies in New Testament Textual Criticism,* EFN (Cordoba: Ediciones El Almendro, 1990), 159–70.

———. *Essays and Studies in New Testament Textual Criticism.* EFN. Cordoba: Ediciones El Almendro, 1990.

———. "An Examination of the 26th Edition of Nestle-Aland *Novum Testamentum Graece.*" *JTS* 32 (1981): 19–49.

———. "An Examination of the Text and Apparatus of the Three Recent Greek Synopses." *NTS* 32 (1986): 557–82.

———. "The Healing of the Leper in the Synoptic Parallels." *TZ* 34 (1978): 175–76.

———. "L'importance de la Critique Textuelle pour le Problème Synoptique." *RevBib* 96 (1989): 56–70.

———. "In Defence of Thoroughgoing Eclecticism in New Testament Textual Criticism." *ResQ* 21 (1978): 95–115.

———. *The Language and Style of the Gospel of Mark: An Edition of C. H. Turner's "Notes on Marcan Usage," Together with Other Comparable Studies.* NovTSup 71. Leiden: Brill, 1993.

———, ed. *The Principles and Practice of New Testament Textual Criticism: Collected Essays of G. D. Kilpatrick.* BETL 96. Leuven: Leuven University Press, 1990.

———. "Printed Editions of Greek Synopses and Their Influence on the Synoptic Problem." In *The Four Gospels, 1992: Festschrift Frans Neirynck,* edited by F. van Segbroeck, C. M. Tuckett, G. Van Belle, and J. Verheyden, 1:337–57. BETL 100. Leuven: Leuven University Press, 1992.

———. "The Relevance of Textual Criticism to the Synoptic Problem." In *The Interrelations of the Gospels,* edited by David L. Dungan, 348–59. BETL 95. Leuven: Leuven University Press, 1990.

———. Review of *Jesus and the Oral Gospel Tradition,* edited by H. Wansbrough. *NovT* 35 (1993): 307.

———. "Thoroughgoing Eclecticism in New Testament Textual Criticism." In *The Text of the New Testament in Contemporary Research: Essays on the Status Quaestionis: A Volume in Honor of Bruce M. Metzger,* edited by Bart D. Ehrman and Michael W. Holmes, 321–35. Studies and Documents 46. Grand Rapids: Eerdmans, 1995.

Ellis, E. Earle. "Gospels Criticism: A Perspective on the State of the Art." In *The Gospel and the Gospels,* edited by Peter Stuhlmacher, 26–52. Grand Rapids: Eerdmans, 1991.

―――. "The Historical Jesus and the Gospels." In *Evangelium, Schriftauslegung, Kirche: Festschrift P. Stuhlmacher,* edited by Jostein Adna, Scott J. Hafemann, and O. Hofius, 94–106. Gottingen: Vandenhoeck and Ruprecht, 1997.

―――. "The Making of Narratives in the Synoptic Gospels." In *Jesus and the Oral Gospel Tradition,* edited by Henry Wansbrough, 310–33. JSNTSup 64. Sheffield: JSOT Press, 1991.

Engelbrecht, J. "The Language of the Gospel of Matthew." *Neot* 24 (1990): 199–213.

Enslin, Morton S. "Luke and Matthew: Compilers or Authors?" In *Aufstieg und Niedergang der romischen Welt,* edited by Hildegard Temporini and Wolfgang Haase, 2358–88. *ANRW* 25.3. Berlin: W. de Gruyter, 1985.

Epp, E. J. "The Eclectic Method in New Testament Textual Criticism: Solution or Symptom?" *HTR* 69 (1976): 211–57. Reprinted in *Studies in the Theory and Method of New Testament Textual Criticism,* edited by E. J. Epp and G. D. Fee, Studies and Documents 45 (Grand Rapids: Eerdmans, 1993), 211–57.

―――. "Issues in New Testament Textual Criticism." In *Rethinking New Testament Textual Criticism,* edited by David A. Black. Grand Rapids: Baker, 2002.

Epp, E. J., and G. D. Fee, eds. *New Testament Textual Criticism: Its Significance for Exegesis: Essays in Honour of Bruce M. Metzger.* Oxford: Clarendon, 1981.

―――. *Studies in the Theory and Method of New Testament Textual Criticism.* Studies and Documents 45. Grand Rapids: Eerdmans, 1993.

Evans, Craig A. *Mark 8:27–16:20.* WBC 34B. Nashville: Thomas Nelson, 2001.

―――. *To See and Not Perceive: Isaiah 6.9–10 in Early Jewish and Christian Interpretation.* JSOTsup 64. Sheffield: JSOT, 1989.

Evans, Owen E. "Synoptic Criticism Since Streeter." *ExpTim* 72 (1960–61): 295–99.

Fanning, B. M. *Verbal Aspect in New Testament Greek.* Oxford: Clarendon, 1990.

Farmer, William Reuben. "Basic Affirmation with Some Demurrals: A Response to Roland Mushat Frye." In *The Relationships Among the Gospels: An Interdisciplinary Dialogue,* edited by William O. Walker Jr., 303–22. Trinity University Monograph Series in Religion 5. San Antonio: Trinity University Press, 1978.

―――. "The Case for the Two-gospel hypothesis." In *Rethinking the Synoptic*

Problem. Edited by David Alan Black and David R. Beck. Grand Rapids: Baker, 2001.

———. *The Gospel of Jesus: The Pastoral Relevance of the Synoptic Problem.* Louisville: WJKP, 1994.

———. *Jesus and the Gospel: Tradition, Scripture, and Canon.* Philadelphia: Fortress, 1982.

———. "Modern Developments of Griesbach's Hypothesis." *NTS* 23 (1977): 275–95.

———, ed. *New Synoptic Studies: The Cambridge Gospel Conference and Beyond.* Macon, Ga.: Mercer, 1983.

———. "The Passion Prediction Passages and the Synoptic Problem: A Test Case." *NTS* 36 (1990): 558–70.

———. "The Present State of the Synoptic Problem." *PSTJ* 32 (1978): 1–7.

———. "The Present State of the Synoptic Problem." *Literary Studies in Luke-Acts: Essays in Honor of Joseph B. Tyson.* Macon, Ga.: Mercer University Press, 1998, 11–36. An updated version can be found at http://www.bham.ac.uk/theology/synoptic-1-farmer.htm.

———. "A Response to Joseph Fitzmyer's Defense of the Two Document Hypothesis." In *New Synoptic Studies: The Cambridge Gospel Conference and Beyond,* 501–23. Macon, Ga.: Mercer, 1983.

———. "A 'Skeleton in the Closet' of Gospel Research." *Biblical Research* 6 (1961): 18–42.

———. *The Synoptic Problem: A Critical Analysis.* Dillsboro, N.C.: Western North Carolina Press, 1976.

———. "The Two-gospel hypothesis: The Statement of the Hypothesis." In *The Interrelations of the Gospels,* edited by David L. Dungan, 125–56. BETL 95. Leuven: Leuven University Press, 1990.

Farnell, F. David. "The Case for the Independence View of Gospel Origins." In *Three Views on the Origins of the Synoptic Gospels,* edited by Robert L. Thomas. Grand Rapids: Kregel, 2002.

Fee, Gordon D. "The Corrections of Papyrus Bodmer II and Early Textual Transmission." *NovT* 7 (1965): 247–57.

———. "Modern Text Criticism and the Synoptic Problem." In *J. J. Griesbach: Synoptic and Text-Critical Studies, 1776–1976,* edited by B. Orchard and T. R. W. Longstaff, 154–69. Cambridge: Cambridge University Press, 1978. Reprinted in *Studies in the Theory and Method of New Testament Textual Criticism,* edited by E. J. Epp and G. D. Fee, Studies and Documents 45 (Grand Rapids: Eerdmans, 1993), 174–82.

―――. "Rigorous or Reasoned Eclecticism—Which?" In *Studies in the Theory and Method of New Testament Textual Criticism*, edited by E. J. Epp and G. D. Fee, 124–40. Studies and Documents 45. Grand Rapids: Eerdmans, 1993. First published in *Studies in New Testament Language and Text: Essays in Honour of George D. Kilpatrick on the Occasion of His Sixty-fifth Birthday*, edited by J. K. Elliott. NovTSup 44 (Leiden: Brill, 1976), 174–97.

―――. "A Text-Critical Look at the Synoptic Problem." *NovT* 22 (1980): 12–28. Reprinted in *The Synoptic Problem and Q: Selected Studies from* Novum Testamentum, edited by David E. Orton (Leiden: Brill, 1999), 163–79.

―――. "Textual Criticism." In *Dictionary of Jesus and the Gospels*, edited by Joel B. Green and Scot McKnight, 827–31. Downers Grover, Ill.: InterVarsity, 1992.

Feuillet, A. "Les Perspectives Propres à Chaque Évangéliste dans les Récits de la Transfiguration." *Bib* 39 (1958): 281–301.

Filson, Floyd V. *The Gospel According to St Matthew*. BNTC. 2d ed. London: Adam and Charles Black, 1971.

Finegan, Jack. *Encountering New Testament Manuscripts: A Working Introduction to Textual Criticism*. Grand Rapids: Eerdmans, 1974.

Fitzmyer, J. A. *The Gospel According to Luke (I–IX): Introduction, Translation, and Notes*. AB 28. New York: Doubleday, 1981.

―――. "Memory and Manuscript: The Origins and Transmission of the Gospel Tradition." *ThS* 23 (1961): 442–57.

―――. "The Priority of Mark and the 'Q' Source in Luke." In *Jesus and Man's Hope*. Vol. 1 of *A Perspective Book*, edited by David G. Buttrick, 131–70. Pittsburgh: Pittsburgh Theological Seminary, 1970. Reprinted (partial) in *The Two-Source Hypothesis: A Critical Appraisal*, edited by Arthur J. Bellinzoni Jr. (Macon, Ga.: Mercer, 1985), 37–52.

Fleddermann, Harry. "'And He Wanted to Pass by Them' (Mark 6:48c)." *CBQ* 45 (1983): 389–95.

Focant, Camille, ed. *The Synoptic Gospels: Source Criticism and the New Literary Criticism*. BETL 110. Leuven: Leuven University Press, 1993.

France, R. T. *The Gospel According to Matthew: An Introduction and Commentary*. TNTC 1. Grand Rapids: Eerdmans; Leicester: InterVarsity, 1985.

―――. *The Gospel of Mark: A Commentary on the Greek Text*. NIGTC. Grand Rapids: Eerdmans, 2002.

―――. *Jesus and the Old Testament*. London: Tyndale, 1971.

―――. *Matthew: Evangelist and Teacher*. Grand Rapids: Zondervan, 1989.

Frye, Roland Mushat. "The Synoptic Problems and Analogies in Other Literatures."

In *The Relationships Among the Gospels: An Interdisciplinary Dialogue,* edited by William O. Walker Jr., 261–302. Trinity University Monograph Series in Religion 5. San Antonio: Trinity University Press, 1978.

Fuller, Reginald H. "Die neuere Diskussion uber das synoptische Problem." *TZ* 34 (1978): 123–48.

———. "The Synoptic Problem: After Ten Years." *PSTJ* 28 (1975): 63–68.

Garland, David E. *The NIV Application Commentary: Mark.* Grand Rapids: Zondervan, 1996.

Gaston, Lloyd. *No Stone on Another.* NovTSup 23. Leiden: Brill, 1970.

Gench, Frances T. "A Response to Donald J. Verseput's 'The Davidic Messiah and Matthew's Jewish Christianity.'" Paper presented at the annual meeting of the national SBL in Philadelphia, 1995.

Gerhardsson, Birger. "The Path of the Gospel Tradition." In *The Gospel and the Gospels,* edited by Peter Stuhlmacher, 75–96. Grand Rapids: Eerdmans, 1991.

Gnilka, Joachim. *Das Evangelium nach Markus.* EKKNT 2. 2 vols. Zürich: Benziger Verlag; Neukirchen-Vluyn: Neukirchener Verlag, 1978, 1979.

Goodacre, Mark. "Fatigue in the Synoptics." *NTS* 44 (1998): 45–58.

———. *The Synoptic Problem: A Way Through the Maze.* London: Sheffield Academic Press, 2001.

Gould, Ezra P. *A Critical and Exegetical Commentary on the Gospel According to St. Mark.* ICC 27. Edinburgh: T. and T. Clark, 1896.

Goulder, Michael. "Some Observations on Professor Farmer's 'Certain Results . . .'" In *Synoptic Studies: The Ampleforth Conferences of 1982 and 1983,* edited by C. M. Tuckett, 99–104. JSNTSup 7. Sheffield: JSOT, 1984.

Greenlee, J. H. *Introduction to New Testament Textual Criticism.* 2d ed. Peabody, Mass.: Hendrickson, 1995.

Griesbach, J. J. "Commentatio qua Marci Evangeluim totum e Matthaei et Lucae Commentariis Decerptum esse monstratur." In *J. J. Griesbach: Synoptic and Text-Critical Studies, 1776–1976,* edited by Bernard Orchard and T. R. W. Longstaff, 74–102. Cambridge: Cambridge University Press, 1978.

Grundmann, Walter. *Das Evangelium nach Markus.* THKNT 2. Berlin: Evangelische Verlagsanstalt, 1977.

———. *Das Evangelium nach Matthäus.* THKNT 1. Berlin: Evangelische Verlagsanstalt, 1986.

Guelich, Robert A. *Mark 1–8:26.* WBC 34A. Dallas: Word, 1989.

Gundry, Robert H. *Mark: A Commentary on His Apology for the Cross.* Grand Rapids: Eerdmans, 1993.

———. *Matthew: A Commentary on His Handbook for a Mixed Church Under Persecution.* 2d ed. Grand Rapids: Eerdmans, 1994.

———. *The Use of the Old Testament in St. Matthew's Gospel.* NovTSup 18. Leiden: Brill, 1967.

Hagner, Donald A. *Matthew 1–13, Matthew 14–28.* WBC 33A, 33B. Dallas: Word, 1993, 1995.

Hamann, H. P. "*Sic et Non:* Are We So Sure of Matthean Dependence on Mark?" *CTM* 41 (1970): 462–69.

Harrington, Daniel J. *The Gospel of Matthew.* Vol. 1. SP. Collegeville, Minn.: Liturgical Press, 1991.

Harris, J. R. "Artificial Variants in the Text of the New Testament." *ExpTim* 24 (1922): 259–61.

Harris, Murray J. "Prepositions and Theology in the Greek New Testament." In *NIDNTT,* edited by Colin Brown, 3:1171–1215. 4 vols. Grand Rapids: Zondervan, 1978, 1986.

Hawkins, John C. *Horae Synopticae. Contributions to the Study of the Synoptic Problem.* 2d rev. ed. Oxford: Clarendon, 1909. Reprint, Grand Rapids: Baker, 1968.

Head, Peter M. "Christology and Textual Transmission: Reverential Alterations in the Synoptic Gospels." *NovT* 35 (1993): 105–29.

———. *Christology and the Synoptic Problem: An Argument for Markan Priority.* Cambridge: Cambridge University Press, 1997.

———. "Observations on Early Papyri of the Synoptic Gospels, especially on the 'Scribal Habits.'" *Bib* 71 (1990): 240–47.

Held, H. J. "Matthew as Interpreter of the Miracle Stories." In *Überlieferung und Auslegung im Matthäusevangelium* [Tradition and Interpretation in Matthew], by Günther Bornkamm, Gerhard Barth, and Heinz Joachim Held. NTL. Translated by Percy Scott. Philadelphia: Westminster, 1963.

Hengel, Martin. *The Four Gospels and the One Gospel of Jesus Christ.* Harrisburg, Pa.: Trinity Press International, 2000.

Hill, David. *The Gospel of Matthew.* NCB Commentary. Grand Rapids: Eerdmans; London: Marshall, Morgan and Scott, 1972.

Holmes, Michael W. "Reasoned Eclecticism in New Testament Textual Criticism." In *The Text of the New Testament in Contemporary Research: Essays on the Status Quaestionis: A Volume in Honor of Bruce M. Metzger,* edited by Bart D. Ehrman and Michael W. Holmes, 336–60. Studies and Documents 46. Grand Rapids: Eerdmans, 1995.

———. "The Text of the Matthean Divorce Passages: A Comment on the Appeal to Harmonization in Textual Decisions." *JBL* 109 (1990): 651–64.

————. "Textual Criticism." In *Dictionary of Paul and His Letters,* edited by Gerald F. Hawthorne and Ralph P. Martin, 927–32. Downers Grover, Ill.: InterVarsity, 1993.

Holtzmann, Heinrich Julius. *Die synoptischen Evangelien.* Leipzig: Wilhelm Engelmann, 1863.

Honoré, A. M. "A Statistical Study of the Synoptic Problem." *NovT* 10 (1968): 95–147.

Hooker, Morna D. *The Gospel According to Saint Mark.* BNTC. London: A. and C. Black. 1982. Reprint, Peabody, Mass.: Hendrickson, 1991.

Hübner, Hans. *Das Gesetz in der synoptischen Tradition: Studien zur These einer progressiven Qumranisierung und Judaisierung innerhalb der synoptischen Tradition.* 2d ed. Göttingen: Vandenhoeck and Ruprecht, 1986.

Hummel, Reinhart. *Die Auseinandersetzung zwischen Kirche und Judentum im Matthäusevangelium.* Beiträge zur evangelischen Theologie 33. 2d ed. München: Chr. Kaiser Verlag, 1966.

Hurtado, Larry W. *Mark.* NIBCNT. Peabody, Mass.: Hendrickson, 1989.

————. *Text-Critical Methodology and the Pre-Caesarean Text: Codex W in the Gospel of Mark.* Studies and Documents 43. Grand Rapids: Eerdmans, 1981.

Jepsen, A. "Anmerkungen eines Aussenseiters zum Synoptikerproblem." *NovT* 14 (1972): 106–14.

Jeremias, J. "Palästinakundliches zum Gleichnis vom Säemann (Mark iv. 3–8 par.)." *NTS* 13 (1966): 48–53.

Johnson, Sherman E. *The Griesbach Hypothesis and Redaction Criticism.* SBLMS 41. Atlanta: Scholars, 1991.

Keck, Leander E. "Oral Tradition Literature and the Gospels: The Seminar." In *The Relationships Among the Gospels: An Interdisciplinary Dialogue,* edited by William O. Walker Jr., 103–22. Trinity University Monograph Series in Religion 5. San Antonio: Trinity University Press, 1978.

Keener, Craig S. *A Commentary on the Gospel of Matthew.* Grand Rapids: Eerdmans, 1999.

Kelber, Werner. *The Oral and Written Gospel: The Hermeneutics of Speaking and Writing in the Synoptic Tradition, Mark, Paul and Q.* Philadelphia: Fortress, 1983.

Kenyon, Sir Frederic G. *Handbook to the Textual Criticism of the New Testament.* 2d ed. London: Macmillan, 1912.

Kiley, Mark. "Why 'Matthew' in Matt 9, 9–13?" *Bib* 65 (1984): 347–51.

Kilpatrick, G. D. "Atticism and the Text of the Greek New Testament." In *Neut-*

estamentliche Autsätze: Festschrift für Prof. Josef Schmid zum 70. Geburtstag, edited by J. Blinzler, O. Kuss, and F. Mussner, 125–37. Regensburg: Friedrich Pustex, 1963. Reprinted in *The Principles and Practice of New Testament Textual Criticism: Collected Essays of G. D. Kilpatrick,* edited by J. K. Elliott, BETL 96 (Leuven: Leuven University Press, 1990), 15–32.

———. "Eclecticism and Atticism." *ETL* 53 (1977): 107–12. Reprinted in *The Principles and Practice of New Testament Textual Criticism: Collected Essays of G. D. Kilpatrick,* edited by J. K. Elliott, BETL 96 (Leuven: Leuven University Press, 1990), 73–79.

———. "The Greek New Testament Text of Today and the Textus Receptus." In *The New Testament in Historical and Contemporary Perspective: Essays in Memory of G. H. C. Macgregor,* edited by H. Anderson and W. Barclay, 189–206. Oxford: Basil Blackwell, 1965. Reprinted in *The Principles and Practice of New Testament Textual Criticism: Collected Essays of G. D. Kilpatrick,* edited by J. K. Elliott, BETL 96 (Leuven: Leuven University Press, 1990), 33–52.

———. "Matthew on Matthew." In *Synoptic Studies: The Ampleforth Conferences of 1982 and 1983,* edited by C. M. Tuckett, 177–85. JSNTSup 7. Sheffield: JSOT, 1984. Reprinted in *The Principles and Practice of New Testament Textual Criticism: Collected Essays of G. D. Kilpatrick,* edited by J. K. Elliott, BETL 96 (Leuven: Leuven University Press, 1990), 250–58.

———. *The Origins of the Gospel According to St. Matthew.* Oxford: Clarendon, 1946.

———. "Some Thoughts on Modern Textual Criticism and the Synoptic Gospels." *NovT* 19 (1977): 275–92. Reprinted in *The Principles and Practice of New Testament Textual Criticism: Collected Essays of G. D. Kilpatrick,* edited by J. K. Elliott, BETL 96 (Leuven: Leuven University Press, 1990), 80–97.

———. "Western Text and Original Text in the Gospels and Acts." *JTS* 44 (1943): 30–34.

Kingsbury, Jack Dean. *The Parables of Jesus in Matthew 13: A Study in Redaction-Criticism.* Richmond, Va.: John Knox, 1969.

Kloppenborg, J. S. "The Theological Stakes in the Synoptic Problem." In *The Four Gospels, 1992: Festschrift Frans Neirynck,* edited by F. van Segbroeck, C. M. Tuckett, G. Van Belle, and J. Verheyden, 93–120. 2 vols. BETL 100. Leuven: Leuven University Press, 1992.

Knowles, Michael. *Jeremiah in Matthew's Gospel: The Rejected Profit Motif in Matthean Redaction.* JSNTSup 68. Sheffield: JSOT, 1993.

Koester, Helmut. "The Text of the Synoptic Gospels in the Second Century." In *Gospel Traditions in the Second Century: Origins, Recensions, Text, and*

Transmission, edited by W. L. Petersen, 19–37. Christianity and Judaism in Antiquity 3. South Bend, Ind.: University of Notre Dame Press, 1989.

———. "Written Gospels or Oral Tradition?" *JBL* 113 (1994): 293–97.

Lagrange, M.-J. *Évangile selon Saint Marc.* Rev. ed. Paris: Librairie Lecoffre, 1947.

Lake, Kirsopp. "ΕΜΒΡΙΜΗΣΑΜΕΝΟΣ and ΟΡΓΙΣΘΕΙΣ, MARK 1, 40–43." *HTR* 16 (1923): 197–98.

Lane, William L. *The Gospel According to Mark: The English Text with Introduction, Exposition and Notes.* NICNT. Grand Rapids: Eerdmans, 1974.

Léon-Dufour, Xavier. "Interprétation des Évangiles et Problème Synoptique." *ETL* 43 (1967): 5–16.

Lindsey, Robert L. "A New Approach to the Synoptic Gospels." *Mishkan* 17.18 (1992): 87–106.

Linnemann, Eta. *Is There A Synoptic Problem? Rethinking the Literary Dependence of the First Three Gospels.* Translated by Robert W. Yarbrough. Grand Rapids: Baker, 1992.

Linton, Olof. "Evidences of a Second Century Revised Edition of St Mark's Gospel." *NTS* 13 (1968): 321–55.

Longstaff, Thomas R. W. *Evidence of Conflation in Mark? A Study in the Synoptic Problem.* SBLDS 28. Missoula, Mont.: Scholars, 1977.

Longstaff, Thomas R. W., and Page A. Thomas. *The Synoptic Problem: A Bibliography, 1716–1988.* New Gospel Studies 4. Macon, Ga.: Mercer, 1988.

Lord, Albert B. "The Gospels as Oral Traditional Literature." In *The Relationships Among the Gospels: An Interdisciplinary Dialogue,* edited by William O. Walker Jr., 33–91. Trinity University Monograph Series in Religion 5. San Antonio: Trinity University Press, 1978.

Louw, J. P., and E. A. Nida, eds. *Greek-English Lexicon of the New Testament Based on Semantic Domains.* 2 vols. New York: United Bible Societies, 1988.

Lowe, Malcolm. "From the Parable of the Vineyard to a Pre-Synoptic Source." *NTS* 28 (1982): 257–63.

Luck, Georg. "Textual Criticism Today." *AJP* 102 (1981): 164–94.

Lührmann, Dieter. "The Gospel of Mark and the Sayings Collection Q." *JBL* 108 (1989): 51–71.

Luz, Ulrich. "The Disciples in the Gospel According to Matthew." In *The Interpretation of Matthew,* edited by Graham Stanton, 98–128. London: SPCK; Philadelphia: Fortress, 1983.

———. *Das Evangelium nach Matthäus (Mt 1–7)* [Matthew 1–7]. Translated by Wilhelm C. Linss. EKKNT. Zürich: Benziger, 1985; Minneapolis: Fortress, 1992.

———. *Matthew 8–20.* Hermeneia. Minneapolis: Fortress, 2001.

———. "The Primacy Text (Matt. 16:18)." *PSB* 12 (1991): 41–55.

———. "Das Primatwort Matthäus 16.17–19 aus Wirkungsgeschichtlicher Sicht." *NTS* 37 (1991): 415–33.

Malbon, Elizabeth Struthers. "TH OIKIA AΥTOΥ: Mark 2.15 in Context." *NTS* 31 (1985), 282–92.

Manek, Jindrich. "Mark viii 14–21." *NovT* 7 (1964): 10–14.

Mann, C. S. *Mark: A New Translation with Introduction and Commentary.* AB 27. New York: Doubleday, 1986.

Manson, T. W. "Mark ii. 27f." *ConNT* 11 (1947): 138–46.

Marcus, Joel. *Mark: A New Translation with Introduction and Commentary.* AB 27. New York: Doubleday, 2000.

Marshall, I. Howard. "How to Solve the Synoptic Problem: Luke 11:43 and Parallels." In *The New Testament Age: Essays in Honor of Bo Reicke,* edited by William C. Weinrich, 2:313–25. Macon, Ga.: Mercer, 1984.

Martini, Carlo M. "Eclecticism and Atticism in the Textual Criticism of the Greek New Testament." In *On Language, Culture and Religion: In Honor of Eugene A. Nida,* edited by M. Black and W. A. Smalley, 149–56. Hague: Mouton, 1974.

McCord, Hugo. "The Synoptic Problem." *ResQ* 1 (1957): 51–69.

McIver, Robert K., and Marie Carroll. "Experiments to Develop Criteria for Determining the Existence of Written Sources, and their Potential Implications for the Synoptic Problem." *JBL* 121 (2002): 667–87.

McKnight, Scot. "A Generation That Knows Not Streeter: The Case for Markan Priority." In *Rethinking the Synoptic Problem.* Edited by David Alan Black and David Beck. Grand Rapids: Baker, 2001.

———. "The Role of the Disciples in Matthew and Mark: A Redactional Study." M.A. thesis, Trinity Evangelical Divinity School, 1980.

———. "Source Criticism." In *New Testament Criticism and Interpretation,* edited by David Alan Black and David S. Dockery, 136–72. Grand Rapids: Zondervan, 1991.

McNeile, Alan Hugh. *The Gospel According to St. Matthew: The Greek Text with Introduction, Notes, and Indices.* London: Macmillan, 1915.

McNicol, Allan J. "The Composition of the Synoptic Eschatological Discourse." In *The Interrelations of the Gospels: A Symposium Led by M.-É. Boismard, W. R. Farmer, F. Neirynck, Jerusalem 1984,* edited by David L. Dungan, 157–200. BETL. Macon Ga.: Mercer; Leuven: Leuven University Press, 1990.

———. *Jesus' Directions for the Future: A Source and Redaction-History Study of the Use of the Eschatological Traditions in Paul and in the Synoptic Accounts of Jesus' Last Eschatological Discourse.* New Gospel Studies 9. Macon, Ga.: Mercer, 1996.

———. "The Two Gospel Hypothesis Under Scrutiny: A Response to C. M. Tuckett's Analysis of Recent Neo-Griesbachian Gospel Criticism." *PSTJ* 40 (1987): 5–13.

McNicol, Allan J., ed. *Beyond the Q Impasse: Luke's Use of Matthew. A Demonstration by the Research Team of the International Institute for Gospel Studies,* with David L. Dungan and David B. Peabody. Valley Forge, Pa.: Trinity Press International, 1996.

Meagher, John C. *Clumsy Construction in Mark's Gospel: A Critique of Form- and Redaktionsgeschichte.* Toronto Studies in Theology 3. New York: Edwin Mellen, 1979.

———. "Die Form- und Redaktionsgeschichtliche Methoden: the Principle of Clumsiness and the Gospel of Mark." *JAAR* 43 (1975): 459–72.

Meier, John P. *Matthew.* New Testament Message. Vol. 3. Wilmington, Del.: Michael Glazier, 1980.

Meijboom, H. J. *A History and Critique of the Origin of the Marcan Hypothesis, 1835–1866.* Translated and edited by J. J. Kiwiet. New Gospel Studies 8. Macon, Ga.: Mercer, 1993.

Metzger, Bruce M. "Explicit References in the Works of Origen to Variant Readings in New Testament Manuscripts." In *Biblical and Patristic Studies: In Memory of Robert Pierce Casey,* edited by J. N. Birdsall and R. W. Thomson, 78–95. Freiburg: Herder, 1963.

———. "The Furniture in the Scriptorium at Qumran." *RevQ* 1 (1958–59): 509–15.

———. "The Practice of Textual Criticism Among the Church Fathers." Chap. 12 in *New Testament Studies: Philological, Versional, and Patristic.* Leiden: Brill, 1950.

———. "St. Jerome's Explicit References to Variant Readings in Manuscripts of the New Testament." In *Text and Interpretation: Studies in the New Testament Presented to Matthew Black,* edited by Ernest Best and Robert McL. Wilson, 179–90. Cambridge: Cambridge University Press, 1979.

———. *A Textual Commentary on the Greek New Testament.* 2d ed. New York: United Bible Societies, 1994.

Metzger, Bruce M., and Bart D. Ehrman. *The Text of the New Testament: Its Transmission, Corruption, and Restoration.* 4th ed. New York: Oxford, 2005.

Moo, Douglas J. "'Gospel Origins': A Reply to J. W. Wenham." *TrinJ* 2NS (1981): 24–36.

Morgan, C. Shannon. "When Abiathar Was High Priest." *JBL* 98 (1979): 409–10.

Morris, Leon. *The Gospel According to Matthew.* Grand Rapids: Eerdmans; Leicester: InterVarsity, 1992.

Moule, C. F. D. *An Idiom Book of New Testament Greek.* 2d ed. Cambridge: Cambridge University Press, 1959.

Moulton, James Hope. *A Grammar of New Testament Greek.* 3 vols. Edinburgh: T. and T. Clark, 1908–63.

———. *Prolegomena.* Vol. 1 of *A Grammar of New Testament Greek.* 3d ed. Edinburgh: T. and T. Clark, 1908.

Moulton, James Hope, and George Milligan. *The Vocabulary of the Greek Testament: Illustrated from the Papyri and Other Non-literary Sources.* Grand Rapids: Eerdmans, 1930.

Mounce, Robert H. *Matthew.* NIBCNT. Peabody, Mass.: Hendrickson, 1991.

Murray, Dom Gregory. "Five Gospel Miracles." *DRev* 108 (1990): 79–90.

Neirynck, Frans. *Duality in Mark: Contributions to the Study of Markan Redaction.* Rev. ed. BETL 31. Leuven: Leuven University Press, 1988.

———. "Les Expressions Doubles chez Marc et le Problème Synoptique." In *Evangelica II, 1982–1991, Collected Essays,* edited by F. van Segbroeck, 293–320. Leuven: Leuven University Press, 1991.

———. "The Matthew-Luke Agreements in Mt 14,13–14/Luke 9,10–11 (par. Mark 6,30–34)." *ETL* 60 (1984): 25–44.

———. "Once More: The Making of a Synopsis." In *Evangelica II, 1982–1991, Collected Essays,* edited by F. van Segbroeck, 363–76. Leuven: Leuven University Press, 1991.

———. "The Order of the Gospels and the Making of a Synopsis." In *Evangelica II, 1982–1991, Collected Essays,* edited by F. van Segbroeck, 357–62. Leuven: Leuven University Press, 1991.

———. "La Rédaction Matthénne et la Structure du Premier Évangile." *ETL* 43 (1967): 41–73. Reprinted in *Evangelica: Gospel Studies—Études D'Évangile,* edited by F. Van Segbroeck, BETL 110 (Leuven: Leuven University Press, 1982), 3–36.

———. "Urmarcus redivivus? Examen critique de l'hypothèse des insertions matthéennes dans Marc." In *L'Évangile selon Marc: Tradition et rédaction,* edited by M. Sabbe, 103–45. BETL 34. Leuven: Leuven University Press, 1974.

Neirynck, Frans, and Frans van Segbroeck. *New Testament Vocabulary: A Companion Volume to the Concordance.* BETL 95. Leuven: Leuven University Press, 1984.

Neville, David J. *Arguments from Order in Synoptic Source Criticism: A History and Critique.* New Gospel Studies 7. Macon, Ga.: Mercer, 1994.

———. *Mark's Gospel—Prior or Posterior? A Reappraisal of the Phenomenon of Order.* JSNTSup 222. London: Sheffield, 2002.

New, David S. *Old Testament Quotations in the Synoptic Gospels, and the Two-Document Hypothesis.* SBLSCS 37. Atlanta: Scholars Press, 1993.

Newman, Robert C. "The Synoptic Problem: A Proposal for Handling Both Internal and External Evidence." *WTJ* 43 (1980): 132–51.

Nida, Eugene A. "The 'Harder Reading' in Textual Criticism: An Application of the Second Law of Thermodynamics." *BT* 32 (1981): 101–7.

Nineham, D. E. *Saint Mark.* New York: Penguin Books, 1963. Reprint, Westminster Pelican Commentaries. Philadelphia: Westminster, 1977.

O'Neill, J. C. "The Lost Written Records of Jesus' Words and Deeds Behind Our Records." *JTS* 42 (1991): 483–504.

———. "The Synoptic Problem." *NTS* 21 (1975): 273–85.

Orchard, Bernard. "Are All Gospel Synopses Biased?" *TZ* 34 (1978): 149–62.

———. "A Demonstration That Mark Was Written After Matthew and Luke (A translation of J. J. Griesbach's Commentatio qua Marci Evangeluim totum e Matthaei et Lucae Commentariis Decerptum esse monstratur)." In *J. J. Griesbach: Synoptic and Text-critical Studies, 1776–1976,* edited by Bernard Orchard and T. R. W. Longstaff, 103–35. Cambridge: Cambridge University Press, 1978.

———. *Matthew, Luke and Mark.* The Griesbach Solution to the Synoptic Question 1. Manchester: Koinonia, 1976.

———. "The Solution of the Synoptic Problem." *ScrB* 18 (1987): 2–14.

———. "The Two-gospel hypothesis or, Some Thoughts on the Revival of the Griesbach Hypothesis." *DRev* 98 (1980): 267–79.

Orchard, Bernard, and Thomas R. W. Longstaff, eds. *J. J. Griesbach: Synoptic and Text-Critical Studies, 1776–1976.* Cambridge: Cambridge University Press, 1978.

Orchard, Bernard, and Harold Riley. *The Order of the Synoptics: Why Three Synoptic Gospels?* Macon, Ga.: Mercer, 1987.

Orton, David E. *The Understanding Scribe: Matthew and the Apocalyptic Ideal.* JSNTSup 25. Sheffield: JSOT, 1989.

Owen, Henry. *Observations on the Four Gospels; Tending Chiefly, To Ascertain the Times of their Publication; and To Illustrate the Form and Manner of their Composition.* London: St. Martin's, 1764.

Parker, David C. *Codex Bezae: An Early Christian Manuscript and Its Text.* Cambridge: Cambridge University Press, 1992.

———. "The Development of Textual Criticism Since B. H. Streeter." *NTS* 24 (1977): 149–62.

———. *The Living Text of the Gospels.* Cambridge: Cambridge University Press, 1997.

Parker, Pierson. "The Posteriority of Mark." In *New Synoptic Studies: The Cambridge Gospel Conference and Beyond*, edited by William R. Farmer, 67–142. Macon, Ga.: Mercer, 1983.

———. "A Second Look at *The Gospel Before Mark*," *JBL* 100 (1981): 393, 408

Peabody, David B. "Chapters in the History of the Linguistic Argument for Solving the Synoptic Problem: The Nineteenth Century in Context." In *Jesus, the Gospels, and the Church: Essays in Honor of William R. Farmer*, edited by E. P. Sanders, 47–67. Macon, Ga.: Mercer, 1987.

———. *Mark as Composer.* New Gospel Studies 1. Macon, Ga.: Mercer, 1987.

———. "A Pre-Markan Prophetic Sayings Tradition and the Synoptic Problem," *JBL* 97 (1978): 409

Peabody, David B., Lamar Cope, and Allan J. McNicol, eds. *One Gospel from Two: Mark's Use of Matthew and Luke.* Harrisburg, Pa.: Trinity Press International, 2002.

Peabody, David B., and Bo Reicke, "Synoptic Problem." In *Dictionary of Biblical Interpretation*, edited by John H. Hayes, 2:517–24. 2 vols. Nashville: Abingdon, 1999.

Pesch, Rudolf. "Levi-Matthäus (Mc 2:14/Mt 9:9; 10:3). Ein Beitrag zur Lösung eines alten Problems." *ZNW* 59 (1968): 40–56.

———. *Das Markusevangelium: Einleitung und Kommentar zu Kap. 1,1–8,26.* HTKNT 2. 2 vols. Freiburg: Herder, 1977.

Pettem, Michael. "Le premier récit de la multiplication des pains et le problème synoptique." *SR* 14 (1985): 73–83.

Petzer, J. H. "Author's Style and the Textual Criticism of the New Testament." *Neot* 24 (1990): 185–97.

———. "Eclecticism and the Text of the New Testament." In *Text and Interpretation: New Approaches in the Criticism of the New Testament*, edited by P. J. Hartin and J. H. Petzer, 47–62. NTTS 15. Leiden: Brill, 1991.

Porter, Stanley E. *Idioms of the Greek New Testament.* Biblical Languages Greek 2. Sheffield: JSOT, 1992.

———. *Verbal Aspect in the Greek of the New Testament, with Reference to Tense and Mood.* New York: Peter Lang, 1989.

Porter, Stanley E., and Matthew Brook O'Donnell. "The Implications of Textual

Variants for Authenticating the Activities of Jesus." In *Authenticating the Activities of Jesus.* Edited by Bruce Chilton and Craig A. Evans. Leiden: Brill, 2002.

Powell, J. Enoch. *The Evolution of the Gospel: A New Translation of the First Gospel with Commentary and Introductory Essay.* New Haven: Yale University Press, 1994.

Powers, B. Ward. "The Shaking of the Synoptics: A Report on the Cambridge Conference on the Synoptic Gospels, August, 1979." *RTR* 39 (1980):33–39.

Pryke, E. J. *Redactional Style in the Marcan Gospel: A Study of Syntax and Vocabulary as Guides to Redaction in Mark.* Cambridge: Cambridge University Press, 1978.

Reicke, Bo Ivar. "The History of the Synoptic Discussion." In *The Interrelations of the Gospels: A Symposium led by M.-É. Boismard, W. R. Farmer, F. Neirynck, Jerusalem 1984,* edited by David L. Dungan, 291–316. BETL. Macon Ga.: Mercer; Leuven: Leuven University Press, 1990.

———. *The Roots of the Synoptic Gospels.* Philadelphia: Fortress, 1986.

———. "The Synoptic Reports on the Healing of the Paralytic: Matt. 9:1–8 with Parallels." In *Studies in New Testament Language and Text: Essays in Honour of George D. Kilpatrick on the Occasion of His Sixty-fifth Birthday,* edited by J. K. Elliott, 319–29. NovTSup 44. Leiden: Brill, 1976.

Riesner, R. *Jesus als Lehrer. Eine Untersuchung zum Ursprung der Evangelien-Überlieferung.* 3d ed. Tübingen: J. C. B. Mohr, 1988.

Riley, Harold. *The Making of Mark: An Exploration.* Macon, Ga.: Mercer, 1989.

Rist, John M. *On the Independence of Matthew and Mark.* SNTSMS 32. Cambridge: Cambridge University Press, 1978.

Robinson, J. A. T. "The Parable of the Wicked Husbandmen: A Test of Synoptic Relationships." *NTS* 21 (1975): 443–61.

———. *Redating the New Testament.* Philadelphia: SCM, 1976.

Rogers, Alan D. "Mark 2:26." *JTS* 2 (1951): 44–45.

Rolland, Philippe. "A New Look at the Synoptic Question." *European Journal of Theology* 8.2 (1999): 133–44.

———. "Les Prédécesseurs de Marc: Les Sources Présynoptiques de Mc, II, 18–22 et Parallèles." *RevBib* 89 (1982): 370–405.

———. "La Question Synoptique Demande-t-elle une Réponse Compliquée?" *Bib* 70 (1989): 217–23.

Ross, J. M. "Some Unnoticed Points in the Text of the New Testament." *NovT* 25 (1983): 59–72.

Royse, James R. "Scribal Habits in the Transmission of New Testament Texts."

In *The Critical Study of Sacred Texts,* edited by Wendy D. O'Flaherty, 139–61. Berkeley: Graduate Theological Union, 1979.

———. "Scribal Tendencies in the Transmission of the Text of the New Testament." In *The Text of the New Testament in Contemporary Research: Essays on the Status Quaestionis: A Volume in Honor of Bruce M. Metzger,* edited by Bart D. Ehrman and Michael W. Holmes, 239–52. Studies and Documents 46. Grand Rapids: Eerdmans, 1995.

Sabourin, Leopold. *The Gospel According to St Matthew.* 2 vols. Bombay: St. Paul Publications, 1982.

Sand, Alexander. *Das Evangelium nach Matthäus.* RNT. Regensburg Verlag Friedrich Pustet, 1986.

Sanday, W. *Studies in the Synoptic Problem: By Members of the University of Oxford.* Oxford: Clarendon, 1911.

Sanders, E. P., ed. *Jesus, the Gospels, and the Church: Essays in Honor of William R. Farmer.* Macon, Ga.: Mercer, 1987.

———. "The Overlaps of Mark and Q and the Synoptic Problem." *NTS* 19 (1973): 453–65.

———. *The Tendencies of the Synoptic Tradition.* Cambridge: Cambridge University Press, 1969.

Schlatter, Adolf. *Der Evangelist Matthäus: Seine Sprache, sein Ziel, seine Selbständigkeit.* 3d ed. Stuttgart: Calwer Verlag, 1948.

Schnackenburg, Rudolf. *The Gospel of Matthew.* Grand Rapids: Eerdmans, 2002.

Schweitzer, Albert. *Von Reimarus zu Wrede: Eine Geschichte der Leben—Jesu—Forschung.* Tübingen: Mohr, 1906.

Schweizer, Eduard. *The Good News According to Matthew.* Translated by David E. Green. Atlanta: John Knox, 1975.

Senior, Donald. *Matthew.* ANTC. Nashville: Abingdon Press, 1998.

Shin, Hyeon Woo. *Textual Criticism and the Synoptic Problem in Historical Jesus Research: The Search for Valid Criteria.* Contributions to Biblical Exegesis and Theology 36. Leuven: Peeters, 2004.

Sibinga, J. Smit. "Matthew 14:22–33—Text and Composition." In *New Testament Textual Criticism: Its Significance for Exegesis. Essays in Honour of Bruce M. Metzger,* edited by E. J. Epp and G. D. Fee, 15–33. Oxford: Clarendon, 1981.

———. Review of Klyne Snodgrass, *The Parable of the Wicked Tenants. NovT* 26 (1984): 383–4.

Snodgrass, Klyne R. "The Parable of the Wicked Husbandmen: Is the Gospel of Thomas Version Original?" *NTS* 21 (1974): 142–44.

———. *The Parable of the Wicked Tenants: An Inquiry into Parable Interpretation.* WUNT 27. Tübingen: Mohr, 1983.

Snoy, T. "Marc 6,48: '. . . et il voulait les dépasser.'" In *L'Évangile selon Marc: Tradition et rédaction,* edited by M. Sabbe, 352–60. BETL 34. Leuven: Leuven University Press, 1974.

Stanton, Graham N. *A Gospel for a New People: Studies in Matthew.* Edinburgh: T. and T. Clark; Louisville: WJKP, 1992.

———. *Gospel Truth? New Light on Jesus and the Gospels.* Valley Forge, Pa.: Trinity Press International, 1995.

———, ed. *The Interpretation of Matthew.* London: SPCK; Philadelphia: Fortress, 1983.

———. "Matthew as a Creative Interpreter of the Sayings of Jesus." In *The Gospel and the Gospels,* edited by Peter Stuhlmacher, 257–72. Grand Rapids: Eerdmans, 1991. Reprinted in *A Gospel for a New People: Studies in Matthew* (Edinburgh: T. and T. Clark; Louisville: WJKP, 1992), 326–45.

———. "'Pray that your flight may not be in winter or on a Sabbath' (Matthew 24.20)." *JSNT* 37 (1989): 17-30. Reprinted in *A Gospel for a New People: Studies in Matthew* (Edinburgh: T. and T. Clark; Louisville: WJKP, 1992), 192–206.

———. "A Response to J. C. Anderson's 'Life on the Mississippi: New Currents in Matthean Scholarship.'" Paper presented at the annual meeting of the national SBL in Philadelphia, 1995.

Stanton, V. H. *The Gospels as Historical Documents.* Part 2, *The Synoptic Gospels.* Cambridge: Cambridge University Press, 1909.

Stegner, W. R. "Lucan Priority in the Feeding of the Five Thousand." *BR* 21 (1976): 19–28.

Stein, Robert H. *The Synoptic Problem: An Introduction.* Grand Rapids: Baker, 1987.

Stendahl, Krister. *The School of St. Matthew and Its Use of the Old Testament.* Rev. ed. Philadelphia: Fortress, 1968. Reprint, Ramsey, N.J.: Sigler, 1990.

Stoldt, Hans-Herbert. *Geschichte und Kritik der Markushypothese* [History and Criticism of the Marcan Hypothesis]. Translated and edited by Donald L. Niewyk. Göttingen: Vandenhoeck and Ruprecht, 1977; Macon, Ga.: Mercer, 1980.

Stonehouse, Ned B. *Origins of the Synoptic Gospels: Some Basic Questions.* Grand Rapids: Eerdmans, 1963.

Streeter, Burnett Hillman. *The Four Gospels: A Study of Origins Treating of the Manuscript Tradition, Sources, Authorship, and Dates.* New York: Macmillan, 1925.

Stuhlmacher, Peter, ed. *The Gospel and the Gospels.* Translated by John Bowden. Grand Rapids: Eerdmans, 1991.

Sturz, Harry A. *The Byzantine Text-Type and New Testament Textual Criticism.* Nashville: Nelson, 1984.

Styler, G. M. "The Priority of Mark." In *The Birth of the New Testament,* by C. F. D. Moule, 285–316. 3d rev. ed. San Francisco: Harper and Row, 1982. Reprinted in *The Two-Source Hypothesis: A Critical Appraisal,* edited by Arthur J. Bellinzoni Jr. (Macon, Ga.: Mercer, 1985), 63–75.

Swete, Henry Barclay. *The Gospel According to St Mark: The Greek Text with Introduction, Notes and Indices.* 3d ed. London: Macmillan, 1913. Reprint, Grand Rapids: Eerdmans, 1952.

Talbert C. H., and E. V. McKnight, "Can the Griesbach Hypothesis Be Falsified?" *JBL* 93 (1974): 338–68.

Taylor, Vincent. *The Gospel According to St. Mark: The Greek Text with Introduction, Notes, and Indexes.* 2d ed. London: Macmillan, 1966.

Thomas, Robert L. "Discerning Synoptic Gospel Origins: An Inductive Approach." *The Master's Seminary Journal* 15 (2004): 3–38.

———. ed. *Three Views on the Origins of the Synoptic Gospels.* Grand Rapids: Kregel, 2002.

Thomas, Robert L., and F. David Farnell, *The Jesus Crisis.* Grand Rapids: Kregel, 1998.

Tischendorf, Constantin von. *Codex Sinaiticus: The Ancient Biblical Manuscript Now in the British Museum: Tischendorf's Story and Argument Related by Himself.* 8th ed. London: Lutterworth, 1934.

Tov, Emanuel. "Criteria for Evaluating Textual Readings: The Limitations of Textual Rules." *HTR* 75 (1982): 429–48.

Tregelles, Samuel P. *An Account of the Printed Text of the Greek New Testament.* London: Samuel Bagster, 1854.

Tuckett, Christopher M. "The Griesbach Hypothesis in the 19th Century." *JSNT* 3 (1979): 29–60.

———. "Mark and Q." In *The Synoptic Gospels: Source Criticism and the New Literary Criticism,* edited by C. Focant, 155–76. Leuven: University Press, 1993.

———. "Response to the Two-gospel hypothesis." In *The Interrelations of the Gospels: A Symposium Led by M.-É. Boismard, W. R. Farmer, F. Neirynck, Jerusalem 1984,* edited by David L. Dungan, 47–62. Macon Ga.: Mercer; Leuven: Leuven University Press, 1990.

———. *The Revival of the Griesbach Hypothesis: An Analysis and Appraisal.* SNTSMS 44. Cambridge: Cambridge University Press, 1983.

———. "Synoptic Problem." In *Anchor Bible Dictionary,* edited by D. N. Freedman, 6:263–70. 6 vols. New York: Doubleday, 1992.

———, ed. *Synoptic Studies: The Ampleforth Conferences of 1982 and 1983.* JSNTSup 7. Sheffield: JSOT, 1984.

———. "The Two Gospel Hypothesis Under Scrutiny: A Response." *PSTJ* 40 (1987): 25–31.

Turner, C. H. *The Gospel According to St. Mark: Introduction and Commentary.* London: SPCK, 1931.

———. "Marcan Usage: Notes, Critical and Exegetical, on the Second Gospel." *JTS* 25 (1923–1924): 377–86.

———. "Marcan Usage: Notes, Critical and Exegetical, on the Second Gospel." *JTS* 26 (1924–1925): 12–20, 145–56, 225–40, 337–46.

———. "Marcan Usage: Notes, Critical and Exegetical, on the Second Gospel." *JTS* 27 (1925–1926): 58–62.

———. "Marcan Usage: Notes, Critical and Exegetical, on the Second Gospel." *JTS* 28 (1926–1927): 9–30, 145–58, 349–62.

———. "Marcan Usage: Notes, Critical and Exegetical, on the Second Gospel." *JTS* 29 (1927–1928): 275–89, 346–61.

Turner, Nigel. *Grammatical Insights into the New Testament.* Edinburgh: T. and T. Clark, 1965.

———. *Syntax.* Vol. 3 of *A Grammar of New Testament Greek,* by James Hope Moulton. Edinburgh: T. and T. Clark, 1963.

———. *Style.* Vol. 4 of *A Grammar of New Testament Greek,* by James Hope Moulton. Edinburgh: T. and T. Clark, 1976.

Tyson, Joseph B. "Order in the Synoptic Gospels: Patterns of Agreement Within Pericopes." *SecCent* 2 (1987–88): 65–109.

Tyson, Joseph B., and T. R. W. Longstaff. *Synoptic Abstract.* The Computer Bible 15. Wooster, Ohio: Biblical Research Associates, 1978.

Vaganay, L. *Le Probleme Synoptique: Une Hypothèse de Travail.* Bibliothèque de Théologie Série III. Théologie Biblique 1. Paris: Desclé and Co., 1954.

Vaganay, L., and C. B. Amphoux. *An Introduction to New Testament Textual Criticism.* 2d rev. ed. Translated by Jenny Heimerdinger. Cambridge: Cambridge University Press, 1991.

van Segbroeck, F., C. M. Tuckett, G. Van Belle, and J. Verheyden, eds. *The Four Gospels, 1992: Festschrift Frans Neirynck.* 2 vols. BETL 100. Leuven: Leuven University Press, 1992.

Vincent, M. R. *A History of the Textual Criticism of the New Testament.* New York: Macmillan, 1899.

Walker, Norman. "After Three Days." *NovT* 4 (1960): 261–2.

Walker, William O., Jr. "Order in the Synoptic Gospels." *SecCent* 2 (1987–88): 83–97.

―――, ed. *The Relationships Among the Gospels: An Interdisciplinary Dialogue.* Trinity University Monograph Series in Religion 5. San Antonio: Trinity University Press, 1978.

―――. "The Son of Man Question and the Synoptic Problem." In *New Synoptic Studies: The Cambridge Gospel Conference and Beyond,* edited by William R. Farmer, 261–302. Macon, Ga.: Mercer, 1983.

―――. "The State of the Synoptic Question: Some Reflections on the Work of Tuckett and McNicol." *PSTJ* 40 (1987): 14–21.

―――. "An Unexamined Presupposition in Studies of the Synoptic Problem." *Religion in Life* 48 (1979): 41–52.

Wansborough, Henry, ed. *Jesus and the Oral Gospel Tradition.* JSNTSup 64. Sheffield: JSOT Press, 1991.

Weisse, C. H. *Die evangelische Geschichte: kritisch und philosophisch Bearbeitet.* 2 vols. Leipzig: Drud und Berlag, 1838.

Wenham, David. "The Interpretation of the Parable of the Sower." *NTS* 20 (1974): 299–319.

―――. *The Rediscovery of Jesus' Eschatological Discourse.* Gospel Perspectives 4. Sheffield: JSOT, 1984.

―――. "The Synoptic Problem Revisited: Some New Suggestions about the Composition of Mark 4.1–34." *TynBul* 23 (1972): 3–38.

―――, ed. "Tradition and Redaction in the Parables of the Gospel of Thomas." In *The Jesus Tradition Outside the Gospels,* 189–90. Gospel Perspectives 5. Sheffield: JSOT, 1984.

Wenham, John W. "Mark 2.26." *JTS* 1 (1950): 156.

―――. *Redating Matthew, Mark and Luke: A Fresh Assault on the Synoptic Problem.* Downers Grove, Ill.: InterVarsity, 1992.

―――. "Why Do You Ask Me About the Good? A Study of the Relation Between Text and Source Criticism." *NTS* 28 (1982): 116–25.

Westcott, B. F. and F. J. A. Hort, *Introduction to the New Testament in the Original Greek, with Notes on Selected Readings.* New York: Harper, 1882. Reprint, Peabody, Mass.: Hendrickson, 1988.

Wettstein, Johann Jakob. Η ΚΑΙΝΗ ΔΙΑΘΗΚΗ: *Novum Testamentum Graecum.* 2 vols. Amsterdam: Dommeriana, 1752. Reprint, Graz, Austria: Akademische Druck und Verlagsanstalt, 1962.

Wheeler, Frank. *Textual Criticism and the Synoptic Problem: A Textual*

Commentary on the Minor Agreements of Matthew and Luke Against Mark. Ph.D. dissertation, Baylor University, 1985.

Wilkins, Michael J. *Following the Master: A Biblical Theology of Discipleship.* Grand Rapids: Zondervan, 1992.

——. *The NIV Application Commentary: Matthew.* Grand Rapids: Zondervan, 2004.

Williams, C. S. C. *Alterations to the Text of the Synoptic Gospels and Acts.* Oxford: Basil Blackwell, 1951.

Williams, Matthew C. "The Case for the Markan Priority View of Gospel Origins: The Two-/Four-Source View." In *Three Views on the Origins of the Synoptic Gospels,* edited by Robert L. Thomas, 19–96. Grand Rapids: Kregel, 2002.

——. "The OWEN Hypothesis: An Essay showing that it was Henry Owen who first formulated the so-called 'Griesbach Hypothesis.'" *JHC* 7 (2000): 126–58.

——. Review of Eta Linnemann, *Is There A Synoptic Problem? Rethinking the Literary Dependence of the First Three Gospels. TrinJ* 14NS (1993): 97–101

Wong, Eric K.-C. "The Matthaean Understanding of the Sabbath: A Response to G. N. Stanton." *JSNT* 44 (1991): 3–18.

Wright, N. T. "Doing Justice to Jesus: A Response to J. D. Crossan: 'What Victory? What God?'" *SJT* 50 (1997): 359–79.

Zerwick, Maximilian. *Biblical Greek: Illustrated by Examples.* Rome: Editrice Pontificio Instituto Biblico, 1963.

Subject Index

Abbott, E. A., 31, 127n
Abiathar, 78, 143–44n, 206, 209
"abomination that causes desolation," 192n
Ahimelech, 78
Aland, Kurt, 42–43
Allen, Willoughby C., 130n, 187n
Allison, Dale C., Jr., 130n, 177n, 178n
"Aloofness of Jesus in Mark" (Cory), 164n
Ambrozic, Aloysius M., 149n
anger of Jesus, 127–28
"Appendix: the Scribes and the Pharisees"
     (Marcus), 139n
Aramaic background, 60, 62
Arndt, William, 87n, 105n, 167n, 183n, 191n
assimilation, 200–1, 220. *See also*
     harmonization; text criticism.
asyndetons, 188, 192
"Atticism" (Kilpatrick), 59n
atticistic improvements, 57–58, 61, 62
     more difficult reading and, 55n
     scribal, 53, 57–58
     text-critical criteria of, 61, 62
     theory about, 132n, 185n
Augustine, 23
authority
     divine, 181
     human, 136–37, 181, 205
author's style
     as text-critical criterion, 58–60, 61,
     119–20, 197–99
     Matthew-Mark differences in, 219
     text-critical changes and, 217, 218

awkward readings
     as text-critical criterion, 118–19,
     196–97, 217
     Matthew-Mark, 219

Barth, Gerhard, 193n
Bauer, Walter, 87n, 105n, 167n, 183n, 191n
Beare, F. W., 145n
Bengel, Johann Albrecht, 51, 55
Black, David Alan, 32–33
Blass, F., 70n, 78n, 85n, 89n, 105n, 191n
blind man healed, 170
Blomberg, Craig L., 37, 164n, 165n, 180n
Boismard, Marie-Émile, 27, 215n
Bonnard, Pierre, 126n
Buchanan, G. W., 143–44n
Burton, Ernest De Witt, 41n
Butler, B. C., 25, 30, 31, 34
Byzantine Text-Type and New Testament,
     The (Sturz), 55n, 56

Caesar, tribute to, 107–8, 184–87
Cambridge Gospel Conference (1979), 26
"Can the Griesbach Hypothesis Be
     Falsified?" (Talbert and McKnight),
     143n
"Can We Recover the Original New
     Testament?" (Elliott), 59n
Carlston, Charles E., 139n, 149n, 152n
Carroll, Marie, 212n
Carson, Donald A., 169n
Cerfaux, Lucien, 150n